JOHN AND POSTCOLONIALISM

TRAVEL, SPACE AND POWER

Edited by

Musa W. Dube and
Jeffrey L. Staley

THE BIBLE AND POSTCOLONIALISM, 7

Series Editor:
R.S. Sugirtharajah

Editorial Board:
Fernando Segovia, Kwok Pui-lan, Sharon Ringe,
Ralph Broadbent and Marcella Althaus-Reid

SHEFFIELD ACADEMIC PRESS
A Continuum imprint
LONDON • NEW YORK

For our mothers, Mary Elizabeth Jean Sheldrake Staley 1924–84, and Agnes Stabatabana Tafa 1930–whose faith and love have nourished us on our spiritual journeys.

Copyright © 2002 Sheffield Academic Press
A Continuum imprint

Published by
Sheffield Academic Press Ltd
The Tower Building, 11 York Road, London SE1 7NX
370 Lexington Avenue, New York, NY 10017-6550

www.SheffieldAcademicPress.com
www.continuumbooks.com

British Library Cataloguing-in-Publication Data

A catalogue record for this book is available from the British Library

Typeset by Sheffield Academic Press
Printed on acid-free paper in Great Britain by MPG Books Ltd, Bodmin, Cornwall

ISBN   1-84127-323-6 (hardback)
       1-84127-312-0 (paperback)

Contents

Foreword

The editors of this volume wish to thank R.S. Sugirtharajah for his initial interest in our project; for the prophetic, postcolonial voice he raised in the early 1990s in the wilderness of biblical studies; and for the encouragement he gave us as this project slowly moved toward publication.

For both Musa Dube and Jeffrey Staley, Tod Swanson's 1994 *JAAR* essay 'To Prepare a Place: Johannine Christianity and the Collapse of Ethnic Territory', was central to their first forays into postcolonial interpretations of the Fourth Gospel. Thus, we are grateful to Oxford University Press for allowing us to use it as our lead chapter. Both Jeffrey Staley's essay '"Dis Place, Man": A Postcolonial Critique of the Vine (the Mountain and the Temple) in the Gospel of John' and Musa Dube's 'Reading for Decolonization (John 4.1-42)' are heavily indebted to his critical reflections on the Johannine sense of place. Since these two essays interact in significant ways with Swanson's essay, it seemed appropriate to place his essay first after the introduction, and then follow his essay with those of Staley and Dube. Luckily for us, Dube's essay on John 4 allowed us to put the remaining essays in 'canonical' order—John 5, 8, 15—concluding with the two more general essays by Reinhartz and Liew.

Finally, we are grateful to Brill for allowing us to reprint Leticia A. Guardiola-Sáenz's essay 'Border-crossing and Its Redemptive Power in John 7:53–8.11: A Cultural Reading of Jesus and The Accused'. Her essay, now slightly revised, appeared in Ingrid Rosa Kitzberger (ed.), *Transformative Encounters: Jesus and Women Reviewed* (Leiden: E.J. Brill, 1999), pp. 267-91.

Abbreviations

AB	Anchor Bible
ABD	David Noel Freeman (ed.), *The Anchor Bible Dictionary* (New York: Doubleday, 1992)
ANRW	Hildegard Temporini and Wolfgang Haase (eds.), *Aufstieg und Niedergang der römischen Welt: Geschichte und Kultur Roms im Spiegel der neueren Forschung* (Berlin: W. de Gruyter, 1972–)
ASNEL	Association for the Study of the New Literatures in English
ATR	*Anglican Theological Review*
Bib	*Biblica*
BSac	*Bibliotheca Sacra*
BT	*The Bible Translator*
BTB	*Biblical Theology Bulletin*
CBQ	*Catholic Biblical Quarterly*
CI	*Critical Inquiry*
CL	*College Literature*
CT	*Christianity Today*
ET	*Eglise et Theologie*
HBT	*Horizons in Biblical Theology*
IAMS	International Association for Mission Studies
JAAR	*Journal of the American Academy of Religion*
JBL	*Journal of Biblical Literature*
JETS	*Journal of the Evangelical Theological Society*
JGS	*Journal of Gender Studies*
JITC	*Journal of the Interdenominational Theological Center*
JRS	*Journal of Roman Studies*
JSNT	*Journal for the Study of the New Testament*
JSNTSup	*Journal for the Study of the New Testament*, Supplement Series
MFS	*Modern Fiction Studies*
NCB	New Century Bible
NTS	*New Testament Studies*
PT	*Poetics Today*
SBLASP	SBL Abstracts and Seminar Papers
SBLMS	SBL Monograph Series
SSEJC	Studies in Scripture in Early Judaism and Christianity
SSR	*Scientific Study of Religion*
USQR	*Union Seminary Quarterly Review*
ZNW	*Zeitschrift für die neutestamentliche Wissenschaft*

List of Contributors

Musa W. Dube, University of Botswana, Botswana

Francisco Lozada, Jr, University of the Incarnate Word, San Antonio, TX, USA

Zipporah G. Glass, Vanderbilt University, Nashville, TN, USA

Adele Reinhartz, McMaster University, Hamilton, ONT, Canada

Leticia A. Guardiola-Sáenz, Andover Newton Theological School, Newton Centre, MA, USA

Jeffrey L. Staley, Seattle University, Seattle, WA, USA

Mary Huie-Jolly, School of Ministry, Knox College, Dunedin, Aotearoa, New Zealand

Tod D. Swanson, Arizona State University, Tempe, AZ, USA

Jean K. Kim, San Francisco Theological Seminary/Southern California, Claremont, CA, USA

Tat-siong Benny Liew, Chicago Theological Seminary, Chicago, IL, USA

Descending from and Ascending into Heaven: A Postcolonial Analysis of Travel, Space and Power in John

MUSA W. DUBE AND JEFFREY L. STALEY*

'*In principio erat Verbum*'. Think of Genesis. Think of how it was before the world was made. There was nothing, the Bible says. 'And the earth was without form, and void; and darkness was upon the face of the deep'. It was dark, and there was nothing. There were no mountains, no trees, no rivers. There was nothing…

Now, brothers and sisters, old John was a white man, and the white man has his ways. He talks about the Word. He talks through it and around it… [He] deals in words and he deals easily, with grace and sleight of hand. And in his presence, here on his own ground, you are as children, mere babes in the woods.[1]

In the beginning was the word, and the Word was with God, and the Word was God. All things came into being through him and without him not one thing came into being. What has come into being in him was life and the life was the light of all people. The light shines in the darkness, and the darkness did not overcome it… He was in the world, and the world did not know him (Jn 1.1-5, 9-10).

Going up that river was like travelling back to the earliest beginning of the World, when vegetation rioted on earth and the big trees were kings. An empty stream, a great silence, an impenetrable forest. The air was warm, thick, heavy, sluggish. There was no joy in the brilliance of sunshine.[2]

Postcolonialism and Earthly Journeys of Power

The word 'postcolonialism' originated about 25 years ago[3] among certain travelers who claimed to be crucibles of light and knowledge; with

---

* The bulk of this essay represents Musa W. Dube's work. Jeffrey Staley functioned primarily as editor.

1. N. Scott Momaday, *House Made of Dawn* (New York: New American Library, 1966), pp. 85, 87-88.

2. Joseph Conrad, *Heart of Darkness and the Secret Sharer* (New York: Bantam Classics, 1902), p. 53.

the desperate search for liberation among the 'visited', those defined as the 'darkness' and 'the ignorant', but who could be rescued and raised as 'children of God' if only 'they believed'. The visited were the dominated, the colonized, the collaborators who stood up to political domination and colonization and argued for their right to be called human; to sanctify their geographical spaces that had been mapped out as land of darkness, as the abode of the powerless and the godless. But the visited, the colonized, eventually began to take the 'voyage in/to' the geographical spaces of their former colonizers—more often as powerless visitors trying to assert their right to be, than as powerful travelers who claimed light and knowledge.

Such struggles for power characterize our contemporary world as well as the text of John. Postcolonialism is thus attested by massive traveling, by the crossing of boundaries, by the continued contested relationships between the colonized, the collaborators and the colonizers.[4] In Fernando Segovia's words, 'at the core of the imperial/colonial phenomenon, indeed through all its various stages, lies the reality and experience of the diasporic phenomenon: unsettlement, travel, resettlement'.[5]

The essays in this volume trace the journeys within John's narrative in order to examine the making and distribution of power on earthly spaces. This power is often distributed unevenly between the powerful and powerlessness, and between the colonized, the colonizer and the collaborator. The authors seek to identify the many 'heavens' that we have created—the ones from which we can speak and claim power— sometimes justly and sometimes unjustly. The authors show how the Johannine text empowers certain travelers to invade foreign peoples and

3.   The term 'postcolonialism' began as an expression describing a particular literary practice, but as an act of resistance to colonialism, postcolonialism's origins can be traced back to the day the colonized came in contact with the colonizer. For example, see Bill Ashcroft, Gareth Griffiths, and Helen Tiffin, *The Empire Writes Back: Theory and Practice in Post-Colonial Literatures* (New York: Routledge, 1989), pp. 1-13.

4.   Introductions to and definitions of postcolonialism are many, and it is not the purpose of this introduction to replicate the work of other, more knowledgeable scholars in the field. Nevertheless, a few recent works are well worth mentioning for their breadth and critical insight: The online journal *Jouvert* (http://152.1.96.5/jouvert/), a recent volume of the journal *Ariel* (30 [1999]) entitled 'Postcolonial and Queer Theory and Praxis'; Leela Gandhi's *Postcolonial Theory: A Critical Introduction* (New York: Columbia University Press, 1998); and a collection of essays edited by Monika Reif-Hülser entitled *Borderlands: Negotiating Boundaries in Post-Colonial Writing* (ASNEL Papers, 4; Atlanta: Rodopi, 1999).

5.   Fernando F. Segovia, *Interpreting Beyond Borders* (Sheffield: Sheffield Academic Press, 2000), p. 14; cf. Mark Raper, 'Refugees: Travel under Duress', *The Way* 39 (1999), pp. 27-38.

lands and how these foreign peoples can re-read John for decolonization (Tod Swanson, Jeffrey Staley, Musa W. Dube and Francisco Lozada Jr). Some authors seek to identify the exclusive boundaries we have put up that bar others from our heavens (Zipporah Glass and Tat-siong Benny Liew). Others seek to open up closed boundaries so that all travelers can descend from heaven to earth (or if you like, so that all travelers can spread heaven on all earthly spaces [Leticia Guardiola-Sáenz]). Still others trace the journeys and places occupied by women in the Johannine story and in colonial settings (Jean Kim). Finally, some authors highlight how colonial history has changed the reading practices of certain communities (Mary Huie-Jolly), while others read John in order to understand the complex power relations that characterize us as colonizers, collaborators and colonized (Adele Reinhartz).

All the writers in this collection challenge readers of the Fourth Gospel to take responsibility for the journeys they make and for the power they claim over earthly spaces. They seek to clear a small space where members of our differing worlds can be involved in creating a world of liberating interdependence; a world of balanced co-existence, where all 'is good'; where none are involved in the exploitation or suppression of others. Basically, the authors of this collection are involved in earthly struggles for liberating power. And this effort is expressed with the paradigm of postcolonialism, a framework that was awakened by the desperate, unequal distribution of power over the face of the earth.

Postcolonialism is thus a paradigm that involves many different disciplines.[6] It seeks to examine how the colonizer constructs and justifies domination of the other in various places and periods of history; how the colonized collaborate, resist and assert their rights to be free in various places and periods of history; and how both parties travel and cross boundaries. Postcolonialism examines the role of narratives in colonizing, decolonizing and nation-building. It is concerned about economic, political, cultural and social justice in the world. But above all, postcolonialism proposes many different ways to co-exist on earth without having to suppress and exploit the other. The essays in this volume address the concerns mentioned above and overlap at many points.

---

6.   For a more detailed description of postcolonial studies and its influence upon biblical studies, see Segovia, *Interpreting Beyond Borders*, pp. 11-15; and Stephen D. Moore, 'Postcolonialism', in A.K.M. Adam (ed.), *A Handbook of Postmodern Biblical Interpretation* (St Louis: Chalice, 2000), pp. 182-88.

The Contribution of Postcolonialism
to Contemporary Biblical Studies

In a previously published article, I noted that I have come out of a historical experience where the Bible functioned as an imperialist text. And thus

> I know that the biblical story is a story that is acted out in history. I have, therefore, journeyed with some sense of injustice and emptiness in my academic biblical studies, where the Bible became an antiqued text, firmly contextualized in ancient times... To be sure, this approach of situating biblical studies in ancient times has facilitated many liberating and helpful discoveries for me. Nevertheless, I have discovered that privileging the ancient historical setting in the academic interpretation of the Bible is a powerful tool that divorces my experience and my questions from the field. By privileging the ancient history in biblical interpretation, the biblical text is perfectly shielded from its various historical reader-actors. The question of confronting the imperialist manifestation of the text is neatly bracketed.[7]

In the same essay I held that 'the biblical story is at times a travel narrative; it commands its readers to travel. Consequently, the privileging of one historical [period (i.e. ancient times)] in determining its meaning is ideologically suspect'.[8] This volume goes a long way toward addressing this ideologically suspect reading strategy. For although historical criticism has yielded many useful insights for readers of the Bible, many other readings from different settings, and by different readers in different histories deserve equal attention. These historically mediated readings and equally contextualized readers illumine the text in ways that we could not have imagined with traditional historical criticism. Not that the essays in this volume disavow historical criticism.[9] Rather, they find practical ways of integrating other times, places and readers into the interpretation of the biblical text. For example, some of the contexts (i.e. geographical spaces) that inform these interpretations of John are

1.   Modern colonization of Africa, Asia, Latin America and Australia (Swanson, Dube, Huie-Jolly)

7.   Musa W. Dube, 'Towards a Post-colonial Feminist Interpretation of the Bible', *Semeia* 78 (1997), p. 13.
8.   Musa W. Dube, 'Towards a Post-colonial Feminist Interpretation of the Bible', p. 23.
9.   Echoing the fear of many historically trained biblical scholars, Heikki Raisanen is concerned that postcolonial approaches may disparage traditional historical criticism (*Reading the Bible in the Global Village, Helsinki* [Atlanta: SBL, 2000], pp. 7-28; R.S. Sugitharajah, 'Critics, Tools and the Global Village', pp. 49-60.

2. Settler colonies of Canada and the USA (Reinhartz and Staley)
3. Contemporary nation-states such as Germany and the USA (Glass and Tat-siong)
4. Borderlands of Latin America and the USA (Guardiola-Sáenz)
5. Japan and Korea in the Second World War and afterwards (Kim)
6. Christian and Moslem cultural worlds (Lozado).

The historical readers (i.e. other than those of ancient biblical times) and contemporary readers who bring their particular meanings to John are

1. Modern-day colonizers and their colonizing acts
2. The colonized of various contexts
3. Women in colonized settings
4. Minority races in the colonizers' centers
5. Natives within settler colonies
6. Christian readers and their attitude towards non-Christian readers
7. Borderland dwellers.

Mary Huie-Jolly describes how 'certain Maori who had earlier been regarded as converts of the missionaries, now in response to colonial practices which undermined their tribal lands and way of life, called themselves "Jews" and began to leave the way of the son' (pp. 104-106). This is an excellent testimony to the underlying theme of these essays—that victims of colonialism will read from a variety of time settings and often will identify with 'unorthodox' characters in the biblical text.[10] Indeed, most readers of this volume who come from colonized lands would testify to the Maori approach and say that it applied to them as well. For most of them read in identification with those who are marginalized from power (the visited, the Samaritans, the woman caught in adultery, etc.), and they too read in search of international justice. The postcolonial approach of these essays thus helps inform biblical studies of actual lived relationships and places. And it calls upon the biblical scholar in the new millennium to do a kind of scholarship that is socially engaged and ethically committed to creating a just world.

---

10. See also Musa W. Dube, 'Towards a Post-colonial Feminist Interpretation of the Bible', p. 11. There I argue that my experiences as a colonized subject have led me to read in solidarity with the discredited Pharisees of Mt. 23 and with Paul's foolish Galatians (Gal. 3.1).

Johannine Journeys into Heaven and Earth: A Postscript

Unlike any of the other canonical gospels, the narrative of John opens by locating its story and its protagonist, the Word, at the beginning of everything. The first verse takes the flesh-and-blood reader back in time, to the time where everything began—'the beginning'. The narrator informs the reader that the Word, whom we later know is Jesus (1.16-18), was there at the beginning. The narrator then goes on to say that the Word was 'with God'; and, in fact, 'the Word was God' (1.1). To emphasize further the status of the Word, the narrator states 'all things came into being through him and *without him not one thing came into being*' (1.3). This brief, narrative opening the story takes the reader/s on a journey back into time; back to the time when it all started—when all things came into being. The narrator highlights the presence, role and power of the Word/Jesus in the clearest of terms. And the reader is left with little or no doubt that according to this author, 'there is no other creator' but God, and Jesus stands very close to this God—so close that a distinction between the two is nearly impossible to make. For 'the word *was* God'.

Yet if Jesus/Word was the creator of all things, something must have gone awry. For the narrator also tells the reader/s that 'he was coming into the world…and the world came into being through him, yet *the world did not know him*. He came to what was his own, and his own people did not accept him. But to all who received him, who believed in his name, he gave them power to become the children of God' (1.10-14).

A number of things have happened or are happening in the narrative world of this pre-existing creator-Word. First, the world does not know him. Second, his people do not receive him. Third, the Word/Jesus is forced to embark on a campaign of conferring childhood rights on all those who believe in him. These images hint at the possibility that the Word/Jesus may not be as powerful as the narrator first claimed, for the Word/Jesus descends from heaven into the world as an unknown and rejected traveler.

The intertwining of absolute power and peculiar powerlessness in the characterization of the Word/Jesus is telling. Could it be that the Word/Jesus's powerlessness provides the reader/s with a hint as to why he was first characterized as one who was 'with God', 'as God', and 'creator?' Is it merely a rhetorical claim of power for Jesus? Can the reader/s completely rule out the possibility that the Word/Jesus might be the tragically dispossessed and forgotten creator; the dispossessed owner? Whether powerful or powerless, the prologue's contradictions signify the Word/

Jesus's *struggle* for power more than they signify his secured position.

Yet the Johannine narrative continually emphasizes the power of the Word/Jesus rather than his apparent powerlessness. Thus in Jn 3.13, Jesus informs the reader/s that '*No one* has ascended into heaven except the one who descended from heaven, the Son of Man...' The narrator then makes the connection between place of origin and power explicit, by arguing that 'The one who comes from above is above all; the one who is of the earth belongs to the earth and speaks of about earthly things...' (3.31-32). Far from being indicative of powerlessness, Jesus's journeys from heaven, to the earth, and back into heaven highlight his power over earthly creatures, for '*the one who comes from above is above all*'.[11] Different spaces confer different levels of power over their occupants and travelers.[12] Heaven is a place of the highest power as compared to the earthly places and their occupants. Heaven thus confirms unparalleled power to Jesus as compared to those who occupy earthly places. The followers of Jesus are also promised access to heaven (14.1-7).[13]

As postcolonial readers, we are aware that 'the created', 'the visited', those whose darkness is supposedly broken into by the Word's light and

---

11. For a detailed analysis of the Word/Jesus's journeys in John, see Fernando F. Segovia, 'The Journey(s) of the Word: A Reading of the Plot of the Fourth Gospel', *Semeia* 53 (1991), pp. 23-54; and Adele Reinhartz, *The Word in the World: The Cosmological Tale in the Fourth Gospel* (Atlanta: Scholars Press, 1992).

For a more detailed analysis of the relationship between space/place and the claims of power in John's gospel, see Musa W. Dube, 'Savior of the World but not of this World: A Postcolonial Reading of Spatial Construction in John', in R.S. Sugirtharajah (ed.), *The Postcolonial Bible* (Sheffield: Sheffield Academic Press, 1998), pp. 118-35; esp. pp. 121-25.

12. The theoretical distinction between 'space' and 'place' is an important one in contemporary debates among geographers, but it has yet to be addressed fully by postcolonial biblical scholars. For example, Doreen Massey argues that 'in the pair space/place it is place which represents Being, and to it are attached a range of epithets and connotations: local, specific, concrete, descriptive. Each of these carries a different burden of meaning and each relates to different oppositions. The contrary to these classically designated characteristics of place are terms such as: general, universal, theoretical/abstract/conceptual... It is interesting...to ponder the gender connotations of these pairings' (Doreen Massey, *Space, Place, and Gender* [Minneapolis: University of Minneapolis Press, 1994], p. 9; cf. Patricia Yaeger, 'Introduction: Narrating Space', in Patricia Yaeger [ed.], *The Geography of Identity* [Ann Arbor: University of Michigan Press, 1996], pp. 18-30; and Tim Cresswell, *In Place/Out of Place: Geography, Ideology, and Transgression* [Minneapolis: University of Minnesota Press, 1996], pp. 149-62).

13. In his essay included in this volume, Tat-siong Benny Liew likens this promise to the rhetoric of 'upward mobility' ('Ambiguous Admittance: Consent and Descent in John's Community of "Upward" Mobility').

life, and those occupants of earthly places, do not speak for themselves in this narrative. Were these worldly occupants created by the Word/Jesus as the Johannine narrator argues, or are they only claimed to be such? Were they really the darkness that was conquered by the light as the narrator characterizes them? Were they lifeless until Jesus became the light that embodied their life at creation? Why are they characterised as such? Were they ignorant of their creator? These are questions that every reader should grapple with in their reading practices, for undoubtedly the Johannine narrative is told more from the perspective of the Word/Jesus than from the perspective of the ones visited.

Journeys of the Reader: What Kind of Travelers Are We?

Undoubtedly the journey of the Word/Jesus from heaven to earth is an assertion of power over space and time; over people, and over the earth. It is a claim of power where power is not guaranteed and where power has been denied or lost. There are a number of questions that arise from this characterization of the Word/Jesus, which the reader should put to the text. These are

1. What is the significance of Jesus claiming power over all people and all space if he is powerful or powerless, in different contexts and times?
2. How do we, as contemporary interpreters of John's narrative, read this language of power?
    a. Do we read as powerful travelers who, like Jesus, come to their own and are above all?
    b. Or do we read as the once powerful owners who come to reclaim their possessions?
    c. Do we read as the silenced, the created, the ignorant; those characterized as the darkness, who are supposedly overcome by the light?
    d. Or do we read as people who interrogate the gates to 'childhood rights' (1.12), the rites of passage that make one a child of God on earth?
    e. Do we read as hybrid travelers, whose constant journeys between heaven and earth blur the boundaries between power and powerlessness or make them more distinct?
    f. Do we read as men—as fathers and sons—who are characterized as inhabiting the realm of power, heaven, creating, traveling and struggling for power in earthly spaces, or do we also read as women—mothers and daughters—whose

place in heaven and earth remains invisible, suppressed, and unknown?

g. Must a woman reader of John undertake male journeys? Or are there other options?

h. Can women and men read as creators who pause at every moment, judging and searching to see if all 'is good', inter-dependent, and not in violation of the rights of the Other?

3. How do the contemporary power relations of our various worlds help us to understand, illumine and interpret the Johannine narrative?

4. What kind of journeys do we undertake as readers of John? What spaces (and times) do we inhabit in our reading practices?[14]

5. What borders do we cross, patrol or inhabit in our reading practices?[15]

These questions emphasize that in our reading practices, as citizens of the world, we also become particular travelers across space and time. We search for power within the struggles that characterize our worlds and texts. We are involved in traveling—descending from and ascending into 'heavens'—wherein we can claim or grant certain powers. As readers from various backgrounds, we are involved in journeys that reflect struggles for power in earthly spaces. We are involved in

1. Returning to the beginnings of time.[16]
2. Asserting our being with God[17] and *being* God.
3. Recounting our power to create ourselves and others—literally and figuratively—in order to reclaim our lost power, to retain

14. For a more detailed discussion of readers' journeys, see Musa W. Dube, 'Batswakwa: Which Traveler Are You (John 1:1-18)?', in Gerald West and Musa W. Dube (eds.), *The Bible in Africa* (Leiden: E.J. Brill, 2000); and Jeffrey L. Staley, *Reading with a Passion: Rhetoric, Autobiography, and the American West in the Gospel of John* (New York: Continuum, 1995), pp. 148-70, 179-85.

15. For a further development of this question, see Leticia Guardiola-Sáenz's essay in this volume ('Border-crossing and Its Redemptive Power in John 7.53–8.11: A Cultural Reading of Jesus and the *Accused*'); cf. Leslie Marmon Silko, 'Fences against Freedom', *Hungry Mind Review* (Fall 1994), http://www.bookwire.com/hmr/Review/silko.html.

16. Joseph Conrad characterizes traveling to Africa as 'traveling back to the earliest beginning of the world' (p. 53). This characterization then refigures Marlow and Kurtz, the colonizers, as the creators who will be involved completing the creation of Africa.

17. The rhetoric of claiming to be 'with God' is a characteristic of colonial literature and its heroes. See Musa W. Dube, 'Saviour of the World', pp. 122-24.

our power, to take power from others, or to underline our unpronounceable power.
4.   Seizing geographical worlds and dispossessing the original natives/creators.

The narrative of John is, therefore, a site of struggle for power. And it does not propose democratic power. The Word/Jesus who comes from heaven does not seek to spread democracy or equal rights to all the inhabitants of the earth. Instead, he claims 'absolute power' in all spaces and over all things through his pre-existent, creator status. This same Word/Jesus laments dispossession and rejection within his own created world. The Word/Jesus thus has conflicting faces as the possessor (the pre-existing creator), the dispossessed (his own did not know him or accept him), the struggler (the one who tries to win believers). Since the narrative prompts the reader/s to identify with the creator, the light and life; to believe and to distance themselves from the ignorant who do not believe, it follows that identification with the Word/Jesus could turn readers into possessors of others, possessing the dispossessed and displaced. Identification with the creator can render readers as settlers who have displaced the natives. Readers of the Fourth Gospel often claim such absolutizing powers over others, undertake quests into unknown territories and establish settlements. *The journey we choose to participate in, and the space we choose to inhabit in our reading practices are, therefore, acts that have an impact on our worlds and our neighbors' worlds*. So the Johannine narrative is best seen as a site of struggle for power amongst different parties. And we, as readers, cannot be neutral in this struggle.

To Prepare a Place: Johannine Christianity and the Collapse of Ethnic Territory

Tod D. Swanson

At least since Mircea Eliade's early work in *Cosmos and History*,[1] it has been recognized that communal orientation in space is central to what religion is about.[2] But with a few notable exceptions, Peter Brown's work on the graves of martyrs and Jonathan Z. Smith's essays on fourth-century Jerusalem and Constantinople in *To Take Place*, very little attention has been given to early Christian construals of space.[3] The reason seems obvious. Christianity does not claim ties to any particular territory. But that only begs the question: What was it about early Christian interpretations of space that made it seem so universal and transplantable? That question is important for moral reflection on the colonial expansion of Christianity into the Americas, Australia, Africa, and elsewhere. Why have Christians so often thought it permissible and even morally imperative to carry their message across all boundaries, invading the homelands of other communities?

The question is also important for the study of religion as religion because the discipline has arisen within a predominantly Christian milieu. Thus it is likely that unexamined Christian assumptions about space still serve as the lenses through which historians of religion interpret the exotic spaces of the post-colonial world. It is because of my

---

1. Mircea Eliade, *Cosmos and History: The Myth of the Eternal Return* (trans. Willard R. Trask; New York: Harper Torchbooks, 1959).

2. This article originally appeared in *JAAR* 62 (1994), pp. 241-63. At that time Jacob Neusner raised questions as to whether any Jewish community could actually have existed in the first century with an attachment to place in the way I had reconstructed it (personal communication). However, even if he were right in his challenge to my reconstruction, my main argument would still remain unchanged. For the rhetoric of the Fourth Gospel would function in the same way even when the community was only a stereotypical foil constructed by the author of John.

3. Peter Brown, *The Cult of the Saints: Its Rise and Function in Latin Christianity* (Chicago: University of Chicago Press, 1981); Jonathan Z. Smith, *To Take Place: Toward Theory in Ritual* (Chicago: University of Chicago Press, 1987).

interest in Christian effects on the study of sacred space that I approach the Gospel of John through what might otherwise seem like a circuitous route—the early work of Mircea Eliade. In doing so my intent is not to interpret John through the work of Mircea Eliade but rather to use Eliade as a modern example of the gospel's influence on modern thinking about sacred places. In *Cosmos and History* Eliade implies that the history of religions as he practiced it was made possible by a profound change in the religious evaluation of space that began with the Hebrew prophets and culminated in Johannine Christianity.

Although Eliade formulated his original argument in terms of the shift from cyclical to historical time, it was clearly intended to apply to space as well, i.e. to the move from 'archaic' sacred centers to Judeo-Christian notions of decentralized space.[4] Reformulated in terms of space, here is Eliade's argument. The orienting power of the so-called 'archaic' religions was always precarious because they had no positive way of valuing the strange places outside the orbit of local sacred centers. These foreign spaces could be interpreted only as profane spaces, and their threatening character could then be abolished only dialectically through periodic reenactments of the origin at the center. The problem was that in times of catastrophic dislocation, such as the Judean exile to Babylon, traditional rituals lost their power to reestablish the center. As a result, space threatened to become permanently emptied of meaning. In temporal terms Eliade called this 'the terror of history', but it could equally be called the terror of secular space.[5]

In response to this situation, the Hebrew prophets began to see history itself, and by analogy one could say the decentralized spaces of their exile, as the place where Yahweh appeared.[6] According to Eliade, this new way of valuing novel places came to its fullest expression in the Christian myth of the incarnation. He does not explicitly cite the Gospel of John at this point, but John is the earliest systematic articulation of Christian thought on the incarnation. With the faith that God was incarnate in history, it became possible to recognize every place as a potential space for revelation. For the first time a religious community had freed its own center from attachment to any particular place.[7] The new became meaningful.

This Christian insight into the potential sacrality of all spaces made

4. Eliade, *Cosmos and History*, pp. 141-62.
5. Eliade, *Cosmos and History*, p. 108.
6. Mircea Eliade, *The Sacred and the Profane: The Nature of Religion* (trans. Willard R. Trask; New York: Harcourt Brace, 1959), p. 137.
7. Eliade, *The Sacred and the Profane*, p. 137.

Christianity exportable. And this same insight, historically at least, pro-vided the ground of possibility for the history of religions as practiced by Eliade. In the archaic religions the symbols of diverse sacred centers could not be gathered into a cumulative list or morphology because their meanings seemed to clash. For example, one of the archaic sacred centers cited by Eliade is the famous Samaritan well encountered in John 4. Its claim to be the center would have competed with the claims of other sacred centers such as the healing waters in Jerusalem or (if they had ever come into historical contact) even Lake Titicaca, the sacred center of the Inca universe.

But with the changing evaluation of spaces that culminated in the incarnational insights of Johannine Christianity, all of this changed. Because the incarnational insight allowed the symbols of diverse centers to be delocalized without loss of meaning, in principle at least, the cen-ters ceased to clash among themselves or to cancel each other out. Appearances of the sacred across the globe could finally be recognized as cumulative rather than competitive. This is why Eliade saw the delocaliz-ation of sacred meanings in Christianity as the fulfillment of 'primitive' religious thought about space. As he put it, the 'universal aquatic symbolism' of sacred centers, like Lake Titicaca or the Well of Samaria, 'was neither abolished nor dismembered by the historical...interpret-ations of baptismal symbolism'. In fact, 'It could even be said that...aqua-tic symbolism awaited a fulfillment of its deepest meaning through the new values contributed by Christianity.'[8]

Put in more secular language, the new value that Eliade thought Christianity contributed was the recognition that ordinary places and ordinary 'history constantly add new meanings, but they do not destroy the structure of the symbol'.[9] This insight made possible Eliade's mor-phological approach of gathering into a pattern the sacred symbols scattered across space and time. And although Eliade usually avoided explicitly Christian language, fundamentally Christian notions gave him the confidence to proceed with his morphology. 'It is the incarnation of God in historical time [and decentered space]', he wrote, 'that, in the Christian view, guarantees the validity of symbols.'[10]

In this essay I examine the meaning of sacred spaces and spacelessness that emerges from the interplay of certain key passages in the Gospel of John, especially the prologue, and two of the signs performed in chap-ters four and six. I choose the Fourth Gospel because it is the text in

---

8. Eliade, *The Sacred and the Profane*, p. 137.
9. Eliade, *The Sacred and the Profane*, p. 137.
10. Eliade, *The Sacred and the Profane*, p. 137.

which the Christian language of incarnation first emerges and because, more than any other, it foreshadows the universalizing direction of later Christian attitudes toward space. While I am aware of the source critical problems, I intend to leave them aside in order to examine the text as a whole. For it is, after all, as a whole that the Gospel has had its impact on the Christian tradition.

For the purposes of this essay I will assume that some sort of Johannine community behind the Gospel of John did indeed exist, more or less along the lines posited by Raymond Brown. As a kind of thought experiment, I interpret the Fourth Gospel anthropologically, almost as though it were a cycle of Native American culture hero stories foundational for a community. In other words, I want to interpret the gospel as the collection of origin narratives that reflect and determine a community's orientation in space. My argument does not really depend on Brown's position, however, because even if it should turn out that no distinctively Johannine community actually existed in the early second century, it remains the case that the Fourth Gospel has played a foundational role for Christianity as a whole, and thus all later Christian movements are, at least in part, Johannine communities.

How, then, does the Johannine 'culture hero' orient his community in space? On the eve of his death Jesus tells his disciples that his exit is required in order 'to prepare a place' for them in the Father's House (14.2). No doubt he is speaking about some kind of spiritual place, but the steps he took to prepare it had very real consequences for this-worldly construals of ethnic territory. Most important, the opening of a spiritual place in 'the Father's House' seems to have required an end to the sacred topographies of this world. The clearest passage to this effect is Jesus' announcement to the Samaritans that true worship would no longer take place 'on this mountain [Mt Gerizim, the center of Samaritan identity], nor in Jerusalem [the center of Jewish identity]', but 'in spirit' (4.21-23). That statement is provocative because it posits the place-bound character of ethnic identity as something to be overcome in the newly opened placeless place of Johannine worship. Why did this particular Christian community want to abolish the privacy and polite distance sustained by ethnic territories, and what were the ethical consequences of doing so?

Judging from the few statements of purpose that appear in the Gospel, the Johannine community seems to have seen the fracturing of social harmony as a primary symptom of the world's separation from God. One important piece of evidence for this is Caiaphas's statement that Jesus must die in order 'to gather into one the scattered children of God'. If the gathering together announced by Caiaphas is indeed the salvific act that was foundational for the Johannine community, then scatteredness was their perception of the cosmic problem Jesus was to overcome. Ordinarily we might suspect such a statement because it is the speech of an enemy, but the text explicitly tells us that Caiaphas spoke not of his own accord but by revelation. It therefore requires us to interpret Caiaphas as a mouthpiece of the author.

That the scattered children in question are not just individuals but separated communities might be inferred from the speech of the Samaritan woman in John 4. She announces that when the Messiah comes he will overcome the split between Jews and Samaritans. Her concern, which seems to mirror the concern of the Johannine community, is clearly with the separated condition of whole communities. The Samaritan woman's view of the Messianic task seems to be seconded by Jesus himself when he says that he has come to create 'one flock and one shepherd', presumably out of various flocks and various shepherds (10.16).

But what caused the scattering? How is it related to religious attitudes toward space? And how exactly was it to be overcome through the acts of Jesus? To be sure, the scattering in question involved other dimensions of religious life besides space. But to anticipate my argument, one reason for divisiveness identified by the Johannine community seems to have been the mistaken attachment of ethnic identity to concrete sacred places, especially to places of origin. Consequently, the Johannine Jesus gathers at least some of the 'scattered children of God' by abolishing the territorial markers that had divided them into separate ethnic communities. He does this by reenacting in reverse certain foundational acts through which the patriarchs had differentiated ethnic space in the beginning.

Before turning to John, it may be helpful to review some of the common cultural resources used by Hellenistic thinkers to link the ethnic territories to a common center. Although a brief sketch is bound to distort, it will at least provide a context within which a more careful analysis of the Johannine passages can be carried out. According to Peter Brown, hellenized Jews, Christians, and pagans alike linked ethnic territories to semi-divine patrons called 'gods' or 'angels'.[11] Thus the author of the Apocalypse could write to 'the seven angels of the seven churches' of seven cities of Asia Minor. And rabbinical writers could speak of the angel of Egypt, the angel of Babylon, or the angel of Rome. In the Greco-Roman world, the gods around which the nations formed were often imagined to have been divinized emperors or hero founders such

---

11. Peter Brown, *The Cult of the Saints*.

as Romulus and Remus. Influenced by these ideas, Christians, and to a lesser extent Jews, began to think of their own founding fathers and mothers in a similar light. The graves of the patriarchs, the places they prayed, and the relics they left came to distinguish particular territories in the manifold world. Because the fathers were also oriented toward the One God, these same patriarchal shrines also served as beacons of light to draw their descendants back from the manifold world to the unity of the One God. In retrospect, the legendary twelvefold division of the tribes could therefore be imagined as a stylized image of the One in the many.

Plotinus distinguished this mediating layer of patron 'gods' or national founders by their more stable attachment to the One. Although all souls ought to orbit harmoniously, 'only the souls of gods do so always'. 'It is this that makes them gods,' he writes, 'for a god is closely attached to this center, those further from it are average men...'[12] The average citizens of each nation, then, orbited around the local shrines of their own god, and the gods in turn orbited around the One.

For our purposes, a particularly important example of this Hellenistic reinterpretation of national founders is Philo's portrait of Moses. It was Moses' journey out of Egypt to the boundaries of Canaan that had established the mythic geography of the wilderness so important to post-exilic Israelite piety. In Philo's hellenized thought, however, the earthly places marked out by that journey become pointers for a different kind of journey—an ascent from the manifold places of the bodily world to the spiritual 'place which is...the Logos':

> [T]he work proper to those who serve Being [the Hebrews] is not...to shape...bodily things like brick, [the jobs performed by the slaves in Egypt] but to ascend in mind to the ethereal height, setting before them Moses, the God-loved type, as leader on the road. For then they will behold the 'place' which is really the Logos, where God the immovable and immutable, stands...[13]

For Philo, the founder of the Israelite nation becomes a 'God-loved type' or embodiment of the Logos, 'a leader on the road' who turns Hebrew eyes from their physical homeland toward the One whom Plotinus called 'our true country'. Consequently the Mosaic spaces of this world (Egypt, the Red Sea, Sinai, the wilderness) all become signposts to the true country, 'the place which is the Logos', where all physical divisions of the

---

12. *Enneads* 6.9.8; Willis Barnstone, *The Other Bible: Ancient Esoteric Texts* (San Francisco: Harper & Row, 1984), p. 730.

13. 'The Confusion of Tongues', in *Philo*. IV. *Loeb Classical Library* (trans. F.H. Colson and G.H. Whitaker; Cambridge, MA: Harvard University Press, 1932), pp. 95-97.

manifold world are left behind.[14] It is within this broad framework of Hellenistic thought on unity and the nature of ethnic territories that the problem of attachment to sacred space presupposed by John will best be understood.

The Prologue

Unlike the birth narratives of Matthew and Luke, the Johannine prologue is not related to the acts of Jesus as first in a series, but rather as a key to their meaning. It tells the reader what to expect in the series of *semeia*, or 'signs', that Jesus is about to perform. Evoking certain Hellenistic interpretations of Genesis, the prologue identifies Jesus with the light of creation, probably a gentile version of the Torah light. In the beginning, this light shone out into the darkness to create the world. Each part of the manifold world would therefore seem to be a crystallization of the Torah's light. As such, all spaces in this world would presumably have had the potential to act as a kind of mirror to the source of light from which they were created.

Although this light of creation enlightens every place and every person it creates, it has a special relation to its 'own' people, who are later identified with the Jews. There is no evidence that the Johannine community knew of the rabbinic traditions that Israel was the center of creation and the place from which the creation began, but it seems likely that the territory of the Jewish people was also imagined to have had a special relation to the light, because throughout the Gospel the *Ioudaioi* are identified with a certain mythic geography.[15] They in particular kept the memory of the various patriarchs, the holy places, the written Torah itself—all signposts orienting the world back toward the light from which it came.

The problem presupposed by John includes a breakdown in this orienting function of the Jewish people and thus of the patriarchal memories that their spaces had preserved. For reasons still to be examined, the *Ioudaioi* had evidently cut themselves off from the unifying light of creation. Primordial conditions returned and the children of God were scattered in darkness. In the acts of Jesus which the prologue introduces, the light of creation is said to return to the world, probably to gather its scattered children back into one as predicted by Caiaphas

14. Philo, 'The Confusion of Tongues', p. 61.
15. I retain the untranslated term *Ioudaioi* here in order to bracket the question of whether the term actually refers to Jews in anything like the modern sense at a time when rabbinic Judaism was still in an incipient phase.

later in the Gospel. But how, exactly? Some of the signs that Jesus
performs are clearly dramas that reenact the foundational deeds of local
patriarchs. Their purpose, as I will argue later on, seems to be to reconnect the fathers of specific places with the one Father, and the geographies they founded with the one true country.

The prologue alerts us to expect two opposing responses to these
semeia. On the one hand, the light of creation will come to its own home,
its own place, but there it will not be received. The light will then come
to others who evidently are not its own, but they will respond and
become children of God. The first are clearly the *Ioudaioi*, while the
second are the members of the incipient Johannine community most
clearly represented in the gospel by the Samaritans. It is my thesis that
these contrasting responses are in fact two opposing attitudes toward
ethnic territory. As such, they provide a key to the religious meaning of
space in the early Johannine community.

Since the prologue clues us to expect this two-fold response to the
semeia, I will use it as the structuring principle of the essay. My strategy
will be to examine the meaning of ethnic territory in two of the *semeia* or
patriarchal mini-dramas Jesus performs: first, a Jacob-like performance
at the Well of Samaria, and second, a Moses-like performance to *Ioudaioi*
in their special territory, the wilderness. In each case I will be looking for
correspondences between the patriarchal signs which distinguish the
territories and the unity of all places in 'the Father's House' to which
they point.

Jesus and the Samaritan Jacob (John 4)

As the scene opens, the stage is very clearly described as the patriarchal
space of Samaritan identity: 'He came to a city of Samaria called Sychar,
near the field that Jacob gave to his son Joseph. Jacob's well was there.'
At this patriarchal relic he appears to a woman who is identified only
generically, as a Samaritan. Because her conversion immediately results
in the conversion of the entire town, the woman seems to represent the
Samaritan people as a whole.

In the course of their short dialogue, the woman identifies two prom-
inent features of the landscape which were formative of Samaritan
identity, and both of them are relics of the patriarch Jacob. Mt Gerizim
is the place where Jacob prayed. Fidelity to that ritual center is what
stigmatizes local worship as Samaritan, separating them off from the
Ioudaioi. The well itself is identified as the 'gift of our father Jacob', a
center of local hagiography. Significantly for our larger argument,
Mircea Eliade cites this very well as one of his examples of a sacred

center that oriented a community in space and time. According to a tradition (which unfortunately he does not cite), the well was believed to be located at the very center of the world, and its waters were the primordial waters of creation. But even if that tradition was unknown to the Johannine community (as is likely), Jacob is clearly not just any patriarch, but the founder whose acts of bequeathing fields, digging wells, and praying on mountains had created the spaces of Samaritan identify. One need not have read Eliade to see that in drinking from the well Samaritans were linked to the formative age of the patriarchs and to Jacob, founder of their town.

What is the plight of this woman, who is identified only as a Samaritan whose identity is formed by the Jacob relics? Whatever her plight is, it is symbolized by her only other salient characteristic: she has five husbands. However the author may have intended it, the Gospel's Hellenistic audience would not have seen physical polyandry as the woman's greatest problem.[16] It is more likely that they would have identified the woman as the Samaritan *pysche* and her many husbands as the dispersed loves that separated her from the One—her spiritual bridegroom.

The problem of the Samaritan people as represented by the woman is not only that the dispersal of her loves separates her from the One, but that her attachment to the Samaritan Jacob shrines separates her from other ethnic communities, especially the *Ioudaioi*. As we will see in a moment, the woman explicitly comments on the divisive function of both Jacob's well and Mt Gerizim. Thus we may have a picture of the Samaritan community as a woman, who, forgetful of her true origins, is lost in the promiscuous multiplicity of ethnic spaces. The entanglement of her identity with two shrines that mark off Samaritan territory has obscured the true origin and goal of her love: the One Father to which the relics of 'our father Jacob' ought to point. And the result is ethnic discord.

How does the Johannine Jesus overcome this problem? His first act is to make a request that blurs ethnic boundaries. Appearing as one of the *Ioudaioi*, he asks for a drink of the sacramental waters that bind Samaritans to their territory and their patriarch. As one might expect, the confused woman doesn't know how to respond except to remind him of

16. According to Heracleon, for example, the question 'Where is your husband?' is meant to wake up the pneumatic and recall her love to her true counterpart—her spiritual husband in the *pleroma*. The many husbands represent the dispersal of her loves in the ignorance of the psychic realm. See Elaine H. Pagels, *The Johannine Gospels in Gnostic Exegesis: Heracleon's Commentary on John* (SBLMS, Atlanta: Scholars Press, 1973), pp. 87-88.

the ethnic difference that separates them: 'How is it that you, a *Ioudaios*, ask me, a woman of Samaria, for a drink?' If the water of John 4 is parallel to the manna of John 6, then a Jew asking to drink of the Samaritan Jacob water is a little like an Egyptian asking for some of the manna given to the fleeing children of Israel. It upsets ethnic boundaries.

He then further confuses things by suggesting that if her understanding had not been so clouded she would have asked him for water—a petition ordinarily appropriate only to 'our father Jacob', patron of the Samaritan well. The woman makes the connection, of course, and asks him straight out if he is someone greater than Jacob, i.e. the one to whom Jacob points. Since greatness is measured comparatively and from the perspective of an observer, the connotation seems to be 'Are you claiming to outdo Jacob? To be a more powerful source of our life as Samaritans than our founder Jacob is?'

In reply, Jesus makes a contrast between the physical water to which the Samaritans must return again and again and the permanent well of living water which Jesus gives. The speech closely parallels the contrast made to the *Ioudaioi* between the perishing manna which their father Moses gave and the living bread from heaven made present in the *semeion* Jesus performed. Evidently the living well is the Logos or spiritual place to which the physical place points. By asking for water, the woman implicitly assents to this claim, shifting her allegiance from the patriarch Jacob and the physical well that had centered Samaritan space to this new returning Jacob and his spaceless living well.

At this point Jesus further opens her eyes to the scattered character of her loves by asking her to call her husband. It is unclear what the husbands refer to, but certainly Jesus does not ask her to be reconciled with some actual man from which she has been separated. It may be that in asking the question Jesus makes her recognize that, although her true husband is the One Father, her loves have been promiscuously attached to the many Jacob signs intended only to point to that One.

What suggests this interpretation is that the woman responds to Jesus' revelation of her many husbands with a question about competing loyalties to ethnic shrines: 'Sir, I perceive that you are a prophet. Our [Samaritan] fathers [or patriarchs] worshiped on this mountain; and you [Jews] say that in Jerusalem is the place where men ought to worship' (Jn 4.19-20). Jesus then makes it perfectly clear that overcoming the problem of dispersed loves entails the transfer of loyalties from the patriarchal geography that had divided ethnic territories to the spiritual place of the Father: '[T]he hour is coming when neither on this mountain nor in Jerusalem will you worship the Father... God is spirit and those who worship him must worship in spirit and truth' (Jn 4.21-24).

Jesus' response causes the woman to long for the end time when the Messiah would unify the disparate communities by providing the final answer. Only then does Jesus say to her, 'I...am he.'

The drama ends when the woman directs the townspeople to the one who had made her Samaritan life transparent. The town as a whole then transfers its allegiance from the patriarchal relics that mark their territory to the Father as embodied in the Jacob drama performed by Jesus. The separatist space marked off from Jewish territory by the Jacob shrines now collapses, and the encounter between Jesus and the Samaritan becomes a sign of the Messianic overcoming of ethnic separation.

Jesus and the Mosaic Space of the *Ioudaioi*: 'He Came to his Own but his Own did Not Receive Him'

In the Gospel of John the term '*Ioudaioi*' gains its meaning through a contrast not to 'Christians', but to 'Samaritans'. The irony of the contrast seems to depend on the previous reputations of the two groups. While the *Ioudaioi* were traditionally the beacons of unity, the Samaritans had a reputation for being schismatic. Yet their respective response to the *semeia* or drama/signs of Jesus is exactly the opposite of what their reputations might lead one to expect.

Just as the *semeion* performed in John 4 depends on a previous identification of Jacob as the founding father of the Samaritan people, so the *semeion* performed in John 6 depends on identifying Moses as the patriarch of the *Ioudaioi*.[17] Our comparison will focus on the way Jesus now evokes the acts through which Moses had founded the special space of the *Ioudaioi*. Since there is every reason to believe that the writer of the Gospel had no firsthand knowledge of Palestinian geography, what I intend to examine is not Jesus' relation to the actual shrines of Palestine, but to the special space of the *Ioudaioi* as it might be reconstructed theologically from the Septuagint. One might immediately think of Canaan. For some of the prophets, however, such as Hosea, as well as for later reform groups such as the Essenes, the followers of the Baptist, and certain early rabbinic circles, it was the wilderness between Egypt and Canaan that represented Hebrew identity at its most pristine.

17. See Wayne Meeks, *The Prophet King* (Leiden: E.J. Brill, 1967). Meeks argues that the kingly character of Moses in the Johannine Gospel points to a Samaritan component or origin for the Gospel. In the history behind the text that may be the case, but in the text itself Moses is contrasted as patron of the *Ioudaioi* to Jacob, patron of Samaria. If Meeks is right in identifying a Mosaic prophet-king tradition with Samaria, this would only indicate that the writer of the Fourth Gospel had little knowledge of the historical Jewish and Samaritan communities in Palestine.

The tractate *Bahodesh* of the *Mekilta de-Rabbi Ishmael* is particularly significant in this regard because it argues that the wilderness became the foundational place of Judaism for reasons that closely parallel Johannine concerns with ethnic territory. 'The Torah was given in public, openly in a free place', it reads. 'For had the Torah been given in the land of Israel, the Israelites could have said to the nations of the world: You have no share in it.'[18] In other words, the Jews as keepers of the Torah are to be keepers of a utopian, that is placeless, testimony to the unity of God. And this testimony is to form the basis for a unity of nations that transcends territory. Although it is a space in this world, the religious purpose of the wilderness space is to signify no place. Its meaning is derived by contrast to the ethnic territory of any one nation and especially to the territory of Israel. Nevertheless the wilderness is a *Ioudaioi* space in a peculiar kind of way because it is the *Ioudaioi* whose ancestors wandered through the wilderness and received the law there. The wilderness is therefore still the special placeless place of the Jews as witnesses to the unity of God.

This wilderness holy land was not the wilderness as completely empty space, however, but the wilderness as marked out by concrete memories of the acts of Moses. Its port of entry is the Reed or 'Red' Sea as opened by Moses, and its center is Mt Sinai as marked out by the ascent of Moses to receive the Torah. Two things were especially important as material relics of this wilderness space: the written Torah brought down from the mountain and the manna with which Moses fed the children of Israel. According to tradition, some of that bread was preserved along with the Torah as a relic in the Ark of the Covenant and was carried before the Hebrew tribes as they conquered the land of Canaan. It is this space as evoked by the acts of Moses, the manna and the Torah, the sea and the mountain, that the Johannine community seems to envision as the special place to which Jewish identity is attached.

We can now examine how the *semeia* or sign/drama performed by Jesus plays on these formative acts of Moses. As the scene opens, Jesus simply appears in the wilderness without announcing who he is and begins to feed miraculous bread to a crowd of *Ioudaioi*. The allusion to manna is unmistakable. The *Ioudaioi* seem to recognize the performer as a returning Moses and attempt to make him king. But Jesus immediately withdraws. We will return to the manner of his withdrawal because it is crucial. But before we can understand the exit, it is necessary to see what Jesus was doing in the manna drama itself.

18. *Melkita de Rabbi Ishmael. II* (trans. Jacob Z. Lauterbach; Philadelphia: The Jewish Publication Society of America, 1976), p. 198.

Some clues are provided by a second encounter. On the following morning the same *Ioudaioi* accost Jesus on the other side of the sea, but significantly they now contrast Moses' act of feeding manna to Jesus' action the day before: 'Our fathers ate the manna in the wilderness as it is written', they say, 'but what signs can you perform?' Speaking in the first person from within the Mosaic persona, Jesus then interprets his own performance of the preceding day: 'Your fathers ate the manna in the wilderness and they died… I am the living bread which came down from heaven' (6.51). Evidently Jesus's reenactment of the Moses drama is meant to reconnect the physical manna and the wilderness place it evoked with its true Logos, the spiritual place 'in the Father's House' with its spiritual bread, which it was Jesus' mission to embody.

The impact of this scene seems to depend on assigning Moses a function similar to that given him by Philo.[19] The true Moses is the 'God-loved type' of Jewish identity, the 'leader on the road' who causes their minds to ascend 'from bodily things' to 'the place of the Logos, where God the immovable…stands…'[20] By portraying a heavenly Moses who will not be made an earthly king, the *semeia* now forces a choice between Moses as beacon of the reunified Logos and the separatist use of Moses as founder of ethnic identity. Similarly it is a choice between the wilderness as a road to unity and the wilderness as the space of a separatist identity. In direct contrast to the Samaritans of John 4, the *Ioudaioi* of John 6 opt for the wilderness as the this-worldly space of their earthly patriarch, with its physical bread and its written Torah, over the heavenly space of unity to which it points. In light of the charges and defense later made in the execution scene, it seems likely that the initial attempt by the *Ioudaioi* to crown the manna provider is to be understood as an attempt to make him defender of a this-worldly *Ioudaioi* territory represented by the wilderness.

From the Johannine perspective this disqualifies the *Ioudaioi* as true heirs of the fathers and as true heirs of the wilderness space they bequeathed. Speaking in the first person as mouthpiece of the living Torah, Jesus announces the judgment of Moses against the *Ioudaioi* who claim his name: 'Do you think that I shall accuse you to the Father? It is Moses who accuses you, on whom you set your hope. If you believed Moses you would have believed me, for he wrote of me.'

It is to act out this rejecting testimony of the patriarch Moses and of the wilderness space he bequeathed that Jesus had withdrawn from the *Ioudaioi* on the previous day. And as I have said, the manner of his

19. Philo, 'The Confusion of Tongues', p. 61.
20. Philo, 'The Confusion of Tongues', pp. 95-97.

withdrawal is crucial. Continuing to play the Mosaic persona, but now in reverse, he first retreats away from the *Ioudaioi* and up a mountain to pray. Since the Johannine author has made it clear from the beginning that Jesus embodies the heavenly light and Logos associated with the Torah, his flight evokes the retreat of the Torah from those who try to make it a physical relic. In fact, a few verses earlier Jesus says explicitly, 'You search the scriptures because you think that in them you have eternal life; and it is they that bear witness to me [the eternal Torah evoked by the *semeia* of Jesus]; yet you refuse to come to me that you may have life' (5.39-40).

After retreating up the mountain, Jesus then exits the wilderness by miraculously walking back across the sea in a manner that would allow no people to follow him. It may be remembered that it was Moses' crossing of the Sea that first opened up the wilderness as the place where the *Ioudaioi* walked with God. Now, by retracing the patriarch's foundational journey in reverse, the Logos of Moses embodied in the performance of Jesus unravels the mythic geography of the Torah and withdraws the material culture of the Hebrew people. By taking the true Logos of the Torah and the manna with him, Jesus severs the ties that had bound the *Ioudaioi* wilderness to 'the Father's House' it had once imaged.

But what does all this have to do with the central theme of disunity and discord between groups? In the Johannine scheme of things, to prefer the physical territory of a patriarch over the unity to which it pointed was to be a schismatic. And to be a schismatic led to hatred of neighboring territories like Samaria and finally to murder—especially to the murder of all those who chose unity. In Jn 8.12-29 the *Ioudaioi* advance a claim to patriarchal identity: 'Abraham is our father.' Jesus' answer is blunt: 'If you were Abraham's children, you would do what Abraham did.' It is not clear from the text just what deeds of Abraham the writer has in mind, but they must have been similar to what Philo's Moses did: to point to 'the "place" which is really the Logos, where God...stands'. It is in contrast to this that Jesus accuses the *Ioudaioi*, 'you [on the other hand] try to kill me, because my Logos finds no place (or does not fit, *ou chorei*) in you'. Their father is therefore not Abraham, the beacon of unity, but the patriarch of all schismatics. 'You are of your father the devil', Jesus says to them, 'and your will is to do your father's desires. He was a murderer from the beginning.'

In accord with this principle that schismatics are murderers, the killing of Jesus finalizes the judgment of the *Ioudaioi* because it pushes their rejection of unity to its murderous conclusion. On the eve of Passover, the same Mosaic performer whom they had earlier tried to crown king of the *Ioudaioi* territory is offered to them again. Their response, 'We have no king but Caesar', could be read as an ironic inversion of the *Shema* with its confession of allegiance to the unity of God. The Roman claim that Caesar was the divine one on whom the unity of the *pax romana* hinged was clearly seen by early Christians as an idolatrous claim to occupy the place of God. The *Ioudaioi*, by contrast, had been given the special task of confessing the unity of God. They were the Logos's own (*idioi*) people to whom the blueprint of unity, the written Torah, had been entrusted. Hence the creedal formula in the *Shema*: 'Hear O Israel the Lord your God is one.' Now, with the pledge to Caesar on their lips, the *Ioudaioi* finally align themselves with the idolatrous claims of the fragmented gentile world and its attempt to kill Jesus, the dramatist who embodies 'the Father's House', the place of unity where the Logos stands. The prologue says cryptically that the Logos came to his own and his own received him not. Their place as beacons of unity is forfeited to the Johannine community.

Of particular importance for our purposes is the way in which the authority of Jesus is derived from the authority of places in John 4 and John 6. Jesus claims to speak nothing but what he has heard from the Father. But in both John 4 and John 6, the script of the *semeia* is supplied neither by Jesus himself nor directly by the Father but by the patriarchal acts which were foundational for the particular ethnic territory in which the *semeia* was performed. Without adding new content, the dramas Jesus performs seem merely to extract the Logos or symbolic meaning from a concrete place. The authority of a very real well located in a field just outside of Sychar is extracted and transformed into the authority of a spring of living water welling up into eternal life.

If the authoritative power of the dramas comes from preexisting sacred places, why does the text insist that the authority of Jesus comes from the Father? It can only be that for the Johannine community the term 'father' derives its meaning by analogy to the fathers: 'our father Jacob', 'our father Abraham', 'our fathers who ate manna in the desert'. Jesus embodies the spaceless Logos of the Father because his performances extract the *logoi* of the fathers from their entanglement in territorial shrines. After watching Jesus perform numerous *semeia*, the rather obtuse disciple Philip asks Jesus to show them the Father. Jesus responds, 'He who has seen me has seen the Father.' But what has Philip actually seen? The dramas. Jesus can say, 'I and the Father are one', because the dramas also reveal that the fathers Moses, Abraham, and Jacob are one with the performer.

The link that Jesus establishes between the fathers and the Father implies a relationship between two kinds of space: the patriarchal homelands and the Father's House, that spaceless place in which all who worship the Father worship neither on the Samaritan Mt Gerizim nor on the *Ioudaioi* Mt Zion but 'in spirit and in truth'.

On the eve of his death Jesus tells his followers that he must exit this world in order to 'prepare a place' for them in the 'Father's House'. By performing the *semeia*, Jesus had already transferred ethnic allegiance from the territorial shrines to his own body. But his body was still one space in the world alongside other competing spaces. As long as his body is there incarnating the *logoi* of the patriarchal territories, no 'true country', no unembodied 'space' for unity could really emerge. In order to open the spaceless rooms of the Father's House, the body space of the one who had incarnated the symbols of the patriarchal homelands also had to be erased. And in fact it is the dissolution of Jesus' body that finally clears a space for the coming of the unifying Spirit. It is only with Jesus' death, therefore, that the epiphany of the Logos recounted in the prologue is complete. And with this completion on his lips the Johannine Jesus dies: '*tetelestai*, it is finished'. The 'children of God' who were 'scattered abroad' entangled in their various territories have now been gathered into one spaceless place of the Spirit.

A Concluding Critique of the Myth

Like many origin myths, the narrative cycle we have just examined is the story of how an earlier people, the *Ioudaioi*, failed to maintain the created order, leading to the return of a chaotic darkness. It then orchestrates a return of the culture hero whose miraculous performances unravel the spaces of the old world. By extracting the true meanings of sacred spaces from the territories that divide, he gathers the scattered children of God into a community of the end time where there is one flock and one shepherd without mediations. The result is the Johannine community, vanguard and continuing agent of the unity that represented the end time return of the many to the One.

But even as utopian a religion as Johannine Christianity sustains an ethos, and every ethos competes for space in this world. Ironically, therefore, the very preparing of the nonterritorial place for unity actually remapped the world in a way that displaced completing religious cultures. By delegitimizing all territorially based religions it actually staked out a new kind of Christian claim to all of the territories of this world. There is, therefore, also a darker side to the Johannine myth that follows from its mapping of the outside world, and this is how I think it worked.

Since the Johannine sect probably did not have recent or direct roots in Palestine, 'Samaritans' and '*Ioudaioi*' would have worked structurally, or metaphorically, as the contrast terms for construing the possible non-Johannine stances toward spaces presently occupied by neighboring communities. It was only against these present representatives of the Samaritans and *Ioudaioi* from the mythic past that Johannine Christians living in a quite different time and place could act out their identity as sparks of light recalled from the darkness of their schismatic homelands into an unmediated fellowship with the One.

Like any mythical map of the world, the Johannine map is a plan of action. Coloring a territory 'Samaritan' would have equated neighboring communities with the pre-conversion past of the Johannine community itself—marking the inhabitants as potential converts still enmeshed in sacred geographies. The term conveys a hope that the ethnic homeland of the community to which it is applied may yet be abolished. For those surrounding communities colored 'Samaritan', Christian love was expected to erase the boundaries of ethnic space, drawing them into the utopian community. Put more suspiciously, Christian love was expected to expand the Johannine ethos into 'Samaritan' territories.

At this point one might ask what would become of the rich religious meaning embedded in the territories into which Johannine Christianity might expand. If meanings of the old sacred places comparable to the Samaritan well or Mt Gerizim are simply abandoned for a new and more abstract consensus, a tremendous impoverishment of religious imagination would result. In fairness to the Johannine community, however, that seems not to have been their intent. By prefixing Neoplatonic terms such as *alethos* (true) or *pneumatikos* (spiritual), the symbols of diverse ethnic origins were to be assimilated without loss of meaning to enhance the expanding universal community's power to imagine, and so to embody the One. But although the intent might be laudable, a tremendous impoverishment of meaning does in fact occur. Despite being eternal, 'living water' is flatter than actual well water. People don't sweat on the dusty pilgrimage to draw it. They aren't shocked by its coldness. They can't smell the camel dung around it that so forcefully recalls Jacob's camels, and so the sense of drinking together with Jacob pales. Like the Samaritan well that became 'living water', the disembodied symbols of other sacred centers would be similarly impoverished.

But impoverishment is not the only issue. Coloring a territory Samaritan also marked the sacred centers of a territory as power symbols to be appropriated or co-opted through a process of spiritualization—a process Augustine was later to call 'despoiling the Egyptians'. By taking over the authority of centers comparable to Mt Gerizim or the well of Sychar, Christians disenfranchised the natives of those places from the symbols that had empowered their ownership of a territory. In short, coloring a territory Samaritan marks it for a loving, but perhaps still unwanted, invasion.

The parallel myth of the rejecting *Ioudaioi* has, of course, played a sobering part in the history of Christian anti-Judaism. By representing Jews as the ultimate betrayers of unity, it transferred the heirship of Hebrew monotheism to what was probably a gentile community. Applied symbolically, the term *Ioudaioi* would have transformed any neighboring community that rejected Christian attempts to co-opt its territory into murderous *Ioudaioi* schismatics who as such forfeited their right to a territory.

This essay is not, however, about anti-Judaism per se, but about the role played by Johannine Christians in the western collapse of ethnic space. My intent has been to question the modern idea that meaning is separable from place by examining the early Christian origins of that idea. The point is certainly not simply to blame the Johannine Christians of the first and second centuries. Their attitudes toward sacred places were part of a much broader Hellenistic trend that included pagans like Plotinus and Jews like Philo. And undoubtedly, the Johannine vision of a harmony gained by transcending attachment to sacred territories has challenged less utopian versions of Christianity in salutary ways, contributing to periodic outbreaks of communitarianism and internationalism.

Nevertheless, the Johannine quest for boundary-less harmony misjudges the human need for private places. Sacred places mark off the boundaries of ethnic territories, and an ethnic territory is in turn like a room adorned with private memories. Such rooms with their pictures are partly meant to shut people out, of course. As such they seem to exclude outsiders from love. But relatedness depends on this privacy. It is out of the identity formed in the privacy of a room, of a home, or of an ethnic shrine that people enter into productive relations with each other. Therefore, the most public symbols are also the most derivative. Their shared meanings are powerful only if they evoke, without exposing, the most cherished private memories of a birthplace, an old hometown, a private room.

The early Johannine Christians over-identified fidelity to one's own room or home ground with divisiveness. By abandoning the boundaried world of ethnic territories, they also abandoned the private places and middle grounds needed to nurture diversity. In the spaceless world the Johannine Christians had hoped for, room for unity had actually shrunk, relatedness was asphyxiated, and divisiveness exacerbated. The first epistle of John concludes sadly, 'We know that we are of God and that the whole world is in the power of the evil one' (5.19).

The historical effects of this Johannine remapping of the world have been significant. There are, of course, complex economic and political reasons for colonialism. But Christian perspectives on sacred places that marked the centers and boundaries of ethnic territories certainly played an important part. Since the heirs of the Johannine tradition no longer recognized the distinctiveness of the space they occupied, there was no longer any way of mediating respectful relations between ethnically Christian spaces and those of African or of American tribes. The sacred spaces marked out by foreign culture heroes could only be recognized as mission fields, and the Christian ethos which imagined itself to occupy no place overran the globe.

Although it would take a different essay, I would argue that the Gospel of John is of particular interest to mission historians because of the way it influenced missionary approaches to local culture heroes and the sacred geographies they establish. Just as Samaritan attachment to Mt Gerizim was transcended in the true worship of the Father in spirit and in truth, so American Indian attachment to this or that sacred mountain was also to be transcended. Although this modern use of the Fourth Gospel is beyond my present scope, the intent of this essay has been to examine the religious meaning of ethnic space and spiritual placelessness within the Gospel itself so that the reasons for such later effects can be more easily understood.

The novel Christian perspectives on space that derived in part from the Johannine community also influenced some of the great historians of religion, Mircea Eliade in particular. These scholars certainly did not desire to abolish sacred territories, but like that Johannine community and like much of Protestant and Orthodox thought, they were convinced that the true meaning of sacred places was detachable from the places themselves. Far from conflicting with each other, the holy places of the diverse tribes shed light on space as a universal category of human imagination.

In Eliade's view, the gathering of the diverse symbols from sacred centers around the world into patterns had the potential to expand the imaginative capacity of human beings, thus opening a way for a new humanism.[21] As he saw it, this new humanism provided a third way between the inherently precarious 'primitive' religions and a paralyzing terror of secular space and history. As we have already seen, the Well of

21. Eliade's theory of this new humanism is most clearly articulated in his essay 'A New Humanism', in *The Quest: History and Meaning in Religion* (Chicago: The University of Chicago Press, 1969), pp. 1-11. His practice of gathering the symbols into patterns is best exemplified in *Patterns in Comparative Religion* (trans. Rosemary Sheed; New York: Sheed & Ward, 1958).

Samaria is one of the many symbols Eliade arranges alongside others to reveal the meaning of the center. He could argue that the 'universal aquatic symbolism' revealed in sacred centers like the Samaritan well 'was neither abolished nor dismembered by the historical…interpretations of baptismal symbolism'.[22] Historically, at least, it was the master symbol of God's incarnation into profane space, an idea which first appears in the Gospel of John, which made this new way of studying religion possible.

Jonathan Z. Smith has pointed out certain troubling dimensions of the break between symbol and place which the modern study of religion has inherited from Christianity. The study of myths abstracted from places 'was conceived, from the beginning, as the study of belief, and enterprise of a "hermeneutic of recovery"'.[23] But in the process of being 'recovered', that is, cut apart and exported from their ethnic terrain to enhance the meaningfulness of a supposedly global human community, indigenous symbols were co-opted. If the myths were co-opted, then the rites, which were less separable from the territory then were myths, fared worse. Smith does not use the example of Jacob's well but it fits his argument. Once the spiritual meaning of water had been divorced from the physical Samaritan well itself, any ritual which remained connected with that place would have been perceived as empty, a mere leftover formality, a *superstition*. So, too, once the meaning of American Indian or African sacred places has been 'retrieved', that is extracted and appropriated, the rituals still associated with those places begin to seem empty. The modern study of such rituals, Smith argues, 'was born as an exercise in the "hermeneutic of suspicion", an explanatory endeavor designed to explain away'.[24] The typical colonial stance toward ritual was extirpation.

In conclusion, the Samaritan woman who represented the Johannine community may have thought that if Jesus gave her spiritual water there would no longer be any reason for the journey to Jacob's well, that the rite of going there would become pointless, but in light of subsequent history she turned out to be wrong. The meaning of a place is not transferable. It is in the memories of the dead who are buried there. It is in the blood of victims that has been shed there. It is in the taste of that particular spring. It is in the way the dirt and heat combine with the footprints of ancestors on that particular pilgrimage road. And it is part of the meaning of such sacred places that their presence is irreplaceable. One either has to go there or not be there. Rituals are irreplaceable

22. Eliade Smith, *The Sacred and the Profane*, p. 137.
23. Smith, *To Take Place*, p. 101.
24. Smith, *To Take Place*, p. 102.

responses to these irreplaceable places. There is simply no substitute for walking to a grave and crying there, for praying at the place where victims fell, for tasting the water from the well of one's ancestors. Despite the Johannine hope, modern people will continue to fight for such things with good reason.

This non-transferable quality of sacred places certainly does not mean that they cannot or ought not be compared. But it does change the way in which comparison should be done. Mircea Eliade's comparative work on sacred centers has undoubtedly increased the capacity of western culture to imagine space. And it has also done much to increase the respect in which native traditions are held. But it was motivated by some of the same utopian hope that motivated the Johannine community. The meaning of sacred places cannot really be extracted and captured in a text or a photograph or a recording. Photographs and recordings taken from holy places and arranged into the morphological patterns of the imagination cannot really capture the meaning of a place. In fact, they will only make pilgrims feel the absence of the place more acutely. And therefore the best comparisons will happen when the pictures and the texts are recognized for what they are: the comparative signs of the absence of irreplaceable places.

'Dis Place, Man':[1] A Postcolonial Critique of the Vine (the Mountain and the Temple) in the Gospel of John

JEFFREY L. STALEY

Place is the beginning of our existence, just as a father (Francis Bacon)

She lived divided, straining to adjust to this place where she seemed to float, never to light... (Michelle Cliff)

'Dis Place'[2] of Mine

I have been thinking a lot about fatherhood and place lately, since fatherhood has been my primary vocation for the past few years, and since my family recently moved from Portland, Oregon to Seattle, Washington. For the last ten years I have been flitting between a number of part-time and temporary teaching positions while my wife has worked

---

1. This phrase is intended to evoke both Jacques Derrida's concept of 'déplacement' and the problems of deferral (see Patrick Chatelion Counet, *John, A Postmodern Gospel: Introduction to Deconstructive Exegesis Applied to the Fourth Gospel* [Biblical Interpretation Series, 44; Leiden: E.J. Brill, 2000], pp. 158-61), and a postcolonial reading context (see Smadar Lavie and Ted Swedenburg [eds.], *Displacement, Diaspora, and Geographies of Identity* [Durham, NC: Duke University Press, 1996]). And speaking of déplacement, my present essay is displacing an earlier version which appeared as 'The Politics of Place and the Place of Politics in the Gospel of John', in Fernando F. Segovia (ed.), *'What is John'*. II. *Literary and Social Readings of the Fourth Gospel* (Symposium Series, 7; Atlanta: Scholars Press, 1998), pp. 265-77.

2. For the complex, postcolonial meaning of 'dis place' that informs this essay, see Michelle Cliff, *No Telephone to Heaven* (New York: Penguin, 1996); esp. pp. 14-16, 117-18, 189. On the more specific significance of 'dis', dialects, accents and 'lingua vernacula', see Cliff, *No Telephone to Heaven*, pp. 38-39, 74-75; Mikhail Bakhtin, *The Dialogic Imagination: Four Essays* (ed. Michael Holquist; trans. Caryl Emerson and Michael Holquist; Austin: University of Texas Press, 1981), pp. 301-31; and Douglas Burton-Christie, 'Words Beneath the Water: Logos, Cosmos, and the Spirit of Place', in Dieter T. Hessel and Rosemary Radford Ruether (eds.), *Christianity and Ecology: Seeking the Well-Being of Earth and Humans* (Cambridge, MA: Harvard University Press, 2000), pp. 324-25.

full time outside our home. Every few months I have sent out my *Vita*—my 'Innagaddadavida, baby'—looking for the Garden of Eden, the abundant life Jesus was talking about in John 10—tenure, a real salary with health benefits, a retirement plan, and tuition-less college education for my children. I have spent countless hours sitting by the telephone, pretending to write scholarly essays while waiting for that special phone call.

Jesus! It's beginning to ring! Is it really you?

'Yes, I sent you my *Vita* a few months ago. Yes, I'm the one with the PhD in Biblical Studies (New Testament) from the Graduate Theological Union in Berkeley, California. I finished my degree back in 1985. Before that I did an MA in Theology at Fuller Theological Seminary, in Pasadena, California. I finished that in 1979, and my first degree was a BA in Greek and Religion from Wheaton College in Illinois. You can see from my transcript that I graduated in 1973 with High Honors.'

Over the years I have gotten a few campus interviews, but never the final call that ends, ' Τετέλεσται' (Jn 19.30). 'The nightmare is over. We want you.'

There is 'no telephone to heaven. No voice to God'.[3]

Now I'm beyond desperation. Things have gotten so bad that I've taken to posting my *Vita* in the bathroom stalls of all the gas stations on Interstate 5 between Seattle and Tacoma, Washington, where I've been teaching lately.[4] Using my car keys, I scratch my vital records into the gray metal dividers next to those racks of fluorescent-colored condoms and plastic joy rings.

'For a good time, call Dr Jeffrey L. Staley, PhD, at (425) 485-2278, or find him on the Worldwide Web at: http://www.sarweb.org/staley/staley. htm'. Or is it http://www.staleywise.com/ or http:// or http://www.igc.org/ staley/? How about trying http://artists.mp3s.com/artists/144/staley_ thomsen_audiocan.html, http://cnews.tribune.com/news/story/0,1162, wphl-sports-76155,00.html, or http://www.u.arizona.edu/~rstaley/? I must confess that I've been teaching in so many different places that half the time I don't have a clue as to who or where I am. So I dive into the nearest bathroom stall or log into cyberspace and pick out whatever custom-made identity seems to fit at the moment.

---

3.   Cliff, *No Telephone to Heaven*, p. 16.

4.   I am part of what William Leach calls 'the new labor pools [which] include native-born Americans, skilled and unskilled, who work under contract for short periods of time, travel anywhere to take up temporary employment, and often live hand-to-mouth' (*Country of Exiles: The Destruction of Place in American Life* [New York: Random House, 1999], p. 66, cf. 73-74).

For the moment I am living in Bothell, Washington, a suburb of Seattle; near the corporate headquarters of Amazon.com and Microsoft, and a leisurely bike ride away from Chateau Ste. Michelle Winery and the Red Hook Brewery. As a result of this recent displacement, I have decided to put aside for awhile my dream of securing a full-time, tenure-track position in New Testament.[5] Instead, I have turned to writing about fatherhood and the politics of place;[6] and in particular, the politics of 'dis place' as it relates to postcolonial studies of John.

'Dis Place' of My Fathers

When my grandfather Lloyd Malcolm Staley sold his father's house and farm in Franklin County, Kansas at the beginning of the Great Depression, he could not have foreseen that he would be the last Staley to make a living at horticulture.[7] Four generations earlier, in 1833, his ancestor Abraham Staley had packed up his family and meager belongings and moved west to central Indiana from a farm on the Roanoke River in Franklin County, Virginia.

Like his namesake of the Hebrew Bible, Abraham Staley traveled as if by faith, to a land he had never laid eyes on. The only possessions he passed on to his descendants were a few scraps of paper—one, a creditor's note, reads

---

5.   'Moving is often synonymous in our culture with 'getting ahead'. We often admire and aspire to emulate those whose frequent moves signal boldness of vision, dynamism, upward mobility, willingness to stride forth into the expanding horizons of the future', writes Douglas Burton-Christie ('Living Between Two Worlds: Home, Journey and the Quest for Sacred Place' *ATR* 79 [1997], p. 419).

6.   The expression 'politics of place' comes from an important collection of essays on postmodern geographies, entitled *Place and Politics of Identity* (New York: Routledge, 1993) where the editors, Michael Keith and Steve Pile, divide their introduction into two parts, 'Part 1: The Politics of Place', and 'Part 2: The Place of Politics'. Cf. Mary Ann Tolbert, 'Afterwords: The Politics and Poetics of Location', in Fernando F. Segovia and Mary Ann Tolbert (eds.), *Reading from this Place: Social Location and Biblical Interpretation in the United States*, I (Minneapolis: Fortress Press, 1995), pp. 305-17.

7.   On the etymology of the word culture (Latin 'colere'), and its relationship to husbandry and colonialism, see Terry Eagleton, *The Idea of Culture* (Malden, MA: Blackwell, 2000), pp. 1-2, 27.

> *On demand I promise to pay or cause to be*
> *paid unto Christan Vineyard the sim*
> *of eight shillings and 2 pense for valu[.]*
> *rec'd of him as witness my hand and si[...]*
> *January 29ᵗʰ 1812 A[...]*
>
> *Test William Richardson*

I suspect that Mr Vineyard never received the eight shillings and two pence owed him before my great, great, great, great grandfather left Virginia, for Abraham Staley died and was buried in central Indiana.

Abraham's son, Isaac, remained on the lush, verdant land just east of Indianapolis, growing wheat and corn, and working as a toll keeper on the National Road (that marvelous symbol of American 'Manifest Destiny') until his death in 1887. Isaac's son, Abraham E. Staley farmed in nearby Hancock County until moving to Missouri in 1867. Nine years later Abraham E. bought a farm in eastern Kansas, where my great grandfather, grandfather, and father were all raised.

Although my grandfather was forced to sell the family home and farm in 1929, he never lost his love for the earth or for growing things. Whether living in the suburbs of Kansas City, Kansas or in the central coast range at Atascadero, California, he would spend his leisure hours turning small plots of ground into thriving vegetable gardens. Today, as high-maintenance, luxuriant vineyards creep ever closer to the central California house where he and his wife spent their retirement years, I can still recall one peculiar detail of his gardening. His gardens were always laid out in the same order: onions, radishes and lettuce on one side; beans, tomatoes, and corn on the other. For years my father and I have followed the furrows of his dirt-encrusted fingernails without fail, even though I don't particularly like green onions or radishes. It is a planting tradition that probably goes back generations to the gardening mothers in the Staley family.

For me, vegetable gardens have been an unconscious symbol of family rootedness. More than a source of vitamins and fresh produce; more than a way of reducing weekly food costs; vegetable gardening has been a natural, physical way for me to say 'This is my place, my home. This is where I have put down roots and will stay.'[8]

8. 'To be rooted', says geographer David Sopher, 'is the property of vegetables' (quoted in Douglas Burton-Christie, 'Living Between Two Worlds', p. 419). But 'to be rooted is [also] perhaps the most important and least recognized need of the human

In my adult life I have had vegetable gardens in only three locales: in sunny southern California, where I lived for five years and borrowed a small plot from a friendly neighbor; in northern California where I went to graduate school; and in Portland, Oregon, where I lived for eleven years. In southern California I had to pull out yards of tangled, matted bermuda grass and pieces of old concrete in order to grow a few wizened carrots and phallus-shaped zucchini. In northern California I appropriated a piece of ground in my girlfriend's parents' backyard. While I was planting that passion fruit known as the tomato, Barbara and I announced our engagement to my future mother-in-law. In Portland, we bought our first house in part because of its large, raised-bed garden. There I taught my two children how to plant beans, carrots and radishes.

I do not have a vegetable garden in dis new Seattle place.[9] The soil is a thick stew of glacier deposited gravel and stone, fit only for growing horsetail ferns and marshland buttercups.

'Dis Place' in Two Recent Johannine Studies

In a provocative essay entitled 'Territorial Religion, Johannine Religion, and the Vineyard of John 15', Gary M. Burge argues that the christology of the Fourth Gospel is oriented toward displacing the significance of place in the Christian experience.[10] Burge's article picks up a theme from Raymond Brown's commentary that is well known to Johannine scholars, one in which the Johannine Jesus is viewed as replacing Jewish institutions and religious views.[11] But Burge takes this replacement theme in a new direction by focusing on Judaism's identity with the land of Israel and showing how that identity is uprooted by Johannine

---

soul' (Simone Weil, *The Need for Roots: Prelude to a Declaration of Duties toward Mankind* [trans. Arthur Wils; New York: Harper, 1952], p. 43).

9.   James Combs writes that '[i]n the final analysis, gardening perpetuates that most civilized and mature of emotions: hope. At every uncertain moment of individual or social life, there is the potential to abandon hope for despair... Gardening gives credence to holding out hope, since eventually it does rain, and the heat wave passes, and the buttercups return, and the seasons heal the wounds of the land and of the soul' ('Gardens of Earthly Delight', *The Cresset* 63 [2000], p. 30).

10.   Burge argues, 'John finds in his christology an answer to the Jewish yearning for *place*. Christ is *the place* of God's promise' (his emphasis), in 'Territorial Religion, Johannine Christology, and the Vine of John 15', in Joel B. Green and Max Turner (eds.), *Jesus of Nazareth, Lord and Christ: Essays on the Historical Jesus and New Testament Christology* (Grand Rapids: Eerdmans, 1994), p. 389.

11.   *The Gospel According to John* (AB, 29a; Garden City, NY: Doubleday, 1966), pp. cxliii-cxliv. See also R. Alan Culpepper, *Anatomy of the Fourth Gospel: A Study in Literary Design* (Philadelphia: Fortress Press, 1983), pp. 199-202.

christology. Building upon insights gleaned from Walter Brueggemann's and W.D. Davies's studies on Israel's ideology of the land,[12] Burge gives Brown's 'replacement theme' an important political twist, setting it in the context of contemporary Israeli–Palestinian territorial battles and arguments over land—especially as these quarrels are portrayed within American evangelical Protestantism.

Gary Burge's argument for how the land of Israel is displaced in Johannine christology is intertwined with Jesus's use of the vine metaphor in John 15. Burge attempts to show that scholars who have focused only on a Christian, eucharistic context for the Johannine metaphor have limited themselves much too narrowly and have missed its important Jewish context.[13] He argues that the 'vine had a far more diverse and popular usage' in Judaism, where it can refer to the land of Israel, wisdom, and the messiah.[14] But for Burge, the vine image refers primarily to the land of Israel and reflects 'the Fourth Gospel's most profound theological relocation of Israel's 'Holy Space',[15] since Jesus 'chang[es] the place of rootedness for Israel'.[16] Thus, 'the people of Israel cannot claim to be planted as vines in The Land; they cannot be *rooted* in the vineyard unless first they are *grafted* into Jesus' (Jn 15.6).[17] *'In a word, Jesus spiritualizes The Land.'*[18]

Although it is not Burge's explicit intention to refocus contemporary discussions of Johannine christology, his emphasis on the significance of territory and place in ancient Jewish and contemporary Israeli politics

---

12. W. Brueggemann, *The Land: Place as Gift, Promise, and Challenge in Biblical Faith* (Philadelphia: Fortress Press, 1977); and W.D. Davies, *The Territorial Dimension of Judaism* (Minneapolis: Fortress Press, 1992).

13. Burge, 'Territorial Religion', p. 392.

14. Burge, 'Territorial Religion', p. 392. Cf. Craig R. Koester, *Symbolism in the Fourth Gospel: Meaning, Mystery, Community* (Minneapolis: Fortress Press, 1995), pp. 244-47.

15. Burge, 'Territorial Religion', p. 392.

16. Burge, 'Territorial Religion', p. 393. However, Edward Casey reminds us that 'the Hebrew word *Makom*, the name of God, means precisely Place', and that '[a] rabbinical commentary on Genesis exclaims, 'Why is God called Place? Because He is the place of the world, while the world is not his place.' Philo of Alexandria follows suit, [arguing] 'God Himself is called place, for He encompasses all things, but is not encompassed by anything' (*Getting Back into Place: Toward a Renewed Understanding of the Place-World* [Bloomington: Indiana University Press, 1993], p. 17); cf. Jonathan Z. Smith, *To Take Place: Toward Theory in Ritual* (Chicago: University of Chicago Press, 1987), p. 88; and Douglas Burton-Christie, 'A Sense of Place', *The Way* 39 (1999), pp. 59-72.

17. Burge, 'Territorial Religion', p. 393 (his emphasis).

18. Burge, 'Territorial Religion', p. 395.

points Johannine christology in an important new direction. The politics of place is a topic of crucial importance in our postcolonial world, at a time when many immigrant American families are beginning to explore the spirituality of their rootedness in 'the land',[19] at a time when white, upper middle-class citizens of the United States have appropriated Native American expressions of geographical and tribal spirituality,[20] and at a time when daily news reports remind us of the struggle of people for land and independence in such far off places as Bosnia and Herzegovina, Kosovo, Arizona, Rwanda, Iraq, East Timor, South Dakota, Chechnya, Palestine, Northern Ireland, Nevada, Liberia, Turkestan, Sudan, the Amazon rain forests of Brazil—and the list goes on.[21]

But in an article published the same year as Gary Burge's essay, Tod Swanson appraises the Johannine sense of place more critically.[22] Swanson is particularly concerned with the question 'What is it about early Christian interpretations of space that made it seem so universal and transplantable?', and he begins his discussion with a summary of Mircea Eliade's *Cosmos and History*. In this early work Eliade argued that ancient Judaism and Christianity set in motion a process of desacralizing space in the West, a process which ultimately made possible modern comparative studies of religion and ritual.[23] Eliade's fleeting reference to

19. Wendell Berry, *A Place on Earth* (San Francisco: North Point, rev. edn, 1983) and Wallace Stegner 'The Sense of Place', in *Where the Bluebird Sings to the Lemonade Springs: Living and Writing in the West* (New York: Penguin, 1992), pp. 199-206.

20. For example, see Fred Pfeil's chapter entitled 'Guerrillas in the Mist: Wild Guys and New Age Tribes', in *White Guys: Studies in Postmodern Domination and Difference* (New York: Verso, 1995), pp. 167-232.

21. As Doreen Massey writes, 'Since the late 1980s the world has seen the recrudescence of exclusivist claims to places—nationalist, regionalist and localist. All of them have been attempts to fix the meaning of particular spaces, to enclose them, endow them with fixed identities and to claim them as one's own' (*Space, Place, and Gender* [Minneapolis: University of Minnesota Press, 1994], p. 4; see also Patricia Yaeger, 'Introduction: Narrating Space', in Patricia Yaeger [ed.], *The Geography of Identity* [Ann Arbor: University of Michigan Press, 1996], pp. 9-17; and Mark Raper, 'Refugees: Travel under Duress', *The Way* 39 [1999], pp. 27-38).

22. 'To Prepare a Place: Johannine Christianity and the Collapse of Ethnic Territory', *JAAR* 62 (1994), pp. 241-63; reprinted by permission in this volume.

23. Burge, 'Territorial Religion', p. 241. See also Musa Dube's response to Swanson's essay, 'Savior of the World but not of this World: A Postcolonial Reading of Spatial Construction in John', in R.S. Sugirtharajah (ed.), *The Postcolonial Bible* (Sheffield: Sheffield Academic, 1998), pp. 118-35.

Mary Ann Tolbert reflects on similar issues, but without reference to the influence of Johannine theology, in 'Afterwords: Christianity, Imperialism, and the Decentering of Privilege', in Fernando F. Segovia and Mary Ann Tolbert (eds.) *Reading from this*

the Samaritan woman's question about the place of proper worship leads Swanson on a quest through the Fourth Gospel to find the clues to the Johannine reinterpretation of place.[24] Swanson does not claim to be a Johannine scholar, and he seems to depend too much on a Neoplatonic reading of the Fourth Gospel in order to prove his points about the Johannine ideology of place.[25] Nevertheless, he poses important questions for the contemporary interpreter of John's Gospel. He notes in his conclusion that

> even as u-topian a religion as Johannine Christianity sustains an ethos, and every ethos competes for space in this world. Ironically, therefore, the very preparing of the nonterritorial place for unity actually remapped the world in a way that displaced competing religious cultures. By delegitimizing all territorial-based religions it actually staked out a new kind of Christian claim to all of the territories of this world. There is, therefore, also a darker side to the Johannine myth that follows from its mapping of the outside world...[26]

Provocative as Swanson's and Burge's studies are, their essays begin outside their own physical worlds. They pull up colonialist and imperialistic elements from early Christianity and ancient Judaism that are beyond the realm of their own personal experience, and with these in hand they seek to cultivate John's Gospel in such a way that it can reconfigure contemporary colonialist and imperial situations. My strategy, however, is different. For here, in this essay, my scholarly voice and academic agenda is fractured by a personal story—the story of my own reading experience[27]—a reading where ancestral uprootedness and experiences of displacement resonate with other, older memories of 'dis place'. For 'dis place' is as much about the colonized space of the Navajo

---

Place: Social Location and Biblical Interpretation in Global Perspective, II (Minneapolis: Fortress Press, 1995), pp. 347-61.

24. I am using the word 'place' instead of Swanson's less precise use of the term 'space', since many postmodern geographers have been quite careful to distinguish between the meaning of the two terms (for example, see Massey, *Space, Place, and Gender*, pp. 4-10; cf. Yaeger, 'Introduction: Narrating Space', pp. 18-30; and Tim Cresswell, *In Place/Out of Place: Geography, Ideology, and Transgression* [Minneapolis: University of Minneapolis Press, 1996], pp. 149-62).

25. For example see Swanson, 'To Prepare a Place', pp. 246-47, 258.

26. Swanson, 'To Prepare a Place', p. 257.

27. See especially Diane P. Freedman, Olivia Frey, and Frances Murphy Zauhar (eds.), *The Intimate Critique: Autobiographical Literary Criticism* (Durham, NC: Duke University Press, 1993); Paula Gunn Allen, *Off the Reservation: Reflections on Boundary-Busting, Border-Crossing Loose Canons* (Boston: Beacon Press, 1998); and Heather Kerr and Amanda Nettelbeck (eds.), *The Space Between: Australian Women Writing Ficto-criticism* (Nedlands: University of Western Australia, 1998).

Reservation in northeastern Arizona where I grew up, as it is about my own personal sense of 'dis place'-ment. In that former place where I was raised by fundamentalist Protestant missionary parents, we learned to quote Jn 3.16 in Navajo and would recite it to illiterate Native Americans living in a place named 'San Juan' by Spanish Catholic *conquistadores*.

I believe that 'dis place'—especially those fantastic landscapes of the American Southwest—have had a significant impact on how I read the Gospel of John. And so I seek to relate New Testament texts to the contemporary political context of those still living on the Navajo Reservation.[28] However, most of my hermeneutical effort has been directed toward illuminating how *my own personal understanding* of Johannine narrative can be read out of the parched physicality of the San Juan valley which surrounded my childhood home. I have not attempted a political reading of the Gospel of John for those Euro-Americans and Native Americans who lived or presently live in the San Juan region of the American Southwest.[29] Yet Gary Burge's and Tod Swanson's essays provoke other Johannine scholars and me to ask new questions about the place of 'dis place' in the Fourth Gospel. What, for example, would a reading of the Fourth Gospel look like if we were to attempt to read its ideology of geography in the context of our own national story and its postcolonial contexts?

Leaving 'Dis Place' Behind

I am confused by 'dis place'. I thought this old Portland house would be our home forever. But today we are moving, leaving our ten-year μονή behind. The house is now empty, and it echoes hollowly as I pull the door shut and lock it so that no thief can sneak in. This is the only house my children have known, and I have lived in it longer than I have lived anywhere else.

We are moving to Seattle because of my wife's recent promotion. We both think that there might be more job opportunities for me in a larger metropolitan area. We will be 'homeless' during Christmas vacation,

28. Jeffrey L. Staley, *Reading with a Passion: Rhetoric, Autobiography, and the American West in the Gospel of John* (New York: Continuum, 1995), esp. pp. 192-98. See also my more recent reflections regarding the mapping narratives and landscapes in 'Narrative Structure (Self Stricture) in Lk. 4.14–9.62: The United States of Luke's Story World', *Semeia* 72 (1995), pp. 173-76, 206-209. Cf. Swanson, 'To Prepare a Place', pp. 260-61.

29. On the problem of speaking for others, see my *Reading with a Passion*, p. 227 n. 88; p. 237 n. 4; cf. my 'Changing Woman: Postcolonial Reflections on Acts 16.6-40', *JSNT* 73 (1999), pp. 113-35.

living in a condominium in downtown Seattle while we wait for the purchase of our new house to close.

After three months of desperate searching, we have finally settled on a $180,000, six-year-old house that seems to be slowly sinking into a marsh just beyond our backyard fence.[30] We are twenty miles from my wife's workplace in downtown Seattle. Our real estate agent is congratulating us on our purchase; trying, unsuccessfully, to convince us that the house is a great deal.

'You know, the Seattle housing market is supposed to take off in the spring. You're doing the wise thing, buying now.'

Three days after we move in we have to replace a 150-foot-long leaking water line. Maybe that's why the house is sinking into the marsh.

'No, no, no', our new neighbors exclaim, 'That's not a marsh. It's a protected wetlands! Can't you read the signs? Now the wild blackberries that have invaded your backyard are another matter. The county has listed them as a "noxious weed". So you can go in there and hack away at them to your heart's delight'.[31]

But I can't do that. An environmentalist friend of mine has told me that they are Himalayan Giant blackberries. And legend has it that the thorny vines slipped over to this country on nineteenth-century Pacific steamships; on the backs of Chinese immigrants who, like my wife's ancestors, were seeking wealth on the rail lines and mines of California and the great Northwest. So I can't uproot them. They're almost family. Besides, I have promised my children blackberry pies for Halloween and Thanksgiving.

Eventually I will discover that this particular blackberry probably originated in Iran and was introduced to Europe by Theodor Reimers of Hamburg, Germany. From there the famous nineteenth-century

30. 'The place between water and land functions most overtly as a threshold. Its presence signifies the necessity of passing from one state to another', writes Margaret Anne Dooley in *The True Story of the Novel* (New Brunswick, NJ: Rutgers University Press, 1996), p. 321. And again, 'The muddy margin is a place to start from—perpetually a point of departure and rebirth' (335). Douglas Burton-Christie adds, 'To inhabit such a world means learning to dwell in a landscape where borders are fluid and permeable, where life unfolds in unexpected ways in the continuous movement of species back and forth across the borders' ('Into the Body of Another: *Eros*, Embodiment, and Intimacy with the Natural World', *ATR* 81 [1999], p. 13).

31. On the ecological significance of borders and centers, see Gary Meffe and Ronald Carroll, *Principles of Conservation Biology* (Sunderland, MA: Sinauer Associates, 1994), pp. 237-64. These authors make a strong argument that ecosystems with weak centers and active borders are much more likely to be destroyed than ones with strong centers and undisturbed borders.

American horticulturist Luther Burbank introduced it to the Pacific
Northwest wilderness. And there it took off—like, like a wild blackberry.[32] So two years after we move into our house I spend six back-
breaking months of labor cutting down and digging out the vines from
my property that borders on the wetland. But I do not attempt to eradi-
cate the plants from the officially designated wetland itself. I need them
for the blackberry pies I promised my children.

Challenging 'Dis Place'-mentalism in the Gospel of John

Gary Burge's and Tod Swanson's articles offer me a hint of what future
postcolonial readings of John's Gospel might look like. But can the
biblical canon—and the Gospel of John in particular—really displace the
imperialist cannons of a postcolonial world? Or will the Fourth Gospel's
politics of place continue to be used largely to cultivate colonialist and
hegemonic agendas?

A number of years ago Ernst Käsemann argued that John's christology
was radically spiritualized and naïvely docetic in nature.[33] Does Burge's
argument that 'Jesus spiritualizes the Land' imply that the Fourth
Gospel also hides a docetic geography behind its docetic christology?[34]
Or is his essay overly naïve in its rejection of territorialism? In her book
The Humanity of Jesus in the Fourth Gospel, Marianne Thompson disputes
Käsemann's claim of the Fourth Gospel's naïve docetism. She writes that
Jn 1.14 'insists on the reality of Jesus' humanity and flesh, and is actually
anti-docetic, combating either the kind of view of Jesus which Käsemann
delineates in *The Testament of Jesus* or an even more emphatic denial of
his true incarnation'.[35] In view of this classic christological argument, my
questions are these: If docetism represented a radicalizing of Johannine
spirit christology in the early centuries of the church, a radicalizing that
was alien to the intention of the Fourth Gospel, could the spiritualizing
of Johannine geography in our day be equally alien to its intention, and
thus be wrongly implicated in the demise of cultures and peoples struggling to maintain their land and identity? And could we then maintain
an *incar/national* theology that would be authentically Johannine; one
that could be developed into a postcolonial geography of John's Gospel

32. D.L. Jennings, *Raspberries and Blackberries: Their Breeding, Diseases, and Growth*
(New York: Academic Press, 1988), p. 46.

33. *The Testament of Jesus: A Study of the Gospel of John in Light of Chapter 17* (trans.
Gerhard Krodel; Philadelphia: Fortress Press, 2nd edn, 1968), p. 26; cf. pp. 66, 70.

34. Burge, 'Territorial Religion', p. 395.

35. Marianne Thompson, *The Humanity of Jesus in the Fourth Gospel* (Minneapolis:
Fortress Press, 1988), p. 122.

that was neither imperialistic nor territorial?[36] Is it possible to uphold an integral reading of the Fourth Gospel that values *terra/tory* without participating in terrorist activities?

In *Place and the Politics of Identity*, Michael Keith and Steve Pile argue for a much more complex view of land, territory and place than either Burge or Swanson can envision; where multiple spatialities show that

> the metaphoric and the real do not belong in separate worlds; that the symbolic and the literal are in part constitutive of one another. That meaning is never immanent, it is instead not just *marked* but also in part *constituted* by the spaces of representation in which it is articulated. These spaces of representation subvert the representation of spaces so that the ground we stand on becomes a mongrel hybrid of spatialities; at once a metaphor and a speaking position, a place of certainty and a burden of humility, sometimes all of these simultaneously, sometimes all of them incommensurably.[37]

I return briefly to my own childhood place on the Navajo Reservation; to the politics of my own national geographics and muddled memory. In a world where European conquerors seized territory from the Navajo people (land which the Navajo doubtless took from earlier peoples) and renamed it St John, I find troubling Gary Burge's description of Johannine christology as one that spiritualizes place. What does it mean to be the conqueror, the colonizer, the dominant people and say to those you have conquered, ' "Dis place" has been superseded by Christ'? That 'dis place' you once called Jerusalem is now 'Aelia Capitolina'; or that the place you once called 'Old Age River', or 'One with a Long Body', has now become the 'San Juan River'?[38] That the Four Corners National Monument is more important than the Bear's Ears? What happens to a people when borders, once signaled by obvious, topographical markers,

36. This question essentially turns Culpepper's discussion of Johannine exclusivism and universalism on its head ('The Gospel of John as a Document of Faith in a Pluralistic Culture', in Fernando F. Segovia [ed.], *'What is John?': Readers and Readings of the Fourth Gospel* [Atlanta: Scholars Press, 1996], pp. 121-25).

37. 'Introduction', p. 23 (their emphasis). Cf. Swanson's more simplistic assessment where 'taking over the authority of centers comparable to Mt Gerizim or the well of Sychar [implies that] Christians disenfranchised the natives of those places from the symbols that had empowered their ownership of territory' ('To Prepare a Place', p. 259; cf. Aleida Assman, 'Space, Place, Land—Changing Concepts of Territory in English and American Fiction', in Monika Reif-Hüsler [ed.], *Borderlands: Negotiating Boundaries in Post-Colonial Writing* [ASNEL Papers, 4; Atlanta: Rodopi, 1999], pp. 57-68; esp. pp. 62-64).

38. Robert S. McPherson, *Sacred Land Sacred View: Navajo Perceptions of the Four Corners Region* (Charles Redd Monographs in Western History, 19; Salt Lake City: Charles Redd Center for Western Studies, Brigham Young University, 1992), p. 49.

now invisibly bisect the land as mysteriously as the doctrine of the two natures divides Christ?[39]

In 1864 General James H. Carleton brought together his own staunch Presbyterianism with United States's expansionist land policies. His plan was to convert the Navajo people to Christ by exiling them to the Bosque Redondo, three hundred miles from their traditional homeland.[40] The theory was that if you could get the natives off their land and turn them into Christian farmers, they would be convinced that the one God was not tied to territory. But as Robert McPherson notes,

> [t]he Holy Land in the Middle East with its Jerusalem, Garden of Geth-
> semane, and Golgotha, are of no greater import to Christians than the
> Diné's holy land is to them, circumscribed as it is by sacred mountains and
> containing the junction of the San Juan River and Mancos Creek, where
> Born for Water invoked supernatural aid to overcome danger and death,
> and the Bear's Ears, where good triumphed over evil.[41]

Within a few short years the US government experiment was deemed a failure, and the decimated, destitute Navajo tribe was allowed to return to its native land.

So how can one say to peoples, ancient or modern, that 'dis place' is unimportant and has been superseded by a spiritual reality that appears to be only tenuously connected to the physical world? Burge fails to recognize the implications of his territorial arguments when he observes in a footnote that the 'passion for "historic land ownership" pervades the cultures of the Middle East and lies at the heart of the Israel/Palestinian struggle', but 'Western culture has few parallels to this experience.'[42] Although Burge does not mention what those 'few parallels' in Western culture might be, I would venture a guess that there are more than a few parallels to the Palestinian experience in Western culture. The continu-ing arguments of the United States's government over Native American land rights are one of the most obvious connections.

One way dispossessed people have maintained a connection to 'dis place'-ment is by giving names to future generations of children that express the experience of exile. These people's names function as verbal

39. Staley, 'Narrative Structure (Self-Stricture) in Luke 4.14–9.62', pp. 174-76.

40. Clifford E. Trafzer, *The Kit Carson Campaign: The Last Great Navajo War* (Norman: University of Oklahoma Press, 1982), pp. 83, 239.

41. McPherson, *Sacred Land Sacred View*, p. 73; cf. Casey, *Getting Back into Place*, pp. 34-37.

42. 'Territorial Religion', p. 386 n. 12. Cf. Rashid I. Khalidi, 'Contrasting Nar-ratives of Palestinian Identity', in Yaeger (eds.), *The Geography of Identity*, pp. 187-222. On the slow development of Christian holy places, see Blake Leyerle, 'Landscape as Cartography in Early Christian Pilgrimage Narratives', *JAAR* 64 (1996), pp. 119-43.

testimonies to, and as witnesses against, ongoing colonialist and imperialist policies. This is what Isaiah the prophet seemed to be doing when he named his children 'Shearjashub' and 'Mahershalalhashbaz' (Isa. 7.3-9; 8.1-4). Not insignificantly, one of the most outspoken representatives of Native American theology and United States's colonialism was given the name Vine Deloria Jr by his parents, thus evoking Jesus' famous 'I am' saying of Jn 15.1.[43] The vine—cut off, uprooted, and displaced from the land by three hundred years of United States colonial, imperial polices, has now become an individual's name, a living person, a flesh-and-blood testimonial; a prophetic witness against colonialist displacement.[44]

While Burge ends up with a naïvely docetic, de-politicized view of 'the Land' in Johannine theology, Swanson ends with its opposite; with a Thomas-like credo that would seem to state 'Unless I see the lay of the land with my own eyes, and put my toes in the dirt of that place, and my fingers in its streams, and my nose in its indigenous plants, I will not believe.' Thus Swanson's concluding critique of the Johannine ideology of place argues that

> [t]he meaning of a place is not transferable. It is in the memories of the dead who are buried there. It is in the taste of that particular spring. It is in the way the dirt and heat combine with the footprints of ancestors on that particular pilgrimage road. And it is part of the meaning of such sacred places that their presence is irreplaceable.[45]

Contrary to Burge's and Swanson's arguments, I believe that the rhetorics related to ubiquitous and localized places in the Fourth Gospel can also be played out in at least two other important ways, and that the

43. For a brief biography of Vine Deloria Jr, see Jace Weaver, *That the People might Live: Native American Literatures and Native American Community* (New York: Oxford University Press, 1997), pp. 124-32. The origin of Vine's first name was related to me in a conversation with Jace Weaver, in 1998.

44. Regarding naming in Native American cultures, Gail Guthrie Valaskakis argues, 'Old names are uttered and new names are formed in the experience of everyday life and the ideological struggles of continually-constructed identity and community. These names speak of the reality of the personal and the public in the discord of lived experience' ('Indian Country: Negotiating the Meaning of Land in Native America' in Cary Nelson and Dilip Parameshwar Gaonkar [eds.] *Disciplinarity and Dissent in Cultural Studies* [New York: Routledge, 1996], p. 162).

45. Swanson, 'To Prepare a Place', p. 262. Or as Jonathan Z. Smith writes, 'Place is not the creation of personality; it is what forms or imprints personality', *To Take Place*, p. 30. To be fair, Swanson has added a footnote to the current version of his *JAAR* essay (reprinted in this volume). That footnote describes the conflicting complicities of Johannine 'dis place'-ment in a more nuanced manner.

image of travel implicit in Swanson's pilgrimage metaphor may open up a way to critique them both.[46] In the first scenario, after the invaders have appropriated the land of the vanquished, they can say, as Jesus does to the Samaritan woman, 'Why should you be concerned with land and "dis place"? The hour is coming when you will worship the Father neither on this mountain nor in Jerusalem' (Jn 4.21).

'Place is unimportant', say those conquerors like Jesus, who, to the Samaritan woman, must have represented the typical Judean—responsible for destroying her people's temple in 128 BCE. 'Those Judeans are all alike', I can hear her muttering under her breath. 'They take away more and more of our land, and then turn around and tell us that place doesn't matter. We've heard it all before. It's a different face, but the same old shit they're feeding us.'

On the other hand, Jesus's statement '...neither on this mountain nor in Jerusalem...' can sometimes have a totally different meaning when spoken by one victim of oppression to another. And both Jesus and the Samaritan woman fit this description. Both have fallen under Roman domination, that ruthless imperialistic regime which will not stop its quest for power until the entire Mediterranean region is under its sway.[47] And just as the Samaritan temple had once been destroyed, so also will the Jerusalem temple one day be destroyed (Jn 11.48). Furthermore, although Jesus's own words suggest that he displaces the displaced, Jerusalem temple (Jn 2.19-22), he also will be destroyed, displaced by that same *pax romana* (19.10).

But one victim of oppression can also say to another *victim* what Jesus

46. As Neil Smith and Cindi Katz write, 'The notions of travel, travelling identities and displacement represent another response to the undue fixity of social identity. 'Travelling' provides a means for conceptualizing the interplay among people that are no longer so separate or inaccessible one to another. Travel erodes the brittleness and rigidity of spatial boundaries and suggests social, political and cultural identity as an amalgam, the intricacy of which defies the comparative simplicity of 'identity' ('Grounding Metaphor: Towards a Spatialized Politics', in Keith and Pile [eds.], *Place and the Politics of Identity*, p. 78; cf. Casey, *Getting Back into Place*, pp. 273-314; Philip Sheldrake, 'Travelling Through Life? Subversive Journeys' *The Way* 39 [1999], pp. 5-15; and Valaskakis, 'Indian Country', pp. 160-61).

47. As Musa W. Dube so forcefully argues, 'It is...quite tempting to locate the conflict in the Gospel [of John] as a reflection of conflict between national Jewish groups or conflict within the Johannine community itself, while overlooking a very important factor: the presence of empire... The presence of the imperial power, the Roman Empire, is the catalyst for the vicious competition of local groups' ('Savior of the World but not of this World: A Postcolonial Reading of Spatial Construction in John', in R.S. Sugirtharajah [ed.], *The Postcolonial Bible* [Sheffield: Sheffield Academic Press, 1998], p. 128).

says to the Samaritan woman, and it can be heard as a liberating voice. No place—neither the sacred places that have been wrested from the victims *nor the ancient places that the oppressors view as sacred*, are unique, special places of the gods' presence and power.[48] Thus, the gut-wrenching experience of being ripped from one's land can sometimes be assuaged by the voices of other alienated, dispossessed peoples who are witnesses to God's subversive activity on behalf of the oppressed—an activity that is quite separate from any authorized sacred space.[49] For Rome is no more the center of God's power and activity than is Jerusalem, Antioch or Nazareth (Jn 1.46).

Can we, as Johannine interpreters, nuance the ideology of Johannine topography in such a way that it can be liberating for oppressed peoples without seeming to grant theological license to the conquerors? Is a reassessment of Johannine christology possible, one that challenges contemporary scholarly 'orthodoxy' (which dismisses Johannine temporal, geographical and religious portrayals of Jesus's life in favor of the Synoptic view) without succumbing to a naïve docetism?

Toward a Renewal of 'Dis Place'

Three months after moving we are beginning to feel at home on our new cul-de-sac in Bothell. In my morning walks around the neighborhood, I discover that 'dis place' is truly a postcolonial community—despite the cookie-cutter sameness of the two-story, pastel-painted houses in the new development. Next door and just down the street from us are recent immigrant families from the Ukraine, India and Russia. In the other direction, homes are inhabited by Thai, Pakistani, Chinese, Hispanic and African-American families. I think there are only three 'fully white' families in the subdivision of 40 houses.

On the hill behind our house are spiked Nike missile silos, pointed at the former Soviet Union. They are momentos from the Cold War of the 1950s–80s and the United States' imperialist attempts to 'overcome' the world (Jn 16.33). Ironically, our former hometown, Beaverton, Oregon was the corporate world headquarters of Nike shoes. The remnants of that other, more sinister Nike overshadows our backyard, reminding us

48. Douglas Burton-Christie notes that '[i]n the New Testament we also see resistance to the wrong kind of attachment to place...[when] Jesus declares to the Samaritans that soon true worshippers will look neither to the Samaritans' holy mountain nor to the Jewish holy city of Jerusalem, but will worship "in spirit and truth"' ('Living Between Two Worlds', p. 426).

49. See, for example Anton Shammas, 'Autocartography: The Case of Palestine, Michigan', in Yaeger (ed.), *The Geography of Identity*, pp. 466-75.

that invisible power—whether military or economic—is not easily destroyed (Jn 19.10-11). It quietly mutates and reconfigures itself. Like blackberries that build up tolerance to pesticides.

Our friendly Ukrainian neighbors tell us that if we need anything, 'just give us a call'. We don't, but we watch their two old aunts who live with them plant cabbage and garlic in their backyard in February, next to our overgrown patch of 'noxious weeds'. The former citizens of the Soviet Union work hard for the multinational computer companies and 'dotcoms' sprouting like viney blackberries around the suburbs of Seattle.[50] The Indian family works for a pharmaceutical company, trying to patent a new generation of Viagra look-alike drugs. 'Livin' the vida loca'. They are all busy making the world safe for American capitalism, while I struggle to find a part-time teaching position.

Within three months, two of the families have moved up and out of the neighborhood as they quickly climb the corporate ladder of success and excess. They are fast learners. Much quicker than I.

I remember when we first broke the news to our children that we would be moving from Portland to Seattle. My eight-year-old daughter sobbed the entire evening and could not be consoled.

'But this is the only house I know!' she wailed. 'All my friends are here! And what about my treehouse and the garden? What will happen to them?'

I tried to comfort her, but I didn't do a very good job. After all, I had never lived for more than ten years in the same house, and I had no full time job keeping me in Portland. So why should we stay? Yes, we did have a remarkable, close-knit neighborhood; wonderful friends; a progressive, caring church; and the marvelous scenery of Oregon's rocky seacoast—all which we still miss from time to time. So perhaps, like those wetland blackberry vines, we have left rhizome fragments[51] still deeply sunk in Oregon soil.

So why, indeed, did we move? And who are we becoming in dis new place to the north? Who can tell?[52] Can the God of Abraham, Jacob, Isaiah and the Samaritans trace our sinewy, woody roots to Seattle and

50. Leach, *Country of Exiles*, pp. 71-73.

51. On the image of the rhizome in postcolonial theory and its relationship to ideas of space and displacement, see Jaishree K. Odin, 'The Edge of Difference: Negotiations Between the Hypertextual and the Postcolonial', *MFS* 43 (1997), pp. 598-630; esp. pp. 606-607; and Stuart Moulthrop, 'Rhizome and Resistance: Hypertext and the Dream of a New Culture', in George P. Landow (ed.), *Hyper/Text/Theory* (Baltimore: The Johns Hopkins University Press, 1994), pp. 299-319.

52. This is a paraphrase of Douglas Burton-Christie's questions in 'Into the Body of Another', p. 23.

make us whole in the transplanting aftershocks of new schools, neighbor-
hoods, friendships and careers?

'Of course!' I say to myself, without really thinking. Yet I am afraid
that perhaps we have lost something vital in the move, in this
displacement.

As we were loading the final boxes in our van, I had a sudden urge to
leave a mark behind—a finger in the dust of our Portland property. I
called to my children, and took them out to the treehouse that their
uncle had built for them in our backyard when my son was just a toddler.
We climbed up into it and sat and carved our names on its living walls
with a Boy Scout pocketknife: 'Ben and Allie played here, 1986–1996.
BWS/AJS/JLS.'

I want my children to remember their lives there as parts of themselves cut deeply into 'dis place'. And I want them to go back and visit
that place at least once before they die; to trace strong fingers in darken-
ing wood. I want them to tell their children stories about a father who
lived there with them; who once believed, and so planted a garden,
weeded it, and watched it grow good things, strong things—life-sustain-
ing things.

I recall my family history with its slow, plodding movements across the
great expanse of this continent: The family roots in Virginia, in Indiana,
Missouri and Kansas; my grandfather's sadness in selling the family farm
during the Great Depression; his vegetable gardens. Will I find in this
new place solid ground to plant a new garden and a new life? Is there a
politics of place, a theology of space in the Gospel of John that can move
people beyond their own clinging, human desire to be here, here and
now? 'Can one be simultaneously at home and on the way, secure and
unstable, located within clear boundaries and constantly moving across
boundaries, attached to place and yet detached, grounded in the present
and stretching toward the future'?[53] These questions are at the heart of
contemporary understandings of rhizomes, diasporic communities and
globalization, and no doubt the twenty-first century will see an increase
in the number of down-to-the-earth, 'dis placed' political readings of the
Fourth Gospel. Like the essays in this collection, they will be readings
that are critically resistant to the dangerous edges of Johannine
ideology, and at the same time they will be nurtured and sustained by
the book and by a wide variety of Christian faith communities.

I am a selfish person. I want to see readings of the Gospel of John that
will revitalize the Gospel in the experience of the church. These readings
will bridge the gap between the distancing effects of historical-critical

---

53. Douglas Burton-Christie, 'Living Between Two Worlds', p. 428.

methodologies and the personalizing, pietistic and 'orthodox' readings of the church that have so often gotten mired down in the Fourth Gospel's ideology of 'dis place'. I want to plant native vines and restore a struggling wetland. I want to repay my ancestors' debt to Christan Vineyard and to Vine Deloria Jr, then sit down on my deck and watch a wild, untamed fecundity take over.

Reading for Decolonization (John 4.1-42)*

MUSA W. DUBE

> When the white man came to our country he had the Bible and we had the land. The White man said to us, 'let us pray'. After the prayer, the white man had the land and we had the Bible (a popular African saying).

> Modern imperialism was so global and all-encompassing that virtually nothing escaped it; besides, as I have said, the nineteenth-century contest over empire is still continuing today. Whether or not to look at the connections between cultural texts and imperialism is therefore to take a position in fact taken—either to study the connection in order to criticize it and think of alternatives for it, or not to study it in order to let it stand (Edward Said, *Culture and Imperialism*, p. 68).

Introduction: Imperialism(s), Space and Texts

Imperialism is an ideology of expansion that takes diverse forms and methods at different times, seeking to impose its languages, its trade, its religions, its democracy, its images, its economic systems and its political rule on foreign nations and lands.[1] The victims of imperialism become the colonized, that is, those whose lands, minds, cultures, economies and political institutions have been taken possession of and rearranged according to the interests and values of the imperializing powers.[2] Imperialism is, therefore, about controlling foreign geographical spaces and their inhabitants. By its practice and its goals, imperialism is a relationship of subordination and domination between different nations

---

An earlier version of this essay appeared in *Semeia* 74 (1996).

1.   For different types, methods and definitions of imperialism(s), from ancient to contemporary times, see René Maunier, *The Sociology of Colonies: An Introduction to the Study of Colonies*, Vol. 1 (London: Routledge, 1949), pp. 133-260; Robert Delavignette, *Christianity and Colonialism* (New York: Hawthorn Books, 1964), pp. 1-46; Edward Said, *Culture and Imperialism* (New York: Alfred A. Knopf, 1993), pp. 9-13; Ngugi wa Thiong'o, *Decolonising the Mind: The Politics of Language in African Literature* (London: James Currey, 1986), pp. 1-3.

2.   V.Y. Mudimbe, *The Invention of Africa: Gnosis, Philosophy and the Order of Knowledge* (Bloomington: Indiana University Press, 1988), pp. 1-2.

and lands, which actively suppresses diversity and promotes a few universal standards for the benefit of those in power. It involves the colonized and the colonizer, the ruler and the ruled, the center and the periphery, the First World and the Two-Thirds World, relationships which define our current world; and relationships that are closely related to, although not identical to, particular physical places of the earth.

In this introduction, I briefly discuss different imperialist movements and cultural strategies of dominating foreign spaces, the Bible and empire-building before I turn to John 4. Throughout this essay, the term 'imperializing texts' designates those literary works that propound values and representations that authorize expansionist tendencies grounded on unequal international/racial relations. Decolonizing, on the other hand, defines awareness of imperialism's exploitative forces and its various strategies of domination, the conscious adoption of strategies of resisting imperial domination as well as the search for alternative ways of liberating interdependence between nations, races, genders, economies and cultures.

Imperialism is certainly an ancient institution. The Babylonian sovereign Hammurabi, for example, 'gave himself the title of "King of the Four Corners of the World"'[3] to describe his profession of disavowing boundaries. The Babylonian empire had a line of successors in the Assyrian, Hellenistic and Roman Empires. In a tradition that is akin to Hammurabi, Roman emperors were also called 'Saviour(s) of the World'.[4] 'World' in these titles symbolizes the claim to unlimited access to foreign geographical spaces. 'King' and 'Saviour' articulate the claims of power by certain subjects and their followers (races and nations) over unlimited geographical spaces—over the world and its inhabitants. While 'king' implies dominion over space and people—which may be just or unjust—'saviour' also implies power. But it carries an imperial ideology that came to a full-fledged maturity in modern centuries, whereby the violence of imperialism was depicted as a redeeming act for the benefit of the subjugated, or the so-called 'duty to the natives'.

But it is in Alexander the Great's career that we encounter a well-known and ancient example of what it takes to be a king or saviour of the world. His career makes it evident that military might is as central to

3.   René Maunier, *Sociology of Colonies*, Vol. 1, p. 19.

4.   For a more detailed discussion of this title, see Richard J. Cassidy, *John's Gospel in a New Perspective: Christology and the Realities of Roman Power* (Maryknoll, NY: Orbis Books, 1992), pp. 6-16; Craig Koester, 'The Saviour of the World (John 4.42)', *JBL* 109 (1990), pp. 665-80; Charles Talbert, *Reading John: A Literary and Theological Commentary on the Fourth Gospel and the Johannine Epistles* (New York: Crossroad), pp. 118-19.

empire building as are cultural texts. David Quint's study *Epic and Empire* highlights how Alexander drew his inspiration from the literary characters of *The Iliad*.[5] Alexander reportedly carried *The Iliad* in his conquest journeys and 'kept it under his pillow together with a dagger'.[6] Prior to his attack on Persia and Asia, he visited Troy where he 'honored the memory of the heroes who were buried there, with solemn libations; especially Achilles, whose grave he anointed'.[7] In so doing, Alexander was making the literary character of 'Achilles at Troy a model for the conquests carried out by his armies'.[8] Here a literary text that glorifies military might and conquest comes to legitimate and further imperial agendas in a different history. Conquest in empire building becomes a strategy for becoming king or saviour over the world by annihilating its inhabitants or by initiating a powerful death threat against them.

Quint's extensive study goes on to show that the travel and triumph of epic heroes through untold dangers; the characterization of its heroes as people immensely favored by divine powers; and the characterization of foreigners as either dangerous, evil cyclopes, or women/goddesses desperate to hold on to traveling heroes; have provided imperial travelers of different centuries and empires with a language for representing foreign lands and peoples up until the introduction of the novel. Imperial traveling agents and heroes drew their inspiration from epic characters and plots and so were able to withstand and endure their travel tribulations. Such epic characters and plots inspired them to regard themselves as divinely favored, destined and chosen to survive and conquer against all odds.

Not only do certain values of cultural texts inspire imperialism; the cultures of the empire are also used to maintain power over the colonized. Alexander's empire building project thus entailed an elaborate program of Hellenizing his conquered subjects. Alexander 'established a network of routes from Egypt to India and sprinkled cities throughout out Asia to radiate Greek culture'.[9] He founded Greek cities at 'strategic points, to serve as administrative centers but also to provide a focus as beacon of Greek culture in the alien lands of the Orient'.[10] The three

5. David Quint, *Epic and Empire* (Princeton, NJ: Princeton University Press, 1993), pp. 1-18.

6. Quint, *Epic and Empire*, p. 4.

7. Quint, *Epic and Empire*, p. 4.

8. Quint, *Epic and Empire*, p. 4.

9. Calvin J. Roetzel, *The World that Shaped the New Testament* (Atlanta: John Knox Press, 1985), p. 2.

10. David L. Balch and John E. Stambaugh, *The New Testament in its Social Environment* (Philadelphia: Westminster Press, 1986), p. 14.

generals who succeeded him 'encouraged solidarity of Greek culture by
building cities on the old model, just as Alexander had done'.[11] Even the
Roman Empire pursued the program of 'instilling a sense of pride in
traditional Greek civilization'.[12] These ancient cases indicate that a cultural program serves to tame both the physical and mental space of the
colonized. They also indicate that traveling and travelers are not neutral
subject.[13] Imperial travelers depart from their familiar places to unfamiliar people and lands with goals of subjugating the later. The colonizing
travelers, as indicated by the titles of king and saviour of unlimited
spaces, construct themselves in particular fashions to validate their travel
and to confront unfamiliar places and people. Physical lands and minds
are thus 'spaces' that are subject to remolding through cultural texts and
structures such as cities gymnasiums, markets and so on.

In contemporary times, Spain, Belgium, Portugal, Russia, Germany,
France and Britain established empires of unparalleled magnitude, leaving little or no part of the earth untouched. Modern empires took
different forms and methods from the ancient empires. Their unique
strategies assumed the sophistication of dressing military might and
economic greed in the guise of evangelical zeal, moral-rhetorical claims,
technological, racial and cultural claims of superiority. Modern empires
also differed according to each colonizing country as well as according to
the particular culture and geographical area of the colonized. Temperatures that were similar or hospitable to the colonizing countries, for
example, were much more likely to result in settler colonialism, while
areas with non-hospitable temperatures were likely to lead to indirect
rule. The struggle for independence has ever since been wedged and
won by what largely constitutes the Two-Thirds World countries. Many
of the formerly colonized nations are, nonetheless, undergoing new
forms of imperialism, neo-colonialism or globalization. Globalization
here defines the 'process which has led to the creation of a single, international (global) financial or capital market',[14] and landed most Two-
Thirds World economies in huge debts and worse situations than in
colonial times. The latest form of imperialism is also evident in ecological control, military muscle, universal media, and economic domina-

11. Balch and Stambaugh, *The New Testament*, p. 14.

12. Balch and Stambaugh, *The New Testament*, p. 14.

13. See Alison Blunt, *Travel, Gender and Imperialism: Mary Kingsley and West Africa*
(New York: Guilford, 1994), pp. 15-19.

14. Ngugi wa Thiong'o, *Moving the Centre: The Struggle for Cultural Freedoms*
(London: James Currey, 1993), pp. 12-13; and Christopher Lind, *Something is Wrong
Somewhere: Globalization, Community and the Moral Economy of the Farm Crisis* (Halifax:
Fernwood, 1995), pp. 26-43.

tion by the former and new imperialist powers.[15] Neo-colonization, in particular, underlines the differences that characterizes imperialist movements, for unlike ancient and modern empires, globalization largely excludes geographical occupation, or colonization proper, and, to some extent, it excludes government as transnational cooperations take the lead.[16] The dominated countries in the globalization era seemingly retain their own political leadership, and appear to be under control. These mutations of empires make it difficult to posit imperialism as a transhistorical institution even with a series of their reoccurrences. Nonetheless, it is hardly debatable that imperialisms of different times, forms, and strategies have affected and continue to affect this world on a global scale. Imperial images and structures of domination continue to affect the lives of billions of men and women, both the subjugated and the subjugator. How the people of the First World and Two-Thirds World perceive each other, how their cultural, economic and political institutions are structured, for instance, is inseparably tied to the imperial movements and the strategies that have been employed to control foreign geographical spaces and its inhabitants.

The above prefatory quotations attest that cultural texts were also central to the strategies of modern imperialism. Elleke Boehmer's study on *Colonial and Postcolonial Literature* indicate that modern imperial agents employed older and familiar narratives to read and to tame the 'new' and strange spaces. A textual strategy assisted the traveling colonial agents to cope and to colonize strange geographical places. As in Quint's findings on epic and empire, writing in modern empires has become an art of tapping

> the energy of metaphoric borrowings and reproductions within the wider tradition of colonial romance and adventure writing. Motifs of shipwreck, resourceful settlement and cultivation, treasure, slaves, and fear of cannibalism resurfaced time and again in boys' stories... [T]he pairing of white master and black slave/servant became an unquestioned commonplace.[17]

15. Lind, *Something is Wrong Somewhere*, p. 31.

16. See Appadurai in Laura Chrisman and Patrick Williams (eds.), *Colonial Discourse and Postcolonial Theory: A Reader* (New York: Columbia University Press, 1994), p. 273, who has suggested five landscapes that help to highlight the different levels and departments of modern imperialisms: 'ethnoscape(especially groups in movements), technoscape (institutions of technology and its informational flows), "financescape" (the disposition of global capital). "mediascape" (both images produced and the mode of production), "ideoscape" (ideologies)'.

17. Elleke Boehmer, *Colonial and Postcolonial Literature* (New York: Oxford University Press, 1995), p. 47.

Boehmer's analysis further highlights that this web of intertextual repro-
ductions was accompanied by a reproduction of certain cultural symbols
and structures in different areas.[18] Architecture, plantations, magic
lanterns, foods, clothes and names of European origin were transferred
to various parts of the world.[19] Through this uniform transference of a
few cultural structures and the reproduction of the same textual representations, different geographical spaces of the world and its inhabitants
are homogenized, or colonized.

Both Quint and Boehmer highlight the wide range of imperializing
texts, their production and their authors. They are largely written during
the peak periods of imperial movements about the colonized and the
colonizer, but mostly for and by the colonizing nations. The later are
exemplified by the likes of *The Aeneid*, *Heart of Darkness*, *The Tempest* and
Kipling's classic poem, 'The White Man's Burden'. They also include
literary works that imperial powers bring and give to the colonized.
Good examples of these fall within the so-called humanist tradition,
which, as Ngugi aptly argues, was a powerful form of colonizing the
minds of African students for 'bourgeois Europe was always the center of
the universe'.[20] In the latter case, imported texts function as forms of
displacing local cultures and colonizing the minds. Imperializing texts,
however, take many forms and are written by a variety of people. Sometimes even by the colonized who either collaborate with the dominant
forces or yearn for the same power.[21] Regardless of who writes imperializing texts, they are characterized by literary constructions, representations, and uses that authorize taking possession of foreign geographical
spaces and people.

One of the strategies of imperializing texts is the employment of
female gender to validate relationships of subordination and domination.[22] Quint's study on the genealogy of the epic and its role in the

18. Boehmer, *Colonial and Postcolonial Literature*, pp. 51-59.

19. See V.Y. Mudimbe, *The Idea of Africa* (Bloomington: Indiana University Press,
1994), pp. 105-53, whose exposition on missionary strategies shows how domesticat-
ing both people's physical space and their minds sets up cultural structures such as
houses, gardens, and schools that serve as beacons of colonial cultures.

20. Ngugi wa Thiong'o, *Decolonising the Mind*, p. 17.

21. As I will show below, New Testament texts are a good case in point. They were
indeed produced by the colonized, yet they subscribe to the ideology of expansion to
foreign lands based on relationships of unequal power (Mt. 28.16-20; Jn 4.1-42). Commenting on the tendency of the colonized to assume strategies that befriend the
colonizers' methods, David Quint (*Epic and Empire*, p. 18), holds that 'the losers who
attract our sympathies today would be—had they only power—victors of tomorrow'.

22. For further reading on gender roles, representations, and politics of reading in

empires, for instance, finds a sustained recall, rewriting, and reproduction of the figure of a fleeing Cleopatra on Aeneas shield in *The
Aeneid* and its association with eastern nations. Maunier's sociological
study of colonial processes and literature finds that 'native women have
often been the first agents of contact', providing what he calls a 'classic
literary motif of the tragic romance' between the European man and
native women'. Thus, Sigmund Freud, speaking within the imperial
perspective of his time, could describe a 'woman as the dark continent'.[23]
The use of female gender to describe the colonized serves the agendas of
constructing hierarchical geographical spaces, races, and cultures,[24] but
it also comes to legitimate the oppression of women in societies where
these narratives are used.

In sum, texts that legitimate and authorize imperialism include most
canonized classics of ancient and contemporary times—regardless of
discipline or genre.[25] Classical texts such as the Bible, *The Iliad, The
Odyssey* and *The Aeneid* have inspired and participated in different historical processes of imperialism.[26] Contemporary texts range from modern
English and French novels, travel narratives, anthropological documentation, and world maps to missionary reports, paintings, tourist photography, museum collections, and intelligence satellite photography.[27]
The ensemble of these texts authorize imperialism through assuming
various values and strategies: the glorification of military might and
conquest; the promotion of travel that characterizes the travelers as
authoritatively above foreign lands and their inhabitants; and the construction of foreign people and spaces in specific legitimizing forms.
Foreign people are often characterized as inferior, dangerous, diseased,
ungodly, kind, lazy and helpless in these texts, while their lands are constructed as empty, feminine, available, harsh, full of evil and profitable
for the colonizing powers. These imperializing textual representations

imperializing texts and contexts, see Alison Blunt, *Travel Gender and Imperialism*; Alison
Blunt and Gillian Rose (eds.), *Writing Women and Space: Colonial and Postcolonial Geo-
graphies* (New York: Guildford, 1994); Laura Donaldson, *Decolonizing Feminisms: Race,
Gender, and Empire-Building* (Chapel Hill: University of the North Carolina Press, 1992).

23. Laura Chrisman and Patrick Williams (eds.), *Colonial Discourse and Postcolonial
Theory: A Reader* (New York: Columbia University Press, 1994).

24. Quint, *Epic and Empire*, pp. 31-41.

25. See J.M. Blaut, *The Colonizer's Model of the World: Geographical Diffusionism and
Eurocentric History* (New York: Guildford, 1993), pp. 1-124, for the construction of hierarchical geographies that legitimate the hierarchical racial constructions accompanying
contemporary empires.

26. See Quint, *Epic and Empire*, for the role of epics.

27. See Said, *Culture and Imperialism*, for the role of the novel.

depend on sharply contrasting the colonizer's lands and people with those of the colonized. The colonized spaces and inhabitants are basically subjected to the standard of the colonizer, and difference is equated with deficiency.

Because of the centrality of cultural texts to imperialist projects, the struggle for liberation is not limited just to military, economic and political arenas. It necessarily requires and includes a cultural battle of reader-writers who attempt to arrest the violence of the imperializing texts. The centrality of literary texts in imperialism has, therefore, stimulated a literary response from the subjugated at different places and periods of time.[28] The colonized reread the imperializing texts and write new narratives that affirm the adequacy of their humanity, the reality of global diversity, and their right to independence.[29] They write in search of liberating ways that will affirm the interdependence of nations, races, genders and economies, ways which do not depend on oppressive and exploitative relationships.[30] The formerly colonized, who approximate the majority of the Two-Thirds World countries, therefore constitute communities of reader-writers who struggle to decolonize. Their practice challenges the Western or the so-called First World academic cultural texts, exposing and rejecting the literary forms of imperialism, or they admit their acceptance of it. As Said points out, a neutral position is not possible: to read or write for or against imperial domination is an unavoidable position—one that is already taken.[31]

Biblical Texts and Empire-building

The prefatory African saying highlights the Bible as one imperializing text. It emphasizes that for many African nations the success of

28. See Bill Ashcroft, Gareth Griffiths, and Helen Tiffin, *The Empire Writes Back: Theory and Practice in Post-Colonial Literatures* (New York: Routledge, 1989), pp. 1-109; Barbara Harlow, *Resistance Literature* (New York: Methuen, 1987), pp. 1-75; and Said, *Culture and Imperialism*, pp. 1-150.

29. See Chinua Achebe, *Hopes and Impediments: Selected Essays* (New York: Doubleday, 1989), pp. 1-20; and Ngugi wa Thiong'o, *Moving the Centre*, pp. 12-25, for their readings of *Heart of Darkness* and the investigation of the function of its constructions.

30. See Said, *Culture and Imperialism*, pp. 3-43; 303-36, on the concept of interdependence, interconnectedness and the overlapping of territories, histories, cultures and identities. Said holds that interdependence is unavoidable. It is a necessary form of survival sought by both the colonizer and the colonized. The question, therefore, is to seek liberating forms of interdependence since, as he says, survival is about 'connections of things', people, nations, genders, economies rather than independence from one another.

31. Said, *Culture and Imperialism*, p. 68.

colonization is inseparably linked with the use of the Bible. Ngugi wa Thiong'o, a Kenyan writer, underscores this experience by holding that the 'English, French, and the Portuguese came to the Third World to announce the arrival of the Bible and the sword.'[32] Ngugi insists that in the modern colonization of Africa, 'both William Shakespeare and Jesus Christ had brought light'.[33] This synoptic paralleling of military might and the biblical text, of Shakespeare with Jesus, does not exempt the Bible from imperialist violence. David Livingstone, for example, is a renowned colonial hero who championed the colonization of Africa and who made it an open secret that in colonization, 'civilization—Christianity and commerce—should ever be inseparable'.[34] In 1820 missionary Pringle could proudly say

> Let us enter upon a new and nobler career of conquest. Let us subdue Savage Africa by justice, by kindness, by the talisman of Christian truth. Let us thus go forth, in the name and under the blessing of God, gradually to extend the territorial boundary also of our colony, until is shall become an empire.[35]

Both Livingstone and Pringle found no contradiction, no secrecy, nor any reason to separate their Christian missions from the imperialist agendas of their countries. Now many people might dismiss the time of Livingstone as a period of church history which has little or nothing to do with the biblical period. Yet the question remains as to whether the travels of Livingstone and others were also sanctioned by Christian texts and whether the mission texts they used advocate liberating ways of interdependence or the suppression of difference. The question remains as to when and where 'the talisman of Christian truth' is located.

If Livingstone and Pringle can be dismissed as zealous church missionaries, figures such as Albert Schweitzer, who acted as a colonial envoy and influenced academic biblical studies in a big way,[36] hardly exempts academic biblical studies, scholars, their interpretations, or indeed, the texts themselves from the violence of imperialism. Modern European and American colonizing powers openly defined their task as a Puritan 'errand to the wilderness', 'a duty to the natives', or 'a mission to

32. Ngugi wa Thiong'o, *Moving the Centre*, p. 31.

33. Ngugi wa Thiong'o, *Decolonising the Mind*, p. 91.

34. Norman E. Thomas, *Classic Texts in Mission and World Christianity* (New York: Orbis Books, 1995), p. 68.

35. Quoted in Mudimbe, *The Invention of Africa*, p. 47, without giving Pringle's second or first name.

36. Marcus Borg, *Jesus in Contemporary Scholarship* (Valley Forge, PA: Trinity Press International, 1992), pp. 3-4, 18.

civilize'—moral claims derived from Christian texts, which beg to be investigated.[37]

Reading the Bible and other cultural texts for decolonization is, therefore, imperative for those who are committed to the struggle for liberation. Why the Bible is a usable text in imperial projects and how it should be read in the light of its role are central questions to the process of decolonization and the struggle for liberation. As a Motswana woman of Southern Africa, my reading for decolonization arises from the historical encounter of Christian texts functioning compatibly with colonialism; of the Bible functioning as the 'talisman' in imperial possession of foreign places and people. While history attests to the 'use' of biblical texts, and while the Bible may have been one of the Western texts that helped imperial travel to perceive and to domesticate unfamiliar strange places, my reading seeks to investigate whether its use is supported by the ideology of Christian mission texts. My reading seeks to interrogate the travel/mission texts of the Bible and the power relations between different cultural lands and people that they advocate.

In reading a mission text for decolonization, however, I am not denying that cross-cultural exchanges between races and nations has gone on, still goes on, and must continue to go on outside imperialist contexts. Neither am I equating with imperialism every attempt to spread one's influence to other cultures and lands. Rather, my reading seeks to confront the imperialist projects of biblical texts and to investigate the grounds of their dramatic, historic partnership.[38] Thus I have chosen the story of the Samaritan woman for obvious reasons: it is a mission narrative; one that authorizes its reader-believer to 'go forth', so to speak. Furthermore, my reading will interrogate and highlight the power relations John 4 proposes for international cultural relations and exchanges.

37. See Rudyard Kipling, 'The White Man's Burden'. The poem demonstrates dependency on biblical images: colonizing travelers are portrayed as the light to the heathen and half-devil people. Like Moses, the colonizer is confronted with the complaints of the colonized who wish to return to the night and bondage of Egypt. In short, modern colonizers' projects are equated to the Christian mission.

38. Elsewhere I have tabulated the following questions as criteria for identifying imperializing texts: (1) Does this text have a clear stance against the political imperialism of its time? (2) Does this text encourage its readers/hearers/believers to travel to distant lands and how does it justify itself? (3) How does this text construct differences? Is there dialogue and liberating interdependence, or is there condemnation and replacement of all that is foreign? (4) Does this text employ gender and divine representations/claims to construct relationships of subordination and domination? See further, Musa W. Dube, *Postcolonial Feminist Interpretations of the Bible* (St Louis: Chalice, 2000).

Reading for Decolonization: John 4.1-42

My reading attributes the construction of this story to the Johannine community and their missionary vision, rather than the historical Jesus and his disciples. In reading for decolonization, I will deal with the imperial setting, hidden interests, travelers, geography/lands, expansion, and the construction of the Samaritan woman/people/land. I will conclude by looking at one Two-Thirds World woman's attempt to decolonize the story. Throughout the explication of these factors, I will use particular quotations from the story as subtitles to highlight some of the main imperial ideological constructions of the narrative. Despite my attempt to treat each point independently, the reader will find them closely intertwined.

'The Pharisees had heard Jesus is making and baptizing more disciples than John...!' (John 4.1)

The mention of Pharisees, Jesus and John the Baptist highlights an intense struggle for power directly related to imperialist occupation. Historically, the gospel is written several decades after the Roman Empire had destroyed Jerusalem and the Temple in 70 CE. The destruction of the central Jewish symbols of meaning has contributed to creating an intense inter-group competition for power, characterized by negotiation, collaboration and revolt against the Roman Empire by various national groups. Evidently, in Jn 4.1, three movements/interests groups are vying for power in Palestine: The Pharisees, Jesus and his disciples, and John the Baptist and his disciples. As the first verse clearly indicates Jesus is fleeing from the Pharisees, who have heard he 'is making and baptizing more disciples than John' (v. 1). I will now briefly explicate these competitions and how they are related to imperialist presence.

First, there is competition for power between the disciples of John the Baptist, a representative of one interest group, and the disciples of Jesus. Thus the text of John rhetorically subordinates John to Jesus. In the prologue, the narrator states that John the Baptist 'was not the light, but he came to testify to the light' (1.6-9). On two other occasions, the Baptist is characterized as devaluing himself to underline the superiority of Jesus. First, he says 'this is he whom I said after me comes a man who ranks ahead of me because he was before me' (1.29-37). Later, he says Jesus 'must increase, but I must decrease' (3.22-30). However, many scholars argue that there is good reason to suggest that John and his disciples were an independent movement. This textual subordination of John to Jesus simplifies the conflicts as one between the Pharisees and

Jesus and his disciples, who are, no doubt, the biggest rivals within the Gospel of John.

Second, there is competition between the disciples of Jesus and the disciples of Moses, the Pharisees. In the post-70 CE period the Pharisees were not only another interest group, but were also the officially recognized power in Palestine (3.1, 7.48, 12.42). Therefore, the Pharisees and the Sadducees appear as a united authoritative power in John's gospel (7.32, 45; 11.47, 57), a construction which tries to be faithful to Jesus's times and the author's times. As the gospel attests (7–12.50), competition for power and enmity between the disciples of Jesus and the disciples of Moses (Pharisees) has reached its peak with dire consequences. The disciples of Jesus have lost their influence and have been thrown out of the synagogue (9.22, 35; 12.42). Some may even have died (16.2).

Third, when we enter the story of Jn 4.1-42, we witness the consequences of imperial disruption and inter-group competition at two levels. First, the disciples of Jesus are extending their influence to Samaria because they are losing the national competition to the Pharisees. Second, we enter into centuries of imperial subtexts of disruption, alienation and resistance that strains the relationships of the Samaritans and Jews (4.9, 20-23). This tension goes back to the period of the Assyrian Empire. Through intermarriages and the adoption of some of the religions of their Assyrian colonial masters, Samaritans became what some have termed 'despised heretics' and 'despised half-breeds'. As a result, the Samaritan Jewish ancestors distanced themselves from Samaritans on the grounds of religious impurity. Their strained relationship highlights the extent to which imperial domination has affected and influenced the relationship of different people at different centuries in the world.

In sum, imperial domination is central to the story of the Samaritan woman and to John's gospel as a whole. The local leaders who plan the death of Jesus, for instance, are characterized as in genuine fear that his fame will bring a Roman attack on the nation (11.48-53). At his trial, faithfulness to Roman imperial power is evoked to justify the guilt of Jesus (19.12, 15); and Pilate insists on crucifying Jesus as the awaited political liberator—a Jewish king—despite the chief priests' resistance to the inscription, 'Jesus of Nazareth, the King of the Jews' (19.19-22). All these factors highlight how the Roman imperial expansionist agendas and the imposition of its own cultural symbols and power stimulated a response and led to inter-group competition within Jewish society.[39]

---

39. See Andrew J. Overman, *Matthew's Gospel and Formative Judaism: The Social World of the Matthean Community* (Minneapolis: Fortress Press, 1990), for an illuminating

Likewise, Jesus and his disciples' turn to the despised land of Samaritans is linked to the competition for power between the Pharisees and Christian Jews. Both Pharisees and Christian Jews are trying to define Jewish identity during the Roman occupation of Palestine; in particular, after the destruction of their religious symbols—Jerusalem and the Temple. And it is important that this competition for power between local interest groups is not be divorced from the real enemy—from its root cause: the Roman empire. The story of the Samaritan woman illustrates how imperialism affects people in general: it leads the colonized to fight back, to collaborate with the enemy, or to fight among themselves, as in the case of Pharisees and Jesus's disciples.

It seems safe to say that Jesus's disciples are losing (6.66; 12.42-43). They are not making many disciples as other groups (4.1), and so they turn to proselytize the Samaritans. In other words, the alternative vision of the Johannine community ironically embraces an ideology of expansion, despite the fact that it, itself, is the victim of imperial expansion and is struggling for its own liberation.[40] But as is common in imperial ideologies of expansion, the Johannine search for influence is not openly expressed. And so I come to a point in my argument where the hidden interests in the ideology of imperialism can finally be explicitly addressed.

'Look!... See how the fields are ripe for harvesting...!' (John 4.35)
The ideology of imperialism typically conceals its interests and presents its project in rhetorical terms such as the 'duty to the natives', who 'require and beseech domination'.[41] Similarly in John 4, the Johannine community conceals its interests through the literary characterization of Jesus and his disciples. First, the narrator states that Jesus is in transit through Samaria. But his real destination is Galilee. Thus at Sychar, we meet Jesus sitting by the well—notably, outside the village—because 'he is tired out by his journey' to Galilee (vv. 5-6). The refusal to admit to any intention to enter and missionize is further underscored by the fact that Jesus only enters the village when the Samaritans themselves 'asked him to stay with them' (v. 40). Thus the narration of Jesus's journey

discussion on the impact of imperial forces on first-century Palestine. In particular, how it led to conflict, competition and fragmentation of Jewish society as each interest group attempted to define the cultural boundaries, and how such a competition included collaborating with the imperial powers.

40. See Craig Koester, 'The Saviour of the World (John 4.42)', *JBL* 109 (1990), pp. 665-80, whose article highlights Jn 4's direct borrowing of imperial ideology to express the Christian identity.

41. Said, *Culture and Imperialism*, p. 9.

resists any open acknowledgment of an intention to evangelize Samaria. The story prefers to hold that the Samaritans need Jesus's missionary work (v. 22); they follow Jesus of their own accord (v. 30); and they asked for Jesus's message (v. 40).

The hidden interests are also evident in the characterization of the disciples in the story. First, they appear as a faint background of the story. They have gone to buy food in the city *not* to missionize (v. 9). The dialogue between Jesus and the Samaritan woman takes place in their absence. When they return, she departs, and Jesus begins to speak to them about his food, that is, 'to do the will of him who sent me and to complete his work' (v. 34). In this discussion, they are notably puzzled by Jesus's talk, which turns into a monologue. In general, his disciples remain silent and they never openly question or seem to understand. All these literary constructions distance the disciples from any intention to missionize the Samaritans. The evangelization of Samaritans thus falls squarely on the Samaritans themselves: it is the woman and the villagers who beg Jesus to enter the village and stay with them.

Jesus's response to the disciples in this short scene (vv. 31-38), however, is central to the whole story of the Samaritan woman. The scene provides the disciples with an interpretive grid through which they must understand their food, that is, like Jesus who is sent, they are sent, (vv. 34, 38). They are authorized to go, to enter, and to teach other nations. It is in this scene that the rhetoric of interests and power is aggressively articulated; yet it remains concealed by an ideology of disinterest. Jesus says to them: 'Look around you, and see how the fields are ripe for harvesting... One sows, another reaps. I sent you to reap that for which you did not labor. Others have labored, and you have entered into their labor' (vv. 37-38). Many scholars have wrestled with these sayings.[42] Two factors are pertinent to my reading. First, the fields are ripe for harvest. The statement articulates an evident search for profit and a desire to take possession of something. Regardless of whether the possession is spiritual or material, it involves a will to power which is invested in real people and affects real people. Second, the legitimation of the disciples' power entails frightening values: the disciples are *sent to reap that for which they did not labor*. Such a statement reflects the intensity of com-

---

42. The main problem lies in the contradictory statements about the sowers. At first, it seems there is equal division of labor and rewards (vv. 36-37), but the concluding verse suggests otherwise (v. 38). While the reapers are disciples, the identity of sowers remains ambiguous. Jesus has been suggested, but since the verse speaks of 'many other sowers', other explanations—such as former prophets, Hellenist evangelists, or the Samaritan woman herself have been suggested.

petition and struggle for control and, of necessity, depends on unequal relationships.

Consequently, the Samaritans are construed as passive fields to be entered and harvested.[43] Yet, these fields are not limited to Samaria. They include the whole world (v. 42). But once more, this 'global' vision is placed in the mouth of the Samaritans who must proclaim him 'the Saviour of the World'. This characterization distances the disciples from any self-interest and projects an imperial ideology that portrays the colonized as people who 'require and beseech for domination' and the colonizers as people with a moral 'duty to the natives'.

We must remember that historically the story represents a much later vision of the mission (v. 38) arising, as I said, from the Johannine community rather than from the historical Jesus and his disciples. It is therefore striking how the disciples (or the Johannine community) who are most probably the proponents of the missionary vision and authors of the story, present themselves as mute and puzzled by Jesus's talk of ripe fields. Through this literary presentation, the disciples (Johannine community) rhetorically distance themselves from their own vision precisely in order to conceal their interests until the very end. For instance, if the disciples are going to take all the credit for the Samaritan woman's work, the Samaritan people themselves will discredit her importance (v. 42).

Although the rhetoric of concealment pervades the narrative, the story authorizes the Christian disciples/readers/believers to travel, enter, educate and to harvest other foreign lands for the Christian nations. And it does this in a literary fashion that is openly modeled on imperialist values. This is evident both in the saying, 'I have sent you to reap that which you did not labor. Others labored, and you have entered into their labor' and in the title 'Saviour of the World', as a designation of Jesus. Notably, the saying evokes Josh. 24.13, where the Lord God speaks to the Israelites through Joshua saying, 'I gave you a land on which you had not labored, and towns that you had not built, and you live in them; you eat the fruit of vineyards and olive groves that you did not plant.' The book of Joshua is a highly dramatized and idealized capture of the Canaan. It is a narrative that glorifies conquest and openly advocates violent colonialism in the name of God.

43. According to Raymond Brown (*The Gospel and Epistles of John* [Collegeville, MN: Liturgical Press, 1988], p.18), 'the disciples must learn to harvest the crop of believers even though they have not sowed the seed'. He goes on to point out that 'in Acts 8.4-25, Phillip the Hellenist evangelizes Samaria, and then the Jerusalem apostles send Peter and John to confirm the conversion'. Although Brown mentions that both the sower and reaper must rejoice together, his interpretation leans toward validating hierarchical structures.

As noted above, 'Saviour of the World' was a title used to refer to the Roman emperors in the first century. Surprise, surprise! The Johannine Jesus now emerges fully clothed in the emperor's titles.[44] Thus, Jesus also lays claim to unlimited access to all geographical spaces and foreigners. In evoking Joshua's narrative and borrowing the titles of emperors to articulate the Christian mission and to characterize Jesus, John 4 models its vision along imperial goals, strategies and values. The mission is portrayed as a violent entry and domestication of foreign lands and people. It involves reaping fields that one did not plant. This finally brings me to the travelers themselves and their role in the imperialist project. My points will be developed by focusing on Jesus and his disciples as travelers.

'My food is to do the will of him who sent me… I send you…!' (John 4.34, 38)
Imperialism as an ideology of expansion involves superior travelers who reflect the superiority of their origin. Similarly, Jesus and his disciples are the authorized travelers 'from above' (3.34, 8.26; 20.21-23). Their travel is linked with expansion, and it is both locally and 'globally' oriented. First, they are traveling because the expansion of their mission has brought them trouble (v. 1); but soon thereafter, their departure results in further expansion (vv. 30, 39). Jesus's commission to the disciples to harvest the ripe fields, and the Samaritans' declaration that Jesus is the 'Saviour of the World' indicates that their expansion espouses 'global' levels. The disciples of Jesus are 'global travelers', as it were. Like their master, they are authorized from above; hence, they are superior to everyone else.

Jesus and his disciples are travelers invested with high authority far above their hosts. To begin with, Jesus is a very superior traveler. His superiority is communicated through the literary style used for his identification: a gradual unfolding which shows his superiority at every stage of the story. The Samaritan woman, who first thought he was just a simple Jewish man, discovers that Jesus can give her living water which leads to eternal life (v. 10); he is greater than Jacob (vv. 12-14). And he is not only a prophet (v. 19) or a Messiah (v. 26), but the 'Saviour of the World' (v. 42). This gradual unveiling of Jesus's identity characterizes him as an extremely superior traveler who surpasses all other local figures.

The characterization of Jesus in John 4 is consistent with his portrayal in the rest of the gospel of John. For instance, Johannine scholars have

44. Talbert, *Reading John*, p. 118; Koester, 'The Saviour of the World', pp. 665-80, and Cassidy, *John's Gospel*, pp. 6-16.

noted how Jesus is compared to other Christological figures such as the Word, the Lamb of God, the King of Israel, Moses and the Messiah/ Christ. This is a literary device designed to show that he is well above all these figures.[45] The comparison is a rhetorical ladder for his elevation: it foregrounds his superiority and almost equates him with God (1.1; 20.28) while it derogates the validity of all others.

While the disciples are rhetorically obscured in the story of the Samaritan woman, they nevertheless travel with Jesus. The story serves to give them the right to travel with authority (v. 38). Their authority is derived from and is closely related to that of Jesus (v. 34, 20.21-23). It is authority from above, from God. However, such authority can only be justified by a negative portrayal of those nations and lands that must be entered, taught and converted. This brings to me to the characterization of the Samaritan woman, or, as some have noted, the Samaritan land.

'If you knew… You worship what you do not know… We worship what we know!' (John 4.10, 22)

Imperialism expounds an ideology of inferior knowledge and invalid religious faith for those who must be colonized. Authoritative travelers depend heavily upon constructions of ignorant natives. There is a sharp division between those who know, the colonizers, and those who know nothing, the colonized. Thus the Samaritan woman is characterized as an ignorant native (v. 10) and in need of help (v. 10). She is constructed as morally or religiously lacking something; that is, she has had five husbands, and the one she has now is not her own (vv. 17-18). Furthermore, she does not know what she worships (v. 22). By way of contrast, Jesus, a superior traveler, is knowledgeable (vv. 10, 22); powerful (vv. 14, 25, 42); sees everything about her past (vv. 17-18, 29); knows and offers answers to her community (vv. 21-26); and teaches her and her people (vv. 21-23). The ignorance of the Samaritan woman is pathetic. Despite all these revelations (v. 26), she remains ignorant to the end. That is, she is still uncertain and asks, 'he cannot be the Messiah, can he?' (v. 29).[46] As Gail O'Day's analysis correctly notes, the Samaritan woman's inability to understand is well above that of the male disciples (vv. 27, 31-33).[47]

45. See Robert Kysar, *John: The Maverick Gospel* (Louisville: John Knox Press, 1976), pp. 22-46; and J.L. Martyn, *The Gospel of John in Christian History: Essays in Interpretation* (New York: Paulist Press, 1978), pp. 9-54.

46. See Gail R. O'Day, *Revelation in the Fourth Gospel* (Philadelphia: Fortress Press, 1986), who focuses on the Samaritan woman and gives an extensive analysis of her character.

47. See Gail R. O'Day, *The Word Disclosed: John's Story and Narrative Preaching* (St Louis: CBP, 1987), pp. 48-49.

Here, ignorance is furthered by employing the feminine gender. In the mission story, a narrative that authorizes traveling to and entering into foreign lands and places, it is significant that she becomes a first point of contact. As in imperializing narratives, this pattern is a statement about the targeted land and its inhabitants. Like the woman who represents them, the foreign land must be entered, won and domesticated. And so the next subtitle highlights the rhetoric of hierarchical geographical spaces.

'Are you greater than our ancestor Jacob, who gave us this well and…drank from it?' (John 4.12)
Authoritative travelers also depend on an ideology of hierarchical geographical spaces. Jesus is the highest authority and the most authoritative traveler in John's gospel. Consequently, a specific geography had to be constructed for him. That is, he has descended from the Father and will ascend to the Father.[48] His origin allows him to become a 'World Saviour' because he is not of the world. However, this also necessitates that the world should be constructed negatively (8.12, 23; 9.39; 12.31; 13.1).

Within the story of the Samaritan woman, hierarchical constructions of geographical spaces are also evident. There are Judea and Galilee, lands that are much holier than Samaria and Sychar; lands which are best avoided (v. 9). Concomitantly, the occupants of Samaria are also of questionable value. The negative characterization of the Samaritans allows Jesus to assert his religious superiority (v. 22), even when he is discrediting both Gerizim and Jerusalem (v. 21). Jacob's well in Samaria (v. 12) pales beside Jesus's spring of superior waters (v. 13). Ripe fields must be entered and harvested by those who did not sow them (vv. 35-38). And, lastly, the world must be saved (v. 42). These hierarchical, geographical constructions authorize travelers of superior origins and values (Jesus and his disciples) to expand, enter and control, at both local and 'global' levels, those geographical areas that are depicted as inferior in their systems of value (Samaria and the world).

48. See Fernando Segovia, 'Journey(s) of the Word: A Reading of the Plot of the Fourth Gospel', *Semeia* 53 (1991), pp. 23-54, for an extensive treatment of journeys and origins embedded in the plot of John's gospel. For the concept of descending and ascending and its sociological function, See Wayne Meeks, 'The Man from Heaven in Johannine Sectarianism', *JBL* 91 (1972), pp. 44-72.

'You will worship the Father neither on this mountain nor in Jerusalem...!' (John 4.2)

The imperialist ideology of expansion uses the promotion of its own cultural values to devalue, replace and suppress diversity. Its strategy is characterized by a massive inclusivity, but not equality. Similarly, in Jn 4.1-42 the mission expands from the well to the world. Notably, the expansion declares the cultural centers of Jerusalem and Gerizim as inadequate and replaces them with Spirit and truth.[49] This apparent inclusive replacement maintains the religious/racial superiority of Jesus (v. 22), a characterization that clearly shows that imperialism's universal standards never intend to create relationships of equals, but intend to win devotees. Therefore, the transcendence of both Jewish and Samaritan cultural spaces by the realm of Spirit and truth (vv. 23-24), in fact, installs Christianity in the superior position. And as we now know, this installation proceeds by discrediting all other religious cultures for its own interests. We perceive this unequal inclusion through the discursive use and final dismissal of the only female gendered character in the story.

'They said to the woman, "It is no longer because of what you said that we believe"' (John 4.42)

Imperialist ideologies of subjugation construct extremely gendered discourses. The lands that must be subjugated are equated with women, and narratives about the penetration of distant lands feature women. Ancient epic texts feature numerous goddesses and women at the shores of foreign and distant lands. Biblical examples are the stories of the Jericho prostitute (Josh. 2) and the Canaanite woman (Mt. 15.21-28). Like a woman, the target of colonialism is entered, conquered and domesticated. Thus many scholars have noted that the Samaritan woman represents her land. She is the point of entrance, and she is finally domesticated (v. 41). Moreover, those who did not sow, the male disciples, are invited to move in to reap the harvest, while she is dismissed (vv. 37-38).[50]

49. See Jerome Neyrey, 'Jacob Traditions and the Interpretation of John 4.10-26', *CBQ* 41 (1979), pp. 419-37, on this point.

50. Although some readers compare the Samaritan woman's story to John the Baptist or the disciples, who point others to Christ, her story is somewhat different. John the Baptist is at least given a chance to speak for himself and to say that it is his honor to decrease while Jesus Christ increases (3.28-30). The disciples continue to follow Christ and are finally commissioned (20.21-23). The Samaritan woman, however, is never given a chance to say a word after returning from the city. Instead, there is an open dismissal or devaluation of her work (v. 42). If her story represents a later time, when the church

As previously mentioned, imperialist expansion suggests a massive inclusion of races, lands, genders and religions, but not equality. The inclusion is intended to legitimate control, and control depends on unequal relationships. The unequal inclusivity of this narrative is grounded in the very literary device employed. E. Fuchs's research on the betrothal type-scene is instructive here.[51] Fuchs notes that betrothal type-scenes are a constellation of literary motifs employed to mark the launching of a young patriarch's career. The type-scene begins with a young man's journey to the outside world where he meets his future bride at the well. As the scene proceeds, the status of the woman decreases into obscurity. Men take over to discuss her future and her family's wealth. She marries and departs with her husband. Thus as Fuchs notes, betrothal type-scenes are not about the woman but about the launching of a patriarch's career.

The story of the Samaritan woman is built on the same literary foundation. At first, the narrative leads the reader to celebrate her role (and other relationships involving worship, sowers, and reapers). Yet after she finishes announcing Jesus Christ to her townspeople, she never speaks out again. The discussion of her work and its product is transferred into the hands of Jesus, his male disciples, and the village converts—who, after meeting with Jesus—relegate her work to secondary status (v. 42). Here we perceive the launching of Jesus's career outside his home; that is, the birth of his bride (the church or the Johannine community). Jesus's relationship—and by extension Christianity's relationship to foreign people and lands—is, unfortunately, grounded on a very unequal foundation, as attested by the portrayals of race, gender, and geography in the Gospel of John. Accordingly, what seems to be an inclusive gospel of Spirit and Truth is the reverse. It reflects the installation of Christianity as a universal religion: an installation that proceeds by disavowing all geographical boundaries in order to claim power over the 'world' and relegate all other religions and cultures to inadequacy.

Yet as Jeffrey Staley catalogues the uniqueness of the Samaritan woman's story, it is more than just betrothal type-scene.[52] Gary Phillips also notes that 'against the backdrop of the traditional women at the well

began to seriously consider the mission to the Gentiles, then her dismissal is a serious statement on the role of women, rather than just a Johannine pattern of discipleship.

51. Esther Fuchs, 'Structure and Patriarchal Functions in Biblical Betrothal Type-Scenes: Some Preliminary Notes', *Journal of Feminist Studies in Religion* 3 (1987), pp. 7-13.

52. See Jeffrey Staley, *The Print's First Kiss: A Rhetorical Investigation of the Implied Reader in the Fourth Gospel* (Atlanta: Scholars Press, 1988), pp. 95-103, for a detailed comparison between the standard betrothal type-scene and the story of the Samaritan woman.

screen, the Samaritan woman's actions are disturbingly different'.[53] The significant diversion of the Samaritan woman's story points to its wider literary category, one which I have called a type-scene of land possession. For the Samaritan woman and Jesus do not end up married, like in most betrothal stories. The Samaritan woman is not even a marriageable virgin, but a woman who has had five husbands and is living with another one who is not hers. She represents her land. If, as some scholars have noted, her characterization is a statement about Samaria, then Jesus is 'another bridegroom'; another husband. Hence, like other emperors, Jesus is entitled to unlimited access to all the geographical spaces of Samaria and the world, as his new title expressly says. The ideology of this story is that foreign lands are immoral women which await taming by foreign saviours.

In this story, therefore, patriarchal and imperial literary-rhetorical methods of domination are intertwined, making a feminist appropriation of the story a precarious and critically demanding exercise. Undoubtedly, the use of a female figure to articulate relationships of subordination and domination also encourages the oppression of women wherever these texts are used. Therefore, focus on the patriarchal aspect of this narrative, to the exclusion of its imperial aspects, will effect a feminist reading that baptizes colonial oppression and reinscribes the oppression of women.

Given the global experience of imperial and patriarchal domination, its persistence, and the real suffering and exploitation of those who are at its receiving end, how can one read the story of the Samaritan woman for decolonization and for the empowerment of women? How can one foster a new narrative of liberating interdependence that recognizes and nurtures diversity? In searching for the answers to some of these questions, I turn to one Two-Thirds World woman's attempt to rewrite the story for decolonization and the empowerment of women.

One Woman's Decolonizing Reading of John 4.1-42

The Victims' setting is pre-independent to post-independent Botswana and apartheid South Africa. Mositi Totontle's major concerns are the settler colonial practices of the white apartheid regime and their effects on the whole region of Southern Africa; in particular, the breakdown of

53. Gary Phillips, 'The Ethics of Reading Deconstructively or Speaking Face-to-Face: The Samaritan Woman Meets Derrida at the Well', in Edgar V. McKnight and Elisabeth Struthers Malbon (eds.), *The New Literary Criticism and the New Testament* (Valley Forge, PA: Trinity Press International, 1994), p. 303.

family life due to structurally coerced mine labor immigration. As one of the characters describes it, it 'is a sick land and a broken people' in need of healing, for the 'whole society has been shaken, shattered and scattered'.[54] Within this setting of brokenness, Torontle re-writes the story of the Samaritan woman as follows:

> Mmapula...went down the river to fetch water for her plants. Beside the well sat a still woman dressed in white clothing. Her head was bowed and focused in her open hands. Mmapula trod slowly, wondering who she was and what she was doing at this place and time. Mmapula sat down by the well and began to fill her container with water. Just when she was about to leave, the woman in white looked up and said, 'Samaritan woman, give me a drink'. Mmapula gave her a drink. 'Samaritan woman, go and call your husband', she said retaining Mmapula's gourd without drinking the water. 'I am not a Samaritan woman and I have no husband'. The woman in white closed her eyes for some seconds and said, 'You have spoken well, Samaritan woman. You have no husband. In fact, the husband that you have does not belong to you but to the mines. I have come to give you a drink of living water', she said handing Mmapula the same gourd of water. 'Go back to your village and announce that a prophetess has come bringing healing to the broken hearted'. 'A prophet has come bringing healing to Borolong'. The news spread at the speed of a veld fire through the small village.[55]

Totontle's decolonizing reading of Jn 4.1-42 recognizes and makes attempts to arrest the imperializing aspects of the story. But I wish to show how she arrests the oppressive constructions of gender, race, geography and religion. Lastly, I will discuss the author's use of the Samaritan identity as an ideal space to emphasize interconnections in a world constructed by imperialism.

Central to Totontle's rereading is her attempt to decolonize hierarchical gender and race. First, she arrests gender superiority by featuring a female character in the place of Jesus.[56] Second, the Samaritan woman is explicitly 'sent', and so has the status conferred upon male the

---

54. See Sandra Schneiders, *The Revelatory Text: Interpreting the New Testament as Sacred Scripture* (San Francisco: HarperCollins, 1991), pp. 190-91, for an interpretation that reads the husbands as representations of the different empires of the past. In her reading, the current husband would be the Roman Empire.

55. Mositi Totontle, *The Victims* (Gaborone: Botsalo, 1993), pp. 57-58.

56. See Mary Ann Tolbert, 'Protestant Women and the Bible: On the Horns of a Dilemma', in Alice Balch (ed.), *The Pleasure of her Text: Feminist Readings of Biblical and Historical Texts* (Philadelphia: Trinity Press International, 1990), pp. 18-19, who suggests 'imagining Jesus and the twelve as women and a man anointing her head with oil (Mk 14.3-9)' and holds that such a reversal of characters can create a new way of viewing some of these biblical stories.

disciples in Jn 4.38. There is also a clear attempt to decolonize the construction of racial superiority. For example, when asked for water, Mmapula responds positively without any questions. Mmapula's response challenges and dispenses any claims of cultural purity or impurity; hence, it undercuts the ideology of superior and inferior races that heavily depends on such dichotomies. Her response is subversive with regard to the imperial ideology that heavily depends on the claims of racial superiority and chosenness—as attested by the histories of North American and South African colonization. Yet Mmapula denies her Samaritan identity, while the prophetess insists on it. Her insistence is a point I shall revisit later. Totontle's reading also decolonizes geographical hierarchy by offering the Samaritan woman living water from her own well on her own land. The geographical affirmation of her land serves to affirm its occupants and the adequacy of their cultural values. To accentuate this point, nothing is said about Mmapula's possession of many husbands—although we are informed that she has no husband. Furthermore, prophecy—that is, social criticism and the search for new visions of reconstruction—is preferred over universal salvation. Therefore, the woman in white is notably a prophetess and not a Saviour of the World. She has come to bring healing to the village, and her style of healing affirms that the villagers already have strength and abilities in and among themselves. With regard to religion, Totontle's decolonizing reading avoids any replacement or rejection of other faith orientations. In fact, the prophetess, who is later identified as Mother Mary Magdalene, is also a preacher and a faith-healer. In her preaching, she retells biblical stories from her memory, and in her healing she calls on the African Ancestral Spirits and Jesus to heal the land and bind its wounds.[57] In short, she does not privilege the Christian stories over the religious stories of Africans; she uses them both as she finds them useful. Thus the characterization of Mary Magdalene as a decolonizing interpreter serves to underline and to embrace the identity of Mmapula as despised heretic. The despised heretic becomes the ideal model for a truly post-colonial and inclusive world![58] This latter point brings me to the category/identity of the Samaritan as the ideal space for acknowledging cultural interconnections, as well as for nurturing differences.

57. Mositi Totontle, *The Victims*, pp. 60, 73-76.

58. Mositi Totontle, *The Victims*, p. 71. Her description of Mother Mary Magdalene's attire depicts her remarkable diversity: She 'was wearing a white turban, a red cape, a rosary, white and red beads on her writs and held a Zion hymn book in her hands. Dineo tried to place her various lines of faith and found that her dress pronounced her a mixture of various things and follower of none.'

Despite Mmapula's denial of her Samaritan identity, Mother Mary Magdalene's insistence on it implies an emphasis on the imperialist setting. Like the biblical Samaritan woman, Mmapula is a despised heretic, an outcaste half-breed; she cannot claim any purity of race or religion, and she has lived through several types of imperialist domination. Various forms of imperialism have affected and constructed Mmapula as well as the Fourth Gospel's Pharisees, John the Baptist, Jesus, and his disciples. The Samaritan identity is, therefore, highlighted as the reality of both the biblical characters of John 4 and Mmapula. Totontle's decolonizing reading shows that imperialism is the reality for those nations and races who claim purity and those who cannot claim it; for those who are consciously aware of imperialism as a pervasive reality in the world, and for those who are not aware of it. It is indeed a reality for First World biblical readers and for Two-Thirds World biblical readers.

Mmapula's final response underscores the pervasity of imperialism: in the end she does not deny her Samaritan race. In short, she comes to the reality of who she is—a mixture of many different things: a despised heretic and an outcaste half-breed.

Conclusion

Many biblical narratives are imperializing texts insofar as they use history to propound power relations. The mission passages—which can be fairly termed the central Christian narratives that authorize traveling and entering into foreign cultures and lands exemplified by John 4— hardly propose relations of liberating interdependence between races, cultures and genders. Both the prefatory African saying and the words of missionary-colonial agents attest to the participation of biblical texts in colonial projects; they bind the Bible to the history of subjugation and exploitation. This obligates First World and Two-Thirds World communities of reader-writers to interrogate the biblical ideology of travel, expansion, representations of differences, and their various functions.

Because of the historical reoccurrences, the contemporary persistence, and the mutations of imperialisms, imperialism will not be easily bracketed from the critical practice of academic biblical interpretation. Therefore it is imperative that biblical scholars take cognizance of the world that is wedged between imperial domination, collaboration and resistance. It is also imperative that biblical scholars take cognizance of texts that, more often than not, offer models of international relationships which are less than liberating; which have served in different imperialist projects and lift up writing-reading communities which are calling for decolonization. Totontle's decolonizing reading of John 4 challenges biblical readers, hearers, believers and writers to acknowledge and to embrace their Samaritan social spaces of heretics and half-breeds. Similarly, biblical critical practice must be dedicated to an ethical task of promoting decolonization, fostering diversity, and imagining liberating ways of interdependence.

Contesting an Interpretation of John 5:
Moving Beyond Colonial Evangelism

Francisco Lozada, Jr

Introduction

In a recent essay entitled 'Missions and the Servants of God (John 5)', Everett W. Huffard explores the theme of servanthood in John 5.[1] Huffard's main argument is that John 5 encompasses a model of servanthood for Christians that can be used to evangelize Muslims.[2] To support this reading, Huffard establishes two main assumptions with regard to the suitability and purpose of the Fourth Gospel for Muslims.

First, in exploring the suitability of the Fourth Gospel in the history of Christian missions, Huffard, in agreement with other missionaries, maintains that the Gospel is a good place to start converting Muslims to Christianity. The primary reason for such a position is that the Gospel 'records more of the words of Christ, making it more compatible to their view of revelation'.[3] However, he does disagree with other fellow missionaries in that he believes neither the prologue (1.1-18) nor the eternal life maxim (3.16) are appropriate starting points for evangelizing Muslims. John 5 is a bit better because it suits his interest in developing the theme of servanthood.[4] The prologue is just too 'meaty' for their monophysitic theology and 3.16 is too offensive to Muslims' cultural values.[5] Second, after reviewing the two dominant positions regarding the intent of the Gospel narrated in 20.30-31, Huffard works with the assumption that the Gospel was written as 'an evangelistic tract to reach

---

1. E.W. Huffard, 'Missions and the Servants of God (John 5)', in J. Priest (ed.), *Johannine Studies: Essays in Honor of Frank Peck* (Malibu: Pepperdine University Press, 1989), pp. 84-96.
2. Huffard, 'Missions and Servants of God', p. 89.
3. Huffard, 'Missions and Servants of God', p. 86.
4. Huffard is also interested in studying how Jn 5–8 can be contextualized for Muslim evangelism, although he focuses only on Jn 5 in this article. Huffard, 'Missions and Servants of God', p. 90 n. 21.
5. Huffard, 'Missions and Servants of God', p. 86.

the unbelieving', rather than as an apologetic or polemic against 'the Jews' in order to maintain the faith of the believers.[6] Both of these underlying assumptions support Huffard's primary thesis that the servant motif in John 5 is a mandate for Christians to carry on the mission to convert Muslims.

Such a conclusion, I believe, is not only dangerous to Muslims but to all people of faiths or religious perspectives differing from Huffard's. Unwittingly, no doubt, and with the best intentions, Huffard's reading of John 5 nevertheless is pernicious because it aims to solidify and perpetuate the superiority of Christians over the majority of people who are not Christians and, at the same time, to recast these people and their culture in an inferior mold. In other words, Huffard's interpretation of John 5 both embodies and legitimizes a colonialist theological hierarchy with Christians at the top and people of different faiths underneath— depicting them as inferior and immoral.[7] It is a strategy that many take, unconsciously or consciously, to justify cultural imperialism by means of the biblical text. By correlating the religious differences between Christians and 'non-Christians' along the lines of a superior–inferior scheme, one can easily legitimize a superior–inferior scheme with Christians as superior and 'non-Christians' as inferior.

Unlike Huffard, I question whether John 5, or any part of the Gospel for that matter, should be used to evangelize or 'to convert' cultures of different faiths. Rather, texts provide a means for readers/hearers to recognize or to liberate; this liberation entails economic, gender, sexual, racial/ethnic and political freedom for all peoples.[8] However, such recognition of liberation, I would argue, is not inherent in the authority of the text per se, but rather in the reading practice itself.[9] In this essay, therefore, I will contest Huffard's colonial use of John 5 and instead provide a postcolonial reading of it.[10] That is, I attempt to challenge an

6. Huffard, 'Missions and Servants of God', p. 87.

7. R.S. Sugirtharajah, *Asian Biblical Hermeneutics and Postcolonialism: Contesting the Interpretations* (Maryknoll, NY: Orbis Books, 1998), p. 62; see also J.L. Comaroff and J. Comaroff, *Of Revelation and Revolution: The Dialectics of Modernity on a Southern African Frontier* (vol. 2; Chicago: University of Chicago Press, 1997), p. 21, who confirm that colonialism does not simply refer to the political order but also the state of mind of a person.

8. For a focus on the relationship between the use of recognition and revelation in biblical hermeneutics, see D. Culbertson, *The Poetics of Revelation: Recognition and the Narrative Tradition* (Studies in American Biblical Hermeneutics, 4; Macon, GA: Mercer University Press, 1989).

9. Sugirtharajah, *Asian Biblical Hermeneutics*, p. x.

10. This strategy of reading emanates from one of the following postcolonial

interpretation of John 5 associated with the legacy of colonialism that keeps a hierarchy of superiority alive and well as an active force of modern, colonial evangelism. As such, I will employ the postcolonial task of first, critically examining the superior–inferior scheme present in John 5; second, contesting Huffard's interpretation of it; and third, providing an ethical critique of three colonial assumptions.[11] The overall hope is to provide a reading of John 5 that can contribute toward restructuring the world free of colonialism.

To support this postcolonial reading of John 5, in what follows, I will first delineate an important literary device, *anagnorisis*, that will guide my reading of John 5 and expose the superior–inferior structure in it; second I will provide a literary reading of John 5, informed by post-colonial criticism, in relationship to Huffard's critical reading of John 5; and third I will present a ethical critique of the colonial superior–inferior mentality in relationship to colonial missionary endeavors.

Anagnorisis

John 5 encompasses the literary device known as *anagnorisis* or recognition.[12] *Anagnorisis* is 'a change from ignorance to knowledge, tending either to affection or to enmity; it determines in the direction of good or ill fortune the fates of the people involved'.[13] Based on this definition of *anagnorisis*, the Gospel comprises crisis moments of successful, partial or unsuccessful recognition scenes.[14] To recognize or not to recognize Jesus as the Christ is a matter of life or death.[15] *Anagnorisis* also affects the degree of knowledge that has occurred among intratextual recognizers (interlocutors in the story) as well as extratextual recognizers (modern interlocutors like Huffard and myself).[16] For instance, on the intratextual

strategies outlined by R.S. Sugirtharajah, 'A Brief Memorandum on Postcolonialism and Biblical Studies', *JSNT* 73 (1999), pp. 3-5 (5). For an excellent understanding of colonialism, see J.L. Comaroff and J. Comaroff, *Of Revelation and Revolution*, pp. 1-62.

11. Sugirtharajah, *Asian Biblical Hermeneutics*, pp. 18-20.

12. Culbertson, *The Poetics of Revelation*; R.A. Culpepper, *Anatomy of the Fourth Gospel: A Study in Literary Design* (Philadelphia: Fortress Press, 1983); *idem*, *The Gospels and Letters of John* (Interpreting Biblical Texts; Nashville: Abingdon Press, 1998); F. Lozada, Jr, *A Literary Reading of John 5: Text as Construction* (Studies in Biblical Literature, 20; New York: Peter Lang, 2000).

13. Culpepper, *The Gospels and Letters of John*, p. 72; J. Hutton, *Aristotle Poetics* (New York: W.W. Norton, 1982), p. 46.

14. Terence Cave, *Recognitions: A Study in Poetics* (Oxford: Clarendon Press, 1988), p. 489.

15. Culbertson, *The Poetics of Revelation*, p. 156.

16. Culpepper, *The Gospels and Letters of John*, p. 77; and Cave, *Recognitions*, p. 33.

level, I will argue below that John 5 does comprise a failed recognition scene because the recognizers (the disabled man and 'the Jews') fail to recognize the intended recognized (Jesus). In effect, *anagnorisis* works with certain rules of recognition in the Gospel that discriminate against those who do not recognize the identity of Jesus, by portraying them as ignorant, controlled by evil, and inferior.[17] Such portrayal reinforces the superior–inferior scheme in the Gospel.

However, on the extratextual level, the reader becomes a 'meta-narratival recognizer who may or may not then also recognize the implications of his or her recognition'.[18] For instance, Huffard and I do recognize the recognized (Jesus), yet, in the Gospel, to recognize, does not simply mean one has discovered the identity of Jesus. Recognition can involve associating with the principle of promoting violence rather than peace. I do not mean physical violence, but rather mental violence that leads to 'a lack of respect for another person's right to exist and be different'.[19] In other words, Huffard's recognition leads to setting people apart, rather than creating a sense of belonging. This exclusive 'we–they' perspective is what Huffard is carrying over into the missionary arena.[20]

Anagnorisis, therefore, serves as a vehicle of change from ignorance to knowledge within a context of crisis, not only for the intratextual inter-locutors in the Gospel, but also for the extratextual interlocutors reading this text. However, like many *anagnorisis* plots, recognition is not always achieved, even when an intratextual or an extratextual reader thinks she or he has achieved it.[21]

A Contested Interpretation of John 5

A servanthood model for mission is strongly supported in Huffard's reading of John 5. His first move to support such a model is to show briefly how the servanthood model in the Gospel is parallel to the servanthood model present in Isaiah. Huffard justifies his reading using a prediction fulfillment scheme.[22] In other words, the servanthood model that is predicted in the 'Old Testament' through Isaiah is fulfilled

The terms 'recognizers', 'interlocutors' and 'readers' are used interchangeably.

17. M. Desjardins, *Peace, Violence and the New Testament* (The Biblical Seminar, 46; Sheffield: Sheffield Academic Press, 1997), pp. 100-10.

18. Culpepper, *The Gospels and Letters of John*, p. 73.

19. Desjardins, *Peace*, p. 101.

20. Desjardins, *Peace*, p. 100.

21. Culbertson, *The Poetics of Revelation*; T. Cave, *Recognitions*.

22. Michael Prior, *The Bible and Colonialism: A Moral Critique* (The Biblical Seminar, 48; Sheffield: Sheffield Academic Press, 1997), p. 278.

in the New Testament through Jesus, when in the Gospel, he accomplishes the eternal will and mission of God.[23] Such fulfillment serves as a catalyst for the disciples (as well as today's Christians) to become witnesses sent from God to reveal God's glory.[24] Huffard's second move is to proceed to a reading of John 5 in its entirety. Focusing primarily on the theme of servanthood as his guiding principle, he delineates the structure into a threefold structure: 5.1-21 ('Let God be God'); 5.22-29 ('Glorifying God: The Task of Servanthood'); and 5.30-47 ('Partnership in Missions'). In my narrative reading of John 5, I will provide a different structure, guided by a 'judicial process' that is centered on the conflict of belief and unbelief as successful, partial, or unsuccessful recognition responses.[25] I will follow my reading with a contested reading of Huffard's study of John 5. The purpose is to uncover the interpretative practices that legitimate a colonialist mentality of superiority–inferiority.

Narrative of Action (5.1-9a)

John 5 occurs during the second Jerusalem journey of Jesus in the Gospel. After spending some time in the region of Galilee (Jn 4), Jesus enters Jerusalem during an unnamed Jewish festival.[26] The narrator states: 'After these things there was a feast of the Jews, and Jesus went up to Jerusalem' (5.1). Like most observant Jewish people of his time, Jesus is traveling to Jerusalem (cf. 2.13) to celebrate a major festival. This constant journeying from place to place will make it difficult for intratextual interlocutors to recognize his origins. However, when he does stay in one location for a while as in John 5 (Jerusalem), Jesus will respond with an invitation to recognition.[27] Such invitation to recognition occurs with the disabled man, the first interlocutor, he encounters.

The first encounter occurs near the Sheep Gate at a pool named Bethesda, which in turn is distinguished by its five porticoes and their occupants: namely, the physically disabled, such as the blind, lame and withered (5.2-3). Among the physically marginalized at the pool, there is an anonymous disabled man, who has been there for 38 years. Jesus, traveling through Jerusalem, comes upon this disabled man and extends an invitation to him to recognize his divinity. The narrator states: 'When Jesus saw this man lying and learned [recognized] that he had been

23. Huffard, 'Missions and Servants of God', pp. 89-90.
24. Huffard, 'Missions and Servants of God', p. 90.
25. Lozada, *A Literary Reading of John 5*, pp. 57-64.
26. For a brief discussion on the identification of the feast, see Lozada, *A Literary Reading of John 5*, p. 107 n. 25.
27. Culbertson, *The Poetics of Revelation*, p. 158.

there already for a long time, he said to him, "Do you want to be well?"' (5.6).[28] Jesus' initiative to come to know the disabled man indicates to the extratextual reader that Jesus wishes to have a relationship with the man. In other words, Jesus welcomes recognition. This implies that recognition is a very important theme in the Gospel. As in the scenes, for example, with Nathaniel (1.47-48) and the Samaritan woman (4.18), it is clear here that Jesus wants a relationship with the disabled man and anyone else who recognizes his identity. Full comprehension is not always required.[29]

The disabled man, not recognizing who Jesus really is, responds with a statement that does not address Jesus' question directly but indirectly. His indirection is a statement: 'Sir, I have no one to put me in the pool when the water is stirred; but while I am coming, another goes down before me' (5.7). In other words, the disabled man is abandoned; he is dependent upon himself and therefore not fast enough to reach the water in the pool and be healed of his physical condition. His failure to admit needing help from Jesus indicates that he also fails to recognize Jesus. In the Gospel, intratextual interlocutors who do not recognize Jesus never admit to needing healing, help, or anything for that matter.[30]

It has been argued that the disabled man does recognize Jesus' identity but is instead setting up a competition between two creative powers: the healing power of water versus Jesus' healing words—both of which are already noted in the first two miracle scenes (2.1-12 and 4.43-54)—in order to learn which power will make him well first.[31] If this is the case, the disabled man surely recognizes Jesus but fails to complete the recognition with a positive response, or any direct response for that matter, to Jesus' question of wanting to be made well (5.6). Perhaps the disabled man is simply confused as to what he wants. I am not totally convinced by either lines of interpretation. However, I am more likely to agree with the former in that I do believe that the disabled man recognizes Jesus yet prefers not to accept the invitation of recognition and to remain an unbeliever.

For instance, Jesus next commands the man, through his authoritative words, to get up and walk, thus revealing to the disabled man his true identity (5.8). The narrator then closes the narrative of action with the

28. The Greek word for learned is 'gnosis', a cognate of the word *anagnorisis*.

29. Culbertson, *The Poetics of Revelation*, p. 158.

30. Culbertson, *The Poetics of Revelation*, p. 170.

31. J.H. Neyrey, 'Jesus Equal to God: John 5', in *An Ideology of Revolt: John's Christology in Social-Science Perspective* (Philadelphia: Fortress Press, 1988), pp. 9-36.

result: 'And immediately the man became well and he picked up his pallet and he began to walk' (5.9a). What is interesting here is that the disabled man never asks for a healing. Jesus, uninvited, takes the initiative to heal—a common pattern in the Gospel (cf., 4.52; 9.6-7). It is unclear at this point in the narrative whether the disabled man recognizes Jesus' identity or not. For the narrative in 5.9a gives no clear indication. Recognition or non-recognition will be decided in the following narrative of accusations. What is clear, nevertheless, is that Jesus extends an invitation to the disabled man to recognize him and to establish a relationship with him through the healing miracle.

I believe, however, that Huffard's reading of Jn 5.1-9a encourages the establishment of relationships along the lines of superiority–inferiority. Huffard uses the 'pericope' of the disabled man as an archetype for why contemporary missionaries should 'take the initiative to immerse themselves into the life of a new community, to build relationships and serve people—because our Lord would have done the same'.[32] In other words, Jesus took the initiative to heal without a request, so therefore today's missionaries should also do the same with no need to wait for an invitation to heal or provide help. This strategy of correlating the actions of Jesus in the Gospel with our duty as Christians today, without critical reflection upon the ethical implications, is dangerous. Although, I agree with the idea that one does not need to wait for an invitation to help, I do not agree that the help should require a corresponding belief in Jesus. Recognition, on the intratextual level, does demand belief. However, recognition, on an extratextual level, does not have to require belief, though at many times it follows belief. It can also include recognizing one's own oppressive attitudes and outlook toward interreligious and cultural contacts. In short, even though Huffard and I probably agree that the disable man, as we will soon see, fails to believe, we differ on the point of whether the narrative of action should be used as a point of departure to initiate help on the prerequisite that belief will follow assistance.

Narrative of Accusations (5.9b-18)

The narrative of accusations (5.9b-18) introduces the basis for the hostile conflict of 'the Jews' towards Jesus. It is also here that both the disabled man, now healed, and 'the Jews' resist recognizing the identity of Jesus, thus supporting my argument that John 5 is a non-recognition text.

The narrative opens with the narrator informing the intratextual and extratextual readers that Jesus had just completed a gross violation of

32. Huffard, 'Missions and Servants of God', p. 91.

Jewish custom. Jesus healed the disabled man on the Sabbath, an egre-
gious illegal act against Jewish law.[33] Moving quickly to unfold this
narrative, the narrator introduces the third character of John 5, 'the
Jews'. 'The Jews' enter the narrative by way of a statement addressed to
the healed man: 'It is the Sabbath, and it is not lawful for you to carry
your pallet' (5.10b). The healed man, realizing that he is in violation of
the Sabbath law, responds by insinuating that Jesus is the cause of his
violation. In other words, the healed man eludes responsibility himself
for violating the Sabbath. The healed man states: 'The one who made
me well, even he said to me, "Pick up your pallet and walk"' (5.11). Since
Jesus is the cause of the violation, he rather than the healed man is in
effect the transgressor of the law.

'The Jews' agree with this cause-and-effect argument by asking in their
next question for the identity of the person who originated the violation:
'Who is the man who said to you, pick up [your pallet] and walk?' (5.12).
The question confirms that the healed man is indeed shifting blame
from himself to Jesus. This act of not taking responsibility indicates that
the healed man either resists recognizing the identity of Jesus or, perhaps, really does not recognize the identity of Jesus. The next statement
by the narrator seems to support the latter situation. The narrator
abruptly jumps in the conversation and advises the intratextual and
extratextual readers not to judge the healed man so quickly, for Jesus
quickly fled the scene after the miracle was completed (5.13). In other
words, the narrative suggests that the healed man surely does not
recognize who Jesus is because Jesus, the elusive hero that he is, slipped
away from the scene to avoid perhaps attention or to wait until his 'hour'
comes.[34] However, his anonymity does not last very long, Jesus again
extends another invitation to the healed man to recognize him.

Jesus approaches the healed man, who is now at the Temple (5.13),
and inquires about two aspects concerning the healed man's condition.
On the one hand, Jesus reminds the healed man of his improved
physical condition; on the other, Jesus warns the healed man of his
lapsed moral state. Jesus states: 'See you are well, do not continue to sin
any longer, lest something worse happens to you' (5.14). This command
by Jesus functions as a sign or marker of Jesus' identity. It is not an
obvious sign as the miracle itself, yet it is more revealing, for the healed

33. Francis J. Moloney, *Signs and Shadows: Reading John 5–12* (Minneapolis: Fortress Press, 1996), p. 6.
34. M.W.G. Stibbe, 'The Elusive Christ: A New Reading of the Fourth Gospel', *The
Gospel of John as Literature: An Anthology of Twentieth-Century Perspectives* (Leiden: E.J.
Brill, 1993), pp. 231-47.

man will go to the 'the Jews' and notify them of Jesus' identity: 'The man left and told the Jews that it was Jesus who made him well' (5.15). It can surely be said at this time that the healed man, who just now discovers Jesus' identity, resists recognizing him. The healed man accuses Jesus to the 'the Jews' as the one who is the cause of the Sabbath violation. Unlike the blind man in John 9, the healed man resists to recognize Jesus because he decides not to follow Jesus, but 'the Jews'.[35] However, just because the healed man chooses to side with 'the Jews', does not mean that he is not grateful for Jesus' help. It is fair, on the other hand, to characterize him as irresponsible for not acknowledging a mutual responsibility for breaking the Sabbath. Nevertheless, in keeping with the plot, since the healed man does not acknowledge Jesus' true identity nor defend him (despite Jesus' healing his physical condition), the healed man is cast, just as the 'the Jews' will soon be, as one who does not recognize Jesus.

In the following text, 'the Jews', who now know the cause of the Sabbath violation, decide to charge or prosecute Jesus for violating the Jewish Sabbath law (5.16).[36] This hostile charge leads Jesus to a defense of his identity: 'My father himself is working until now, and I myself am working' (5.17). This defense is at the same time a marker of his true identity; it is an invitation to recognize that Jesus is truly the Son of God. However, 'the Jews' resists to accept the invitation and thus decline to recognize Jesus, for the concluding statement of the narrative of accusations closes with a twofold charge by 'the Jews'. The narrator states: 'For this reason, therefore, the Jews all the more aimed to kill him, because he not only broke the Sabbath, but he also was calling God his own Father, making himself equal to God' (5.18). The charge is amended to include death not only for his previous violation (5.1-9a), but also for his present and forthcoming transgression (5.9-17, 19-47). As it will be seen in the passion narrative (chs. 18–19), Jesus releases anyone who chooses not to recognize him. As a consequence, they can exercise any authority they have against him (5.18).[37] Unfortunately, the plot, as well as Huffard, will cast the non-recognizers as inferiors for their choice of not recognizing, and consider 'the Jews', as well as the healed man, as not saved (5.19-47).

The difference between Huffard and I is that Huffard will use this

35. For a contrary position, see J.L. Staley, 'Stumbling in the Dark, Reaching for the Light: Reading Character John 5 and 9', *Semeia* 53 (1991), pp. 55-80.

36. Harvey, *Jesus on Trial: A Study in the Fourth Gospel* (London: SPCK, 1976), pp. 50-51.

37. Culbertson, *The Poetics of Revelation*, p. 167.

recognition–non-recognition scheme to justify his evangelistic mantra to convert the Muslims. Huffard's interpretation of the narrative of accusation focuses on two theological points. Using a strategy of correlation, he first argues, based principally on 5.17, that God, through Jesus, is the source of the healing power.[38] In other words, Jesus as the servant of God never works alone.[39] In like fashion, contemporary missionaries do not work alone. They are engaged in the work of God, that is, evangelizing the Muslims. God is on their side like God is for Jesus. The missionaries and God, like Jesus and God, are dynamic partners, bringing life and faith to the unrecognized. To support his argument further, Huffard goes beyond the Gospel to Acts, and states: 'As God worked with Cornelius before Peter arrived and Lydia before she met Paul, so God works in the lives of the unchurched before the missionary arrives.'[40] Huffard legitimizes his missionary activity to the Muslims based on Paul's missionary activity.[41] For these reasons, Huffard believes that as a Christian, his first duty is to evangelize the unfaithful, rather than to create an interreligious dialogue. Such a perspective, I believe, is grounded in the conviction that Christianity is superior to all other religions. However, true dialogue can function as a missionary activity only if it also works to promote mutual understanding in a context of respecting diversity.

Second, Huffard also argues another theological point based on 5.17-21. He wants a pluralist understanding of God; however, pluralism really means one understanding of God—his own, across cultures and time. In other words, Huffard, in addressing 'non-Christians' like 'the Jews' in John 5 or the Muslims of today, argues that God cannot be confined 'to one's ethnic or cultural tradition'.[42] God cannot be reduced to being understood through just one religious tradition, rather 'non-Christians' must let God be God. If God is not allowed complete freedom, the mystery of God will be limited, for example, to an understanding fastened to the Sabbath law or a temple system just as the 'the Jews' are

---

38. Huffard, 'Missions and Servants of God', p. 91.

39. Huffard, 'Missions and Servants of God', p. 91.

40. Huffard, 'Missions and Servants of God', p. 92. See also Acts 10 and 16.14.

41. The standard reading exercise for justifying missionary enterprises is the strategy of correlation between the historical-literary context of the text and the historical-literary context of the missionaries. See M. Zago, 'The New Millennium and the Emerging Religious Encounters', *Missiology* 28 (1997), pp. 5-18; F.C. George, OMI, 'The Promotion of Missiological Studies in Seminaries', *Mission Studies: Journal of the IAMS* 26 (1998), pp. 13-27; Justin S. Ukpong, 'Towards a Holistic Approach to Inculturation Theology', *Mission Studies: Journal of the IAMS* 26 (1999), pp. 100-24.

42. Huffard, 'Missions and Servants of God', p. 92.

trying to limit God in John 5. Such confinement for Huffard blinds people. Actually, on a surface level, I agree with Huffard. However, on a deeper level, Huffard is also confining God to his own cultural and religions traditions. If God is confined to one ethnic setting, however, the purpose of mission is merely part of the colonial enterprise so typical among missionaries in the history of Christianity.[43]

In short, the narrative of accusations functions as a failed recognition scene (*anagnorisis*). Neither the healed man nor 'the Jews' ever come to recognize Jesus' identity. Such failure to recognize Jesus contributes to exposing the superiority–inferiority mentality present in the rhetoric of the plot. Belief in Jesus means that one is a privileged recognizer, and unbelief, as with the healed man and 'the Jews', means that you are an inferior recognizer. On the extratextual level, Huffard correlates this superior–inferior mentality and applies it to modern-day missionary endeavors. Recognition of Jesus' identity entails a superior status for Huffard and others who engage in conversion of the unfaithful. Without any interreligious dialogue, Muslims and all other unbelievers are perceived as inferior because they do not believe in Jesus. Even believers like myself, who do not ascribe to Huffard's colonialist notion of missionary activity, are cast as inferior.

Narrative of Defense (5.19-47)
The narrative of defense (5.19-47) sets out to defend the identity of Jesus against the accusations put forth by 'the Jews' (5.16, 18). To accomplish this, the narrative of defense unfolds into a threefold argument: (1) a defense by Jesus on his own behalf (5.19-30), (2) a defense through witnesses (5.31-40), and (3) a defense through the condemnation of 'the Jews' (5.41-47).

a. The first part of the narrative of defense (5.19-30) begins with a discourse on the authoritative identity of Jesus as the Son of the Father here and now (5.19-25), and in the future (5.26-30). Jesus begins by addressing 'the Jews'. His statement explains his unique relationship to the Father: 'Jesus therefore answered and was saying to them, "Amen, amen, I say to you, the Son can do nothing by himself, unless he sees his Father doing something; for whatever he does, these things the Son also does likewise"' (5.19). His basic argument is that his work is equal to his Father's works. Jesus is dependent upon the Father and follows the Father, thus suggesting that it is the Father giving him authority. More importantly, Jesus is implying that the God of 'the Jews' is his source of authority. In other words, the God from whom Jesus receives his

43. Ukpong, 'Towards a Holistic Approach', p. 101.

authority and power, is active in Judaism without 'the Jews' realizing it. This line of argument is used today among missionaries.[44]

Jesus continues the discourse by highlighting his identity as the Son of God. As the Son, Jesus has the power to raise the dead and judge all (5.21-22). The Father gives Jesus this authority (giving life and judgment) so that all may honor the Son as God's emissary. The reward for believing in this unique and intimate relationship between Jesus and the Father is eternal life. Those who fail to recognize Jesus will come under judgment and eventual death and/or abandonment (5.24). Yet those who fail to recognize him but come to full recognition and belief will experience eternal life here and now (5.25). The markers offered here are reminders that it is never too late to come to full recognition, and there is no better time than present time.[45] This also functions for the future (5.26-30). Those who recognize with belief will live, but those who recognize with unbelief assure for themselves judgment and death. Jesus concludes the first scene with a reaffirmation that he has the authority to do works and to judge because he is dependent upon and obeys the Father who sent him (5.30). He is the paradigmatic servant in the Fourth Gospel.

Huffard's reading of 5.19-30 builds upon the theme of servanthood. Using 5.19 as his point of departure, Huffard argues that it is here that the task of servanthood is defined. In other words, whereas 5.1-18 serves as the foundation of the task of servanthood through the healing of the disabled man, 5.19 explains how to perform this task. The goal of servanthood for Huffard is to model or imitate Jesus, the humble servant. We are to be humble servants to the unchurched. The way one goes about fulfilling this mission is explained in 5.20-30. Servanthood must accompany honoring (or glorifying) God. In explaining this obligation, Huffard proceeds to clarify honor by focusing on the 'eastern worldview, fundamental value of the father–son relationship'.[46] To understand this relationship, however, requires that one understand the vertical and male relationship between the father and son.

Honor, as interpreted by Huffard, encompasses servanthood. For example, a servant is honorable if he [*sic*] responds with obedience to parents, kings, and masters. However, a servant is dishonorable if he [*sic*] fails to obey or give glory or time to his superiors.[47] Jesus in John 5, thus serves as a model for Huffard. Not only does Jesus honor God through

44. George, 'The Promotion of Missiological Studies', p. 20.
45. Culbertson, *The Poetics of Revelation*, p. 173.
46. Huffard, 'Missions and Servants of God', p. 93.
47. Huffard, 'Missions and Servants of God', p. 93.

his obedience to the evangelistic mission of God, he also upholds the vertical relationship between Father and Son. In other words, sonship and servanthood are maintained in Jn 5.19-29. What is more, according to Huffard, in a Western society where one does not read this narrative through the lens of this vertical relationship, the extratextual reader may be at loss about what it means to be a servant of God.[48] In other words, if one does not maintain a hierarchical or patriarchal notion of servant-hood, one cannot fully recognize the true identity of Jesus. The danger of such a reading is that it reinscribes a superior–inferior mentality that not only effects interreligious dialogue but also intergender dialogue. 'Non-Christians' are cast in an inferior light, and women are as well. They cannot experience what it means to be an honorable son like Jesus because they are women. As a consequence, the task of servanthood does not apply to them. This limited way of looking at servanthood overlooks the fact that women in the churches spread and live the gospel by caring for the poor and oppressed.

b. The narrative of defense continues with a focus on Jesus' four wit-nesses from the Father, as a defense of his authoritative identity which gives life and judges (5.31-40). The intratextual reader learns that the previous defense by Jesus might be perceived as suspect since Jesus himself is testifying for himself, a tradition contrary to Jewish law (5.30). However, the narrator assures 'the Jews' that because the Father has testified on Jesus' behalf (5.32), Jesus is empowered to give his own tes-timony. If 'the Jews' will not believe in their own Father's testimony, there is the testimony of John the Baptist, the first witness, whom 'the Jews' themselves scrutinize concerning the truth of Jesus' identity and mission (5.33-35). If 'the Jews' are suspicious of John, Jesus' works, as the second witness, prove that Jesus is God's emissary (5.36). Even the Father himself, the third witness, functions as a witness (5.37-38), for the Father's sending of Jesus is a testimony to Jesus' true identity and mis-sion of life and judgment. However, to believe in the Father as a witness, 'the Jews' must first respond with belief towards Jesus, which they continue to fail to do. Finally, the very Scriptures themselves, the fourth witness, which 'the Jews' use to understand eternal life, testify to Jesus' identity and mission (5.39-40). All four of these witnesses are presented to 'the Jews' in order to show how Jesus defends against the charge of violating the Sabbath and making himself equal to the Father. In short, 'the Jews' are asked to believe in the above (their own) witnesses.

Huffard sees the theme of witness as vital to understanding Christian mission and servanthood (5.31-40). The essence of the theme of witness

48. Huffard, 'Missions and Servants of God', p. 94.

is found in 5.36: 'But I have a greater witness than John; for the works that the Father has given me to accomplish, the works themselves that I do, bear witness concerning me that the Father has sent me.' For Huffard, the theme of witness is related to the another common theme, that of sending. Both 'to witness' and 'to send' refer to God.[49] In other words, today's missionaries, who are sent out to bear witness to God, through faith in Jesus to the unchurched, should follow the example of Jesus who is sent by God to witness. Unfortunately, Huffard is working with a narrow understanding of mission, one that treats the other as an inferior. To bear witness in Christ should not be forced but rather left up to the person to decide.[50] Muslims or 'non-Christians' should not be seen as a challenge to Christians, but rather as mutual dialogue partners seeking respect and understanding.[51] Otherwise a superior–inferior mentality arises.

c. The last scene of this narrative shows how Jesus uses his opponents, 'the Jews', as a means of defense (5.41-47). That is, Jesus concludes by focusing on the source of authority of 'the Jews', namely themselves. He does not receive authority from another, but rather he receives it from the Father as he already pointed out (5.41). 'The Jews' cannot under-stand this because they do not have the love of God in them. How does Jesus know this? Jesus points out that he has come in their ('the Jews') and his Father's name, yet they still refuse to respond with belief. If another person came in his own name, they would respond with belief toward that person. In other words, Jesus knows that they do not have the love of God in themselves ('the Jews') because they seek honor and authority not from God, but from another authority, themselves. What is more, Jesus points out that their very important authority, whom they hold up, Moses, is actually ignored when it comes to recognizing Jesus' true identity and mission. If they will not believe Moses, whom will they believe? In this last scene, therefore, Jesus turns the tables on 'the Jews' to point to his own authority. In a tone of superiority, Jesus is claiming that 'the Jews' do not believe in Moses because they fail to accept his christological exegesis of the Scriptures.[52] 'The Jews' are representatives (inferior unbelievers) of those who are concerned with receiving honor from others rather than from the Father, or their own interpretation of Scriptures, or even their own authority, Moses. Because their source of authority is really each other, not God, the unbelief of 'the Jews', for

---

49. Huffard, 'Missions and Servants of God', p. 95.
50. Zago, 'The New Millennium', p. 12.
51. Zago, 'The New Millennium', p. 12.
52. Maurice Casey, *Is John's Gospel True?* (London: Routledge, 1996), p. 218.

Jesus, is portrayed as confirming that he is equal to God the Father, his acknowledged authority. Thus, 5.30-40 and 41-47 fail as recognition scenes. For 'the Jews' fail to recognize the true witnesses of God (5.30-40) as well as their own witnesses (5.45-47). 'The Jews' fail because they seek the glory from themselves (5.44), rather than the glory that their own scriptures (5.39-40) and Moses (5.45-47) as evidence of the identity of Jesus.

Similar to Huffard, my reading also examined John 5 as a coherent whole. Jesus performs a healing act (narrative of action). Second, this healing act, now an illegal act performed on the Sabbath, leads to a twofold accusation consisting of Jesus' Sabbath-day violation and his subsequent claim to authority as equal to God (narrative of accusations). Finally, Jesus defends himself against the charges by functioning as a witness himself, by using other witnesses, and by using his opponents to point to his authority and superiority (narrative of defense). Throughout this threefold structure, there is a strategic aim that not only functions to locate the intratextual interlocutors along the lines of belief, but also the extratextual reader as well. In other words, the conflict of belief and unbelief, as response to Jesus' identity throughout all the scenes, warns the extratextual readers to choose between superiority and inferiority. This is the rhetorical aim of *anagnorisis*.

I read this rhetorical aim as an attempt to force readers to accept the discourse of superiority. That is, in John 5's very attempt to situate the extratextual reader on the side of recognition or belief, it also pre-supposes the inequality between those who receive and believe and those who receive and fail to believe, and even those who are deprived of truth like the Muslims. It is no wonder that Huffard uses John 5 to convert Muslims to Christianity, the supposed superior tradition, or at least to proclaim its message of superiority to all peoples, and thereby placing the responsibility to recognize Jesus upon the recognizers.[53] This is not to say that John 5 is void of any liberative significance; it only illustrates the warrant or mandate implicit in John 5 and what happens when one fails to think through the ethical implications of one's position.[54]

The appropriation of this strategic aim, resulting in belief or unbelief, has lasting cultural and religious consequences for the extratextual reader who has to decide whether to be on the side of believers or to reside with the unbelievers (as the healed man and 'the Jews'). On the one hand, if the reader sides with Jesus (belief), eternal life is his/her

53. For an excellent work on inter-religious dialogue and contact from a post-modern perspective, see James B. Wiggins, *In Praise of Religious Diversity* (New York: Routledge, 1996).

54. Wiggins, *In Praise of Religious Diversity*, p. 12.

reward. On the other hand, if the reader sides against Jesus (unbelief), everlasting death is the outcome. The aftermath of this mentality is the appropriation of an ideology of superiority, or an exclusive 'either/or' scenario that leads to a superior–inferior scheme. Either the reader is one of us (child of God), or the reader is one of them (child of Satan). Such a mentality formulates the believer as superior and the unbeliever as inferior (child of Satan). The appropriation of this mentality of superiority–inferiority can have lasting consequences for both the believer and the unbeliever in terms of survival. In the final section, I will carry out a beginning exercise in the ethics of biblical interpretation, along the lines of an ethics of communication.[55] Such an exercise calls into question three assumptions (absolutism, exclusivism and pluralism) that I believe are in step with promoting a superior–inferior construct.

An Ethical Critique

Huffard, in my view, deeply believes that he possesses the absolute and final word of God. This is why he and so many other Christian evangelists (Catholics and Protestants) throughout the colonial history of Africa, Asia and Latin America, and even today in my own Latino/a community, travel fearlessly across cultures and time to proclaim the Gospel.[56] They have reduced missionary passages in the Gospels (e.g. Mt. 28.18-19) into evangelistic mandates to be taken literally and absolutistically.[57] 'They impose the necessity of agreement or submission to their conceptions of truth upon all who would be their adherents, and they claim their truth to be and to have been such in all times and in all places for all people.'[58] The implication of ascribing to absolute statements is the tendency to construct people with differing views as non-human, since their differences in belief are considered inferior. This is most evident in the past. And even today among colonized or oppressed groups throughout the world including in the United States among African-Americans, Native Americans, Asian-Americans, Latinos/as, women, gays, disabled, and many are perceived as non-human for their differing cultures, beliefs or physical capabilities.[59] Absolutism prevents different positions or different people from existing in the same world.

---

55. See Elisabeth Schüssler Fiorenza, *Rhetoric and Ethic: The Politics of Biblical Studies* (Minneapolis: Fortress Press, 1999), pp. 195-98; see also G.A. Phillips and D.N. Fewell, 'Ethics, Bible, Reading As If', *Semeia* 77 (1997), pp. 1-21.

56. Wiggins, *In Praise of Religious Diversity*, p. 15.

57. Wiggins, *In Praise of Religious Diversity*, p. 15.

58. Wiggins, *In Praise of Religious Diversity*, p. 18.

59. Wiggins, *In Praise of Religious Diversity*, p. 19.

Recognition of the relationality of truth-claims is a step away from a superior–inferior mentality and is instead a step forward, toward respecting multiple constructs of diversity.[60] Sometimes I wonder whether what is feared about accepting and respecting diversity is not the 'westernizing' of other religious traditions, but rather the 'orientalizing' of the west.

Another implication of the superior–inferior construct that is a result of the superior–inferior mentality is exclusivism. As mentioned earlier in my reading of Huffard's interpretation of John 5, Huffard reaches back to the Hebrew Bible (Isaiah) to proclaim the uniqueness of the revelation of God in Jesus as the Christ. In so doing, he quietly confirms Jesus to be God, the messiah—the same God of the Jews and the entire world. This conception of a universal and singular God (e.g. Jn 5.17, 19-30; 16.6-7) will be used especially by evangelists against all other gods.[61] It disavows differing expressions of a greater power. Sometimes pluralists argue that the Christian god is the same transcendent source that is experienced in different religious traditions.[62] Unfortunately, this line of reasoning also excludes, for it places Christianity in the center of the discourse, while differing religious expressions of the transcendent are kept from truly dialoguing or co-existing with Christianity. Christians do not need to continue to be a tool of colonialism in converting different religious cultures. In other words, refraining from a superior–inferior construct, Christians can then work toward understanding how society looks through another set of eyes or experiences.

Finally, a third implication is pluralism. Some may find it odd that I include pluralism along with absolutism and exclusivism, however, my intent is to call attention to the implications of this term, especially in the context of colonial evangelism.[63] The introduction of Huffard's reading of the Fourth Gospel and, John 5 in particular, is entitled 'Pluralism and the Gospel of John'. As some modern, colonial missionaries assume today, inter-religious dialogue takes place today in the spirit of pluralism. That is pluralism provides for equal opportunities for diverse viewpoints to be heard and tolerated around the table. However, in my view, pluralism, when understood in the context of colonial evangelism, does quite the opposite. It works to make the religious 'Other' distinctly

60. Wiggins, *In Praise of Religious Diversity*, pp. 15-20.

61. Wiggins, *In Praise of Religious Diversity*, p. 25. See also, Comaroff and Comaroff, *Of Revelation and Revolution*, pp. 6-7.

62. Wiggins, *In Praise of Religious Diversity*, p. 18.

63. For an excellent examination of pluralism, see Chapter 5, 'Pluralism: Christian Triumphalism in New Dress? or, A Christian Anxiety Attack' in Wiggins, *In Praise of Religious Diversity*.

inferior by making the 'Other' assume or assimilate the same identity as the colonialist evangelist.[64] Pluralism is appropriated in such a way that the 'Other' is seen as ' "an ontological cleavage" rather than an "anthropological distinction" '.[65] In other words, the 'Other' is understood in terms of binary opposition, rather than as having a different identity. The result, as I have interpreted in Huffard's reading of John 5, is an understanding of inter-religious contact in the spirit of pluralism that minimizes difference as unimportant.[66] Pluralism understood in this way returns to a colonialist hierarchy of superiority. In other words, pluralism functions to persuade different religious traditions that Christianity is the completion or fulfillment of all religions.[67] If one is arguing that salvation is dependent upon the central tenet that Jesus is Christ, then inter-religious dialogue is pointless.[68] Dialogue must be framed by the conviction that respecting difference of all sorts is very important to bring forth a more respectful (beyond toleration), just and peaceful world. Pluralism, in the context of colonial evangelism, supports a superior–inferior mentality, rather than a world made of difference and a world of increasingly blended identities. Finally, the pluralism that Huffard, for example, is suggesting allows for diversity as long as it does not challenge a hierarchy of superiority

In conclusion, my contested reading of John 5 does indeed aim to show that Huffard and I agree that John 5, as a whole, represents a failed *anagnorisis* scene. We probably also agree that implicit in John 5 is a superiority–inferiority construct. However, where we differ is the appropriation of John 5 and its construct of superiority–inferiority. Huffard uses the text in step with the colonial enterprise to make the 'the non-Westerner' or 'non-Christian' an Other, whereas I aim to use the text as a means to recognize and challenge the reinscription of exclusivity. Recognition of this use is part of the postcolonial task. Huffard's 'manifested' split of humanity along the lines of believers and a non-believer legitimates cultural imperialism. It does so by promoting difference in terms of a colonial binary opposite (superiority–inferiority), rather than promoting difference in relationship to respect. Respecting the diversity of religions is a step toward peaceful co-existence and a step forward toward fighting oppression.[69]

64. Comaroff and Comaroff, *Of Revelation and Revolution*, p. xiv.
65. Wiggins, *In Praise of Religious Diversity*, p. 13.
66. Wiggins, *In Praise of Religious Diversity*, p. ix.
67. Wiggins, *In Praise of Religious Diversity*, p. 30.
68. Wiggins, *In Praise of Religious Diversity*, p. 65.
69. Wiggins, *In Praise of Religious Diversity*, p. 14.

Maori 'Jews' and a Resistant Reading
of John 5.10-47

MARY HUIE-JOLLY

Johannine Christology makes a division between those who honour Jesus, the 'Son', as the equal of God, and those who refuse to accept these claims. It associates 'the Jews' with resistance to Jesus' claims to sonship: 'Whoever does not honour the Son, just as the Father does not honour the Father' (5.23b).[1] Many scholars could argue that social location makes a difference in determining who makes these claims and who does not. When John 5 was first written, exalted claims concerning Jesus as Son of God figured in a feud between a marginal Johannine group and synagogue authorities.[2] Yet in a situation of colonization the Johannine sonship Christology resonates with claims of superiority and dominance.

Interestingly after the Anglo-Maori land wars of the 1860s and early 1870s, in New Zealand's Bay of Plenty region, some Maori referred to themselves as 'Jews' rather than Christians.[3]

---

1.   See also Jn 1.11-12; 8.37-59; 10.31-39.

2.   John Ashton describes it as a 'family quarrel'; see his summary of Johannine scholarship on the conflict with 'the Jews' in *Understanding the Fourth Gospel* (Oxford: Clarendon Press, 1991), pp. 131-59.

   J. Louis Martyn, *History and Theology in the Fourth Gospel* (Nashville: Abingdon Press, 2nd edn, 1979), pp. 29-37, 70; Wayne A. Meeks, 'Equal to God', in Robert T. Fortna and Beverly R. Gaventa (eds.), *The Conversation Continues: Studies in Paul and John in Honor of J. Louis Martyn* (Nashville: Abingdon Press, 1990), pp. 309-21; Jerome H. Neyrey, *An Ideology of Revolt: John's Christology in Social-Science Perspective* (Philadelphia: Fortress Neyrey, 1988); and Bruce J. Malina, *The Gospel of John in Sociolinguistic Perspective* (Protocol of the Forty-Eighth Colloquy; Berkeley, CA: Center for Hermeneutical Studies in Hellenistic and Modern Culture; Graduate Theological Union and the University of California, 1985), see the conflict depicted in the text as reflective of the conflict that defined the Johannine community.

3.   Bronwyn Elsmore, *The Religion of Matenga Tamati* (Auckland: Reed, 1997), p. 23. In the subsequent discussion of this type of response, I focus on certain actions which are not necessarily representative of all or even most Maori. For a fuller account which gives attention to local variations, see the historical studies by Keith Sinclair, *Kinds of Peace: Maori People after the Wars, 1870–85* (Auckland, NZ: Auckland

Chief Tiopira Te Hukiki, a former lay teacher of Anglicans, reasoned thusly with missionary Leonard Williams in 1878: 'You have not visited us for years, and now that you have come to us again you find that we have given up the way of the Son and have adopted instead the way of the Father.'[4] This phenomenon was not new. Four decades earlier Henry Williams of the Church Missionary Society (CMS) found 'about half the people profess Christianity', the other half 'call themselves Jews or unbelievers'; the missionary also found other groups of 'Jews' in the district.[5]

Again, at the beginning of the twentieth century, certain Maori who had earlier been regarded as converts of the missionaries, now in response to colonial practices which undermined their tribal lands and way of life, called themselves 'Jews' and began to leave the way of the Son.[6]

I am not the first to explore the complex historical reasons for this development.[7] My aim is simply to bring the act of 'turning away from the way of the Son' into conversation with a post-colonial reading of John 5, for John constructs a dominating Christology which has affinities with the universalizing claims of later colonialist Christianity. In the Maori act of 'turning away' I do not see any clear historical connection between the particular text of John 5 and the colonization of New Zealand. However, the claims of John 5 that Jesus is the 'Son', just like 'God the Father' are consistent with later Christian creeds. The creeds persisted in the religion associated with British imperialism. This, in turn, supported the attitudes of religious and cultural superiority often associated with colonial expansion. Both John 5 and politically dominant Christianity present a universal absolute claim to the divine sonship of Jesus. I will suggest that the identification with the Jews by certain Maori

University Press, 1991); Bronwyn Elsmore, *Like Them that Dream: The Maori and the Old Testament* (Tauranga: Tauranga Moana, 1985); and Anne Salmond, *Two Worlds: First Meetings Between Maori and Europeans 1642–1772* (Auckland: Viking, 1991).

4.   Judith Binney, *Redemption Songs: A Life of Te Kooti Arikirangi Te Turuki* (Auckland: Auckland University Press, 1995), p. 296.

5.   Elsmore, *The Religion of Matenga Tamati*, p. 22.

6.   The Maori prophet Rua Kanana is a notable example; on his life, see Judith Binney, G. Chaplin and C. Wallace (eds.), *Mihaia: The Prophet Rua Kanana and his Community at Maungapohatu* (Auckland: Auckland University Press, 1996); and Peter Webster, *Rua and the Maori Millennium* (Wellington, NZ: Price Milburn for Victoria University Press, 1979).

7.   For historical accounts beyond the scope of this paper, see Sinclair, *Kinds of Peace*; Binney, *Redemption Songs*; Elsmore, *Like Them that Dream*. The historical novel, *Season of the Jew*, by Maurice Shadbolt (Auckland, NZ: Hodder & Stoughton, 1986), also provides a helpful introduction to this period.

was a decision to 'leave the way of the Son' and to resist colonial domination.

Polarizing 'the Jews' in Constructing Christological Authority
The Johannine group's conflict over sonship claims is presented by the narrator as if it had come from the mouth of Jesus himself (5.17, 19–47). The narrator relates a healing of Jesus and accusations by 'the Jews' concerning his Sabbath action (5.9-10, 16, 18). Jesus replies in the form of a legal defence, arguing that as Son he can do nothing but what the Father is doing (5.17, 19). The adversarial presentation of 'the Jews' as those who persecute, and do not honour Jesus, appears to reflect the drama of the Johannine group in feud with a synagogue community as much or more than events during the time of the life of Jesus.[8] Thus, John 5 represents Jesus as 'the Son' who calls God 'my Father' and acts just like God. And calling God 'my Father', is regarded as 'making himself equal to God' (5.18). It is answered by an even more exalted claim; absolute authority over life, and absolute judgment are given to the Son by the Father (5.21-23).

The exalted Johannine confession of Jesus as Son would have been regarded as an offence within the profoundly monotheistic culture of the synagogue. But the claim of absolute authority over life and judgment given to the Son by the Father, provided legitimacy and a basis for the Johannine community's identity and authority. For the Johannine group that was no longer under the jurisdiction of synagogue observant Judaism, the Son became the authority, independent of the synagogue.

The Sonship claims do not simply argue that Jesus' Sabbath action was justified. Much more than that, they establish a functional unity between the Son and the Father: the Son acts just like the Father in creating life and in judging, thus establishing equality between Father and Son (5.20-22). The exalted claims for Jesus clearly represent the resurrection faith of the Johannine church: Jesus, exalted to the throne of God, is endowed with all the power of God.[9]

---

8.   Jn 7.13, 9.22, 12.42 and 16.2 similarly refer to conflict over the confession of Christ in connection with fear of expulsion from the synagogue.

9.   See Mary R. Huie-Jolly, 'Threats Answered by Enthronement: John 5.17-27 with Reference to the Divine Warrior Myth in Psalm 2 and Daniel 7', in Craig A. Evans and James A. Sanders (eds.), *Early Christian Interpretations of the Scriptures of Israel: Investigations and Proposals* (JSNTSup, 148; SSEJC, 5; Sheffield: Sheffield Academic Press, 1997), pp.196-200.

The Polarizing Structure of John 5.16-47

The Sonship claim intends to make a universal claim: 'that all may honour the son' (5.23); but practically speaking it is unenforceable outside the group. It serves only to draw a boundary between those within and without, labelling the outsiders as under judgment, and pressuring those within to conform utterly or else be condemned. John 5.16-47 thus structures division between those who honour the Son as God, and those who refuse to honour him and the division is made at the expense of people who the text calls 'the Jews' (5.10, 16, 18). Furthermore, the claims concerning Jesus' Sonship are placed within a polarised, trial-like format in which they function as a defence of Jesus in John 5.16-47.[10]

In the supplementary section on authentic witnesses (John 5.31-47) the 'Jews' are blamed for having never even heard the Father's voice, for lacking his word, not believing Jesus whom the Father sent, refusing to come to him, not having the love of God, giving glory only to one another, and not God, and, finally, are accused by Moses for not believing Jesus' words (Jn 5.37-47). By association they are those who, in the hour of judgment, will not hear his voice and having done evil they will face `judgment' (Jn 5.29).

In its original context, Jn 5.16-23 was presented in the literary form of a forensic defence in reply to accusations; but it was not originally enforceable as a law over those 'outside' whom it called 'the Jews'. The forensic reply had teeth only for the marginal group that constructed it. This is in marked contrast with later colonialist situations, where Christianity, with its 'Son equals the Father' Christology, was the dominant religion supported by economic and political powers of imperialism.

Is Jesus' Identity with God a Claim Consistent with Imperial Domination?
John 5.21-23 is consistent with later creedal norms. The creed 'the Son is one substance with the Father' is a derivative statement. It seems to be consistent with the Johannine statement of the son's identity with the action and judgment of God the Father.

> The Son can do...only what he sees the Father doing; for whatever the Father does the Son does likewise... For as the Father raises the dead and creates life so also the Son gives life to whom he will. The Father...has given all judgement to the Son that all may honour the Son even as they honour the Father. Whoever does not honour the Son does not honour the Father... (Jn 5.21-23).

10. Mary R. Huie-Jolly, 'The Son Enthroned in Conflict: A Socio-rhetorical Interpretation of John 5.17-23' (unpublished PhD dissertation, University of Otago, Dunedin, New Zealand, 1994), pp. 235-37.

'I believe in one God the Father Almighty... And in one Lord Jesus Christ, the only-begotten Son of God...God of God, Light of Light, Very God of Very God, Begotten not made, Being of one substance with the Father...' (The Nicene Creed 325 CE).

'We all with one voice teach that it should be confessed that our Lord Jesus Christ is one and the same God...*homoousious* with the Father as to his Godhead, and the Same *homoousious* with us as to his manhood...'[11]

These statements function as theological norms in the institutional church. Because they are similar to Jn 5.17-23, the original text and the derivative creeds reinforce each other and function as one unitary norm of Christian discourse. Statements of Jesus' identity with God, from a position of superior authority and power, were statements well suited to dominance. They presupposed the deity of Christ by relying on concepts of a Johannine logos Christology. This served the imperial councils and creeds as 'the highroad of developing Christian orthodoxy'.[12]

In John 5, the Jews who refuse to confess Jesus' sonship stand before the Son as their judge. The norm set out in Jn 5.21-23 clarifies the institutional status quo. As in the creeds, the role of giving honour to Jesus 'just as' God the Father is honoured. In addition, it explicitly elaborates the role of dishonour which, though not stated in the creed, follows the same structure and is logically its converse: those who do not honour the Son do not honour the Father (5.23b).

In a church associated with imperial political authority this text wields great authority. Its negative characterization of 'the Jews' reinforces contemporary trajectories of anti-Judaism. And its absolutism threatens indigenous cultures and alternative responses to Jesus.

The forensic trappings of John 5 serve to intensify and clarify an ideology of divine expectation for absolute honour for Jesus, and conversely, to blame all who refuse to grant him this honour. To fail to honour Jesus as God is to fail to honour God (5.23). And indirectly such failures are aligned with the 'Jews who sought to kill him', and who refuse to believe his testimony (5.18, 43-47). From a position of political power, the Sonship claim dominates. It is consistent with the institutional creeds of politically dominant Christendom; and its Christology, based on the absolute superiority of divine power, resonates with colonial claims to superior power: 'God gave all power to the Son that they may honour

11. The Definition of Chalcedon 451 CE, cited by Justo L. González, *A History of Christian Thought: From the Beginnings to the Council of Chalcedon* (Nashville: Abingdon, rev. edn, 1987), p. 379.

12. James D.G. Dunn, *Christology in the Making: An Inquiry into the Origins of the Doctrine of the Incarnation* (London: SCM, 2nd edn, 1989), pp. xxx-xxxi.

the Son just as they honour the Father, whoever does not honour the Son does not honour the Father...' (Jn 5.23).

The claim to Sonship draws on the common desire to honour God through obedience to him. According to John's logic, those who do not honour the Son, do not honour the Father, and are identified, within the larger narrative, with the Jews who resist by refusing to accept that the Son is just like God the Father. Likewise, following the loss of their ancestral lands, certain Maori, who were deeply literate in the Maori Bible (a legacy of Christian missionaries) chose to distinguish themselves from the Christianity of the missionaries over the issues of Jesus' Sonship.

Missionary and Maori

From their earliest contact with European missionaries to New Zealand, Maori identified with the biblical accounts of the children of Israel. Like the Israelites, Maori tribes were knit together by their ties of kinship, genealogy, and their lore of sacred journeys.[13] The sense of tribal affinity with the stories of the Hebrews impelled them with a powerful desire to read this sacred lore. Reading and writing also spread rapidly among Maori, in part, because communication by written marks was seen as an almost magical art. Biblical literacy was a factor in their conversion because the printed text was regarded as tapu (holy);[14] and the eventual translation of portions of the Bible into Maori in the 1830s sustained the powerful enthusiasm for literacy.[15]

People took learning back to villages, where the newly literate passed on knowledge to home tribes. By the 1850s Maori were more literate than Pakeha (the Maori name for New Zealanders of European descent).

---

13. Elsmore, *Like Them that Dream*, pp. 62-76.

14. Allan K. Davidson, *Aotearoa New Zealand: Defining Moments in the Gospel–Culture Encounter* (Geneva: WCC, 1996), pp. 6-7.

15. Elsmore describes the hunger for literacy (Elsmore, *Like Them that Dream*, pp. 23-25): Portions of the Scriptures, printed in Maori as early as 1827, fed an amazing eagerness to learn to read: 'Books books... We are ill for want of books' (Elsmore, *Like Them that Dream*, p. 24). Reading and writing were not prized initially for their link to Pakeha religion but because writing itself was seen to be magical. If writing could make one understand another *Atua* [god], then the Pakeha *Atua* must be more powerful than *Atua* Maori. Learning the art of conveying messages through cryptic markings had immense appeal. Missionaries allowed translation of the Scriptures only in Maori to ensure that the literate Maori were kept from non-Christian influences. The books were seen as possessing great power and were in demand for their protective qualities. People from the tribes flocked to mission stations for lessons. In Poverty Bay, for example, after 1840, for example, the Church Missionary Society's Revd Henry Williams taught outdoors with cut out letters.

Literate Maori often became the teachers of others, so that the Scriptures were received and used by Maori for Maori in dynamic interaction with their traditional religion.[16] Biblical messages also spread orally, sometimes preceding the Pakeha missionaries. Occasionally, European missionaries found Maori villages where people could recite whole passages of scripture, and words of hymns from memory, to which they then composed own their tunes.[17] Whole liturgies were memorized by Maori attending Christian services, and they assimilated aspects of their own culture as an indigenous response to Christianity.[18]

However, the enthusiastic reception of the Bible in Maori did not lead Maori to an uncritical acceptance of missionary Christianity. The early missionaries, following the explorers and whalers, were among the first Europeans to live among Maori. The missionaries themselves came from distinct groups representing diverse perspectives,[19] but in general their motivations centred around conversion of the Maori to Christianity. Yet the link between religion and empire was sometimes taken for granted. Samuel Marsden, of the Anglican Church Missionary society (CMS), gives an indication of this attitude in his 1816 account of 'The First Sabbath-day observed in New Zealand':

> On Sunday morning, when I was on deck, I saw the English flag flying, which was a pleasing sight in New Zealand. I considered it as the signal and dawn of civilization, liberty and religion, in that dark benighted land... I flattered myself [the British colours] would never be removed, till the natives of that island enjoyed all the happiness of British subjects... [I preached from Luke]... 'Behold! I bring you glad tidings of great joy...' The natives told Ruaterra[20] that they could not understand what I meant. He replied that they were not to mind that now, for they would understand bye and bye...[21]

16. Allan K. Davidson and Peter J. Lineham, *Transplanted Christianity: Documents Illustrating Aspects of New Zealand Church History* (Palmerston North, NZ: Massey University Printery, 3rd edn, 1995), p. 37.

17. Elsmore, *Like Them that Dream*, p. 25.

18. Davidson, *Aotearoa New Zealand*, pp. 7-8.

19. Allan Davidson, 'The Interaction of Missionary and Colonial Christianity in Nineteenth Century New Zealand', in *Studies in World Christianity*, Vol. 2, Part 2 (Edinburgh: Edinburgh University Press, 1996), pp. 145-66, explores distinctions and confluence between diverse missionaries and their context in relation to the colonial world.

20. A Maori chief, and nephew of Te Pahi and Hongi Hika, Ruaterra taught the Maori language to Marsden and offered him hospitality and protection (Davidson and Lineham, *Transplanted Christianity*, p. 22).

21. Davidson and Lineham, *Transplanted Christianity*, pp. 27-28, citing the *Missionary Register*, November 1816, pp. 470-71.

The missionary's role became more complicated and new conflicts emerged when colonial settlement, beginning in the late 1830s, brought land hungry Europeans to New Zealand. Colonial rule hastened the alienation of land from Maori by legal and illegal means. The sale and confiscation of their lands took the substance of life from the original Maori inhabitants. Furthermore, since law and religion were part of the overall framework of Maori society, mission involvement in religious and moral teaching was easily understood, but the relationship between missionaries and government authorities was ambiguous. The growth of the settler population and the grab for more land conflicted with the missionaries' attempt to safeguard and protect the Maori interests.[22] The missionaries, particularly those from the Church Missionary Society, were caught up in this ambiguity; some of them became land holders in their own right and were accused of duplicity.[23] As a colonial society became established in New Zealand, the initial influence of the missions declined.

Often, missionaries tried to curb the worst excesses of colonial exploitation of Maori land. For example, they were instrumental in negotiating and promoting of the Treaty of Waitangi in 1840. This Treaty between the British Crown and most Maori tribes enshrined protection of Maori forest, fisheries and cultural treasures by law. It turned land purchasing from the Maori into a government monopoly. The Crown bought the land and then sold or leased it to settlers.[24] But the legacy of the treaty was ambiguous. The English version of the Treaty saw it in terms of Maori ceding their sovereignty to the Crown, and yet in the Maori version, it also ensured Maori sovereignty, *rangatiratanga*, over their own lands.[25]

The status of the missionaries with the Maori converts was also ambiguous in the colonial period. Colonial settlement was accompanied by pressure for more land, and land was often confiscated in war even from Maori who had not fought the British. But confiscation as punishment was a clear breach of the treaty. When missionaries acted as chaplains in the wars of the 1860s and accompanied army and government officials in battle, Maori assumed they were in solidarity with the Crown, and that their role would be to recite chants to ensure victory and defeat the

22. Davidson, *Aotearoa New Zealand*, p. 10.

23. Davidson, unpublished personal correspondence to the author, 26 April 2000, p. 1.

24. Sinclair, *Kinds of Peace*, p. 15.

25. Sinclair, *Kinds of Peace*, p. 16.

'enemy'. The missionaries, perhaps naively and mistakenly, assumed that they could act as army chaplains and at the same time act in good faith to protect Maori from colonial exploitation.

Revd J.W. Stack, speaking of such a battle in the Waikato said: 'No wonder the majority of the Maoris lost their belief in the divine origin of the Christian religion which they strongly suspected was a political intervention to beguile the unwary, and to render them more easily subjugated.'[26]

In traditional Maori society, religion and law were one. For as Elsmore observes,[27] the institution of *tapu* (the sacred and off-limits) formed the basis of civil order and its spiritual aspect was seen in ritual practices. This unity did not change with the coming of the Pakeha, since the 'social laws of that society were laid out in the new scriptures'.[28] Added to this was the fact that the missionaries and the early governors were often seen together. These features of Pakeha behaviour reinforced Maori assumptions that for the Europeans as well, the religious and secular laws were not separate.[29]

Missionaries often were held accountable for other problems caused by colonization. They were seen as those who 'induced the people to accept Christianity', then brought in 'arms to oust the simpleton from his land'.[30] One Maori speaker put it in these words: 'The missionaries were sent to break in the Maoris as men break in a wild horse; to rub them quietly down the face to keep them quiet, while the land was being taken from them.'[31]

Missionaries were instrumental in getting people to sign the treaty, believing that it would protect Maori interests.[32] A Maori saying indicates a different interpretation: 'They [the missionaries] made parsons and priests of several members of the Maori race, and they taught these

26. Elsmore, *Like Them that Dream*, p. 48, cites J.W. Stack, *More Maoriland Adventures* (Wellington, 1936), p. 183.

27. Elsmore, *Like Them that Dream*, p. 47

28. Elsmore, *Like Them that Dream*, p. 47.

29. Elsmore, *Like Them that Dream*, p. 47.

30. Elsmore, *Like Them that Dream*, p. 32.

31. Elsmore, *Like Them that Dream*. Elsmore, p. 33, cites Revd T.G. Hammond, *In the Beginning* (Auckland, 1940), p. 72.

32. Settler greed for more land brought more and more breaches in the Treaty and was a major factor leading to sporadic armed conflict and war. Although until the 1980s the Treaty had been regarded with pride as something setting New Zealand apart in its dealings with indigenous peoples. But it carries the painful legacy of promises disregarded and broken.

persons to...look up and pray; and while they were looking up the Pakehas took away our land.'[33]

An old song of the Nga-Puhi people about Samuel Marsden, the first missionary to New Zealand, carries a similar message:

> [Marsden's] message was this: God is in heaven, look therefore to the sky. But the Maori people turned and gazed below to the land, the soil of Aotearoa. They beheld it decayed away with the iron spade, the iron axe, the flaming red blanket and the iron Jew's harp. Thy goods O Governor! Alas the land has gone adrift on the great ocean of *Kiwa*.[34]

Maori saw the *mauri* (the life principle) of anything living or nonliving as the dwelling place of the protecting deities.[35] *Karakia* was a chant or prayer connecting humans to helpful or unhelpful *atua* (deities), by a process of loosing and binding.[36] If connection by *karakia* was polluted in any way, then the deity withdrew and its protection was therefore no longer present.[37] As Michael Shirres explains, the power to make *karakia* effective came from the *atua*. *Mana* (power and status) and the power to reap advantage from *karakia* came from the gods. But most importantly, the failure of *karakia* was linked to acceptance of Western Christianity, indicating that the effectiveness of the chants ceased when people accepted the new faith. The time before *te taenga mai o te Rongopai* (the coming of the good news) was seen as a time when people were *tapu* (sacred) and *karakia* had power. Formerly *karakia* had power and so had people. But from the time the Gospel arrived here sickness commenced. It was because of people being made *noa* (ordinary, no longer sacred) that sickness commenced. From the time the gospel arrived the people were made *noa*.[38]

> This was the spiritual state of the Maori after some decades of continuing contact with the alternative system of the Pakeha... When a cure was sought, a *tohunga* [holy person] might be called in, but the power of these figures was most often inadequate to affect any cure against Pakeha diseases. The *Atua* Pakeha was therefore acknowledged to be stronger than

---

33. Elsmore, *Like Them that Dream*, p. 32, cites *The New Zealand Parliamentary Debates* (1903), Vol. 142, p. 1141.

34. Elsmore, *Like Them that Dream*, p. 32, cites Apirana T. Ngata and I.L.G Sutherland, 'Religious Influences', in Sutherland (ed.), *The Maori People Today: A General Survey* (Wellington, 1940), pp. 346-47.

35. Elsmore, *Like Them that Dream*, p. 43.

36. Michael P. Shirres, *Te Tangata: The Human Person* (Auckland: Snedden & Cervin, 1997), pp. 78, 82.

37. Elsmore, *Like Them that Dream*, p. 43.

38. Shirres, *Te Tangata*, p. 86.

the *atua* Maori, and Pakeha medicine the only remedy against *mate* (diseases, curses and death) of the Pakeha.[39]

Bronwyn Elsmore decries the missionaries' use of this crisis to encourage belief in the superiority of the Pakeha God.[40] When Maori were defeated in battles against Pakeha and Christian Maori who had sided with the government, God was seen to be on the side of the Pakeha.[41]

Europeans often regarded the sacred traditions of the Maori as absurdities in contrast to the biblical epics. All this led to loss of status for the Maori. In a conversation between James Stack, an early Wesleyan missionary to New Zealand, and the son-in-law of Chief Te Puhi from Waitangi, Stack writes:

> The chief's son-in-law requested conversation on the creation, before I commenced he wished to know if after I had done I would listen to his traditions. I endeavoured to speak to him on the Mosaic Creation, Fall of Man etc as far as the Flood. But soon perceived that he had a far greater desire to talk than to listen. Finding his patience beginning to exhaust I finished when he commenced telling me a long round of absurdities but with all the spirit imaginable.[42]

In response to the confiscation of land and loss of *mana*, due to Pakeha colonial domination, some Maori turned away from the religion of the missionaries. Instead, they identified with the political situation of the ancient Israelites. They, too, were captive in their own land, subject to imperial domination by a foreign race.[43] According to Irvine Roxburgh, 'The unconcealed wish of many colonists and even politicians for a war of extermination of the Maori race, went to give a strong colour to the native belief that the white man's desire for land was the controlling factor [in the unjust labelling of Maori as rebels for their defence of their homeland].'[44]

However, Allan Davidson cautions against stereotyping the 'colonial and indigenous worlds' of New Zealand. He notes that the missionaries were in fact influenced by humanitarianism and paternalism. Whereas the colonial world was based on self-interest and aggrandisement, the

---

39. Elsmore, *Like Them that Dream*, p. 43.

40. Elsmore, *Like Them that Dream*, p. 43.

41. Elsmore, *Like Them that Dream*, p. 47.

42. Davidson and Lineham, *Transplanted Christianity*, p. 35, citing W.M.S. NZ Correspondence, J.W. Stack to W.M.S secretaries, 29 March 1826 (Journal No. 1), p. 2.

43. Elsmore, *Like Them that Dream*, pp. 71-72.

44. Irvine Roxburgh, *The Ringatu Movement: A Phenomenological Essay on Culture Shock in New Zealand/Aotearoa* (Christchurch, NZ: Cadsonbury, 1998), p. 39, cites James Cowan, *The New Zealand Wars and the Pioneering Period* (Wellington, 1923), p. 9.

influence of Social Darwinism from the 1870s brought a 'different attitude towards Maori as a dying race and was used to justify assimilationist thinking and actions', says Davidson; there was no one voice in colonialist Christianity, for nineteenth-century colonialism was influenced by a 'growing pluralism, sectarianism and secularism'.[45]

As I have argued, complex social forces led certain Maori in the late nineteenth and early twentieth centuries to identify themselves as 'Jews' as distinct from Christian subjects of the religion of empire. First, the Scriptures had become their own, and they were free to select and adapt them to their particular social, and religious concerns. Secondly, they felt empathy with the stories of the Hebrew tribes, affinity between with the religion of ancient Israel and traditional Maori practices. And thirdly, during and after the wars of the 1860s there was a degree of 'aggressive defiance' in identifying themselves with 'Jews'. This became the Maori way of saying they were 'the chosen people'.[46]

Te Kooti Rikirangi, a member of the Rongowhakaata sub-tribe of Ngati Porou, was a man of no traditional chiefly rank, who was deeply learned in Scripture, having gained literacy in the mission schools. When he was unjustly exiled without trial, he escaped with a gathering of followers around him. By claiming the authority of Jehovah, he led a religious movement called *ringatu* (the word means the upraised hand, recalling Moses's hands upraised as the harbinger of 'the Jews'). Ringatu forays into the 'promised land', which Te Kooti resolved to take back from 'Canaan', as he called the places occupied by the colonial settlers, brought sporadic fighting with the colonists.

After a visit to Te Kooti and his followers around 1877, Missionary Thomas Grace noted that their order of service was based on the prayer-book and their faith was not so different from his own—'except that it did not look to the Christian Saviour in its prayers. Rather it looked directly to God'.[47] Reflecting on his visit, Grace wrote in his annual letter to the Christian Missionary Society in 1877:

> In early years they received Christianity (and I may say Colonization) at our hands, without doubting and to a great extent on credit. Colonization, war, Confiscation…have followed each other in quick succession; while the expectations anticipated from representations made when they signed the Treaty of Waitangi have not been realized. And now they turn and question their first advisers and look at the whole of our connection with

45. Davidson, unpublished personal correspondence to the author, 26 April 2000, p. 2.

46. Davidson, unpublished personal correspondence to the author, 26 April 2000, p. 1.

47. Binney, *Redemption Songs*, p. 297.

them as a scheme to get their lands from them… These things, together with the course some of our brethren took in the [Anglo-Maori] war, has completely changed our position with these people. Nor is the change less than has come over their own minds as regards the management of their religious affairs. Formerly they consulted us in all matters connected with their teaching and worship… Now they assume the entire management of their own spiritual affairs and seem to consider they have a perfect [right] to do so…they have clearly never intended to renounce Christianity and go back to heathenism—on the contrary. Whatever individual exceptions they now make—they have lost confidence in us as a body and look upon us with distrust and suspicion, and have determined to manage their own religious affairs.[48]

Other religious movements associated with prophetic figures like Te Kooti emerged from this period as well.[49] Judith Binney, Te Kooti's biographer, sees the faith of his people as

…Essentially concerned with the problems of the colonised. It gave them the framework for analysing their own situation; it also offered them a unique relationship with God…resting on the covenanted relationship between them and God, or the politics of the Exodus whereby the destiny of the people is urged as being in their own hands.[50]

In conclusion, biblical stories of land and tribal identity connected Maori with Israelite lore and this identity with Israel fuelled the resolve of Te Kooti and others to battle as Israelites for land against the Canaanite (the European settlers) during the time when the settlers' greed led to war and further confiscation of land.

John's Jews and Maori Resistance
From first their first contact with Christianity, Maori were encouraged by the missionaries to believe that their tribes were descendants of the people of Israel.[51] But it was, I suggest, their alienation from colonialism and, by association, Christianity as the colonial religion, which fuelled their identification with the Jews in the negative Johannine sense of

48. T. Grace is cited in Binney, *Redemption Songs*, p. 296.
49. The various Maori prophets and their particular historical contexts are quite distinct. For a fuller historical introduction, see Elsmore, *Like Them that Dream*, and Sinclair, *Kinds of Peace*.
50. Binney, *Redemption Songs*, p. 298.
51. Early nineteenth-century Christian interpretation of Genesis was that all people came from Adam and Eve the first parents. This encouraged missionaries to suggest that Maori might be a lost tribe of Israel. The view was widely accepted by Maori who, from the period of first contact with Europeans, 'firmly believed that his origins were in the same people of which he read in the new scriptures'. Elsmore, *Like Them that Dream*, p. 71.

associating 'the Jews' with unbelief. Maori identification with the New Testament role of the Jew as enemy of the Christians (or in Johannine terms with 'unbelief'), was an act of resistance to colonial Christianity.

Elsmore would seem to support my hypothesis.

> When seen in light of the scriptures, the religious significance between the Maori and Pakeha cultures was major. In the New Testament it was shown that the Christian and the Jews were opposed, and in fact references to the Jews in the later scriptures were to the effect that they were set apart from the Christians for their unbelief. Those termed 'Jews' were those who had rejected both Jesus and his teachings, and had even persecuted and killed him. To give to the Maori the idea that they were descended from this race, and in addition to give him the proof of this in the word of God, was therefore almost the equivalent to instructing him that it was his duty to reject the message of Christianity and become rather, as that people of old.[52]

John 5 initially presents the Jews as the accusers of Jesus who 'seek to kill him' (5.18). But Jesus quickly moves from the role of the accused to the role of all-powerful judge (5.19-23). The claim that Jesus is the Son just like God the Father, turns the tables and the Jews change roles. By questioning and refusing to accept the claim that Jesus the Son is just like God, they refuse to honour the all-powerful judge. Jesus' speech reiterates the dominion of the Son as equal to God. It requires hearers to accept or reject him on these same terms. By implication, to respond appropriately to God's demands, to be just and right, requires one to honour God by also giving honour to the Son in those absolute terms.

The negative role in which John's Gospel casts 'the Jews' is not unlike anti-Jewish attitudes reflected in the correspondence of Henry Williams, an early CMS missionary to New Zealand. Williams recorded in 1839 that he once met a man named Mr. Merning who told Williams of his first arrival in Taranaki, New Zealand. Merning and his companion were greeted by men carrying muskets, so to protect themselves they had called out that they were missionaries, at which point they were heartily welcomed. Williams commented that Merning was 'an infidel and his companion a Jew, both enemies to our cause, but in this instance it was convenient for them to hail for Missionaries'. [53]

The religion of 'the Son just as God', the same substance as the Father, is enshrined in the creeds of Western Christendom where it continued to be normative within the religion of the British Empire during the

---

52. Elsmore, *Like Them that Dream*, p. 88.

53. Elsmore, *Like Them that Dream*, pp.18-19, cites Henry Williams, Journal, 11 November 1839, found in Lawrence M. Rogers (ed.), *The Early Journals of Henry Williams 1826–40* (Christchurch: Pegasus, 1961), p. 450.

colonization of New Zealand. Indirectly, then, to refuse to submit to the Son who is vested with the absolute power of God, is, in the ideology of empire, to associate oneself with those placed outside the realm. It is to identify, as certain Maori did, with the Jews, who are outside the religious ideology of Christendom's loyal subjects. But as Davidson notes: 'it was Maori who identified themselves in this way, they demanded this status for themselves, rather than having it imposed by Pakeha'.[54]

The Jews are marginalized in John's gospel within the legal motif of a trial. Foiled as the unbelievers who accuse and do not believe the testimony of Jesus, they are judged by God for their refusal to accept the equality of the Son with God (5.23). In the symbolic order of later developments in institutional Christianity, their refusal to believe in the Son as one with the Father, places them outside the fold.

Rudolf Bultmann comments on this Johannine line of reasoning as part of what he characterizes as a 'cosmic trial'. The 'trial' is characterized by the witness, accusation and reply format repeated throughout John.

> Just as in the rest of the Gospel, the Jews in John 5 appear as the opponents of Jesus, and as the opponents of his witness. This, then, is the prelude to the struggle which runs through the whole of the life of Jesus: it is a struggle between Christian faith and the world as represented by Judaism. It is a struggle that is continually represented as a trial, where the 'Jews' are under the illusion that they are the judges, whereas in fact they are the accused before the forum of God.[55]

The 'cosmic trial' is a forensic theme in John's Gospel, one which scholars have identified as a device designed to present the reader's decision for or against Jesus in universal terms. The outcome of the cosmic 'trial' is consistent with the plot structure of John 5. A division develops between the approved behaviour of honouring Jesus as God and the reproach and dishonour attending those who refuse to conform to this behaviour as the norm of faith.

John 5.17-23 gives testimony that Jesus is equal to God by arguing in absolute and universal terms for the divine superiority of the Son. In situations of politically dominant Christianity, such texts legitimate an imperial Christology that wields enormous social power when associated with institutions and communities gathered around the traditions of the authority of Jesus.

54. Davidson, unpublished personal correspondence to the author, 26 April 2000, p. 1.

55. Rudolf Bultmann, *The Gospel of John: A Commentary* (trans. G.R. Beasley-Murray; Oxford: Basil Blackwell, 1971), pp. 50, 84-97, 145, 172, 237-84

When, after the missionary period in New Zealand, some Maori who had become Anglicans changed their minds and willingly identified themselves as 'Jews', their identity was tied up with the Israelites in a political sense. On one hand, they identified with the stories of the Israelites whom Scripture presents affirmatively with a divine mandate to drive out the Canaanites (who for them represented the European settlers). But, on the other hand, they were willing to self-identify as 'Jews' in a negative sense as 'unbelievers'. They did this in order to empower themselves.[56] In an age of colonial Christianity. I suggest that their self-identification as 'Jews' who had turned away from the way of the Son, was a defiant act of resistance to the dominant claims of empire.

The Nicene creed is ideologically consistent with Jn 5.17-23 in that both seek to regulate the status of the Son as equal to the status of the Father; thus text and creed function as one unitary norm, as statements ordering discourse.[57] I am not aware of any quotations from John 5 or creeds derivative of it in the historical documents of colonial New Zealand. Yet both John 5 and New Zealand colonial documents reflect attitudes of imperial religious ideology: 'The Father raises the dead and creates life so also does the Son…and the Father does not judge anyone but he has given all judgment to his Son that all may honour the Son just as they honour the Father, whoever does not honour the Son does not honour the Father' (Jn 5.21-23).

On the one hand, the way of the Son equates Christ with the absolute power of God the Father who raises the dead and creates life (5.21). On the other hand, it argues that honouring the power of God as it is given to the Son is the criteria for inclusion as a loyal subject of the Father: whoever does not honour the Son does not honour the Father (5.23).

John's 'high Christology' was not formulated as a challenge to Roman political power. It was formulated in order to counter criticism for linking Jesus with God. It did this by solidifying expressions of Jesus' divine authority in superior, absolute terms. Later, in a Christian imperial context, its exalted image of Jesus as the unique Son, God from above from the beginning, resonated with the culture of subsequent imperial rule, and later Western colonial subjugation.

---

56. Davidson, unpublished personal correspondence to the author, 26 April 2000, p. 2.

57. My discussion is dependent upon Michel Foucault's view of the relationship between social practice and the statements that provide normative shape to their institutions. See Michel Foucault, *The Archaeology of Knowledge* (trans. A.M. Sheriden-Smith; London: Tavistock, 1972).

Davidson affirms that colonial nineteenth-century Christianity was in a 'self-assured expansionist mode' in New Zealand.[58]

> In taking colonialist forms of ministry, its ways of organising the Church, its modes of worship, old world values and ideals dominated Maori Christian behaviour. That is not to say there was not a process of adaptation in the new environment; there was and that is in itself significant. In their expansionist mode, colonial Christians could very easily ride roughshod over the values of indigenous peoples. They were happy to assimilate Maori Christians into their own Church structures on their own terms. But, whenever the question of Maori having some control over their own spiritual destiny was raised, this was largely squelched. It is therefore not surprising that some Maori expressed their Christianity and religious beliefs outside the structures of both missionary and colonialist Christianity.[59]

Former Anglican chief Tiopira Te Hukiki's comment 'You have not visited us for years and now that you have come to us again you find that we have given up the way of the Son and have adopted instead the way of the Father'[60] indicates a change of affiliation. If the 'way of the Son' was perceived as ideologically connected with the claims of superiority presumed and imposed by colonial rule of New Zealand, it may have represented, for some Maori, the way of Pakeha domination; to leave the 'way of the Son' was to refuse to bow to colonialism's claim of absolute power and instead to identify with the Jews as an act of defiance. To do so is to resist absolute imperial claims, just as in John's gospel the Jews refuse to conform to the Johannine ideology that Jesus the Son is equal with God the Father. Some Maori resisted allegiance to the divine Son of God because of the colonial connection. The absolute religious claims and the dominance imposed by the religion of Empire meant that to 'leave the way of the Son' was to challenge the universal and 'superior' claims of colonialist Christianity. Maori who defiantly identifed with 'the Jews' shook the dust of empire from their feet. They challenged the core of colonialist Christian confession, as reflective of the very structure of nineteenth-century British colonial thought. It was a form of resistance to elude the imperial net of social control.

58. Davidson, 'Interaction', p. 162.
59. Davidson, 'Interaction', p.162.
60. Binney, *Redemption Songs*, p. 296, cites the *East Coast Historical Records*, p. 80. Cleric James Stack understood this to be a statement of Maori autonomy from their former teachers, and a powerful belief in their unique relationship with God. The Maori thought that this familial relationship with God their Father 'had been intentionally concealed from them by their English teachers for political reasons'.

Adultery or Hybridity?: Reading John 7.53–8.11 from a Postcolonial Context

JEAN K. KIM

I

The story of the woman caught in adultery continues to hold great fascination for interpreters not only because it stirs up strong feelings of compassion for a human being in a vulnerable situation, but also because it emphasizes the strong conflict between Jesus and the scribes and the Pharisees. The critics who have dealt with this story have thus focused either on the opposition between Jesus and the woman in terms of Jesus' acceptance, wisdom and forgiveness being directed toward a person in a wretched condition, or on the conflict between Jesus and the scribes and the Pharisees.[1]

According to Lev. 20.10, if a man commits adultery with the wife of his neighbor, both the adulterer and the adulteress shall be put to death. Also, according to Deut. 22.22, if a man is caught lying with the wife of another man, both of them shall die: the man who lay with the woman as well as the woman herself. A comparison of John's story with the two Hebrew Bible passages reveals significant differences: in John's story, the subject of the adultery, the person who is the direct target of punishment, is not a man but a woman; there is no mention of the adulterer at all. This strangeness of the text prompts me to raise a question: where was the adulterer? Was he also caught or stoned, or had he already been released?[2] If such was not the case, why was only the woman brought to

---

1. Bart D. Ehrman, 'Jesus and the Adulteress', *NTS* 24 (1988), pp. 24-44; Stephen A. James, 'The Adulteress and the Death Penalty', *JETS* 22 (1979), pp. 45-53; Charles P. Baylis, 'The Woman Caught in Adultery: A Test of Jesus as the Greater Prophet', *BSac* 146 (1989), pp. 171-84.

2. According to J. Duncan M. Derrett, the adulterer was in a better position because the adulteress had no free property of her own with which she might redeem herself from her husband's wrath while the adulterer had his labor to pledge. In J. Duncan M. Derrett, 'Law in the New Testament: The Story of the Woman Taken in Adultery', *NTS* 10 (1964), p. 7.

the ambiguous scene, to be judged or to be forgiven? The text nowhere answers these questions or gives the woman's side of the story. The text shows a similar reticence with regard to what Jesus wrote on the ground. Nevertheless, many scholars have attempted to dissolve the mystery by speculating on what were the exact words that Jesus wrote.[3] In other words, even if the story has attracted much scholarly attention, the woman herself has never been a target of a scholarly focus but has been treated simply as an object whose function in the narrative is to be forgiven by Jesus, or to highlight the supposed hypocrisy of the Pharisees and the Scribes.

The woman does not have a subjective agency in the story itself, and her potential for subjectivity has been ignored in traditional interpretations. Woman's experience has not been central to written narrative and its interpretations. The act of writing and interpreting a text has been one of privilege, practiced by an elite group of *literati* for the use of a like group. As Gail Corrington Streete points out, 'written texts selected from existing oral narratives, lived experiences, and practices by an elite group thus end up privileging certain narratives, experiences, and practices, sometimes to the near or total exclusion of others'.[4] The creation of a canon is an ultimate act of privilege, proceeding from the judgment of an elite: in this way, the Bible shows a narrowed range of vision. In the Christian community, we continue—whether unconsciously or consciously—to authorize biblical texts, conferring on the Bible 'the status of a spiritual guide or manual for politics'.[5] Furthermore, as Regina M. Schwartz warns, 'we often attach ideological formations to the Bible that are alien to it, ones that arose in the course of a long and varied history of interpretation, and that by association and confusion have come to hold the same authority that we attach to the Bible'.[6] The Bible, as a cause of genealogy, has thus been read in order to represent

3.   Some scholars believed that Jesus wrote a list of the sins of his adversaries or some form of the Ten Commandments, while the others insist that Jesus' use of his finger on the ground may be an implicit claim to divine authority. Raymond E. Brown, *The Gospel According to John* (New York: Doubleday, 1966), I, p. 333; James Sanders, '"Nor do I," A Canonical Reading of the Challenge to Jesus in John 8', in R.T. Fortna and Beverly Gavenza (eds.), *The Conversation Continues: Studies in Paul and John* (Nashville: Abingdon Press, 1990), p. 337; Paul S. Minear, 'Writing on the Ground: The Puzzle in John 8.1-11', *HBT* 13 (1991), p. 27.

4.   Gail Corrington Streete, *The Strange Woman: Power and Sex in the Bible* (Louisville, KY: Westminster/John Knox Press, 1997), pp. 20-21.

5.   Regina M. Schwartz, 'Adultery in the House of David: The Metanarrative of Biblical Scholarship and the Narratives of the Bible', *Semeia* 54 (1991), p. 35.

6.   Schwartz, 'Adultery', p. 35.

the origin of a Christian community, and each successive reading appropriates the Bible for the elusive community that it wishes to create or legitimize. This problem is especially visible in the arena of sexual behavior, and continues to arise when interpreters attempt to draw moral absolutes from this culture-bound text. Yet, a destabilization of the elite-produced culture is not impossible. According to Stephen Greenblatt, 'culture' has a twofold characteristic, that is, 'constraint and mobility': the culture is mobile in the sense that it makes possible the production of meaning within a given community; on the other hand, it is constraining in the sense that it defines limits beyond which a set of beliefs can be excluded from the community in question.[7] In other words, when texts and contexts can examine the specific instances of elite cultural production as they refract a socio-historical change, the areas of authority, sexuality and space can be examined from a perspective which, unlike that of previous approaches, is not enclosed within the dominant traditions. The recognition of resisting reading practice from a feminist perspective is therefore inevitable because, as Elaine Wainwright insists, a community-produced or a culture-biased text may only offer an access to dominant traditions.[8]

As a feminist reader belonging to a postcolonial generation, I would like to destabilize the association between the Christian community and the text by articulating women's voicelessness, so that I might proceed to offer a reading of biblical narratives that deconstructs traditional biblical interpretations. By 'voicelessness' I mean not only the historical absence of a woman writer's text but also the silence of articulation which is denied expression and agency. Against the image of woman's silence, feminists have tried to historicize and contextualize a woman's absence and her enforced voicelessness.[9] The concept of voicelessness is indispensable for a discussion of women in a socio-historical context. Filling in the blank spaces of lost story or lost history marks out a space for a woman's presence on the literary scene by exposing her historical marginalization. Because voicelessness, as suppressed history and unacknowledged agency, is a central issue in postcolonial feminist

7.   Stephen Greenblatt, 'Culture', in Frank Lentricchia and Thomas McLaughlin (eds.), *Critical Terms for Literary Study* (Chicago: University of Chicago Press, 1994), pp. 225-32.

8.   Elaine Wainwright, 'Rachel Weeping for her Children: Intertextuality and the Biblical Testaments—A Feminist Approach', in Athalya Brenner and Carole Fontaine (eds.), *A Feminist Companion to Reading the Bible* (Sheffield: Sheffield Academic Press, 1997), pp. 452-69.

9.   Carole Boyce Davies and Elaine Savory Fido (eds.), *Out of Kumbla: Caribbean Women and Literature* (Trenton, NJ: African World Press, 1990), pp. 1-24.

writings/readings, the very fact of presenting the possibility of a woman's narrative is empowering. In other words, the meaning of the story lies in the woman's silence and in the contradiction which the story contains. A marginalized woman's voice not only participates in the reconstruction of the suppressed history of women in the text and challenges the ways in which the past has been encoded, but it also reveals the presence of the subdued voice in the canonized text.

With this deconstructive perspective, I will conduct an 'intercontextual' reading for a postcolonial feminist interpretation of Jn 7.53–8.11. Such a reading, by employing not only a text, but also a context as another text, will enable us to go beyond textual or intertextual limits.[10] For this inter-contextual reading, then, I will utilize a postcolonial context as well as postcolonial literature as a text.[11] In so doing, I will suggest that Jn 7.53–

10. For an intertextual approach to the Bible from deconstructive perspective, see Gary Phillips, '"What is Written? How are You Reading?" Gospel, Intertextuality and Doing Lukewise: Reading Lk 10.25-42 Otherwise', *Semeia* 69/70 (1995), pp. 111-48. The term 'intertextuality' was introduced by Julia Kristeva who used the term in her dialogue with the texts of Mikhail Bakhtin. She then developed Bakhtin's notion of 'dialogism' in order to displace semiotics in favor of an opened ideological criticism that infused ideas from Derridan philosophy, Marxism and Freudian/Lacanian psychoanalysis with linguistic-structuralism (in Toril Moi [ed.], *The Kristeva Reader* [New York: Columbia University Press, 1986]). Since the predominantly literary variant of intertextuality is unable to encourage readers to freely engage in 'political intertextuality', Nicolas Zurburgg suggests that in order to overcome 'the intertextual impasse' readers need to consider an 'intercontextual approach' that is 'a deliberate venturing beyond the over-literary intertextuality confined within writing itself into a more expansive field of studies in which radical intertextual experiments may be best explicated by analogy with the extra-literary conventions informing the literary discourse within which conservative theory and practice locates intertextual relation' (in Nicolas Zurbrugg, 'Burroughs, Barthes, and the Limits of Intertextuality', *Review of Contemporary Fiction* 4 [1984], pp. 88-97). Also, Ellen T. Amour argues that a simple deconstructive approach without an 'extratextual referent to serve as the standard does not distinguish good and bad text, and between good and bad interpretation' (in Ellen T. Amour, *Deconstruction, Feminist Theology, and the Problem of Difference: Subverting the Race/Gender Divide* [Chicago: The University of Chicago Press, 1999], Chapter 2). For *'testimonio'* as a new form of literary narrative, see John Beverley, 'The Margin at the Center: On *Testimonio* (Testimonial Narrative)', *MFS* 35 (1989), pp. 11-28.

11. A written text hardly gives a voice to a forgotten or silent woman, so a history based on the written is no more than the half of history. In order to fill the other half, a postcolonial context as well as a postcolonial literature, which both contain women's social memory, can be effectively utilized: even though postcolonial literatures are fragmented, in them lie histories and the voices of people. For 'Cultural Memory', see Mieke Bal, Jonathan Crewe, and Leo Spitzer (eds.), *Acts of Memory: Cultural Recall in the Present* (Hanover, NH: University Press of New England, 1999). Also, for an application of a modern postcolonial theory to the Roman Empire setting, see Peter Van

8.11 is a story about the legitimate leadership of Israel in a (de)colon-izing context and that the woman caught in adultery may not have been simply a sexually immoral woman but rather a victim used as a site of cultural (im)purity, which is a ground on which competing views of cul-tural or national identity are debated. Then I will suggest that the woman can be a site of hybridity which enables a female reader to lay claim to her own subjectivity.

II

The textual history of this story as a whole is notoriously complex.[12] However, the majority believes that even though the story is an inter-polation, it represents a realistic pericope that can be counted as an early free-floating unit of tradition. When we consider John's Gospel as a narrative, however, the question of whether John found this story in a reliable historical tradition or inserted it himself is not important for the flow of Johannine narrative.[13] Rather, what is more important for a feminist reading is the socio-historical context of John's Gospel which

Dommelen, 'Colonial Constructs: Colonialism and Archaeology in the Mediter-ranean', *World Archaeology* 28 (1997), pp. 305-23; Jane Webster, 'Necessary Com-parisons: A Postcolonial Approach to Religious Syncretism in the Roman Provinces', *World Archaeology* 28 (1997), pp. 324-38; Jean K. Kim, '"Uncovering her Wickedness": An Intercontextual Reading of Revelation 17 from a Postcolonial Feminist Perspective', *JSNT* 73 (1999), pp. 61-81; cf. David Tombs, 'Crucifixion, State Terror and Sexual Abuse', *USQR* 53 (1999), pp. 89-109.

12. For a discussion of textual complexity of John 7.53–8.11, see Barnabas Lind-ars, *The Gospel of John* (NCB; London: Oliphants, 1972), p. 305; Bruce M. Metzger, *A Textual Commentary on the Greek New Testament* (New York: United Bible Societies, 1971), pp. 219-22; C.K. Barrett, *The Gospel According to St. John* (London: SPCK, 1978), pp. 589-92; Brown, *John*, pp. 332-38; R. Schnackenburg, *The Gospel According to St. John* (New York: Crossroad, 1982), vol. 2. pp. 162-71; Ehrman, 'Jesus and the Adulteress', pp. 24-44; J. Ian H. McDonald, 'The So-called Pericope De adultera', *NTS* 41 (1995), pp. 415-27; Philip Comfort, 'The Pericope of the Adulteress', *BT* 40 (1989), pp. 145-47; Zane C. Hodges, 'The Woman Taken in Adultery (John 7.53–8.11): The Text', *BSac* 136 (1979), pp. 318-32.

13. Frederick A. Schilling, 'The Story of Jesus and the Adulteress', *ATR* 37 (1955), pp. 91-106; John P. Heil, 'The Story of Jesus and the Adulteress (John 7.53–8.11) Reconsidered', *Bib* 72 (1991), pp. 182-91; *idem*, 'A Rejoinder to "Reconsidering 'The Story of Jesus and the Adulteress Reconsidered'"', *ET* 25 (1994), pp. 361-66; Zane C. Hodges, 'The Woman Taken in Adultery (John 7.53–8.11): Exposition', *BSac* 137 (1980), pp. 41-53; Allison A. Trites, 'The Woman Taken in Adultery', *BSac* 131 (1974), pp. 137-46; cf. Daniel B. Wallace, 'Reconsidering "The Story of Jesus and the Adulter-ess Reconsidered"', *NTS* 39 (1993), pp. 290-96.

caused the woman's voicelessness; that is, the Roman Empire setting.[14] For by the time of Jesus' ministry, Rome controlled the religio-political sphere of Israel through the patronage of the Jerusalem high priesthood.[15] Through prefects, the Romans directly exerted their power over Palestine, and their power was backed by the Roman auxiliary troops headquartered in Caesarea and by the legions in Syria.[16]

The power relations between the Roman Empire and the colonial Israelites was typically that of patrons and clients. Especially, the patronage of the Roman Empire was almost equivalent to a military patronage, functioning as a protector in time of attack, and as a temporary supervisor of almost every aspect of local government.[17] When the military patrons obtained economic assets in the local country and developed blood ties with the local aristocracy, their patronage became almost complete.[18] This may be compared to the way in which, in modern times, the colonial powers practiced a form of indirect rule—'decentralized despotism'—through local chiefs or headmen.[19] In other words, the strategic logic of political control in the colonial state rested on a practice of

14. Richard J. Cassidy, *John's Gospel in New Perspective: Christology and the Realities of Roman Power* (Maryknoll, NY: Orbis Books, 1992).

15. In order to preserve their own establishment, the high priests cooperated with the Roman governors of their land; they conducted the offering of the daily sacrifice for the well-being of the Emperor and people of Rome. S.G.F. Brandon, 'The Defeat of Cestius Gallus, A.D. 66', *History Today* 20 (1972), p. 38. Joan E. Taylor, *The Immerser: John the Baptist within Second Temple Judaism* (Grand Rapids: Eerdmans, 1997), p. 159.

16. After Herod, the turbulent provinces required the presence of three legions from 67 CE until the Jewish revolt was finally suppressed three years later (V *Macedonia*, X *Fretensis*, XV *Apollinaris*), and the X *Fretensis* alone thereafter; two legions following the outbreak of Bar-Kokba's revolt of 132 CE, and the same two legions (VI *Ferrata*, X *Fretensis*) thereafter. In Edward N. Luttwak, *The Grand Strategy of the Roman Empire: From the First Century A.D. to the Third* (Baltimore: The Johns Hopkins University Press, 1979), pp. 24-25.

17. Josephus, *Ant.* 14.324-467. Luttwak, *The Grand Strategy*, pp. 20-50.

18. Ramsay MacMullen, *Soldier and Civilian in the Later Roman Empire* (Cambridge, MA: Harvard University Press, 1963), p. 160-61; Adrian Keith Goldsworthy, *The Roman Army at War: 100 BC–AD 200* (Oxford: Clarendon Press, 1996), pp. 76-115; K.C. Hanson and Douglas E. Oakman, *Palestine in the Times of Jesus: Social Structures and Social Conflicts* (Minneapolis: Fortress Press, 1998), pp. 86-90.

19. I am indebted to Bruce J. Berman for a comparison of a patron/client system of modern times with that of Roman Empire period. See Bruce J. Berman, 'Ethnicity, Patronage and the African State: The Politics of Uncivil Nationalism', *African Affairs* 97 (1998), pp. 305-41. For a patron/client system of the Roman Empire, see Andrew Wallace-Hadrill (ed.), *Patronage in Ancient Society* (New York: Routledge, 1989), Chapters 7–8.

fragmenting and isolating political activity of the colonized within the confines of local administrative sub-divisions and thereby inhibiting the spread of opposition and resistance to the colonizing power.[20] Each administrative unit attached to a single culturally homogeneous 'tribe' in which people continued to live within the indigenous institutions and were subject to 'tribal discipline' through local structures of authority.[21] In the somewhat analogous case of first-century Palestine, the priesthood and Jewish religious leader groups were the essential linkages between the Roman colonial state and Jewish society.

We can easily find this pattern in the story of the woman caught in adultery. Early in the morning, Jesus is teaching in the temple. As they bring the woman before Jesus, the scribes and the Pharisees ask him 'Teacher, this woman has been caught in the act of adultery. Now in the law, Moses commanded us to stone sinners like this. What do you say?' (8.4-5). In so doing, they clearly set up a trap.[22] If Jesus found her guilty, they would accuse him of seizing the power of Rome; if he let her go free, they would accuse him of breaking the Law of Moses. If their purpose was simply to judge and punish her misconduct according to the Law, they could have done it by themselves. However, they could not perform juridical punishment on the woman because they did not have an official or public authority. The Pharisees are represented as functioning independently only in matters of religious opinion and judgment regarding religious affairs. They were not able to act alone in enacting judgment, but only together with the chief priests, who gained their authority by means of an agreement with Rome in which they undertook to keep the country peaceful in return for being allowed to retain political and religious leadership.[23] The chief priests are brought into combination with the Pharisees precisely at the point where some official action is called for. John regards the alliance between the chief priests and the Pharisees as having been influenced by the ruler of this world, that is the Roman power, which sought the benefits of colonialism by securing the loyalty of the native leaders who shared the resources through the patron/client system.

---

20. Berman, 'The Politics of Uncivil Nationalism', p. 315; Goldsworthy, *The Roman Army at War*, p. 114.

21. Berman, 'The Politics of Uncivil Nationalism', p. 315.

22. Gail R. O'Day, 'John 7.53–8.11: A Study in Misreading', *JBL* 111 (1992), p. 632.

23. Urban C. Von Wahlde, 'The Relationships Between Pharisees and Chief Priests: Some Observations on the Texts in Matthew, John and Josephus', *NTS* 42 (1996), pp. 513-18; Taylor, *The Immerser*, pp. 156-61.

In order to read this religio-political aspect of the story, we need to notice the presence of a larger stage around the story's setting. Although the action is centered in a narrow triangle of parties—Jesus, the accusers, the accused—the audience is far larger than that. When people came to him, Jesus sat down and began to teach them (8.2). It is the whole people, the whole of the nation Israel that is present, and therefore they must be taken into consideration. The place is also significant: the holy city, the temple, which is one of the symbols of Jewish nationalism.[24] In other words, the story makes it clear that the people came to Jesus in the temple in recognition of his role as a promising leader and asked him to teach them. Indeed, Jesus was doing more than evading the trap set by his opponents. Apparently, the central issue was simply a matter of fidelity to Moses and the law (7.19-23). But the authority of teachers and the validity of their teaching are a major point of contention (7.14-17, 28, 8.2, 20). According to Brad H. Young, an exchange of questions and answers was crucial in establishing a foundation of accepted custom within Jewish tradition. The authority of the religious leader was secured by his knowledge of the oral tradition and his ability to interpret the Scripture.[25] In this story, Jesus is called 'teacher' even by the scribes and the Pharisees and is asked to render an interpretation regarding the scriptural commandment to stone a person who commits adultery. Young regards Jesus's answer as a similar 'halachic ruling' or 'legal pro-nouncement' from the oral tradition, which deals with prevailing issues of religious practice.[26] Seeking answers to questions concerning scrip-tural interpretation is a significant part of the Jewish religious custom. In the Jewish interpretation of the Law, according to Young, the oral Law often is regarded as showing the higher intent of the divine revelation.[27] Jesus gives his answer in an oral form, by which he challenged the listeners to reject the authority of those who relied on the written word. If such is the case, Jesus surely mounts a direct attack upon his rivals. The Pharisees, who already called Jesus 'teacher', seem to have been

---

24. According to Doron Mendel, there are four symbols of Jewish nationalism: 'temple, kinship, territory, and army'. Mendel insists that the thought of Jewish nationalism was basic to life in Palestine. See Doron Mendel, *The Rise and Fall of Jewish Nationalism: Jewish and Christian Ethnicity in Ancient Palestine* (Grand Rapids: Eerdmans, 1992), pp. 277-331. In Jesus's day, the temple had already become the center of a 'church-state' compromise. See Carol Stream, 'Jesus vs. Sanhedrin', *CT* 42 (1998), pp. 48-50.

25. Brad H. Young, '"Save the Adulteress!": Ancient Jewish Response in the Gospels?', *NTS* 41 (1995), p. 67.

26. Young, 'Save the Adulteress', p. 67.

27. Young, 'Save the Adulteress', p. 68.

convinced by Jesus' ruling, and to have accepted it as having the authority which the elder has over the younger.

The contest in this story over the legitimacy of Jesus' authority versus that of the established authorities lies in the middle of the increasing hostility surrounding Jesus. The more Jesus teaches, the more his teaching 'sifts' the people, inflaming the opposition of some of the crowd and leading others to believe. In chs. 5–12, the increasing hostility against Jesus is set in the context of the Jewish festivals. At each progression of festivals, Jesus does or says things that show he is the fulfillment of what the festival celebrates (5.1, 6.4, 7.2, 10.22, 12.1). The level of hostility escalates in the ensuing debate. John 8 contains the most hostile exchange between Jesus and the 'Jews', where Jesus declares that their father was the devil (8.44).[28] In response to the healing of the blind man, there is a division even among the Pharisees (9.16) and among the 'Jewish' followers, with some saying that he is a demoniac (10.19), and other defending him. When the 'Jews' again take up stones against Jesus (10.31, 33), he withdraws from Jerusalem (10.41). Mary and Martha send for Jesus because Lazarus is at the point of death. Jesus delays, then returns, and raises Lazarus from the dead. When they receive the report of Lazarus's resurrection, the chief priests and the Pharisees become concerned that everyone may soon follow Jesus (11.45-56). Then they plot to put Lazarus to death as well as Jesus (12.10), because they are afraid of the Romans' intervention which would jeopardize the entire nation: 'the Roman will come and destroy both our holy place and our nation' (11.48). In light of this flow of the story, we can be sure that the real issue in the story of the woman caught in adultery was not a simple interpretation of Moses's Law but a matter of the contest over the legitimate leadership of Israel, such as it was, under Roman control.

To return to the typical colonial patron and client pattern which I described earlier: the native leaders, as the principal clients of the colonial state, become in turn powerful patrons in their own local societies and the central focus of the development of clientelistic patronage networks around political institutions and positions of authority.[29] These networks tended to be ethnically defined within the 'tribal' contexts of local administration.[30] A primary aim of indirect rule was to prevent the

28. In the Johannine narrative, the 'Jews' are almost equal to the Jewish religious authorities (cf. 6.41, 52). Urban C. von Wahlde, 'The Johannine "Jews": A Critical Study', *NTS* 28 (1982), pp. 33-60 (44).

29. As another mode of patronage, a native leader can be the patron of his locale: by building the city of Caesarea, Herod the Great played two roles as client as well as patron (Jos. *War* 1.408-15; *Ant.* 15.331-41); Hanson and Oakman, *Palestine*, p. 76.

30. Berman, 'The Politics of Uncivil Nationalism', p. 317.

mobilization of ordinary people in any anti-colonial struggle, and the patronage networks functioned as fundamentally conservative instruments of political fragmentation. In a colonizing context, however, the invention of tradition and ethnic identities in connection with politics, religions, trading networks and regional economies appears inescapable because the construction of the specific cultural content of ethnic communities and identities can be crucially influenced by the blurred culture of colonialism.[31] Even more than this, as Homi K. Bhabha points out,[32] the 'locality' of national culture itself is neither united nor unitary, because, in a (de)colonizing context, outside and inside are interwoven through a process of hybridity 'incorporating new people in relation to the body politic, generating other sites of meaning and, accordingly, producing unnamed sites of political antagonism in the political process, and unpredictable forces for political representation'. In order to maintain their status quo, however, the native leaders embody the tradition of tribe as the basis of society, custom as the basis of individual behavior, and the continuance of pre-colonial ethnic identities as the basis of a kind of shadow-nationalism. In a colonizing context, therefore, contests over proper leadership become inseparable from debates over the legitimacy of political power. And the definition of moral and political community is cast largely in ethnic terms.[33] In this sense, then, the traditions employed in nationalist discursive practices are Janus-faced because the traditions function not only as a site of struggle against invasive forces from outside but also as a site of contest for leadership within the community. In such a context, women are simply the grounds on which the debates about the traditions are examined; 'women themselves are not significant as human beings; tradition is'.[34]

We can also easily find this pattern in John 8. By calling the Pharisees' law and testimony 'your law' and 'your testimony' in order to contrast it with 'my testimony', Jesus underscores that the Pharisees' appeals to the

31. The notion of 'harem', which is 'home' of other nation ('outside'), is also constitutive of 'home' of its own nation ('inside'). See Inderpal Grewal, *Home and Harem: Nation, Gender, Empire, and the Cultures of Travel* (Durham, NC: Duke University Press, 1996), pp. 7, 13, 54; Trinh T. Minh-ha, *When the Moon Waxes Red: Representation, Gender, and Cultural Politics* (New York: Routledge, 1991), pp. 65-78.

32. Homi K. Bhabha, 'Introduction: Narrating the Nation', in Homi K. Bhabha (ed.), *Nation and Narration* (New York: Routledge, 1990), p. 4.

33. Berman, 'The Politics of Uncivil Nationalism', p. 323.

34. Ketu H. Katrak, 'Decolonizing Culture: Toward a Theory for Postcolonial Women's Texts', *MFS* 35 (1989), pp. 157-79 (168). E. Frances White, 'Africa on my Mind: Gender, Counter Discourse and African-American Nationalism', *Journal of Women's History* 2 (1990), p. 83.

Law are mistaken (8.13-19). As a response, they stir up Jesus' followers, and insist that he is a Samaritan and has a demon. They do this in order to challenge Jesus as a legitimate leader of Israel due to his 'ethnic impurity' and 'uncleanness' (8.48).[35] In reality, the Pharisees might not have possessed a juridical or official power at the time of Jesus. The fact that the Pharisees do not have juridical or official power does not mean that they do not hold social power.[36] Also, the crowd seems to be aware of the Pharisees' authoritative power. When Jewish people lacked a central political authority, their rebels were organized into diverse and 'rival bands' defending individual localities, and the crowd was likely to join whatever side was the strongest.[37] So the crowd begins to speculate about Jesus' identity and whether the authorities might actually know that he is the messiah since they allow him to teach openly. Debate again focuses on Jesus' origin. Finally, they assume they know where Jesus is from and conclude that he cannot be the messiah (8.39-59).

III

If this story is thus about the legitimate leadership of Israel in a colonizing context, which in this case is the colonizing domination of the Roman Empire, we can offer a conjecture as to why there is no mention of the man who was with the woman. The colonial invasion of 'Other' is not a simple invasion of land but includes the invasion of native woman's bodies. The colonial invasion of Other is well reflected in the Forum of Augustus where the statuary on triumphal arches depicting captive women is clearly meant to evoke analogies between the penetration of a woman's body and the breeching of an enemy fortress.[38] This colonial masculine orientation is also well expressed in Augustus' legislation regarding soldiers' marriage. Soldiers' marriages were banned for the duration of their service, and soldiers' wives were not supposed to follow their husbands.[39] The ban was presumably thought necessary for the sake of the efficiency and good order of the army, which would be impeded by the presence of wives and children. Yet the Roman army was

35. Cf. Jn 8.13, 21-26.
36. Taylor, *The Immerser*, p. 159.
37. Goldsworthy, *The Roman Army at War*, pp. 88, 102.
38. Barbara Kellum, 'Concealing/Revealing: Gender and the Play of Meaning in the Moments of Augustan Rome', in Thomas Habinek and Alessandro Schiesaro (eds.), *The Roman Cultural Revolution* (New York: Cambridge University Press, 1997), pp. 167-68.
39. Leo F. Raditsa, 'Augustus' Legislation Concerning Marriage, Procreation, Love Affairs and Adultery', *ANRW*, II. 13, pp. 278-339.

a long-service army in which the average recruit was 18 or 19, an age when very few were already married. The men served for at least 25 years, and often for a great deal longer. If they could not be married officially, the soldiers' answer was obvious: they would be married unofficially.[40] In other words, since the prohibition ran counter to the natural desire of soldiers, sometimes they cohabited with local women or raped them.[41]

In contrast, colonized men who are unable to protect their women tend to feel shame at not being real men, and thus the sexual invasion of their women by foreign men becomes an assault on male and national honor, as Alan Dundes' obervation shows: 'Since ancient times, you get at your male opponent by violating his women. If the women's honor is lost, the man's honor is lost...you conquer enemies by feminizing the men and putting down the women.'[42] So the men of Massada who were afraid of being shamed preferred to kill their wives and daughters rather than allow the Roman troops to rape them.[43] Also, a second-century source tells us that priests' wives were considered unclean collectively as a matter of principle even when soldiers entered a town in large numbers, and this seems to derive from an individual case in which a priest's wife was not raped, but only embraced by a Roman soldier.[44] In a colonizing context, owing to this gendered nationalist ideology, native women's bodies have come to signify sites of cultural (im)purity; bodies polluted

40. George R. Watson, *The Roman Soldier* (Ithaca, NY: Cornell University Press, 1969), pp. 134-35. Craig Koester, *Symbolism in the Fourth Gospel: Meaning, Mystery, Community* (Minneapolis: Fortress Press, 1995), p. 49; *idem*, 'The Savior of the World (John 4.42)', *JBL* 109 (1990), p. 665.

41. In the case of the story of the woman caught in adultery, we can also consider a possibility that the woman might have employed the strategy of 'voluntary rape'. During war times, 'women favored voluntary rape in order to avoid ongoing brutal attacks from numerous soldiers and to obtain assistance in crossing tightly guarded borders. The term 'voluntary rape' suggests the extreme ways that women could have an active will in a context that threatened to dehumanize them completely and render them only as victims' (Marlene Epp, 'The Memory of Violence: Soviet and East European Mennonite Refuges and Rape in the Second World War', *Journal of Women's History* 9 [1997], pp. 67-68).

42. Quoted by Maureen Dowd in *The New York Times*, Sunday, 21 June 1998; see also Alan Dundes, *From Game to War: And Other Psychoanalysis Essays on Folklore* (Lexington, KY: The University Press of Kentucky, 1997), pp. 25-45.

43. Shimon Applebaum, 'The Zealots: The Case for Revaluation', *JRS* 61 (1971), p. 169. See also David Stern, 'The Captive Woman: Hellenization, Greco-Roman Erotic Narrative, and Rabbinic Literature', *PT* 19 (1998), pp. 101-102.

44. Benjamin Isaac, *The Limits of Empire: The Roman Army in the East* (Oxford: Clarendon Press, 1990), 117; see, *y. Ned.* 11.42d, *m. Ket.* 2.9, *y. Ket.* 2.26d, *Git.* 58a.

by disease or by other influences through the hybridized culture resulting from colonialism.[45] Furthermore, only women were expected to bear the burden of cultural tradition by keeping their honor intact, whereas many native males co-opted with and benefited from the colonial occupation.[46] In criticizing the objectification of women in the symbolic equating of sexual aggression against women with colonial aggression against a nation, Nawal El Saadawi attacks the double standard of the patriarchal nationalist: 'The honor of women is preserved or lost depending upon the type of sexual relations which they have with men, rather than on the other aspects of their life.'[47]

However, these are not just old stories that happened long ago. Today, similar incidents often occur, especially in military base areas such as Okinawa, Subic Bay in the Philippines, and South Korea.[48] Since the Second World War, those Asian countries whose women were forcibly recruited as 'comfort women'[49] have hesitated to debate the issue of

45. In a postcolonial literature, the diseases of cultural impurity are manifest as prostitution or whore. In refusing to carry the burden of postcolonial corruption, postcolonial feminists insists that these women can effectively transform their bodies into a site of rebellion whereas the postcolonial bourgeois must recognize the violent structure that produced the victimized women. Gayatri Chakravorty Spivak, 'French Feminism Revisited', in Judith Butler and Joan W. Scott (eds.), *Feminists Theorize the Political* (New York: Routledge, 1992), pp. 54-85. For a postcolonial literature, see Nawal El Saadawi, *Woman at Point Zero* (trans. Sherif Hetata; London: Zed Books, 1983).

46. Therese Saliba, 'On the Bodies of Third World Women: Cultural Impurity, Prostitution, and Other Nervous Conditions', *College Literature* 22 (1995), p. 133. After the First World War, the increase in prostitution around British bases angered the Muslim brotherhood. For the impact of British colonization on Arab life, see Afaf Lutfi Al-Sayyid Marsot, *A Short History of Modern Egypt* (Cambridge: Cambridge University Press, 1985). Tsitsi Dabgarembga attempts to subvert the colonialist metaphor of woman as colonized land and exposes the male elite's collaboration in the colonial process. Tsitsi Dabgarembga, *Nervous Conditions* (Seattle: Seal, 1988).

47. Nawal El Saadawi, *The Hidden Face of Eve: Women in the Arab World* (Boston: Beacon Press, 1980), p. 166.

48. Sandra P. Sturdevant and Brenda Stolzfus (eds.), *Let the Good Times Roll: Prostitution and the U.S. Military in Asia* (New York: The New Press, 1992); Rita Nakashima Brock and Susan Thistlethwaite, *Casting Stones: Prostitution and Liberation in Asia and the United States* (Minneapolis: Fortress Press, 1992).

49. There would have been about 139,000 'comfort women', who were forcibly recruited from among young village girls across Asia. It is estimated that 80 per cent of them were Korean women, because they were preferred by the soldiers after Japanese and Okinawan women. A major obstacle to obtaining a clearer picture of the recruitment process in Korea has been the shortage of official records of draft procedures. All such documentation was systematically destroyed at the end of the

sexually abused women not only because they felt shame for nationalistic reasons but also because they feared upsetting Japan, their most import-ant economic partner.[50] On the other hand, sexually marginalized women continue to exist under a different form of victimization, that of military prostitution in the US military base areas. In these areas, there have been many instances of women who were raped or even killed by the US GIs. However, the GIs who committed the crimes were not tried in a domestic court, because they were under the protection of the host countries' powerful patron.[51] In addition, since nationalism and respect-ability are interwoven as the middle class uses the nation state to impose its notions of the private sphere's proper order on the upper and lower classes,[52] the death of the voiceless women has not received public attention: rather, the public has reviled them by calling them sexually immoral military prostitutes. This danger to colonized women has been overlooked not only because male theorists are indifferent to the gen-dering power of nations but also because western feminism presents itself as a yardstick for a universal sisterhood in suffering, as Anne McClintock points out.[53] Postcolonial feminists observing the dis-placement of the colonized into the colonizer's place have warned that

war, as was the case with all confidential material that could be used as evidence in war-crimes trials. Even until now, the Japanese Education ministry hides the atrocities committed during Japanese colonial rule in Korea and has kept any reference to comfort women out of the nation's textbooks (George Hicks, *The Comfort Women: Japan's Brutal Regime of Enforced Prostitution in the Second World War* [New York: W.W. Norton, 1995], pp. 11-49).

50. Lan Johnson, 'Breaking Silence: Beijing Permits Screening of Najing Massacre Film', *Far Eastern Economic Review* (24 Aug. 1995), p. 40.

51. In June 1977, a sex worker named Pok-Hi Yi was strangled to death and her body was scorched. A month later, another sex worker named Yong-Sun Yi was killed. An American soldier named Steven Warren Towerman admitted killing both women, but at the time of the incident neither Korean police nor the US military police invest-igated the murders, offering the excuse that there was insufficient evidence. For more instances, see Sun-Kum Park, Chan-Kul Kim and U-Sub Kim (eds.), *Our Kum-I* (Seoul: The Committee on the Murder of Kum-I Yun by American Military in Korea, 1993). For postcolonial literatures dealing with asymmetric relationship between the US soldiers and Korean native women, see Junghyo Ahn, *Silverstallion: A Novel of Korea* (New York: Soho Press, 1990); Jeongmo Yoon, *Reins* (Seoul: Poolbit, 1988).

52. See George Mosse, *Nationalism and Sexuality: Respectability and Abnormal Sexual-ity in Modern Europe* (New York: H. Fertig, 1985).

53. Anne McClintock, '"No Longer in a Future Heaven": Gender, Race and Nationalism', in A. McClintock, A. Mufti and E. Shohat (eds.), *Dangerous Liaisons: Gen-der, Nation, and Postcolonial Perspectives* (Minneapolis: University of Minnesota Press, 1997), pp. 90-112.

sexually oppressed women are caught in a no-win situation between foreign and native men.[54]

It is only recently that we have begun to take seriously these incidents of the voiceless women and to articulate their voicelessness as a starting point for a deconstructive reading. The US soldiers' rape of a 12-year-old school girl ignited Okinawan anger against US militarism not only because of the cruel rape of a child but also because the GIs were exempt from being summoned in a Japanese court.[55] Also, the murder of a sex-worker, Yun Kum-I, by a psychotic GI who was also immune from local prosecution inflamed Korean protests against US militarism.[56] Since sexually marginalized women's experiences have not been central to published narratives, Luisa Passerini insists that social memory should be utilized in order to derive meaning from the silenced or hidden history.[57] In fact, a feminist's utilizing of a social memory enables us to depersonalize and place it within an impersonal historical narrative. As a social memory, the death of this voiceless woman (Yun Kum-I) helps us to understand a possible reason why there was no mention of the man who was with the woman caught in adultery.

According to ancient military regulations, a soldier could not be involved in a court case outside camp. The privilege of Roman army is well reflected in Juvenal's description of army life.[58] When a soldier was

54. Gayatri Chakravorty Spivak, *Outside in the Teaching Machine* (New York: Routledge, 1993), pp. 78-82; Elaine H. Kim and Chungmoo Choi (eds.), *Dangerous Women: Gender and Korean Nationalism* (New York: Routledge, 1997); Inderpal Grewal and Caren Kaplan (eds.), *Scattered Hegemony: Postmodernity and Transnational Feminist Practices* (Minneapolis: University of Minnesota Press, 1994).

55. Steven Butler, 'An Alliance under Fire', *U.S. News and World Report* 119 (2 Oct. 1995), pp. 54-56. Cf. Joseph Gerson, 'I Refuse', *The Bulletin of the Atomic Scientists* 52 (1996), p. 26; Dzenita Mehic, 'We are Dying of your protection', *The Bulletin of the Atomic Scientists* 51 (1995), pp. 41-44.

56. On 28 Oct. 1998, a Korean woman named Yun Kum-I was killed by an American soldier named Kenneth Markle. 'Yun was mutilated by a bottle stuck into her vagina, an umbrella stuck into her rectum, matches pushed into her mouth, and detergent powder spread all over her body. Her body was found in a pool of blood in the small room that she rented in the base area.' The death of Yun opened a new way to discuss gender and sexual politics. In Hyun-sook Kim, 'Yanggongju as an Allegory of the Nation: The Representation of Working-Class Women in Popular and Radical texts', in Kim and Choi, *Dangerous Women*, pp. 175-201.

57. Luisa Passerini, *Fascism in Popular Memory* (Cambridge: Cambridge University Press, 1987); *idem*, 'Women's Personal Narratives: Myths, Experiences, and Emotions', in Personal Narrative Group (ed.), *Interpreting Women's Lives: Feminist Theory and Personal Narratives* (Bloomington: Indiana University Press, 1989), pp. 189-97.

58. Juvenal, *Satire*, 16.

summoned in court he had a great advantage over civilian plaintiffs and defendants. The prospects of a civilian were no better even when the soldier was the defendant: the judge was a centurion, and the trial took place in the military camp, circumstances which tended to intimidate and deter potential witnesses. Even if the civilian plaintiff proceeded in a suit against the soldier, he/she was wasting time and faced suffering even worse injury.[59] From Juvenal's conclusion that 'It would be easier to find a witness to perjure himself against a civilian than someone to tell the truth against the interest and honor of a soldier',[60] J. Brian Campbell epitomizes the twofold privilege of Roman army: 'the ability of the soldier to avoid the impartial process of law by being in the military camp with his own comrades, and a civilian's reluctance to face up to soldiers who had a superior status'.[61] From this historical point of view, if the adulterer was a Roman soldier (as we might assume), the Pharisees, scribes, and even Jesus could not do anything to accuse him because he, as a powerful patron, was beyond their control. In a patriarchal society, woman has thus been simply the ground on which competing views of tradition or national identity are debated. In other words, it was only as a site of (im)purity that she was brought to the debate scene in order that the legitimate authority of the colonized Israel might be contested.

IV

For males, this Janus-faced tradition means the conservation of their own tradition and protection from the Others. But for females, it represents an enervating and disabling constraint. So the stereotypical dichotomy between a good woman (e.g. mother or sister) and a bad woman (e.g. whore or adulteress) is used to generate symbols of identification or denunciations in a nationalist discourse. The woman who accepts the role of mother or wife is valorized whereas the 'hybrid' woman who has contacts with 'other ethnic' men becomes the site of cultural corruption and is usually posited as a 'whore'.[62] Nationalist rhetoric thus marginalizes the 'hybrid' woman by deriding her as immoral. Without being aware of the nationalist rhetoric embedded in the Johannine narrative,

59. Juvenal, *Satire*, 16.7-9, 16.13-15, 16.36-38, 16.42-44.
60. Juvenal, *Satire*, 16.32-34.
61. For a more discussion of 'the soldier in court', see J. Brian Campbell, *The Emperor and the Roman Army 31 B.C.–A.D. 235* (Oxford: Clarendon Press, 1984), pp. 254-63.
62. Kim, 'Uncovering her Wickedness', pp. 74-78; Neluka Silva, 'Mother, Daughters and "Whores" of the Nation: Nationalism and Female Stereotypes in Post-colonial Sri Lankan Drama in English', *JGS* 6 (1997), pp. 269-76.

traditional interpretations of Jn 7.53–8.11 have coopted with patriarchal ideology in the text by simply closing the text: as a result, the identity of the adulterer has not been questioned while the woman has been treated as only an object to be forgiven by Jesus' mercy and wisdom.

As Homi K. Bhabha insists, however, 'hybridity' can be envisioned as empowering for a woman's subjectivity because it has the potential to destabilize any form of authority: 'Hybridity moves away from the singularities of race, class and gender as primary and organisational categories and has resulted in an awareness of multiple subject-positions, of race, gender, generation, institutional location, geopolitical locale or sexual orientation.'[63] Bhabha's insightful observation on 'hybridity' is well expressed in Ronyoung Kim's novel *Clay Walls*. In her novel, Kim not only criticizes the irony of (Korean) male's clinging to the Janus-faced tradition but she also offers a hybridity as an empowering site for a woman.

> Her country had fought for its own seclusion, struggling against the penetration of eastern invaders and western ideology. A futile struggle, she thought. Korean walls were made of clay, crumbling under repeated blows, leaving nothing as it was before. Chun has wanted a wall around their house in L.A. Haesu [Chun's wife] remembered, and she had ridiculed him.[64]

When Chun wants to 'put up a fence or wall of some kind' just because he was used to having 'a closed clay wall' around his house in Korea, Kim describes the futility of his clinging to his tradition by contrasting his wife's preferring for 'an open space' (a hybrid space). In the struggle of the displaced, the 'clay walls' to which Chun clings fails to protect him whereas his wife survives successfully, and furthermore she bequeaths her heroism to her children.

As Haesu prefers the open space to the closing wall, I, in order to open the text, have conducted an intercontextual reading from a post-colonial perspective, which applied the social memories of voiceless women to the story of the woman caught in adultery. In so doing, I have attempted to release her body from its imprisonment as a site of cultural (im)purity, and to reclaim it as a site of resistant reading (a site of hybridity) to both the internal disease of patriarchal nationalism (Jewish) and the external disease of colonialism (Roman), which have both been influential on the formation of the text as well as on its interpretations. As Mieke Bal states, 'cultural memorization is an activity occurring in the present in which the past is continuously modified and redescribed and

---

63. Homi K. Bhabha, *The Location of Culture* (New York: Routledge, 1994), p. 1
64. Ronyoung Kim, *Clay Walls* (Sag Harbor, NY: Permanent Press, 1986), p. 103.

on which the future is based'.[65] For the sake of a feminist biblical interpretive task of which the purpose is to claim woman's subjectivity, therefore, we need not only to relieve the woman from the infamous title of
'adulteress' but also to restore the voices of women silenced in the text as
well as in our contexts.

65. Mieke Bal, 'Introduction', in Bal *et al.*, *Acts of Memory*, p. vii.

Border-crossing and its Redemptive Power in John 7.53–8.11: A Cultural Reading of Jesus and the *Accused*

LETICIA A. GUARDIOLA-SÁENZ

Introduction

'Cultural texts do not simply reflect history, they make history and are part of its processes and practices.'[1] The Bible, like any other cultural text, can be studied not only as an archaeological piece that *reflects history* and ideological traces of its time, but also as a text that *makes history* as it does its ideological work.

The influence of the Bible in the formation of Western thought epitomizes the potential that cultural texts have to make histories and conceive ideologies. This influence, however, is not unilateral. The Bible has certainly influenced deeply the history and ideology of the Western world, but equally important has been the influence of the Western world in the history and ideology of biblical interpretation. So closely intertwined are the Bible and the Western thought that it is difficult to conceive one without the other. Because of this 'dangerous liaison' the Bible cannot be read innocently, as a distant text that narrates experiences of a people from the past, as a story detached from our realities. To understand its active role as a text that has made and makes history and ideology in our culture, the biblical text needs to be studied in both its socio-historical conditions of production and its socio-historical conditions of consumption.[2]

---

1. J. Storey, *Cultural Studies and the Study of Popular Culture: Theories and Methods* (Athens: University of Georgia Press, 1996), p. 3.

2. The hybrid reading approach I am proposing in this article has its basis in cultural studies, a critical perspective highly informed by Marxism with a particular interest in the patterns of cultural consumption (see Storey, *Cultural Studies*, pp. 3-7). Within this particular approach, the act of reading is performed dialogically. The reader engages the text in conversation, acknowledging and scrutinizing both the socio-historical context in which the text was written (produced), and the socio-historical conditions in which the text is read (consumed) and interpreted. From this

A text is never read in a vacuum. Every time that a reader encounters a text, a cultural process is set in motion. The act of reading or 'consuming' texts is a cultural practice that exposes the relations of power and politics involved in all cultural transactions aiming at producing meaning. Readers are not disinterested; every reader has a particular agenda which evidences her/his political engagement in society and influences the ways in which texts are read, interpreted, transmitted and used to *make history* and *ideology*.

In some instances, however, there are readers who believe they are immune to our human 'subjectivity' and to the influence of cultural processes. The wide use of the historical-critical method—praised for its objectivity and universality—as the main reading approach to the Bible among Western male scholars proves the point. They have monopolized and manipulated academia in the last decades with the myth of the text-as-window to the past. Blinded, perhaps, by the symbiotic existence of the Bible and their Western thought they seem to overlook the cultural fibers of their readings. Consciously or unconsciously, they hide their agendas under their supposed objective view which can retrieve the 'original' and 'proper' meaning of the text.

Postmodernity, however, has launched into academia, together with new readers and readings, different approaches that reflect the changes of a world that, after all, has always been inhabited by many worlds. The collapse of the latest empires brought to trial the subtle readings that nourished the expansionist spirit of the Christian world. Readings that once were regarded as universal and objective, *reflecting the history* of the text, were later proven to be socially constructed.

In the end, the West has been found guilty of reading the biblical text subjectively, *making history* according to its imperialistic and patriarchal agendas. Today, the exposé of Western subjectivity vindicates the marginalized voices previously dismissed as subjective, non-scholarly readings.

Gradually, the presence of minority voices from the Two-Thirds World doing biblical criticism in the US arena has been increasing. But there are still very few methodological approaches that engage the presence of non-Western subjects and their cultural contexts as seriously as one time the supposedly objective readers were taken. Therefore, the aim of this essay is twofold: first, to present a cultural, regional reading of Jn 7.53–

perspective, the history of scholarship on the biblical text can be examined as the history of consumption (readership) of the text at different points in times, under different cultural circumstances, performed by readers from different social locations with particular perspectives and ideologies.

8.11 from the hybrid experience of a bicultural Mexican-American subject from the borderlands, living in the diaspora; and second, to begin theorizing and systematizing the elements of a reading strategy aimed at empowering minority readers as agents of historical change in the ongoing process of decolonization and liberation of the Two-Thirds World.

This cultural, regional reading of 'Jesus and the Accused' in John 7.53–8.11, represents only an alternative reading, which is by no means objective or universal. Rather, it is an interested reading, performed by a subjective reader from the borderlands.

This essay is developed in five steps. First, I briefly review the old and new critical paradigms at work in biblical criticism as a theoretical framework. Second, I map my hybrid, border identity under 'Cultural Studies and Border Theory' as the basis for my reading strategy. Third, I survey some of the cultural conditions that launched the production of Jn 7.53–8.11. Fourth, I critically read and acknowledge some of the existing interpretations of the text, entering into conversation and reading with other readers as a way of finding my own voice.[3] And finally, I present a reading of 'Jesus and the Accused' from my border perspective, concluding with some remarks on the political ramifications of border-crossing practices.

Mapping Biblical Criticism:
Old and New Territories

Four main critical paradigms have dominated biblical scholarship in the past 25 years: historical criticism, literary criticism, social-scientific criticism and cultural studies.[4] The emergence of these four paradigms can be broadly explained as a direct result of historical and social changes. Particularly, the catalysts that have prompted the shift in paradigms have been the roles that culture and experience have played in reading strategies.[5] As readers have gradually come to recognize the inevitable influence of culture and experience in their readings, they have equally

3. Regarding the importance of acknowledging and affirming the legitimacy of other readings see D.M. Patte, *Ethics of Biblical Interpretation: A Reevaluation* (Louisville, KY: Westminster/John Knox Press, 1995), pp. 113-29.

4. See F.F. Segovia, 'And They Began to Speak in Other Tongues: Competing Modes of Discourse in Contemporary Biblical Criticism', in F.F. Segovia and M.A. Tolbert (eds.), *Reading from This Place*. I. *Social Location and Biblical Interpretation in the United States* (Minneapolis: Fortress Press, 1995), pp. 1-32.

5. Segovia, 'They Began to Speak', pp. 1-32.

come to admit the non-universal view of their perceptions. As a consequence of this process of subjectivization—humanization of the readers—the focus of their approaches has evolved. They have moved from the illusory objectivity inherited from the Enlightenment to the chaotic subjectivity of the *flesh-and-blood-readers* of postmodernity.

First, influenced by the positivism of the nineteenth century, historical criticism focused mainly on the historical context of author and text. The reader, as objective observer, was capable of retrieving the text's original meaning in an almost scientific way. Later on, with the influence of scientific empiricism and its emphasis on semiotics, literary criticism centered on the text. The text, as a literary universe, was isolated from its context of production and studied as a coherent unity, a meaningful whole that responded to an internal structure. In this paradigm the reader is still objective, however, under particular lenses like feminist readings, she/he starts questioning her/his social location. Thirdly, under social-scientific criticism, influenced by a postmodern and fragmented postcolonial thinking, the focus starts consistently moving toward the reader. Now the reader is seen as a subject informed of her/his ability to construct meaning(s) from the text.

It is under this latest focus on the reader that the fourth paradigm of cultural studies emerges, pushing the presence of the *flesh-and-blood reader* into biblical studies. Cultural studies integrates within biblical criticism 'the questions and concerns of the other paradigms on a different key, a hermeneutical key, with the situated and interested reader and interpreter always at its core'.[6]

The evolution of the reader has been gradually changing according to the level of acknowledgment that each paradigm has given to the cultural context and experiences of the reader. Acknowledgment and evolution have come, as mentioned before, through the irruption of marginalized and minority voices in academia. By acknowledging the borders of social location, the *flesh-and-blood reader* has expanded the political horizons of her/his reading, and in so doing has exposed the hidden agendas of presumed apolitical, disengaged readers.

Regarding its political agenda, cultural studies is informed by Marxism in two aspects: first, it takes cognizance of the socio-historical conditions in which cultural texts, practices and events are produced (generated) and consumed (engaged), in order to understand their

6.   F.F. Segovia, 'Cultural Studies and Contemporary Biblical Criticism: Ideological Criticism as Mode of Discourse', in F.F. Segovia and M.A. Tolbert (eds.), *Reading from This Place*. II. *Social Location and Biblical Interpretation in Global Perspective* (Minneapolis: Fortress Press, 1995), pp. 1-17 (8).

meaning; and second, it is aware that capitalistic societies are divided unequally, and thus culture becomes a site of ideological struggle.[7]

In cultural studies, culture is defined as the texts and practices of everyday life. Since different meanings can be ascribed to the same text or practice, minority groups always resist dominant groups and their imposition of meanings. Culture is the terrain where meaning is incorporated or resisted, where hegemony can be won or lost.[8]

The reason why I am using this approach is twofold: first, as a reader I can use my cultural identity both as a hermeneutical lens and as a reading strategy; second, I can read texts from the perspective of the political dimension of everyday life. Under cultural studies, the reader participates openly in constructing meaning, because 'a text does not carry its own meaning or politics already inside itself. [T]exts do not define ahead of time how they are to be used.'[9]

By working under this umbrella paradigm of cultural studies, the text becomes the site where the socio-historical conditions of consumption (in which I read) and my social location as reader merge with the text to produce what I call a hybrid text, a *crossroads-text*. This *crossroads-text* has no fixed meaning, but has multiple meanings produced via the readers' constant readings.

Furthermore, cultural studies fosters the perspectives and realities of diverse groups, like border theory, which emerged from Chicano studies.[10] Border theory 'as analytic tool or as a privileged site for progressive political work',[11] addresses and analyzes the experiences of life in the borderlands. Although border theory has grown out of the studies of 'the hybrid culture from the Tex-Mex region,' as Russ Castronovo asserts, 'other contact zones, such as those between race and gender, or between women's writing and patriarchal canons, raise the contention

7. Storey, *Cultural Studies*, p. 3.
8. Storey, *Cultural Studies*, pp. 1-4.
9. Storey, *Cultural Studies*, pp. 6-7.
10. According to D.E. Johnson and S. Michaelsen, 'Border Secrets: An Introduction', in D.E. Johnson and S. Michaelsen (eds.), *Border Theory: The Limits of Cultural Politics* (Minneapolis: University of Minnesota Press, 1997), pp. 1-39, 'the U.S.–Mexico border [is] the birthplace, really, of border studies, and its methods of analysis' (p. 1) They also say that 'while is true that other critical discourses both implicitly and explicitly have recourse to borders—geopolitical and metaphorical—it is equally true that Chicano studies, more than any other, has refocused critical attention on the concept of the border. Chicano studies—more than ethnic studies or postcolonial studies or U.S.–Mexico border studies—has made the idea of the border available, indeed necessary, to the larger discourses of American literary studies, U. S. history, and cultural studies in general' (p. 22)
11. Johnson and Michaelsen, 'Border Secrets', p. 3.

that culture itself can be mapped only by changing margins of identity and fluctuating fringes of power'.[12]

Surrounded by cultural differences, we operate within all sorts of borders, literal and figurative.[13] Our identity is shaped not only by the limits of the borders we inhabit but also by the political ramifications of respecting or crossing those borders. In speaking of the functions of a border, Alejandro Morales says

> A border maps limits; it keeps people in and out of an area; it marks the ending of a safe zone and the beginning of an unsafe zone. To confront a border and, more so, to cross a border presumes great risk. In general, people fear and are afraid to cross borders. People will not leave their safe zone, will not venture into what they consider an unsafe zone.[14]

For Gloria Anzaldúa 'the borderlands are the privileged locus of hope for a better world'.[15] In a similar way Russ Castronovo celebrates the potential of the contact zone, but he advises us not to forget 'the trappings of power that patrol the boundaries of any area of culture'.[16] The borders, as permeable boundaries, prove advantageous not only for border-crossers, but also for the hegemonic ideologies that structure social realities.[17]

Whether we celebrate the subversiveness of border-crossers or lament the repressiveness of border patrols, it is important when reading cultural maps to 'pay attention to the borders, for it is in these uncertain regions where the landscape of politics is most susceptible to sudden change and reversal'.[18] And to better understand borders, it is vital to pay attention to border identities and the hybrid realities that emerge from the borderlands. The following is a description of some of my hybrid identity parameters for reading texts.

12. R. Castronovo, 'Compromised Narratives along the Border: The Mason–Dixon Line, Resistance, and Hegemony', in Johnson and Michaelsen (eds.), *Border Theory*, pp. 195-220 (9).

13. See R. Rosaldo, *Culture and Truth: The Remaking of Social Analysis* (Boston: Beacon Press, 1993), p. 217.

14. A. Morales, 'Dynamic Identities in Heterotopia', in J.A. Gurpegui (ed.), *Alejandro Morales: Fiction Past, Present, Future Perfect* (Tempe: Bilingual Review, 1996), pp. 14-27 (23).

15. Michaelsen, 'Border Secrets', p. 3.

16. Castronovo, 'Compromised Narratives', p. 203.

17. S. Hall, 'Gramsci's Relevance for the Study of Race and Ethnicity', *Communication Inquiry* 10 (1986), pp. 5-27 (22).

18. Castronovo, 'Compromised Narratives', p. 217.

Border/Hybrid Identity and Reading Strategy

Every reader makes sense of a text in ways in which it seems to fit her/his needs. And each reader uses the interpretive resources that better help her/him to make sense of her/his world.[19] So, as a woman from a border zone, I have chosen to read Jn 7.53–8.11 as a case of border-crossing, bringing into dialogue some aspects of the story that resemble the hybrid reality of the borderlands with its political ramifications, in the midst of an era of trans-national and multi-cultural realities.

With culture and experience as key factors for a *flesh-and-blood reader's* reading strategy, I proceed to explore my own story to ground my hybrid reading strategy.

As a Mexican woman, born and bred in the bi-cultural, neo-colonialist context of the Rio Grande Valley borderlands, and living now as a resident alien in the US, I read the Accused's story as an encounter between two *border-crossers* who defy the politico-religious, moral and cultural borders of their time.

As a child, living ten blocks from the International Bridge of Reynosa, a border zone between Mexico and the US, I grew up well informed of the historical struggle hidden (symbolically) beneath that bridge. That bridge represented the negative result of the rupture we suffered as a nation at the hands of our imperialist neighbour. But, paradoxically, it was also the source of a new connection—a hybrid culture coming out of the encounter of two worlds, one struggling for survival under economic oppression, and the other thrashing about in the waters of interventionism.

Ever since the loss of our territory, feelings of depravity and displacement have haunted our people. However, those Mexicans who ceaselessly cross the US border and succeed in obtaining a better life for themselves and their families represent the silent, gradual victories of those recovering seized territory. Regardless of all the laws and patrols to stop the immigration, the influx of border-crossers searching for a better way of life never stops.

The stubbornness of crossing the border in spite of all the failed attempts, and the ability to camouflage intentions and desires by tricking the system—like a chameleon—have become traits of this community's hybrid identity that feels at home in this ambiguous and divided life. Life in the borderlands is in constant change, from certainty to insecurity, from open lives to hidden identities. Smuggling is the ethos of

19. Storey, *Cultural Studies*, pp. 6-7.

survival. It is not just the material smuggling of goods that is at stake, but the smuggled lives of the risk-takers who dangerously cross the border-lands because, 'to survive the Borderlands you must live *sin fronteras*, be a crossroads'.[20]

Now, the old bridge of my childhood, the site of struggle, rupture and hybridity, depicts not just the broader picture of the divided identity of the Mexican-American population of the borderlands, but it is also a place for dialogue and construction from which I can assemble[21] my hybrid identity, denounce oppression, fight for justice, and call for liberation.

Through my hybrid/border subjectivity, assembled in the political grounds of neo-colonialism, I read and appropriate the texts that sur-round me as hybrid-texts, with a hybridity described by Homi Bhabha 'as the sign of the ambivalent and shifting forces of colonial power which cannot be registered at a purely mimetic level within colonial discourse but exceed it, resisting containment and closure'.[22] Likewise, I read the shifting forces of patriarchal power inscribed in Jn 7.53–8.11 as resisting containment and closure. The revolt of the Accused against patriarchy, evident in the interstices of the Johannine discourse of law and author-ity, proves the hybrid/political value of this text for liberation.

Besides using my hybridity as a reading strategy and as a strategy for survival, I also take it as a model for political change, as Homi Bhabha's hybrid moment, where 'the transformational value of change lies in the rearticulation, or translation, of elements that are neither the One nor the Other but something else besides, which contests the terms and territories of both'.[23]

From my experience as hybrid/border woman I present two basic assumptions for this proposed reading strategy from the borderlands: First, the recognition of the reader's hybridity as a way of avoiding the

20. G. Anzaldúa, *Borderlands/La Frontera* (San Francisco: Aunt Lute, 1987), p. 195.

21. *Assembling* is a very well-known word in the borderlands. One of the main sources of economic survival in the borderlands of Mexico are the Maquiladoras. In the Maquiladoras, people assemble expensive goods which they probably will never use. Maquiladoras are alienating places, not just because of the fragmented work people do, but also because of the fragmented lives they live, for members of a family work different shifts and have no chance to see each other. Maquiladoras have become a world inside the borderlands' world. People struggle daily to assemble their lives while assembling goods.

22. S. Sim (ed.), *The A–Z Guide to Modern Literary and Cultural Theorists* (London: Prentice–Hall, 1995), p. 52.

23. H.K. Bhabha, *The Location of Culture* (London and New York: Routledge, 1995), p. 28.

illusion of universal and objective readings; and also as a way of identify-ing the contesting extremes of her/his different reading axes. Second, the acknowledgment of the text as a hybrid product with different sides and positions in itself, inscribed at the moment of its production, as well as a site where multiple meanings converge and are produced in the context where the text is read/consumed.

I shall proceed now to explore the socio-cultural conditions of pro-duction of Jn 7.53–8.11 within the Johannine community.

Community and Text at the Crossroads:
Context of Production

The Bible, through the centuries, has become a hybrid, crossroads-text. It is not a hermetic self-contained narrative, but a *text* that has been read, translated, represented, interpreted and transmitted in so many ways that it is common to see it in movies/TV, to hear it in songs, to admire it in sculptures and paintings, and to perceive it in such a wide variety of other means that sometimes it is overlooked. The biblical text certainly belongs to the culture that produced it, but now it belongs to us and all the cultures that have consumed it before us, that have re-produced and re-enacted it in various ways. However, to say that the text belongs to the present, or that it is *sin fronteras* and hybrid, does not mean it is ahistor-ical. On the contrary, it is precisely the historical re-enactment of the text throughout the centuries that has emphasized its historical nature and its influence in the process of making history.

The (hi)story of the text shapes the way I read my own story, and my story shapes the way I read the (hi)story of the text. So, to appreciate the strategic value of the pericope's hybrid nature, and the Gospel of John's hybridity as a whole, it is necessary to highlight the socio-historical situation of the community that produced such a text.

According to Raymond Brown, as quoted by Craig Koester, the Gospel of John emerged from and reflects the struggles of a mixed (hybrid) community of Jews, Gentiles and Samaritans who were striving to accommodate to their different theological positions.[24] The Johannine community, constructed here as a marginal group that was expelled from the synagogue, had to deal with issues such as, 'the relationship to Judaism, with questions of self-identity, and with Christian life in a situation of minority status and some oppression'.[25] These sociological

---

24. C.R. Koester, R.E. Brown and J.L. Martyn, 'Johannine Studies in Retrospect', *BTB* 21 (1991), pp. 51-55 (53).

25. R. Kysar, 'The Gospel of John', in *ABD*, III (1992), pp. 912-31 (918). The

presuppositions are used to describe the community that produced (wrote) the Gospel of John and are an attempt to make sense of its surroundings. They also illumine my proposed reading strategy, which is to re-read the text from my hybrid community. Finally, they also help to explain the migratory nature of the Accused's story.

Although the historicity of the incident has been widely accepted as part of the Jesus tradition by most scholars, its textual location is still debatable. What is important from my perspective of border theory in this case is that the story has crossed canonical borders and seized a place in the text for more than sixteen centuries. As Gail O'Day has precisely said: 'John 7.53–8.11 is a story without a time or place, a story to be read on its own terms without sustained reference to its larger literary context'.[26] In a sense, Jn 7.53–8.11 has become a hybrid story in the midst of a Gospel that has been adopting it and rejecting it through the readings of millions of consumers (readers) who have debated the same issue. Thus, this is a *crossroads-text* that depicts the existence and survival strategies of two border-crossers living at the crossroads.

Due to the mobile nature of this pericope in the written sources, the opinions about the spacial location of the text are divided. Frederick Schilling considers the story as an *intrusion* into the original text, since the earliest manuscripts do not include it.[27] Herman Ridderbos says the story is 'a clear *interruption* and it differs sharply in language and style from John'.[28]

H. Riesenfeld explains that the reason for the late inclusion of the pericope in the Gospel of John was the strict penitential discipline at work in the early church. The tolerant forgiveness Jesus gives to the Accused was against the teachings of the church. Later, when penitential practice became more liberal, the story received acceptance in the text.[29] This incident shows how the weight of popular readership/consumption, and not the text itself, is what determines its textual borders. The

---

three most common causes used to explain the expulsion from the synagogue are: the introduction of another group of Christians into the community…, the enforcement of a formal benediction against the heretics…, [and] the destruction of the Temple in 70 CE (p. 918).

26.   G.R. O'Day, 'John', in C.A. Newsom and S.H. Ringe, (eds.), *The Women's Bible Commentary* (Louisville, KY: Westminster/John Knox Press, 1992), pp. 293-304 (297).

27.   F.A. Schilling, 'The Story of Jesus and the Adulteress', *ATR* 37 (1955), pp. 91-106 (92-93).

28.   H. Ridderbos, *The Gospel of John: A Theological Commentary* (Grand Rapids: Eerdmans, 1997), pp. 285-86.

29.   See R.E. Brown, *The Gospel According to John I–XII* (AB, Vol. 29; New York: Doubleday, 1966), p. 335; Ridderbos, *The Gospel of John*, p. 286.

hybridity of this text is evident: the borders of the text were subjected to the interests and values of the culture that consumed (read) the text.

For Rudolf Schnackenburg, the text is not from 'the original fabric of John's gospel'.[30] A similar position is taken by Leon Morris[31] and Daniel Wallace.[32] For Fausto Salvoni[33] the pericope's style is Lukan, and it is, for Eugene Nida and B. Newman who also favor the Lukan origin, an interruption of the sequence of Jn 7.52 and 8.12.[34]

Among the scholars in favor of the present location and its Johannine origins are Allison Trites[35] and Alan Johnson. The latter argues that 'the traditional and popular internal linguistic criticism of this disputed passage is not as strong as it has usually been represented'.[36] Also using linguistic theories, John Paul Heil attests that the narrative sequence in this 'masterfully dramatic story adeptly contributes to rather than disrupts the narrative flow in John 7–8'.[37]

Whether the scholars consider this pericope Johannine or non-Johannine, it is a fact that the text has assured its place in the canon by popular demand, and the choice is now ours, either to read or to reject it. Either way, our decision to accept the conditions of textual production enacts already a cultural reading. Explicitly or implicitly, our rejection or acceptance of the text shows the imprint of our cultural values, political agendas, and in sum, maps the borders of our subjectivities in the context of our cultural conditions of consumption (readership).

Reading the Story of the Accused with Others

Historically, the biblical text has proven to be powerful. The Bible has gone beyond its temporal and spatial boundaries not just for good, but

30. R. Schnackenburg, *The Gospel According to St. John*, II (New York: Seabury, 1980), p. 162.

31. L. Morris, *The Gospel According to John* (Grand Rapids: Eerdmans, 1995), p. 779.

32. D.B. Wallace, 'Reconsidering "The Story of Jesus and the Adulteress Reconsidered"', *NTS* 39 (1993), pp. 290-96 (296).

33. See F. Salvoni, 'Textual Authority for John 7.53–8.11', *Restoration Quarterly* 4 (1960), pp. 11-15.

34. B. Newman and E. Nida, *A Translator's Handbook on The Gospel of John* (New York: United Bible Societies, 1980), p. 257.

35. A.A. Trites, 'The Woman Taken in Adultery', *BSac* 131 (1974), pp. 137-46, (146).

36. A.F. Johnson, 'A Stylistic Trait of the Fourth Gospel in the Pericope Adulterae?', *JETS* 9 (1966), pp. 91-96 (96).

37. J.P. Heil, 'A Rejoinder to "Reconsidering 'The Story of Jesus and the Adulteress Reconsidered'"', *ET* 25 (1994), pp. 361-66 (366).

also for evil, including massive destruction. Because of some evil interpretations of the biblical text, many people have been erased from the
face of the earth. Others have been subjugated and oppressed for not
conforming to hegemonic, often biblically grounded, ideologies.[38] Evidently, there is more power in the way biblical texts are consumed by
readers than we would like to acknowledge. The Bible, read by a variety
of readers, has certainly been proven to be not only redemptive but also
destructive, and all the possibilities in between.

Although interpretations of the story of the accused woman might
seem harmless and might not have caused the physical extermination of
a people, the fact is they have been equally destructive since they reinforce the patriarchal, double-standard morality that oppresses women.
Analyzing some interpretations of Jn 7.53–8.11 done during the last 40
years, I would say that Johannine scholarship has explained the story of
the accused woman by using mainly two scenarios or hypothetical plots.
Not until the last decade has a third or a fourth scenario/hypothesis
joined the academic dialogue. The first interpretive scenario focuses on
God's grace and Jesus' example of forgiveness. The woman in the story
is used to show divine mercy; she is a passive recipient of God's love. The
second scenario is more interactive. God and Jesus call sinners to forgiveness, but it is still God or Jesus who has the central voice in the story.
These first two scenarios assume that the woman is guilty of adultery.
However, in the third scenario, the image of the merciful God dis-
appears. The focus is on the characters, the woman and the Pharisees,
and the equal treatment they received from Jesus. The guilt of the
woman is not the point of entry to the text. In fact, men are also confronted with their sins. Instead, Jesus is seen as sharing the experience of
being on trial together with the accused woman. In the fourth scenario,
the focus is on structural sin: that is, the patriarchal system itself. Jesus
confronts the religiosity of a patriarchal system that has kept women and
men from having a more fulfilling way of life. The following review of
scholars' interpretive scenarios shows their conclusive ideas on the main
teaching of the story, and emphasizes their approaches to the woman. In
the first scenario, focused on God's mercy, Frederick Schilling states that
the purpose of the story is to 'illustrate the principle of forgiveness, the

38. Five centuries ago, while being faithful to the endeavor of Christianizing the
New World (cf. Mt. 28.18-20), the Spaniards massacred hundreds of indigenous
people in Latin America. In the nineteenth century, the US with the myth of the
Manifest Destiny based on the ideology of God's chosen people, seized half of the
Mexican territory as their promised land. The expansionist dreams ended up in mas-
sacres. In both cases the Bible was the excuse to mask political ambitions, justifying
appropriation of lands and subjugation of peoples.

unearned grace of God'.[39] Frederick Schilling's focus on forgiveness, a word never mentioned in the story, ignores the patriarchal oppression inflicted on the woman who is an object to set Jesus on trial. Likewise, for Beverley Coleman the story is about 'our Lord's divine authority as Law-giver, the giver of the love which can save every repentant sinner and give eternal life'.[40] She ignores the woman's dehumanization by the Pharisees. The focus is on the act of repentance, which is not even clear in the story.[41]

For Bart Ehrman, 'the story has to do with Jesus' teaching of love and mercy even to the most grievous of offenders. Judgment belongs to God alone, who forgives sinners and urges them to sin no more'.[42] The woman is the 'offender,' 'urged to sin no more'. The accusers need no forgiveness, they leave free of guilt.

In the second scenario, Rudolf Schnackenburg argues that the theme of the story is not the condemnation of sin but the calling of sinners: 'Jesus accepts sinners in God's name; his will is not to judge but to save'.[43] Rudolf Schnackenburg excludes the male characters from the sinners from the scene.

For Leon Morris 'the guilty woman had as yet given no sign of repent-ance or of faith[,] what Jesus does is to show mercy and to call her to righteousness'.[44] He emphasizes the urgency to call the woman to make a 'clean break with sin,' but there is no such call to the accusers, who enforce the law that gives them the freedom to commit adultery blamelessly.

The shift to the third scenario comes with Patricia Castro. Reading from a feminist perspective, she observes that the presence of the adulterer is neither important nor needed. Jesus, as a man, has sym-bolically taken his place. The accusers 'not only want the death of the woman, but also the death of the man—Jesus'.[45] The woman and Jesus

---

39. Schilling, *The Story of Jesus*, p. 96.

40. B.W. Coleman, 'The Woman Taken in Adultery [John 7.53–8.11]', *Theology* 73 (1970) pp. 409-10 (410).

41. See also in the first scenario: R.E. Brown, *The Gospel According to John* I-XII (AB, vol. 29; New York: Doubleday, 1966), pp. 336-37; B. Lindars, *The Gospel of John* (NCB; Grand Rapids: Eerdmans, 1972), pp. 310-12.

42. B.D. Ehrman, 'Jesus and the Adulteress', *NTS* 34 (1988), pp. 24-44 (38).

43. Schnackenburg, *The Gospel According to St. John*, p. 168.

44. Morris, *The Gospel According to John*, p. 786.

45. P. Castro, 'La mujer en la pastoral de Jesús y de los fariseos', in I. Foulkes (ed.), *Teología desde la Mujer en Centroamérica* (San José: Seminario Bíblico Latino-americano, 1989), pp. 105-19 (113).

are considered equals: two law-breakers, two border-crossers who are judged equally.

Robert Maccini focuses on the woman and addresses gaps in the story that need to be questioned when he states, 'the narrator takes for granted that the woman is guilty of adultery and does not discuss background details or address tangential issues'.[46] The woman who comes into the scene as the pawn of the accusers leaves as a free person. She was silent in the story, and she had not even a chance to defend herself, but 'no one has condemned her...[and] her simple statement to that effect is her only testimony, and her testimony is true'.[47]

Gail O'Day, in her commentary on John,[48] says that the story's structure shows how Jesus' attention is equally divided between the woman and the accusers. Both are treated as social subjects and human beings at equal levels. Jesus speaks to both about their sins. Both receive the invitation to live life anew. When the male accusers dehumanize the woman, Jesus humanizes her by talking to her as equal to the men. Under Jesus' care, women and men are invited to live life anew, to become part of a new system where both are humanized by Jesus. Two years later, in her commentary on the Gospel of John, Gail O'Day inaugurates the fourth scenario. She strongly emphasizes that the story is not about the accusers' sin or self-righteousness, nor about the woman's sexual sin, but is about the structural sin. In contrast to the accusers' religious authority that Jesus challenges, 'Jesus places his authority to forgive and to offer freedom over against the religious establishment's determination of the categories of life and death.'[49] Jesus attacks what needs to be changed— the system—so that men and women can live new lives, a new vision, in a new hybrid age.

By and large, the interpretations that have prevailed in academia and in non-academic forums are the two first scenarios performed by male readers. These readers have taken the woman as sinner and have believed the testimony of the patriarchal accusers, overlooking the fact that the Pharisees are breaking the law by not bringing the adulterer to the trial. They have no regrets in using the woman, whether guilty or innocent, as bait. More work is needed in the third and fourth scenarios to bring about political change or re-articulation and transformation of

46. R.G. Maccini, *Her Testimony is True: Women as Witnesses According to John* (JSNTSup, 125; Sheffield: Sheffield Academic Press, 1996), p. 235.

47. Maccini, *Her Testimony is True*, p. 235.

48. See O'Day, 'John', in *The Women's Bible Commentary*, p. 297.

49. G.R. O'Day, 'The Gospel of John: Introduction, Commentary and Reflections', in *The New Interpreter's Bible*, IX (Nashville: Abingdon Press, 1994), pp. 496-865, (630).

the present, and with it, the fracture of the patriarchal system. Working within the fourth scenario, the proposed hybrid reading seeks to high-light the redemptive power involved in the act of crossing oppressive and tyrannical boundaries. In doing so, new ways of re-defining the bor-ders of marginalized identities will emerge, contouring new territories that invite social transformation and political change.

Crossing Borders with Jesus and the Accused: Reading for Liberation

The first step towards a liberating reading of this story is to approach the pericope with a new title. Whenever a new edition, revision or translation of the Bible is prepared, the cultural context, language, values and preferences of the scholars working on the project permeate the trans-lation of the text and the titles assigned to the pericopes. The suggestive and categorical titles given to Jn 7.53–8.11 in most translations and studies have explicitly proved the readers' common and undisputed biases about the woman's guilt. In order to treat her fairly, giving her the benefit of the doubt, I address her as *the Accused*, not the adulteress.[50] As a way of mapping my reading strategy, I have identified four general contact zones in the story in order to analyze the text from my border perspective: Spacial borders, gender/moral codes, political/religious fac-tions, and communication codes. Regarding space, there are two contact zones in the story: one is public (Mount of Olives, 8.1) and private (people's homes, 7.53), the other is sacred (temple, 8.2) and profane (other than temple). These spacial contact zones are closely related to the second contact zone of gender, which defines the cultural roles for women and men. Women and men had different spacial privileges and different moral codes. The third contact zone is that of politico-religious factions: Moses's law vs Roman ruling, the Pharisees and scribes vs Jesus and the Accused. The fourth and final contact zone is established by the communication codes of groups with their verbal and non-verbal discourses.

Beginning with Jn 7.53–8.1, the first contact zone is one of private and public space: 'Each of them went home, while Jesus went to the Mount of Olives' (7.53; 8.1). Although there is no explicit reference to the time when the people and Jesus withdrew from the scene, it can be inferred

---

50. As far as I know, the only biblical scholar who also mentions something about the bias displayed in the titles given to the pericope is Gail O'Day. See G.R. O'Day 'John 7.53–8.11: A Study in Misreading', *JBL* 111 (1992), pp. 631-40.

that it was at the end of the day, since v. 8.2 refers to the next morning. So, while the multitude from vv. 7.40-44 (and/or the group from 7.45-52)[51] seems to conclude the day in the private spaces of their homes, Jesus spends the night in an open public space, on a hill at the margins of Jerusalem. Jesus, as an alien, non-resident individual of the city, wanders outside the walls of Jerusalem.

Excluded from the private spaces of the people's homes, voluntarily or involuntarily, Jesus takes over some of the public spaces, like the Mount of Olives, and transforms them into his private space/home. He knows well enough how to use public spaces for his benefit so that, whenever he needs to hide from the mob (6.15), he almost becomes invisible, crossing among them without being harmed (8.59, 10.39). According to Renato Rosaldo, 'Immigrants and socially mobile individuals appeared culturally invisible because they [are] no longer what they once were and not yet what they could become.'[52] This is shown in Jesus' life through John chs. 1 to 11. Culturally, as a heavenly immigrant (6.38), Jesus becomes invisible for those who seek to arrest him (7.30). He is no longer what he was with God, and he is not yet what he would become later on. Through the signs he performs, the people begin to believe in him (2.23) and the authorities realize that Jesus is a menace to their culture. He is a powerful leader who could fracture their authority (11.45-53). His presence and identity, although still hybrid, will no longer be invisible to the law-enforcers and the culture's border-keepers. Jesus' hybrid identity helps him survive while crossing borders and moving across frontiers in his subversive acts of creating transformative spaces. In the end, when his hour comes, he will pay a high price for his behaviour as a border-crosser. The next day Jesus comes back to the temple (8.2), the sacred place he has adopted as his teaching space. In the Gospel of John, where the believing community is depicted as a marginal group, Jesus has no synagogue in which to teach. The fact that synagogues, the common forums of Jesus' teaching in the Synoptics, are replaced by the temple in the Gospel of John reveals the tension of a community expelled from the sacred space of the synagogue. This event shaped and moved the Johannine community to construct a Jesus who inhabits not just the margins of the city, but who teaches out of the borders of the sacred place of the

51. When the narratives in 7.45-52 and 7.40-44 are read as separated, but simultaneous stories, verse 7.53 becomes the perfect link between verses 7.44 and 8.1. The narrative ends with the typical Johannine way of concluding conflict scenes (cf. 6.15, 'he withdrew again...'; 8.59, 'Jesus hid himself and went out...'; and 10.39, 'he escaped...'). Reading v. 7.44 as the conclusion of a conflict scene brings a smoother continuity between vv. 7.44 and 7.53, than the one between vv. 7.44 and 8.12.

52. Rosaldo, *Culture*, p. 209.

synagogue, proclaims himself as the temple (2.21), and in fact advocates for an in-between and different worship space (4.21). Living on the fringes of their religious community, the Johannine community re-creates its story in search of its new identity as border people. Its struggles and conflicts are personified in the Johannine Jesus, who creates alternative spaces out of the traditional sites. Jesus, the border-crosser who has come from above, becomes the model for survival in the hostile world which the Johannine community inhabits. Suddenly, the alternative space Jesus opened for all who come to receive his teachings, is invaded (8.3). Those who dare to cross the oppressive boundaries of the system and liberate others by teaching them how to cross those borders, live in constant risk. Thus, the scribes and the Pharisees irrupt into the scene and break Jesus' teaching discourse by imposing their own discourse (8.3-5). Their discourse makes clear that several borders are at stake in this scene, and that care is needed to ensure the borders and the system's order. Scott Michaelsen puts it this way: 'the "border" is always and only secured by a border patrol'.[53] If imposed borders were meant to benefit all the subjects in contact zones equally, there would be no need to secure them; everybody would respect them. The Pharisees, 'ever-watchful and suspicious adversaries of Jesus',[54] know they need to rise as the *border patrol*, ready to secure the benefits of their gender, religious group, and authority. They need to watch over the borders of gender/moral codes established by patriarchy and supported by their interpretations of Moses's law; they have to defend their teaching authority (12.42), which is being threatened by the marginal presence of Jesus' new teachings; and they must secure their political power (endorsed by the chief priests' allegiance with the Roman empire)[55] which is being menaced by Jesus' subversive power.

The Pharisees and scribes bring along with them a woman whom they say has been caught in adultery, and therefore deserves a punishment. They have come to defend the territory that patriarchy has granted them, and do not hesitate to cross personal borders and invade the private space of the woman's house to bring her to trial. Several pieces are missing in the puzzle: Who found the woman and where? Where is the adulterer? Where is the husband? These are some of the timeless questions scholars have been debating without definite answers, for there are several loose strings in the scene.[56]

53. Michaelsen, 'Border Secrets', p. 1.
54. A.J. Saldarini, 'Pharisees', *ABD*, V (1992), p. 297.
55. Saldarini, 'Pharisees', p. 296.
56. For legal details on the arrest and historical considerations on adultery in first-

Scholars have found several reasons to speculate whether the woman was married, and therefore deserved to be punished.[57] Married or not, the fact is that she is there by herself. The adulterer has run away from the consequences of his actions (cf. Deut. 22.22-24), and there is no husband fighting to get her back. Maybe, as Duncan Derrett says, he was the one who arranged the situation to intentionally catch her and benefit somehow from it.[58]

After arresting the woman, the scribes and the Pharisees come to trap Jesus and defend the borders of their religious authority to rule and teach according to Moses' law. They call him 'Teacher,' preparing him to be interrogated and make him prove himself as such. Then the *border patrol* informs Jesus that the arrested woman is accused of crossing the borders of her marriage. By disobeying Moses' law, the woman is practically defying patriarchy's power to control her body and will. The interrogation begins: What do you say? What should we do with such a woman? You know that Moses' law commands us to stone 'such women'. By using the woman as a pawn, they want to trick Jesus and make him confess that he, like her, is also a border-crosser, so that they can accuse him. Likewise, the US immigration patrol uses illegal border-crossers (particularly from Latin America) to catch others in similar situations in order to deport them to their place of origin, once they have confessed where they came from. The Pharisees have cornered Jesus and they are asking him to confess his *place of origin*, just like the border patrol asks the border-crossers. In order to *deport him to where he belongs*, they need to know where is he coming from and whose side is he going to take. They want to know where he belongs. They need to know if he is one of them or if he is against them.

Jesus and the woman are on trial for trespassing boundaries. The Pharisees are expectant, waiting for Jesus' response which will decide his destiny as well as hers. Many possible responses can be concluded from their opening question. Which one do they expect to hear? Evidently, they are looking for one in particular since, 'they said this to test him' (8.6). They could be testing his subversiveness, his knowledge of the law, or his ability to teach. Allison Trites says that the Pharisees see Jesus as a lawbreaker,[59] that is why they go to him with a question regarding

century Christianity, see J.D.M. Derrett, 'Law in the New Testament: The Story of the Woman Taken in Adultery', *NTS* 10 (1964), pp. 1-26.

57. See Schnackenburg, *Gospel According to St. John*, p. 164; Morris, *Gospel According to John*, p. 782 n. 15; Nida and Newman, *Translator's Handbook*, p. 259.

58. See Derrett, 'Law in the New Testament', p. 4.

59. Trites, 'The Woman Taken in Adultery', p. 146.

the law. They want to test him and *catch him in the very act of breaking/ crossing the law*.

According to the historical construction of the story's context, the Sanhedrin no longer had the power of execution under the Roman empire. The trap becomes evident: no matter what Jesus says, he will be wrong. He is between two dangerous borders, the religious border of the Mosaic law, which he will violate if he is in favor of the woman, and the political border of the Roman empire, which he will violate if he orders them to stone her.

Jesus remains silent. His discourse, which is a subversive, liberating message, has been invaded by the Pharisees' discourse of punishment, violence and death. He opens a space of silence between his discourse and theirs when he writes in the dust.[60] It is a space of transformation, a hybrid moment in which they are invited to re-define their own borders, and let the others define their own borders too. In the meantime, the woman is still standing there like a wall in the midst of the crowd, demarcating the borders between Jesus and the Pharisees.

Facing such a wall and listening to the intensity of Jesus' silence, the men are confronted with the validity of their male system. They, like the men in most Mediterranean cultures at the time, are the ones 'responsible for the shame of their women which is associated with sexual purity and their own honor derives in large measure from the way they discharge their responsibility'.[61] However, in this scene there is only an abandoned woman, who is considered by the patriarchal system as someone 'not self-contained, with personal boundaries diffuse and permeable',[62] who stands by herself with no responsible husband fighting for his honor. She is accused of bringing shame to the male system by not living within the established boundaries.

Women were not considered as autonomous beings, self-defined or self-bordered. Therefore, borderless as they were, they had no way to negotiate their existence as equal human beings. Paradoxically, this

---

60. Several versions have circulated about Jesus' writing in the dust, but none of them offers convincing evidence of what Jesus wrote. See Schnackenburg, *The Gospel According to St. John*, pp. 165-66; Derrett, 'Law in the New Testament', p. 19. I agree with the basic idea that 'if what Jesus wrote on the ground had been of importance as far as the account itself is concerned, doubtless the author would have included it' (Nida and Newman, *Translator's Handbook*, p. 260).

61. D.D. Gilmore, 'Introduction: The Shame of Dishonor', in D.D. Gilmore (ed.), *Honor and Shame and the Unity of the Mediterranean* (Washington, DC: American Anthropological Association, 1987), pp. 2-21 (4).

62. C. Delany, 'Seeds of Honor, Fields of Shame', in D.D. Gilmore (ed.), *Honor and Shame*, pp. 35-48 (41).

borderless woman, incapable of mapping out her own identity because her body/territory has been occupied by patriarchy, becomes the metaphorical border between the Pharisees and Jesus. The Pharisees compel Jesus to continue overriding the woman's borders, those they have erased by dehumanizing her and treating her as an object 'to achieve narcissistic gratifications and dominance over other men'.[63] They want Jesus to trespass this woman's will, to ignore her voice, and deny her the chance of breaking out from the oppressive system. If Jesus condemns her, his decision will help the Pharisees to keep their patriarchal privileges, and therefore they will control him and confine him to their borders.

The Pharisees insist on breaking his silence, ignoring the first moment of transformation that Jesus is giving them (8.7). Jesus responds to their shock: 'Let anyone among you who is without sin be the first to throw a stone at her.'[64] There is silence again (8.8), the second hybrid moment. The silence between discourses is a possible interstice to subvert their oppressive system; for them to reflect, transform and break the patriarchal ideology behind their actions.

Unlike those who were afraid to oppose the empire at the expense of their little power, Jesus, having nothing to lose, speaks subversively against the imperial control by telling them, *go ahead, stone the woman, do it*. Even though he lives under Roman jurisdiction he dictates his sentence under the Jewish law. This assertion sounds as if Jesus, by responding positively to the Pharisees' demand, was being insensitive to the woman and was in complete agreement with the law. However, from the border, his response indicates that he does not subscribe to the Roman empire. The empire does not define the limits of who Jesus is; he decides on his borders and constructs his identity. And by the same token, he reveals that he is not subscribing to Moses's law. Jesus offers them a new alternative, a middle ground between their discourses. If they want to follow the law, they can do it; but they need to fulfill the whole law first and obey every single detail in order to be fair. Jesus pushes them to realize that their system is collapsing: first, because they themselves are not respecting the borders they seek to secure; and second, because their interpretations of the law are co-opting the Other's

63. Gilmore, 'Introduction', p. 4.

64. According to Nida and Newman, Jesus was referring to Deut. 17.6-7, 'a person could not be given the death penalty apart from the testimony of two or three witnesses. They were to throw the first stones at the condemned person' (p. 261). But Jesus offers a different interpretation of the law, challenging the system by ironically stating that only a witness who himself is sinless may be the first to throw the stone, implying the need of a new way of life.

opportunity to define her borders and map her own identity. Any system that takes away individuals' privilege of defining their own borders and identities, is an oppressive system.

The teaching space that Jesus opens (8.9), and the hybrid moment provided by his spoken and silent discourses, overcome the Pharisees' intrusion, suppressing their discourse of violence and death. Unable to relinquish their privileges, but aware of their fault in nullifying the borders of the Others—the women—the scribes and Pharisees get out of the hybrid transformative territory Jesus opened. Like the adulterer who fled from the consequences of his action, one by one the accusers disappear silently, running away from their false discourse of righteousness.

Ironically, the leaders who expelled the Johannine community from the sacred space of the synagogue, are expelled by their guilt from the sacred border/space. The space is empty, and only Jesus and the woman remain in that new space, a site for the new community that is 'neither the One, nor the Other, but something else besides which contests the territories of both'.[65] It is one of the sites where the hybrid community of Jesus begins to emerge. By defining the identity borders of those who are willing to live at the crossroads, Jesus begins to map the borders of his new hybrid community. The two border-crossers are left alone, face to face. At a moment when she could have run away like the Pharisees did, the Accused decides to stay. Perhaps she is innocent and has nothing to fear, or maybe she, like Jesus, is tired of the system and wants to change it.

Jesus finally speaks to the Accused (8.10). The woman whose space was invaded, accused, silenced and publicly exposed by the Pharisees and their oppressive system, is now privately addressed by Jesus. She is asked to speak for herself. Freed from her accusers and their criminal charges, she is now invited to the sacred space Jesus offers to those who, oppressed by the structures, are looking for liberating alternatives. The Pharisees and their male system were not treating women as separate entities, as subjects with their own borders who deserved to be respected equally. In addressing the Accused as equal to the Pharisees, Jesus gives her the opportunity to express herself and her identity; to build her own borders, and to reclaim the territory of her body for herself.

'Has no one condemned you?' Jesus asks the woman. And for the first time in the story the woman is enabled to express herself, 'No one, sir' (8.11). She is accused, but not condemned. Jesus releases her from that predicament then respectfully acknowledges her presence and invites

65. Sim, *A–Z Guide*, p. 50.

her to speak for herself. Through the dialogue, 'the potential of borders in opening new forms of human understanding'[66] becomes real for the woman. Only with self-determined borders can respectful dialogue take place and fair demarcation of identities can come true.

The inhabitants of contact zones are at risk of extinction when their particular cultures exist in isolation. It is only through interdependent relationships that such contact zones can save their particular elements and, therefore, the identity and borders of their inhabitants. For borderland subjects, 'salvation involves increasing attention to border crossing: a kind of coming to consciousness of proliferating psychological crossing'.[67] This is part of the salvation that Jesus is granting to the woman, the Pharisees and the rest of the crowd; the realization that contact zones such as gender can only be constructive through interdependency. Crossing systemic borders in order to allow the Other to *assemble* the borders of her identity is the only way in which salvation and liberation can come for all the inhabitants of the borderlands. The scribes and Pharisees do not want to see the redemptive power of bordercrossing which Jesus demonstrates as a possibility for a new way of life. They are certainly crossing the system's borders, but for their own benefit. When Jesus challenges them to subvert the system that oppresses them through their isolation, they refuse to do so and therefore miss the salvation and the opportunity to live in balanced interdependence with the Other.

The Accused is now a free woman. Jesus tells her 'Neither do I condemn you. Go your way, and from now on do not sin again' (8.11). The accusers who had come with a self-righteous attitude end up being accused by their own consciousness and silence and are still bounded to their systemic/institutional sins. They refuse to give up their oppressive borders and miss their chance for transformation. The woman, on the other hand, is freed from the sins of the system, and is told not to return to it; not to sin again by entering into relationships that are dictated by an oppressive and dehumanizing system. She is now a free human being, redeemed and called by Jesus to become a border-crosser in search of new and better ways of life. The Accused, like all the other 'border crossers [who] create new myths...provide[s] radical alternatives to the existing social structures'.[68]

66. Rosaldo, *Culture*, p. 216.
67. Michaelsen, 'Border Secrets', p. 11.
68. A.L. Keating, 'Myth Smashers, Myth Makers: (Re)Visionary Techniques in the Works of Paula Gunn Allen, Gloria Anzaldúa, and Audre Lorde', *Critical Essays: Gay and Lesbian Writers of Color* 26 (1993), pp. 73-95.

By redeeming the border-crosser, Jesus the border-crosser becomes not just the new myth for radical alternatives, but also the new ethos of survival for those who strive for a better world.

Final Remarks

In his broader context, the Johannine Jesus seems to live between borders, in a hybrid space which is an experience similar to that of Hispanics/Latin Americans in the postcolonial and neo-colonial era. Jesus, *the border-crosser*, the traveler between cities and villages, between heaven and earth, between suffering and bliss, comes to redeem the *border-crosser* who refuses to conform to the limits and borders of a society that has ignored her voice, her body and the borders of her identity as the Other.

The hybrid moment of transformation perceived in the story of the Accused is an affirmative statement of the redemptive power involved in the border-crossing behavior. The borders traced in the story become the sites of transformation for the future that emerges in the in-between of the present needs. By confronting the Pharisees and addressing the accused woman, Jesus brings a past of oppressive traditions and a silent present of subversiveness into an 'in-between space that innovates and interrupts the performance of the present'.[69] The new identity of the accused woman announces the interstitial creativity of the future: freed from the oppressive borders of the system, she is sent as a border-crosser, a model for building the future of the hybrid Johannine community and a model for a better life.

On his part, Jesus, the hybrid being par excellence in John's Gospel, contests all contact zones. He removes the structures that have been adopted by those in power and acts in ways that respond to a reality different from the one in which he is located. He is a model of transformation for those readers who, like him, live in the interstices, the in-between, and who look for a political change to alter reality. Reading and inhabiting the interstices that the Johannine Jesus reveals in the text opens the opportunity to trigger a hybrid moment for a political change. It is an invitation to re-articulate or translate the elements of the contact zones which are neither the One nor the Other, but *something else besides* as Homi Bhabha explains, giving way to the transformational value of change.

The relationship of Jesus and the Accused opens some redemptive possibilities for all border-crossers who are looking for another way of

---

69. Bhabha, *The Location of Culture*, p. 7.

being out of the traditional and oppressive boundaries of the present society.

As a Mexican-American I read the story of the Accused as a hybrid subject, living an experience of conflicting border zones like the experience of John's community. In its need for affirmation in a transitional process, the Johannine community constructs a narrative that can help them accept their new identity. The excluded community that once belonged to the official religious institution is now being confronted with the system. They have to decide to go in silence and do nothing to change the system, or be free from condemnation, and be aware of the oppressive borders that need to be transgressed in order to create alternative spaces for liberation.

Building toward 'Nation-ness' in the Vine: A Postcolonial Critique of John 15.1-8

ZIPPORAH G. GLASS

The first stage of a process of de-scribing Empire is to analyze where and how our view of things is inflected (or infected) by colonialism and its constituent elements of racism, over-categorization, and deferral to the centre... The post-colonial is especially and pressingly concerned with the power that resides in discourse and textuality; its resistance, then, quite appropriately takes place in and from the domain of textuality, in (among other things) motivated acts of reading.[1]

Purpose and Argument

This essay employs a postcolonial critique of the modern nation-state's constructs of citizenship and assimilation as a strategy for resisting those discourses in biblical texts. Those discourses constitute a disposition of power along with their warrants for access to power through processes of homogenization. When viewed through this reader's heterogeneous identity, configured in categories of nationality and race, the text of the Fourth Gospel is no exception to the modern nation-state's construct of citizenship. Thus, this essay argues that the discourse of power in Jn 15.1-8 advances a construct of citizenship for establishing positions of inclusion and exclusion. This construct configures nation-ness[2] and assimilation as a selective reduction in diversity in order to found a larger and more dominant homogenized identity similar to that needed in the act of modern nation-building.

The Postcolonial Project

The postcolonial project is most often associated with discourses of the 'other', the 'liminal' and the 'marginalized'. However, if the postcolonial

---

1. Chris Tiffin and Alan Lawson (eds.), *De-scribing Empire: Post-colonialism and Textuality* (London: Routledge, 1994), pp. 9-10.
2. The term 'nation-ness' is borrowed from Benedict Anderson, *Imagined Communities: Reflections on the Origin and Spread of Nationalism* (London: Verso, 1983), p. 16.

project is to be more than an articulation of 'periphery', it must include a re-inscription of heterogeneity that will displace those strategies—which in the past and in the present—have characterized Empire. Thus, the postcolonial project may be conceived not only as a project of de-scribing Empire, but also as re-inscribing its heterogeneous progeny. This is nowhere more true for the postcolonial project than in de-scribing the modern nation-state's constructs of citizenship as member-ship in the nation and assimilation as reduction to the nation. Finally, the postcolonial project must de-scribe the effect of these constructs on discourses of power in enterprises of homogenization.

This Reader

For a person like me, constructing citizenship by becoming a member in a national body of people seems curious. I have moved from a position of multiple jeopardy configured in the nationality and race of one nation, to occupying a precarious position inside another nation-power as defined by DuBois.[3]

I was rescued from occupied, post-Second World War Germany (a nation pervasively marked by National Socialism in its recent past), where a synthesis of African and German *Blut* (blood) was met with the scornful cry of *Mischling* (half-breed). My adopted father, having lived abroad to escape his own questionable status as an American Negro, quickly moved to begin the process of bestowing the rights and privi-leges of citizenship on what was now his *braunkohle* (brown coal) daugh-ter. Ironically, these were the very rights and privileges that he himself had been denied in his country of birth. As a result of his work, today I am no longer Afro-deutsch, but an African American.

Within the paradigms of the modern nation-state, citizenship and assimilation are often constructed as a legitimizing union, having the ability to bestow the privilege of access to power. But in the experience of persons of African descent who live in the modern nation-states of Germany and the United States, these constructs are a part of the discursive practices of nation-building. These constructs sustain the marginalization of heterogeneous identities while simultaneously setting the parameters of power and the privileges of access to power in homo-genizing enterprises.

3. W.E.B. DuBois, 'The Souls of Whitefolk', in *Darkwater: Voices from within the Veil* (New York: Schocken Books, 1920), p. 49.

Citizenship: The Politics of Exclusion and Inclusion

The construct of citizenship, for the purpose of this essay, occurs within the discursive space of polity. Throughout history, the task of many modern nation-states has been to metamorphose heterogeneous identities within their geographical borders (irrespective of social or economic inequalities), into a unified people, sharing the same historical symbols and pursuing the same national interests. This unity is needed to keep alive the ideal of a national identity.

The need for unity accompanied the historical developments that gave rise to the modern nation-state. The formation of the nation-state was attended by the emergence of economic and social phenomena associated with the processes of industrialization. These phenomena proclaimed the approach of modernity and its corresponding demand for standardization and uniformity, and the ideologies needed to legitimate the nation-state. However, more often than not, nation-building led to the need to turn myth into reality with a dominant nationalist ideology that expounded the existence of an integral and undivided nation.[4]

If homogenization is the core of the nationalist project, then the presence of the internal 'other' must be addressed before unity of the nation can be achieved. As Ernest Renan pointed out in his 1882 thesis, 'What Is a Nation', for a nation's identity to evolve, distinctive identities within the nation must be forgotten or repressed, thus making the ideal of a distinctive national identity the underpinning of nation-building.[5] Citizenship, that is, the making of members in the nation, is thus at the very core of national identity. But behind any process of forging a people's unity lies a process of predilection.

Citizenship implies inclusion, yet it is also exclusionary. Citizenship for certain categories of people necessarily implies the non-citizenship for others. Citizenship configured in the exclusionary categories of race, gender or class throughout the modern era bears the impression of its origin in the ancient Greek city-state. It was a privileged status from which slaves, women and aliens were excluded.

Within modern nation-states, two primary principles have acted to exclude the colonized 'other'. The principle of *ius sanguinis* (nationality by blood descent) acts formally to exclude from citizenship mostly

4.   Anderson, *Imagined Communities*, p. 75; Eric J. Hobsbawm, *Nations and Nationalism since 1780: Programme, Myth, Reality* (Cambridge: Cambridge University Press, 1990), p. 14; Ernest Gellner, *Nations and Nationalism* (Ithaca, NY: Cornell University Press, 1983), pp. 19-62.
5.   Ernest Renan, *Qu'est-ce qu'une nation* (Paris: Presses Pocket, 1992), p. 42.

immigrants and the 'mixed blood' progeny resulting from interactions between nations and 'foreign blood'. The second principle is *de facto* exclusion, where statutory citizenship does not provide for full access to the benefits of social, economic or political inclusion. *De facto* exclusion is often masked by the appearance of a cohesive socio-political context, that context being, of course, the nation-state. The dilemma that exclusionary categories and these principles generate for citizenship is typically not apparent until political, economic or social space is contested within the nation-state's dominant culture. Contesting space within nations shifts the focus of attention from overt manifestations of outside invading and colonizing forces to the progressive and subtle forces of colonization from the inside.

DuBois determined that the non-national character or ambiguous political status of colonized peoples within a nation could only be resolved when the 'master nation' (his designation for an imperialist state) 'either integrated their colonial subjects into the polity, or allowed them to become independent, free peoples'.[6] DuBois' statement places African Americans within a puzzling position. Although technically given citizenship in the 1880s, it was not until after the civil rights movement of the 1960s that selective and limited enfranchisement was attained. The historical circumstances and the continuing question of assimilation felt by many Black Americans confirm DuBois' words which prophesied that 'the black people in America are 'a nation without polity, nationals without citizenship'.[7]

In Europe, as in the United States, citizenship/membership has been amply configured by categories of race. The person of mixed African and German heritage is particularly problematic in the German construction of nation, for as early as 1952 the Social Democratic Party of Germany deemed Afro-*deutsch* children, such as myself, as 'form[ing] a special group, presenting a human and racial problem of a special nature'.[8] In a presumptive decision, a people, made up primarily of children, were reputed to be a problem to and in the nation. I and hundreds of other children like me at the time became Germany's 'internal other'. We were an existential and locational paradox, involving being and place.

6.   W.E.B. DuBois, 'The Negro and Imperialism (1944)', in Philip S. Foner (ed.), *W.E.B. DuBois Speaks 1920–1963*, II (New York: Pathfinder, 1970), p. 155.

7.   W.E.B. DuBois, 'The Souls of Whitefolk', p. 49.

8.   May Opitz, Katharina Oguntoye and Dagmar Schultz (eds.), *Showing our Colors: Afro-German Women Speak Out* (trans. Anne Adams; Amherst: University of Massachusetts Press, 1992), p. 80.

To be African and German, in the German mind, is not to be German. German nationhood, being constructed primarily on the basis of the purity of Germanic blood, makes the identity of 'half-German' inconceivable for constructing and maintaining the nation. To be German by participating in the national myth of *Blut*, however, is to hold a priority status. This status is then supported by the nation's political and social institutions, whereby one is worthy of societal benefits. To be not quite German because of African mixture means that the Afro-*deutsch* person stands on the outside of the cultural center that is considered German.

Definitions of Nation

So what exactly is a nation? Seton-Watson describes a nation as 'a community of people, whose members are bounded together by a sense of solidarity, a common culture, a national consciousness'.[9] Walker Connor, however, defines a nation as 'a group of people who believe they are ancestrally related. It is the largest grouping that shares that belief'.[10] Given that few nation-states constitute enough of a homogeneously derived population in order to subscribe to either definition, a crucial question arises. How are ethnic and racial groups within a particular territory to be molded into a nation? One answer to this question borrows from the notion of the *Staatsnation* (state-nation), which disables the need for a common culture, replacing it with the political nation formed through a people's expressed will. Under such circumstances, the individual's will comes into play and the political project of nation-building creates a capacity to transcend the particularism of the *Kulturnation*, thus maintaining the nation as a political unit common in will and purpose.[11] The political unit or 'the nation' is a universal unit, where one is abstracted from cultural particularity and difference. Such an ideal should enable the assimilation of ethnic, racial and religious minorities, but only by subjecting minorities to the dominant group's willingness to assimilate others.

9. Hugh Seton-Watson, *Nations and States: An Enquiry into the Origins of Nations and the Politics of Nationalism* (Boulder, CO: Westview, 1977), p. 1.

10. Walker Connor, as quoted in Daniel Patrick Moynihan, *Pandaemonium: Ethnicity in International Politics* (Oxford: Oxford University Press, 1993), p. 1.

11. Dominique Schnapper, *La communauté des citoyens: Sur l'idée moderne de nation* (Paris: Gallimard, 1994), pp. 83-114.

Nation-Building and the Particular: The German *Kultur*

As Habermas indicates, German national consciousness arose from a 'romantically inspired…notion of a *Kulturnation*', a nation defined by its culture.[12] In contrast to what would evolve as the American ideal, nation-building for Germany did not spring from internal impulses, but rather developed as a reaction to the conquest and restructuring of German lands under Napoleonic armies. In the nineteenth century, the ideological expression of the *Kulturnation* held sway over many parts of Germany. During the Kaiserreich (empire) and Great War (1870–1918), the battle for *Kultur* was waged figuratively and literally. Selective religious, political and ethnic minorities were targeted as hindering the unity of the German *Kultur* and experienced lengthy persecution, stereotyping, or expulsion from the empire. Between 1871 and 1914, much of German history was written in a highly nationalistic vein, particularly seeking to legitimate German dominion. Here, the question to be asked is: does the construction of a national culture in the tradition of Goethe, Schiller and Humboldt—that is German Classicism—leave space for the existence and place of minorities, or does it marginalize minorities? Perhaps history can provide an answer. For example, the unification of the German Reich by Bismarck in 1871 fulfilled the need for national identity. But by 1918, in the final days of the First World War, non-German territories of the Empire seceded to form their own nation-states. Although history may provide hints, sometimes it is not an actual guide. For example, in the 1990/91 Unification Treaty, Germany re-inscribed itself as a cultural [nation] state, thus unifying the old and the new Bundesländer. Contemporary Germany contains some of the largest communities of ethnic minorities and immigrant labor in Europe, many having been born within its borders.[13] Yet, despite the revision of citizenship laws, many do not carry German citizenship or membership.[14] The

12. Jürgen Habermas, 'Struggles for Recognition in the Democratic Constitutional State', in Amy Gutmann (ed.), *Multiculturalism: Examining the Politics of Recognition* (Princeton, NJ: Princeton University Press, 1994), p.146.

13. With the end of the first wave of immigrant labor in the 1970s and the renewed need for labor in the early 1990s, European countries utilizing such labor realized that the departure of these peoples and their families was not inevitable (Organization for Economic Co-operation and Development, *SOPEMI: Trends in International Migration. Annual Report* [Paris: OECD, 1995]), p. 202.

14. With the central objective being to secure social and political order, a majority of the Bundestag passed a bill to overhaul the German citizenship law on 7 and 21 May 1999, respectively. This substantially altered the prior body of law based upon the principle of *jus sanguinis*, 'right of blood'. The new law is modeled, in part, on

exclusion of these 'others' is reinforced by an abiding mythology of national cultural homogeneity.

Nation-Building and the Universal: The American Ideal

While the German example of 'Staatsnation' fits well within a differentialist model of nation-building, where institutions of the state minimalize the assimilation of peoples outside the mainstream of the national culture, the American model is quite different. The 'melting pot' image is still used to describe the American identity. Whereas Germany had Bismarck and its 'thinkers', America's history includes its 'founding fathers' who formed its civic ideology, and inspired a mythology that still pervades the definition of 'American' character.

The American model is, to a great degree, an assimilationist model. It envisions the incorporation of racial and ethnic minorities into the society and state through a process of individual change. This change occurs primarily when the citizen voluntarily abandons his/her distinctive cultural, social or linguistic characteristics and takes on those features that characterize the dominant group. Thus, the model minimizes the potential conflicts between the center and margins. The model, however, leaves little room for retaining distinctive values or practices, if the benefits of assimilation are to be obtained. The model presupposes that those formerly at the margin can indeed move toward the center through assimilation.

The historical process that gave rise to the American nation, however, should not be understood apart from the role of biblical texts in the hands of American missionaries. From the Great Awakening to the rise of the revivalist camp-meetings, history records many religious movements that helped form early America. Historians such as Robert Mitchell and Gregory Nobles, for example, have emphasized the importance of 'religion' as something that stimulates cohesion in the making of the nation by breaking down heterogeneity. For these historians, proclamations of the biblical text acted to unify the nation. They cite the early evangelists' abilities to bring peoples together in a common language of conversion. These historians' perspective is particularly helpful when figuring events such as the Great Awakening. They argue that such events unify Americans in a shared evangelical understanding of the Christian faith and life, creating a universal liberal sentiment and common values. For example, against this backdrop of

American citizenship law, allowing for the granting of citizenship by virtue of birth within the borders of the nation and its territories—regardless of ethnicity.

revivals came a greater sense of the 'white man's responsibility' for the plight of Indians and slaves which offered a sense of religious mission.

George Whitefield, a formidable figure in the movement of the Great Awakening, was among the first to preach to Blacks. However, as the conflict over slavery increased through the news of rebellions such as the Vesey conspiracy (1822) and Nat Turner's uprising of 1831, fear enveloped the nation. Fearing for people's lives, their property and civil peace, laws were instituted that curtailed the rights of Blacks. No longer could they assemble in public or worship in large groups. This fear and anxiety renewed the effort to make Christians of Black slaves in the hope of disarming Black rebellions, and helping them to accept their 'lot in life'.[15]

These events in American history seem far off from the nation's modern context. But from this brief sketch, one thing is clear: the American model of nation-building served to give Blacks and whites a fixed point of reference in the making of the American nation and in the making of their identities.

Configurating Nation, Identity and Assimilation

It may seem obvious that the term 'nation' is not a neutral word, and that it is often appropriated for political ends to give structure to a prescribed social world. Anderson defines the concept of nation as 'an imagined political community', with 'deep horizontal comradeship'.[16] This fellowship of sorts enables peoples, as Anderson argues, not only to kill and harm in the defense of the nation, but to be 'willing to die for such an imagining'.[17]

Anderson's theorizing of nation begins to explain why the notion of nation carried such positive and negative force in my family. My black father once swore his identity as an American with such fist pounding that I wondered why such force was needed when he seemed so sure of his own identity. Now, he is a quiet, elderly man sifting through the numerous military documents that attest to his defense of national interests, and he can finally reveal the subject that was once taboo in our household. The cumulative physical and psychological pains of

15. Robert D. Mitchell, *Commercialism and Frontier: Perspectives on the Early Shenandoah Valley* (Charlottesville: University of Virginia Press, 1977); and Gregory H. Nobles, 'Breaking into the Backcountry: New Approaches to the Early American Frontier, 1750–1800', *William and Mary Quarterly* 46 (1989), pp. 641-70.

16. Anderson, *Imagined Communities*, pp. 6-7.

17. Anderson, *Imagined Communities*, p.13.

segregation and racism placed him at odds with his national citizenship.

As Berlant notes, citizenship can act both as an inclusive and exclusionary notion, 'naming by negation juridically contested racial, gendered and class identities'.[18] Here, then, the visible markers of difference and otherness act as fixed points of reference. They can supercede any privileging of a national identity or claim of citizenship, leading only to a liminal form of membership in a symbolic nation. Thus it seems that assimilation, if obtainable, can only be achieved by 'buying' into the 'system' on the dominant group's terms. However, assimilation (the taking in of the dominant culture's icons and historical narratives) may have no effect on those occupying a liminal position in the symbolic nation. The question, finally, is who is able, and by what means is one able to assimilate into a symbolic nation?

Any carving of a national identity depends on a certain construction of space, of territory and borders within the nation. For African Americans, an essentially uninterrupted internal colonial subjugation serves to crystallize the search for a national identity from Negro, to Colored, to Black and Afro-American, and now finally to African American. These shifting identities attempt to straddle the search for a national identity and a continued status of marginality in the nation. These identities and the historical considerations specific to them reflect a complex negotiation of a place in the nation, since any structuring of membership that is necessary for a sense of belonging, is consistently withheld. Here Anderson argues that for those who occupy a peripheral position in the modern nation-state, membership is a complicated process of ideological negotiation, where statutory citizenship and fabled assimilation can prove to be cruel ideological traps.

This Reader and the Johannine Text

As a real reader of biblical texts, steeped in my own socio-cultural positions, I am keenly aware that the positions imposed on me from past and present identities (both within and between two contemporary nation-powers), affect my encounter with biblical texts. I cannot transcend these positions, nor can I feign objectivity toward the text. My encounter with the Johannine text is directly conditioned by my own positions, and I believe these positions are worth bringing to the text as reading strategies.

18. Lauren G. Berlant, *The Anatomy of a National Fantasy* (Chicago: University of Chicago Press, 1991), p. 9.

My approach to the text falls within the camp of positional criticism,[19] for I try to be conscious of the identities imposed on me, and those I perform within. Hence, my approach does not lie comfortably within formal definitions of autobiographical or reader-response criticism. It is not my purpose to narrate my personal experiences; neither is it my intent to create an implied reader of the text so as to avoid the complications of being a real reader. Instead, my primary approach is hermeneutical. I work within a framework of self-reflection where my own precarious positions frame a bi-racial and bi-cultural experience of citizenship and assimilation. My primary interest in working with the Johannine text is thus my own existential interaction with and relationship to the text.

Selection of the Text

The whole Johannine discourse from 15.1 through 16.33 creates a disjunction between the expected flow of Jn 14.31 to 18.1.[20] However, far from viewing the material of 15.1–16.33 as a digression, I see Jn 15.1-8 as a perimeter around an already well-formed center.[21] As a part of the second unit of discourse, this pericope takes up themes addressed in ch. 14: specifically, the 'indwelling' of Jesus and the Father (14.10).[22] The themes are reintroduced in John 15 as injunctions to members or branches, 'to remain' in the vine.

Proposition

Within Jn 15.1-8, I will focus on the disposition of Jesus as the 'vine', and more importantly, I will explore the warrant for membership and assimilation in the 'vine'. In reading the Gospel text, I liken 'membership' in the vine to aspects that constitute modern notions of citizenship. Here boundaries are erected by constructing and massaging categories of inclusion and exclusion. I find assimilation into the vine akin to a selective reduction in diversity in order to found a larger and more dominant homogenized group identity. I propose that at work in this text are the sort of discursive practices needed in the act of building a new nation-ness—that is, the vine.

19. See Stephen D. Moore, 'True Confessions and Weird Obsessions: Autobiographical Interventions in Literary and Biblical Studies', *Semeia* 71 (1995), p. 25.

20. Fernando Segovia, *The Farewell of the Word: The Johannine Call to Abide* (Minneapolis: Fortress Press, 1991), p. 28.

21. Segovia, *The Farewell of the Word*, p. 326.

22. Segovia, *The Farewell of the Word*, p. 24.

Homi Bhabha has noted that any people who are not 'contained within the *Heim* (home) of a national culture and its unisonant discourse...are themselves the marks of a shifting boundary that alienates the frontiers of the modern nation'.[23] Frontiers exist to define and protect the center. If, however, as Geoffrey Bennington suggests, the frontier can also be described as the region that permits the greatest contact between heterogeneous peoples, then it must of necessity be also the region where the diversities of peoples flow through the frontier's center.[24]

Imagine for a moment the Johannine community not only as a 'shifting boundary' dividing the frontiers of the Roman Empire, but also as a community that has evolved into a focal point itself, a new center, apart from even the authority of the Jewish majority; something that occupies a space within the very frontiers that it divides. The authority of that center can be strengthened in proportion to the homogenization of diverse and fluent peoples. For instance, religious faith and praxis selectively reduces the diversity of peoples characterizing the frontier to a commonality of practice, belief and custom. Here, one center (the *Heim* of a nation culture focused in the Empire and its discourse) is displaced by a Johannine center founded in the frontier. Under such conditions of displacement, the new center assimilates all diversity by expounding an imaginative political vision. This vision merges the discrete identities into one 'people' and becomes the precondition for a new building project that requires a new civic identity.

The 'Vine': A Political Vision

John 15.1-8 proclaims Jesus as the 'vine' in a political vision that unites the particular and the general, the past and the future. It also unites diverse peoples by creating a new civic identity; an identity that evokes its ideals so powerfully that a people are inspired to achieve them. The image of the vine and its branches is presented as peculiar to a place and a people, yet it represents a universal phenomenon. The branches that flow into the vine are seemingly non-essentialist categories; not fixed by notions of race, class or gender.

But a political vision formed in the confines of colonialism, one that invites membership into a new political order over and against that from

23. Homi K. Bhabba (ed.), *Nation and Narration* (London: Routledge, 1990), p. 409.

24. Geoffrey Bennington, 'The Politics and the Institution of the Nation', in Bhabha (ed.), *Nation and Narration*, p. 21.

which its membership derives, requires a dialectic of binary opposites. It demands a clear and value-laden division between the 'main' trunk and the 'other' branches. This is a clear replication of the colonial tactic. The branch's new civic identity as being 'in the vine' is constructed in opposition to the 'other', having inherited the binarism that is fundamental to the colonial situation. Consequently, 'the vine' reinforces and replicates the very categories it organizes against its own oppression.

Here, membership implies inclusion in a new polity, while identity implies recognition of common ties. But of course, membership, of necessity, also entails degrees of exclusion. Thus, in the Johannine metaphor, the definition of membership in the vine increasingly becomes embedded in a politics of identity. What is at stake is the emergence of a corporeality based on a shared political culture.

Founding the Political Body: The Vine

In the farewell discourse, the Gospel writer portrays the disciples as confused by Jesus's words (Jn 13.22; 14.5, 22; 16.17-18). To make the teachings clearer, Jesus is depicted as using the analogy of a vine (v. 1), a figure familiar in Jewish textual and cultural tradition.

In the Hebrew Bible, the nation of Israel is often likened to a vine. For example, Ps. 80.8 speaks of the Exodus story portraying Israel as a vine transplanted from the soil of Egypt to the soil of Canaan. The theme of transplanting is also evident in Ezek. 10-14. There, a vine planted in water flourishes. But a sweeping wind strips it of its fruit, and it is later transplanted in a wilderness where it is consumed by fire. In Isa. 5.1-7, the nation of Israel is equated with a vineyard that yields abnormal fruit; and in Jer. 2.21, Israel is described as a vine that becomes distorted. Clearly, by Jesus's time, the vine had become analogous with the nation of Israel.

Making Binaries: The True Vine

Jesus's relationship to his disciples is described in the symbolic language of a vine and its branches (vv. 1-2). The vine, although not a formal title for Jesus, is used as a metaphor to signify the nature of the relationship between Jesus, the disciples and the Father. Followers of Jesus are the branches in the vine, and the Father is the vine-keeper. The Gospel writer, however, declares Jesus to be the 'true' vine (v. 1).

The Greek word translated as 'true' can be understood in various senses in the New Testament. Firstly, it can be used to emphasize opposition to that which is counterfeit. Secondly, the term can be used to indicate ultimate reality. If the latter sense of the word is applied, then the Gospel writer's depiction of Jesus as the true vine may act to replace the tradition of Israel as the vine with Jesus as the fullest realization of the metaphor. But more fundamentally, the metaphor of the vine is a vehicle for juxtaposing the genuine over against the false. This then produces a binary opposition between the positions of inclusion and exclusion.

Creating Categories: Inclusion and Exclusion in the Vine

The Father is intimately involved in the relationship between the vine and the branches. The Father removes unfruitful branches or members of the vine, and reinforces those that are fruitful so that they may bear more fruit (v. 2). In this narrative, however, to be a branch is not synonymous with sure membership in the vine. Just as physical presence in the United States or Germany does not constitute constituent membership in either nation (nor is it synonymous with the privileging category of 'citizen'), so also the Johannine text opens itself up to the question of whether the portion of membership eventually defined as 'unfruitful' ever did constitute membership in the political body. The answer to the Johannine question seems to be no. Those branches, taking on an inferior status by virtue of their categorization as 'unfruitful', cannot, even for the time of their membership in the vine, lay claim to the privileges which the Father provides and secures for constituent members in the vine (v. 2).

Oddly enough, this design works as a counterpoise to the portrayal of complete dependence of the branches on the vine, where the vine supplies all sustenance to the branches. Apart from the vine, branches cannot have life. Neither can they bear fruit. It would seem, however, from the Johannine narrative that membership in the vine and sustenance from the vine do not guarantee the ability to bear fruit. Without such ability, there is no privileging of the 'cleansing' action of the Father (v. 2). In light of this textual paradox, what is the status of an unfruitful branch in the vine before it is removed from the vine?

Shaping Identity: Universalism and Particularism

Formal exclusion from membership in the political body takes place when the branch is removed from the vine. However, there is a cast of *de facto* exclusion in the text. Dimensions of *de facto* exclusion affect all members declared to be non-fruit-bearing, as with moderns who are stigmatized by race or ethnicity. This situation is, in part, a reflection of the text's portrayal of the new political body striving to achieve solidarity by internal consolidation. This solidarity is achieved by erecting *ein Feindbild*, a concept of enemy, from within the body. Hostility may then be directed against this enemy for failing to meet standards imposed on the membership. If my personal experience can serve here, such hostile actions immediately embroil a group in a politics of identity. When group identity is unstable, a politics of internal positioning is played out.

This emphasis on internal positioning is distinct from what Rensberger points to in the text.[25] For him, the Johannine community looks outside of itself to the non-Christian world for constructing the 'enemy'. Moreover, Rensberger seems to understand the Johannine community as determined to incorporate Jew and Gentile alike into a unified identity. The Johannine text does open up the possibility of a sphere of universalism that would stand above racial, ethnic and cultural particularism, one that would incorporate all the 'children of God' (Jn 1.12; 10.16; 11.52). But just as quickly, it introduces 'difference' as an exclusionary category restricted to those not meeting the definition of membership. With membership in the vine being restricted to those defined as 'fruitful', a site of privileging is created. Those excluded from membership imagine access to the franchise provided by the Father as the only recourse to their ablution. In the Johannine text, as in contemporary settings, membership in a political body implies not only inclusion, but also exclusion.

Moving Towards Homogeneity: Standards for Assimilation

In a broad sense, the fruitful branches reflect their own particular interest in the vine. The branches receive their sustenance from the vine, but such sustenance is subordinate to each branch's fulfillment of the purpose of its existence—bearing fruit. The branches have but one purpose: to produce the fruit that the vine puts forth. The fruit-bearing branches and the vine are thus in conformity with one another.

Deviation is relegated to the non-fruit-bearing branches; those outside of the experiential and historical context of the political body. Lest mentioning the removal of unfruitful branches create doubt or fear, Jesus assures the disciples that they have already demonstrated their genuineness (v. 3). This strengthens the binary opposition between what is genuine and what is false. The disciples, having been 'cleansed' (v. 3)

25. David Rensberger, *Johannine Faith and Liberating Community* (Philadelphia: Westminster Press, 1988), pp. 27-28.

by the hearing of Jesus' message (cf. 13.10), set the standard for a relationship to the message of Jesus; a relationship that permits members to remain in the vine, while simultaneously becoming the locus of historical and participatory identification in the vine. Hence, the Gospel writer inscribes the disciples as the dominant paradigm, documenting their encounter with the message of Jesus. In the impending absence of Jesus (14.30), the sharing of the disciples' experiences and history assimilates one into the cultural life of the group, thus making a homogeneous group.

To be a non-fruit-bearing branch, then, is to be spurious. And one is spurious by virtue of the failure to assimilate into the imagined experiential and historical description of the cultural center. At stake here are the norms by which constituent membership is obtained in the political body, and what it means to be a member of that body. As noted by Park and Burgess, assimilation is an interpretative process and is something that fuses with the 'memories, sentiments, attitudes' of the primary group.[26] However, in modern contexts, and likewise for this ancient text, assimilation suggests an additional criterion: that of structuring relationships. The structuring of relationships can be addressed by reflecting on the practice of the discourse. Here the possibilities of subaltern being and social location are constrained under the mark of authenticity and overridden by a discourse of the main body.

Constructing Authentication:
The Warrant of Access to Power

To be an assimilated member of the 'vine' community is to hold priority status—a status supported by the group politic, and thereby worthy of the privileges that accrue to 'authentic' membership. To be unassimilated in the vine is commensurate with standing outside of the political center of the group. Because of 'inauthenicity', the subject status and presumed unworthiness of access to benefits is upheld by those in the center.

Assimilation in the vine, however, is not a matter of simple affirmation. It must be continually asserted. A member must continually assert his or her authenticity as a branch by conforming to the criterion of bearing 'fruit'. The fundamental meaning of bearing fruit is reflected in v. 15.10 (cf. 13.34-35). But in 15.1-8, 'to bear fruit' is configured as that which authenticates, and is set in counter-distinction to any behavior

26. Robert E. Park and Ernest W. Burgess, *Introduction to the Science of Sociology* (Chicago: University of Chicago Press, 1921), p. 735.

that makes one inauthentic, or lacking the production of 'fruit'. With the 'true vine' being the referent point of authenticity, the binary of authentic and inauthentic becomes the foundation for an additional tightening of access to power and privilege. Inauthentic members' possible claims to authenticity are undermined by dismissing their privilege to make petition and receive the object of their petition (v. 7). This effectively nullifies such members' as legitimate representations of the political body, and positions such members as ones having no meaningful place in the body politic. Here then, the making of a new polity is forged through a system of signification.

Summary

In modern contexts, assimilation and notions of membership in an established or evolving polity, like the Johannine text, underscore and inscribe exclusionary discourse as a system of power. In Jn 15.1-8, a discourse of power is created by an inward dialectic that propels the group towards achieving homogeneity. This is done by reducing and extinguishing differential being and then positioning being through what Stuart Hall calls 'a politics of identification of the imaginary'.[27] Here in the Gospel text (as in German and American history), aspirations for citizenship require imagining a unified group where membership is not only the outcome of political imagination, but where membership is also instrumental in creating the collective identification of the core.

As in this Gospel text, the making of a collective identity in the modern world necessitates distinctive symbolic codes, and these are found in the social construction of boundaries. These boundaries are themselves the social demarcations between aggregated sums of peoples delimited by race, gender and other categories. In the Johannine text, the act of 'fruit bearing' is the primary social demarcation between the aggregate branches that bring glorification to the Father and those who do not (v. 8). Simply put, the boundaries erected for membership in the Johannine community embodied norms for inclusion and exclusion, just as boundaries function in modern contexts of citizenship.

27. Stuart Hall, 'The Toad in the Garden: Thatcherism among the Theorists', in Cary Nelson and Lawrence Frossberg (eds.), *Marxism and the Interpretation of Culture* (Urbana: University of Illinois Press, 1988), p. 22.

Conclusion

This project is not without its historical and cultural challenges. But I have tried to be attentive to the binary thinking that characterizes the closed and protective formations of national identity. Reading the political culture of Jn 15.1-8 with my own hybridity in mind, and perceiving what I believe to be its constructions of identity categories for purposes of exclusion and inclusion, makes me uncomfortable. The text conjures up in me a sense of embeddedness, of metaphysical schemes that derive from forms of cultural and political nationalism; where notions of authenticity and genuineness are tied to group membership and assimilation. And so I have tried to express my concerns with these types of inscriptions by addressing the contemporary and historical settings of two modern nation-states, as I understand them.

For me, the discourse on the vine and the branches describes a process, a building toward nation-ness that bears a resemblance to the making of a contemporary 'imagined political community'.[28] I have argued that Anderson's definition of nation as 'imagined' is productive for opening a critical space where the category of nation itself may be reconsidered. Anderson's definition suggests the idea that a nation is produced in part through representation—that is, through disseminating the idea of community—although the diverse peoples named in and through the idea may not fully participate in the proposed idea. A nation, then, can be constituted in a narrative performance, perhaps even in a Gospel like John. The performance, however, requires the production and assertion of a particular vision of the 'imagined community'. This community, finally, is capable of generating authority through its claims of unity and by dispossessing the diversity of the 'real' community, be it within a modern context or an ancient biblical text.

28. Anderson, *Imagined Communities*, pp. 4, 6.

The Colonizer as Colonized: Intertextual Dialogue Between the Gospel of John and Canadian Identity

ADELE REINHARTZ

Introduction

Like so many of the other 'isms' that have entered the arena of New Testament studies in recent years, postcolonialism defies easy description and direct application to the biblical corpus.[1] According to Gareth Griffiths, Bill Ashcroft and Helen Tiffin, postcolonialist theory applies specifically to the study of history and literature from cultures 'affected by the imperial process from the moment of [European] colonization to the present day'.[2] The postcolonial purview thus includes Canada,[3] but not, or so this definition implies, history and literature from a time before Europe, let alone European colonization, even existed. New Testament scholars, however, have not been daunted by this narrow definition, on the obvious grounds that the New Testament texts themselves testify to the presence of an 'imperial process'. This process was defined by the Roman Empire, long before the 'moment' of European colonization. Hence it is possible to apply a postcolonial approach to the New Testament in general, and, as I intend in this paper, to the Gospel of John in particular.

---

1. There is some debate as to whether the correct term is 'postcolonialism' or 'post-colonialism': 'These terms themselves encapsulate an active and unresolved debate between those who would see the post-colonial as designating an amorphous set of discursive practices, akin to postmodernism, and those who would see it as designating a more specific, and "historically" located set of cultural strategies' (Bill Ashcroft, Gareth Griffiths, and Helen Tiffin [eds.], *The Post-Colonial Studies Reader* [London: Routledge, 1995], p. xv). These authors opt for the hyphen, in keeping with their usage of the term in the specific sense; New Testament scholars, however, seem to prefer the usage without the hyphen, in keeping with a more general, 'amorphous', use of the term. In this paper I follow the latter course.

2. Bill Ashcroft, Gareth Griffiths, and Helen Tiffin, *The Empire Writes Back: Theory and Practice in Post-Colonial Literatures* (London and New York: Routledge, 1989), p. 2.

3. Ashcroft *et al.*, *The Empire Writes Back*.

But how to proceed? Ashcroft, Griffiths and Tiffin speak confidently of postcolonial discourse as a 'methodology for considering the dialogue of similarity and difference; the similarity of colonialism's political and historical pressure upon non-European societies, alongside the plurality of specific cultural effects and responses those societies have produced'.[4] New Testament scholars view postcolonialism more generally as an 'optic' (Fernando Segovia) or as a reading strategy or mental attitude (R.S. Sugirtharajah).[5] In the absence of a handy step-by-step guide— 'Postcolonialism for Dummies' perhaps?—one must extrapolate a method from the work of others in the field. A central point of agreement between postcolonial theory and those who would apply it to the New Testament is that postcolonial readings focus upon the relationship between the centre and the margins, the colonizer and the colonized. Ashcroft, Griffiths, and Tiffin explain that 'What each of these [postcolonial] literatures has in common…is that they emerged in their present form out of the experience of colonization and asserted themselves by foregrounding the tension with the imperial power, and by emphasizing their differences from the assumptions of the imperial centre'.[6] Postcolonial readings of New Testament texts explicitly work from the opposition of margin and centre. R.S. Sugirtharajah, for example, describes postcolonial reading as an oppositional reading practice, or, following Said, as a contrapuntal reading that encourages the experiences of the exploited and the exploiter to be studied together.[7] For Fernando Segovia, the key questions include the following:

> How do the margins look at the world—a world dominated by empire— and fashion life in such a world? How does the center regard and treat the margins in the light of its own view of the 'world' and life in that world? What images and representations of the other-world arise from either side? How is history conceived and constructed by both sides? How is 'the other' regarded and represented?[8]

4.   Ashcroft *et al.*, *The Post-Colonial Studies Reader*, p. 56.
5.   Fernando F. Segovia, 'Biblical Criticism and Postcolonial Studies: Toward a Postcolonial Optic', in R.S. Sugirtharajah (ed.), *The Postcolonial Bible* (The Bible and Postcolonialism, 1; Sheffield: Sheffield Academic Press, 1998), pp. 49-65; Fernando F. Segovia, 'Notes Toward Refining the Postcolonial Optic', *JSNT* 75 (1999), pp. 103-14; R.S. Sugirtharajah, 'A Postcolonial Exploration of Collusion and Construction in Biblical Interpretation', in Sugirtharajah (ed.), *The Postcolonial Bible*, p. 93.
6.   Ashcroft *et al.*, *The Empire Writes Back*, p. 2.
7.   Edward Said, *Culture and Imperialism* (London: Chatto & Windus, 1993), p. 59.
8.   Segovia, 'Biblical Criticism', p. 57.

These comments suggest, if not a clear-cut method, then at least a starting point for a postcolonial reading of the Fourth Gospel. Step one is to identify the centre and the margins. Step two is to read from the point of view of the margins over against the centre.

Two problems arise immediately. First, it is not obvious, at least to me, where the centre and the margins lie. When I consider Johannine Christianity within the larger context of the Roman empire, it is clear that Rome is the centre, and the Johannine community is the margin. From this point of view, to read from the margins means reading 'with' the Johannine community in relation to imperial Roman rule. On the other hand, when I consider the language of Johannine christology, which identifies Jesus as the Son of God and claims that he is the one and only path to salvation for all humankind, then Johannine Christianity becomes the centre, and those groups whose views are challenged and delegitimized within the Gospel, such as the Jews and the Samaritans, become the margins. From this point of view, reading from the margins means reading through the eyes of these groups over against Johannine Christianity.

Second, the Gospel of John, unlike the postcolonial literatures considered by Ashcroft *et al.*, does not explicitly reflect upon the relationship between the fledgling Christian movement and the vast Roman Empire.[9] Nor does the Gospel preserve the authentic voices of the Johannine Jews or other groups who are marginal to the christological vision expounded by the Gospel. Rather, these groups as represented in the Gospel speak the lines assigned to them by the narrator, which may not at all express the views of their 'real life' counterparts. The stubborn silences of the Fourth Gospel turn the attempt at a postcolonial reading into an uncomfortably speculative exercise.

These two problems threaten to block any efforts at a postcolonial reading of the Fourth Gospel from the outset. Perhaps the postcolonial optic should be left to those who study the literatures of former European colonies after all. I eye the delete key with longing. What stays my hand, however, is not yet another work of postcolonial theory or interpretation, but a column in *The Globe and Mail*, 'Canada's National Newspaper', entitled 'Un-American Activities'.[10] It begins as follows:

9.   I follow J.L. Martyn (*History and Theology in the Fourth Gospel* [Nashville: Abingdon Press, 2nd edn, 1979]) in seeing the Fourth Gospel as a work that reflects the experience, however indirectly, of a historical community.

10.   Jeffrey Simpson, 'Un-American Activities', *The Globe and Mail* (23 December 1998).

> Whether Canada constitutes a cultural colony of the Unites States depends,
> I suppose, on your definition of a colony. In a formal sense, the United
> States does not occupy or control Canadian culture, but the US presence is
> powerful, omnipresent and defended by the US government and repre-
> sentatives of US cultural industries.

For the author, and many other Canadian nationalists including myself, the US often appears as a powerful centre, with Canada at its margins.

Yet there are groups within Canada that perceive Canada herself as a colonizing power. Canada's First Nations were dispossessed of their lands and deprived of their culture by European settlers, and later, by Canadian policy. Older Newfoundlanders still remember a time when their province was independent of Canada. On the occasion of the 50th anniversary of Newfoundland's entry into Confederation (31 March 1999), Marjorie Doyle asks Canadians to imagine 'that Canada is sub-sumed by the United States. How many years would it take before you felt about 4 July as you now feel about 1 July?' Modern Canada, like the ancient community implied by the Gospel of John, can be seen as both the colonizer and the colonized.

Perhaps, then, the interplay between the Fourth Gospel and a variety of Canadian voices can be called upon to break the impasse brought on by my readings in postcolonialism.[11] The Canadian scene presents the same problem of definition that impedes a postcolonial analysis of the Fourth Gospel. But in contrast to the Fourth Gospel, the corpus of Canadian literature gives ample expression to the relationships between the margins and the colonizing centre, whether the centre be under-stood as Canada or the United States. Perhaps, then, the Canadian voices can help to tease out the voices of the 'colonized' within the Fourth Gospel.

In this paper, then, I attempt a twofold reading of the Gospel of John. In the first case, I will look at the Gospel as an expression of a colonized Johannine community, and consider how it might have functioned as a response to Roman imperial rule. Second, I will look at the Gospel as an expression of the christological vision of the Johannine community, and the ways in which non-believers responded to this colonizing language from the margins. In each case I begin with Canadian examples that reflect explicitly on issues of colonization from the perspective of the margins.

---

11. In his exposition of the 'postcolonial optic', Segovia ('Notes', p. 108) asserts that 'texts of any length or sort, from across historical or cultural distances, can be brought together in dialogue to see what sparks are generated in the process'.

The Gospel of John as a Gospel of the Colonized

The communities implied by the Fourth Gospel and the country of Canada have this much in common: they both occupy a position that is subordinate to a large empire. Canada exists at the margins of the United States, not only geographically, but also economically, culturally, and in many other ways both obvious and subtle. This marginal position is taken for granted by many Canadians much of the time. Nevertheless, it has a significant effect on Canadian identity, and periodically becomes the topic of national debate. One such period occurred in the late 1960s, when Canada celebrated its centennial at the same time as she faced serious and violent threat from extremists within the Quebec separatist movement. Meanwhile, the United States was heavily involved in the Cold War and economic expansion. The year 1968 saw the publication of a book entitled *The New Romans*, a volume of reflections on Canada–US relations edited by the poet Al Purdy. The book was intended as a wakeup call to Canadian nationalism, said Purdy, but he feared that

> All this book may do is register a sullen protest, a belated yap from a captive dog. It will scarcely raise more than an eyebrow on the big real estate dealers in the Ottawa who have sold this country down the river to the Americans for the last 30 years. In fact, I think the book will be amusing to those citizens of a second-class nation who are unable to comprehend their own subservience or their own naive stupidity. But for some Canadians, the book will not be amusing.[12]

Farley Mowatt's contribution to *The New Romans* expressed both the hope of resistance and also despair of its possibility. In a 'Letter to My Son', he described what he called his naive conviction 'that the people of this land would not forever continue to acquiesce in this piecemeal betrayal of themselves and of their country'. He feared that 'We have become a prostrate people—by our own volition. Actually the only time Canadians even raise themselves on their elbows these days is to *defend* their chosen masters and to attack, with the bitter hostility only known to turncoats, those who dare reproach them for their spineless espousal of slave status' (emphasis his).[13]

And indeed, there were many who reproached Mowatt and other Canadian nationalists for such views. Mowatt himself quoted the prag-matic and 'fatherly' lecture that Joey Smallwood, the first Premier of

---

12. A.W. Purdy (ed.), *The New Romans: Candid Canadian Opinions of the U.S.* (Edmonton: M.G. Hurtig, 1968), p. iv.

13. Farley Mowat, 'Letter to my Son', in Purdy, *The New Romans*, p. 3.

Newfoundland, once gave him: ' "What the US wants, it will get," he told me. "And if we don't *give* them what they want, they'll take it anyway. And what they want—is most of what we've got." '[14]

Many others dismissed the writings of Mowatt and Purdy as anti-American rhetoric. In his contribution to a volume entitled *The Star-Spangled Beaver*, F.S. Manor responded vigorously to the title and premise of Purdy's book.[15] In his view, Purdy's collection

> is not history but hysteria... The book is a vehicle for a collective psychosis that seems endemic among Canada's literate classes...all the recurrent boasts about our alleged Canadian superiority...would not be worth a Prague intellectual's cuss were it not for the benevolent power south of the border that indeed stands 'on guard for thee'.[16]

The allusion is to the American stance against Communism, which, Manor believed, safeguarded the freedom that allowed Canadians to write misguided and hysterical books about the American menace. He concluded with an anecdote:

> In my student days I attended a course where the teacher discussed the problem of Roman intellectuals who became so fascinated with the barbarians, intent upon destroying the Roman civilization, that they acted as their fifth column, and often defected to them. The eventual triumph of the barbarians brought on the dark ages. I wish somebody would revive this course at our universities.[17]

This brief survey illustrates the two facets of the Canadian stance towards their position on the margins of the US. Those who accept this marginal position focus both on the power and inevitability of its impact on Canada and on the benefits that accrue to Canada from the American centre. Those who deplore American expansionism, and urge the Canadian government and people to resist it, particularly in areas of economics and culture, fear a loss of Canadian identity and autonomy. The latter group frequently expresses its views using the rhetoric of colonization, illustrated in book titles such as *The New Romans* and *The Star-Spangled Beaver*.

Unlike Canadians, who still retain sovereignty while living in America's shadow, the community implied in the Fourth Gospel existed as a tiny group within the Roman Empire; sovereignty for this small group was not a possibility or even an issue. The Roman presence is felt

14. Mowat, 'Letter', p. 2.

15. 'Are They Really the New Romans?', in John. H. Redekop (ed.), *The Star-Spangled Beaver* (Toronto: Peter Martin Associates, 1971), pp. 106-13.

16. Manor, 'New Romans?', p. 107.

17. Manor, 'New Romans?', p. 113.

in the Gospel, particularly in the passion narrative where Jesus is
arrested by Roman soldiers and tried by the Roman governor, Pilate.
There is little explicit reflection, however, on the stance of the Johannine
community, or the Evangelist himself, towards Roman domination. The
Canadian parallel, imprecise as it is, emboldens us to look for at least
some hints of both acceptance of Roman domination and also resistance
to it.

Acceptance of Roman Hegemony

The relative silence of the Gospel may in itself be evidence of an acceptance of Roman rule as an unalterable fact of life, and acceptance of the
impracticality or undesirability of active resistance. There are, however,
are a number of potentially subversive narrative threads and christological claims within the Gospel that are defused or disarmed within the
Gospel itself. We look briefly at three examples: the christological claim
that Jesus is King, the absence of a mission to the Gentiles, and the role
attributed to Pilate in Jesus's crucifixion.

a. *Jesus as King*
In 1.49, Nathanael declares Jesus to be the Son of God and King of
Israel. A similar declaration later appears on the lips of the Jerusalem
crowd, which 'took branches of palm trees and went out to meet him,
shouting, "Hosanna! Blessed is the one who comes in the name of the
Lord—the King of Israel!"' (12.13). Jesus affirms this accolade; he sits
astride a young donkey, thereby fulfilling the biblical prophecy: 'Do not
be afraid, daughter of Zion. Look, your king is coming, sitting on a
donkey's colt!' (12.14-15, citing Zech. 9.9).

The application of the royal title to Jesus might imply that Jesus
intends to liberate his people from Roman oppression and set himself
up as king in the political and military sense. Such an interpretation, or
hope, is implied in 6.15, according to which the witnesses to Jesus's
multiplication of the loaves and fishes (6.1-14) come to crown him king.
But their political hopes are dashed: Jesus withdraws from the people
rather than allow himself to be crowned.[18]

Jesus's withdrawal implies that the royal title as it applies to himself is
not to be understood in nationalist or political terms. In his interview
with Pilate, Jesus makes this point clear:

18. Other titles may also have direct political implications in the context of the
Roman Empire. Craig Koester argues that the title 'Saviour of the World' in 4.42 can
be read as a polemic against the emperor, for whom this title was sometimes used. See
Koester, 'The Savior of the World (John 4.42)', *JBL* 109 (1990), pp. 665-80.

> Then Pilate…summoned Jesus, and asked him, 'Are you the King of the Jews?' Jesus answered, 'Do you ask this on your own, or did others tell you about me?' Pilate replied, 'I am not a Jew, am I? Your own nation and the chief priests have handed you over to me.What have you done?' Jesus answered, 'My kingdom is not from this world. If my kingdom were from this world, my followers would be fighting to keep me from being handed over to the Jews. But as it is, my kingdom is not from here'. Pilate asked him, 'So you are a king?' Jesus answered, 'You say that I am a king. For this I was born, and for this I came into the world, to testify to the truth. Everyone who belongs to the truth listens to my voice' (18.33-37).

In this passage, Jesus asserts that his kingship is not from this world, that is, the royal claim is not a threat to Roman political and military hegemony. It is not clear, however, whether Pilate believed either Jesus's denial of his own political aspirations or Jesus's self-proclaimed role as a 'king not from this world'. The fact that Pilate crucified him under the title 'King of Jews' may hint that Pilate accepted Jesus's spiritual kingship; it may also indicate that, despite Jesus' best attempts to qualify his understanding of kingship, Pilate nevertheless saw him as a threat to Rome and crucified him as such (19.19).

b. *No Mission to the Gentiles*
Despite the universal language of Johannine christology, the Gospel narrative pays scant attention to the Gentile majority of the population of the Roman world. The only individual Gentile featured in the Gospel may be the royal official whose son is healed in 4.46-53, though it is possible that he too is a Jew.[19] In contrast to the Samaritan woman who shares his chapter (4.1-42), the official does not bring along any other believers beyond his immediate household. According to 12.10, some Greeks, who had come up to worship at the Temple for Passover, wanted to meet Jesus. Whether these Greeks are Gentiles or Greek-speaking Jews is not certain; I incline to the view that they are Gentiles, an interpretation that is consistent with the universal tone of Johannine soteriology.[20] In any case, Jesus does not meet with them, but instead postpones

19. The term that is translated 'royal official' is βασιλικός. This term can refer to a court official, or possibly a military man. Although it is often assumed that he is a Gentile, the Evangelist does not evince any interest in his ethnic identity. See Rudolf Schnackenburg, *The Gospel According to St. John*, I (New York: Crossroad, 1982), pp. 465-66.

20. R.E. Brown (*The Gospel According to John: I–XII* [AB, 29; Garden City, NY: Doubleday, 1966], pp. 314, 466), is typical of the many scholars who view the 'Greeks' as Gentiles. Scholars who argue that the Gospel is a missionary document directed at Diaspora Jews, on the other hand, generally see the 'Greeks' of 12.20 as Greek-speaking Jews. See W.C. van Unnik, 'The Purpose of St. John's Gospel', in Kurt Aland

their encounter to some future time: 'The hour has come for the Son of Man to be glorified. Very truly, I tell you, unless a grain of wheat falls into the earth and dies, it remains just a single grain; but if it dies, it bears much fruit' (12.23-24). This passage suggests that the Gentiles, if such they were, will come in at some future time, but not now.

The Gospel's general lack of interest in the Gentiles may simply reflect its genre as a story of Jesus set in first-century Palestine, where Jews outnumbered Gentiles. But given the diaspora provenance of the Gospel itself, it is possible that this silence intends to suggest that Christians were innocent of attempts to attract large numbers of Gentiles to their movement.

c. *Lack of Roman Responsibility for Jesus's Death*
Although crucifixion is a Roman form of execution, the Gospels mini-mize the Roman role and magnify the Jewish role in the events cul-minating in Jesus's crucifixion. Whether this apportioning is historical or not, it circumvents the potential accusation that the Christian scriptures preach hatred of Rome as their leader's executioners. John is explicit in this regard. Pilate finds no case against Jesus (18.38) and offers to release him according to custom (18.39). The Jews refuse: 'Not this man, but Barabbas!' (18.40). Finally, they cry out: 'Away with him! Away with him! Crucify him!' Pilate gives them one more chance: 'Shall I crucify your King?' The chief priests answer, 'We have no king but the em-peror'(19.15). Only then does he hand Jesus over to be crucified (19.16). Though the Roman soldiers mock and scourge Jesus (19.1-3), Pilate himself, the representative of the Roman empire in Palestine, is not held responsible for the fact of his death.

Resistance to Roman Hegemony

The above comments suggest that some elements of the Gospel narrative and theology can be read as evidence of the Gospel's acceptance of Roman rule as an unalterable fact. Other aspects, however, allow us to view the Gospel as the voice of a marginal group attempting at least a limited and specific form of resistance to colonizing forces. Again we

et al. (eds.), *Studia Evangelica: Papers presented to the International Congress on 'The Four Gospels in 1957' at Oxford, 1957* I (Berlin: Akademie-Verlag, 1959), p. 408; J.A.T. Robinson, 'The Destination and Purpose of St. John's Gospel', *NTS* 6 (1959–60), p. 121; H.B. Kossen, 'Who Were the Greeks of John xii 20?', *Studies in John* (Leiden: E.J. Brill, 1970), pp. 97-110. Robinson ('Destination', p. 119) reinterprets all of the apparent references to Gentile figures and on this basis claims that 'the world of the Gospel narrative is a wholly Jewish world'.

look briefly at three examples: the Gospel's use of spatial language, the tension between future and realized eschatology, and the Gospel's adoption of colonizing rhetoric.

a. *Spatial Language*

The power differential between the Roman center and the Johannine margins rendered direct forms of resistance to colonization impractical. But the Gospel's use of spatial language implies that if one cannot change the world, perhaps there is a way to leave the world behind. The most explicit expression of a hope for exit from the world is 14.2: 'In my Father's house there are many dwelling places. If it were not so, would I have told you that I go to prepare a place for you?' The movement from a current reality to a future, better one, is evident in other references to departure, such as 10.1-3: 'Very truly, I tell you, anyone who does not enter the sheepfold by the gate but climbs in by another way is a thief and a bandit. The one who enters by the gate is the shepherd of the sheep. The gatekeeper opens the gate for him, and the sheep hear his voice. He calls his own sheep by name and leads them out.' These passages are often read cosmically, as a promise that the disciples would join Jesus and the Father in the place in the heavens from which Jesus had come.[21] But if Rome represents the known world in political and imperial terms, then the notion of leaving this world for another dwelling place may also imply at least a desire to escape from the landscape as shaped by Roman imperial rule.

More elusive is the question of whether the 'world' as used in this Gospel includes a reference to the Roman empire. After the Jewish crowds cheer Jesus at his triumphal entry (2.18), for example, the Pharisees fret: 'You see, you can do nothing. Look, the world has gone after him!' (12.19). The very next verse recounts the attempt of 'the Greeks' to meet Jesus (12.20). If these Greeks are Gentiles, then the order of events from 12.18-20 implies that 'the world' encompasses both Jews and Gentiles, and hence, by implication, the Roman empire as a whole. If so, then we have some, admittedly slim, basis on which to read a critique of Rome in those passages that depict the world in negative terms. One such is Jesus's declaration to the disciples:

> If the world hates you, be aware that it hated me before it hated you. If you belonged to the world, the world would love you as its own. Because you do not belong to the world, but I have chosen you out of the world—therefore

21. For a summary of scholarly views on this passage, see Adele Reinhartz, *The Word in the World: The Cosmological Tale in the Fourth Gospel* (SBLMS, 45; Atlanta: Scholars Press, 1992), pp. 50-62.

the world hates you. Remember the word that I said to you, 'Servants are not greater than their master'. If they persecuted me, they will persecute you; if they kept my word, they will keep yours also (15.18-20).

Another example is Jesus's prayer and final request to God:

I have given them your word, and the world has hated them because they do not belong to the world, just as I do not belong to the world. I am not asking you to take them out of the world, but I ask you to protect them from the evil one. They do not belong to the world, just as I do not belong to the world (17.14-16).

These passages posit a dissonance between the current world order, in which the disciples are persecuted, and an alternate world, in which God is ruler and the values and world view of the Gospel are decisive. While one cannot be certain that Rome is the primary target of the negative connotations of 'world' in this Gospel, it is certainly possible that she is included, along with other groups, such as the unbelieving Jews, in this negative portrayal.

b. Realized and Future Eschatology

The dissonance between the present and future orders is also reflected in the eschatological language of the Gospel, which is characterized by the paradoxical proclamation that 'the hour is coming and now is'. John 5.25 promises that 'the hour is coming, and is now here, when the dead will hear the voice of the Son of God, and those who hear will live...' This formulation suggests that the disciples are to live in this world as if they are not of this world, in the present as if it is the future, and cope with physical death as if they are already experiencing eternal life. In a situation in which they are powerless to defeat the current world order, realized eschatology may be a form of spiritual resistance to the current world order as defined by the Roman Empire.

c. Colonizing Language

But these small and ambiguous hints of acceptance of and resistance to Roman rule become even less impressive when compared to the explicit, extended, and formative role played by the conflict between Jesus and the unbelieving Jews. On the narrative level, the Gospel portrays the Jews and their leadership as the primary opposition to Jesus and his message. Within the theological discourse, the Evangelist places the Jews at the negative pole of a dualistic rhetoric, thereby identifying the Jews with the devil (8.44), flesh (1.13) and death (5.40).

As Musa Dube notes, 'the Gospel of John engages in a long and extended subordination of all other Jewish figures and the cultural spaces of power associated with them'.[22] In Dube's view, John redraws the spatial maps in a quest for power on the same terms as its imperial oppressors and their collaborators.[23] Further, the Gospel's strategy of elevating Jesus above any other cultural figure among the Jews and in the world is a colonizing ideology.[24]

This colonializing rhetoric of the Gospel may itself be seen as a form of resistance to Roman imperial rule. Not only is the imperial power a catalyst for the vicious competition of local groups, as Dube notes,[25] but it also provides a model that a group in the process of developing its own self-identity may adopt. In doing so, this group forges an identity that does not derive from subordination to the imperial powers but rather from its sense of spiritual superiority over other subordinate groups and indeed the dominant group itself. We may conjecture that the implied community's primary means of coping with its colonized state was to take on the role of colonizer, at least in its theology, language and narrative.

With this observation, our focus shifts from the Fourth Gospel at the periphery of the Roman Empire to the groups that are marginalized by the Gospel's own colonizing rhetoric.

The Gospel of John as a Colonizing Text

The message of the Fourth Gospel is universal: Jesus is the only Son of God; he was sent into the world to provide salvation for all humankind (1.9-13). The goal of the book, as stated in 20.30-31, is to provide a means through which readers, *all* readers, can believe in Jesus as Christ and Son of God, and can thereby have life in his name. The Gospel is a colonizing text in that it asserts the primacy of its message, and its absolute truth, to the exclusion of all others. The Gospel narrative depicts Jesus's efforts in this direction, and provides examples of both the desirable (faithful) and the undesirable (faithless) response to Jesus.

Two types of colonizing activity may be discerned. One is exemplified by Jesus's adversarial contacts with the Jews, another, by his far more harmonious relationship with John the Baptist. In neither case do we have access to the direct response of the 'colonized'. Canadian examples, however, will direct us to some clues within the Gospel itself regarding the range that responses to Johannine colonization may have taken.

22. Musa W. Dube, 'Savior of the World but not of this World: A Post-Colonial Reading of Spatial Construction in John', in Sugirtharajah (ed.), *The Postcolonial Bible*, p. 125.
   23. Dube, 'Savior of the World', p. 121.
   24. Dube, 'Savior of the World', p. 129.
   25. Dube, 'Savior of the World', p. 128.

a. *Jesus and the Jews*

Throughout the Gospel, Jesus is presented as usurping Jewish symbols, identity markers, and sacred spaces, and thereby denying their ongoing use to the Jews themselves. In effect, the Johannine Jesus claims that with his coming, the Jews have been expelled from their covenantal relationship with God and replaced by those who believe Jesus to be God's own son. This religious colonization is depicted most clearly in the 'Temple Cleansing':

> The Passover of the Jews was near, and Jesus went up to Jerusalem. In the temple he found people selling cattle, sheep, and doves, and the money-changers seated at their tables. Making a whip of cords, he drove all of them out of the temple, both the sheep and the cattle. He also poured out the coins of the moneychangers and overturned their tables. He told those who were selling the doves, 'Take these things out of here! Stop making my Father's house a marketplace!' (2.13-16).

In this passage, Jesus is depicted as making the Temple pilgrimage at the Passover, as Jews were commanded to do (Exod. 23.14; 34.23). He finds the merchants and bankers firmly in position at their tables. This position not only implies that they are entitled to be present in the Temple but also that their very roles as merchants and bankers make it possible for the pilgrims to do the obligatory sacrifices.[26] Jesus's act raises the 'Jesus flag' over the Temple and asserts Jesus's legitimacy while denying that of the merchants and bankers, and, by implication, those who make use of their services. Jesus thus stakes his claim to this house as the legitimate son of its divine owner (cf. 8.34-35); those visitors who are not in Jesus's service do not belong.

The Johannine Jesus not only evicts the Jews from their sacred place, but also denies their self-identification as children of Abraham (8.39), for 'If you were Abraham's children, you would be doing what Abraham did, but now you are trying to kill me, a man who has told you the truth that I heard from God. This is not what Abraham did' (8.49-50). He also denies them their role as sons of God in covenantal relationship with God: 'Very truly, I tell you, everyone who commits sin is a slave to sin. The slave does not have a permanent place in the household; the son has a place there forever' (8.34-35). Far from being sons of God, the Jews are children of the devil, as evidenced by their continued rejection of Jesus and his message (8.44).

Canadian history provides an obvious parallel to this colonizing act. From the time that the British and French staked their claim to Canada,

---

26. E.P. Sanders, *Judaism: Practice and Belief 63 BCE–66 CE* (Philadelphia: Trinity Press International, 1992), p. 68.

the Native peoples have been taken from and manipulated out of their land and settled in reserves. The official position of the British and, later, Canadian, governing bodies was that aboriginal peoples should either be removed to communities isolated from whites or else be assimilated into white society. Large scale land cessions took place, as in 1790 when the Ojibwa, Odawa and Potawatomi, who lived between Lake Erie and the Thames River in Upper Canada (now Ontario), surrendered two million acres of land for £1200.[27] Native Canadians were to be 'civilized' by settling them on lands as farmers; education was to be provided by Christian missionaries, who induced them to give up their own language and culture, and replaced their sacred symbols, spaces and gods, with Christianity.[28]

The writings of Howard Adams, a Native Canadian activist, describe the ways in which Indians (his preferred term) initially accepted but now are resisting the strong forces at the centre. Adams writes of his own youthful work experience as an example of the passive acquiescence that the Canadian 'white supremacists' aimed to inculcate in the Native peoples:

> I was a fully colonized native at that time, pathetically subservient and silently hostile. I accepted my inferior place as an Indian. There was no desire or confidence to stand up to this powerful boss, confront him, and struggle for justice. I wanted to do my work, quietly collect my pay, and sneak back home. Although my hostility seethed, I controlled it and submitted to racial indignities. Because I postponed any confrontation with this white oppressor, I postponed decolonizing myself. Is there a right time for decolonization? I don't know. It depends very much on the conjunction of personal feelings and political circumstances. This judgment is hard to arrive at, because of the personal unworthiness and social inferiority a native person experiences with regard to himself and his people.[29]

Adams also gives expression to the hope for liberation. He views the struggle of the Native peoples as similar to the revolutions of other colonized peoples, in which violence is a likely but perhaps not inevitable outcome. Writes Adams:

> It might be possible to achieve liberation in an orderly, systematic manner. First, it must be recognized that attempts to decolonize Indian and Métis by integration into [the] mainstream will only be self-defeating, because white supremacy and the white-ideal reinforce and perpetuate colonization

27. Olive Patricia Dickason, *Canada's First Nations: A History of Founding Peoples from Earliest Times* (New York: Oxford University Press, 1992), p. 190.

28. Dickason, *First Nations*, p. 225.

29. Howard Adams, *Prison of Grass: Canada from the Native Point of View* (Toronto: General Publishing, 1975), p. 191.

and inferiorization. When the white-ideal is gradually destroyed, a reformed education system, a re-created economy, and a spirit of purpose could be regained. This would lead to a genuine sense of confidence, personal skills, and self-esteem. From there, social action could begin in a meaningful way to restructure native society.[30]

Because the Fourth Gospel writes explicitly from the point of view of belief in Jesus as Messiah, it does not provide insight into Jews' subjective responses to Jesus. But one can discern a similar twofold response. Some Jews accept Jesus's negative judgment on the viability of a covenantal relationship with God apart from Christ and thereby become believers; others, including most of the Jewish leadership, actively resist Jesus' claims for his own identity and thus repel his attacks on their own legitimacy.

1. *Acceptance of Colonization.* Among those who accept Jesus's position are the first disciples, the Bethany siblings (Mary, Martha and Lazarus; 11.1-44), and Mary Magdalene (20.1-18). All of these characters make statements of faith in Jesus as the Christ and Son of God. True, they are not portrayed as relinquishing their Jewish identities. Within the polarized terms set up by the Gospel itself, however, believing Jesus to be the Christ and Son of God also entails belief in the various claims that Jesus makes, including the idea that he is the only path or gate, or means to salvation, and the only source of knowledge of the Father. By definition, therefore, all other paths—including those taken by the Jews—are dead ends.

Other characters are shown at various stages of acceptance. Nicodemus, a Jewish leader who initially comes to Jesus at night (3.1-2), later defends him before the Jewish authorities (7.51), and finally comes to anoint Jesus's dead body (19.39). Some, such as Joseph of Arimathea (19.38) and perhaps also Nicodemus,[31] become secret believers—including some Jewish leaders (12.42) who maintain secrecy 'for fear of the Jews' (19.38). The possibility of a widespread acceptance of Jesus's message is implied by the interest of the crowds at the Feast of Tabernacles in Jerusalem, who wonder whether Jesus does in fact fulfill the various criteria that they associate with the Messiah (7.27). The

30. Adams, *Prison of Grass*, p. 192.

31. On Nicodemus as a secret Christian, see Sarah J. Tanzer, 'Salvation is for the Jews: Secret Christian Jews in the Gospel of John', in Birger Pearson (ed.), *The Future of Early Christianity: Essays in Honor of Helmut Koester* (Minneapolis: Fortress Press, 1991), pp. 285-300.

widespread acceptance is implied even more by those who come to faith after witnessing the raising of Lazarus (11.45; 12.17).

2. *Resistance to Colonization*. While some Jewish characters therefore accept the Gospel's colonizing message, the majority, including the leadership, do not.[32] The resistance of these Jews takes three forms. One is verbal, as in John 8. Here the Jews insist on their right to self-identification as children of Abraham and children of God, in the face of Jesus' attempt to undermine their claims to these identity markers. To Jesus' contention that they must be set free (8.32), the Jews reply that they are descendants of Abraham and have never been in bondage to anyone (or anything; 8.33). In response to Jesus's accusation that they cannot be children of Abraham because they seek to kill him, they insist that Abraham is their father (8.39). To Jesus' observation that they do not behave as Abraham did, they reply that their father is God (8.41).

A second form of resistance is violence. According to the narrator, Jesus refrains from going about in Judea 'because the Jews were looking for an opportunity to kill him' (7.1). When words of resistance are not effective, the Jews pick up stones to throw at Jesus (8.59). They are also portrayed as expelling Jesus' followers from the synagogues (9.22, 12.42, 16.2). This expulsion mirrors Jesus's expulsion of the merchants and bankers from the Temple, and contributes to the legitimacy theme that weaves through the narrative.

The most extreme mode of resistance is betrayal to the Roman authorities. It is perhaps paradoxical that resistance to one source of colonization (the Jesus movement) required collusion or collaboration with another (the Roman authorities). The betrayal motif is explicitly associated with Judas. The Gospel portrays Jesus as knowing that Judas would betray him (6.70-71, 13.11), even before the evening when 'Satan entered into him' (13.27) and Judas left to contact the imperial authorities (13.18-30; cf. 18.2-5). Later, at the trial of Jesus itself, it is the Jewish authorities as a whole who betray him, by not taking the various avenues that Pilate provides for releasing Jesus. This helps both to demonstrate the lengths to which the Jews would go to be rid of this man, and also, as noted earlier, the innocence of the Romans: 'So Pilate went out to them and said, "What accusation do you bring against this

---

32. Note that the followers closest to Jesus are not explicitly referred to as Jews, though we know that in the story of the Gospel they must have been Jews by birth. Rather, the term 'Jew' is associated most frequently with that group that resisted Jesus's message, and that expressed such resistance in violent terms.

man?" They answered, "If this man were not a criminal, we would not have handed him over to you"' (18.29-30).

Of course, from the point of view of the narrative, the outcome is a tragedy, and the Jews are to blame for an act that has no rival in its wickedness. But if we turn the tables and view Jesus' comments to the Jews as part of a theological program intended to colonize the Jews, spiritually if not (yet) politically, then actions and words attributed to the Jews imply a not unreasonable program of resistance.

This perspective suggests a reevaluation of Judas's role in the drama. Although the Gospel attributes Judas's change of heart to the work of Satan, we may ask whether the Johannine Judas in fact was evil, or whether he simply 'saw through' or changed his assessment of Jesus's message. Perhaps we should not entirely dismiss, as the Evangelist does, his reported response to Mary's anointing of Jesus: '"Why was this perfume not sold for three hundred denarii and the money given to the poor?" (He said this not because he cared about the poor, but because he was a thief; he kept the common purse and used to steal what was put into it)' (12.5-6). Although the narrator views Judas's concern for the poor with some skepticism, we might consider whether, within the story world at least, Judas may indeed have objected to Jesus's apparent lack of concern for the poor, as evidenced by Jesus's words: 'You always have the poor with you, but you do not always have me' (12.7).

That there was some tension between those who accepted and those who resisted the colonizing message of the Johannine Jesus is suggested in a number of exchanges between the Jewish leadership that is intent on having Jesus killed, and those who are attracted to his movement. In 7.47, for example, the Pharisees describe the crowd that has been hanging on Jesus's every word during the Feast of Tabernacles as ignorant of the law and accursed.

b. *Jesus and the Baptist Movement*

The Gospel symbolizes the 'colonization' of various other groups without resorting to the language and narrative of violence. The Samaritan group, for example, is brought to Jesus simply through the words of the Samaritan woman and a first-hand encounter with Jesus (4.39-42). A more detailed account is given of Jesus's relationship with the Baptist movement and its leader, John.

That John had gathered a group around him is clear from the reference to his disciples (1.35; 3.25). That these disciples may have made special claims for him is implied by the efforts of the Jewish leadership to discover his identity, and, more specifically, to inquire whether he is the Messiah, Elijah or 'the' prophet (1.19-21). John himself describes his primary role as that of a witness to 'the one who is coming after me', whose sandal thong John feels unworthy to untie (1.27). This role had already been assigned to him in the Prologue: 'There was a man sent from God, whose name was John. He came as a witness to testify to the light, so that all might believe through him. He himself was not the light, but he came to testify to the light' (1.6-8).

Thus from the first chapter, the Gospel emphasizes the harmonious but hierarchical relationship between John as witness and Jesus as the one to whom he bears witness. The colonizing undertone to this relationship is evident in 3.30, in which the Baptist declares that 'he must increase, but I must decrease'. The obvious meaning is that with the coming of Jesus, the Baptist's own following must dwindle, presumably because of their transfer to the Jesus movement itself. The full replacement is hinted at in 10.40-41, which describes how Jesus 'went away again across the Jordan to the place where John had been baptizing earlier, and he remained there. Many came to him, and they were saying, "John performed no sign, but everything that John said about this man was true."'

What did the Baptist's followers themselves think about this? Our discussion to this point would suggest that some would acquiesce and some would resist this message. More specific insight can be provided by a situation that is analogous in some ways to that faced by the Baptist's group: the debate within Newfoundland over whether to join Canadian Confederation. Most Canadians living outside of Newfoundland and born after 1949 take Newfoundland's presence as the tenth province for granted. But a look at the history and the writings of Newfoundlanders even today suggests that this historical event was not as inevitable or as welcome as it might seem to those of us in the rest of Canada.[33] From 1832 until 1855, Newfoundland was governed by a governer and council appointed by the British government. In 1855, this system was replaced by 'Responsible Government', based on the British parliamentary system. This is the same system that operated in what was then Upper and Lower Canada, and paved the way for a peaceful transition to Confederation in 1867. 'Responsible Government' refers to a government by elected legislature. This principle gave colonists responsibility for their own affairs; Britain's representatives simply followed the advice and policies of the legislature for all domestic matters. Local control was enlarged by degrees, allowing Canadians, as well as Newfoundlanders, to

33. For a historical survey, see St. John Chadwick, *Newfoundland: Island into Province* (Cambridge: Cambridge University Press, 1967).

acquire command of their own political concerns thereby achieving national self-direction without revolution.

Thus, beginning in 1855, Newfoundland's relations with Britain were on a par with those of other British colonies in North America. After Confederation, she was equal under the law to the rest of Canada. But the situation changed in 1934. In the aftermath of the Depression, Responsible Government was suspended and Newfoundland reverted to Crown-colony status. Newfoundland was now governed by a commission consisting of a British governor, three British commissioners, and three Newfoundlanders, all appointed by the British government. In 1948, after the Newfoundland economy improved greatly, the commission held a referendum to allow the residents of Newfoundland to choose their form of government. Few were in favour of continuing the Commission. The choices therefore came down to either a return to Responsible Government or Confederation with Canada. The campaign for Confederation was led by Joey Smallwood, and was successful by a slim margin: 78,323 for Confederation and 71,334 for Responsible Government. Newfoundland became the tenth province on 31 March 1949.

Some historians insist that the hostility between those for and against confederation is all but dead.[34] But a recent memoir by Wayne Johnston, entitled *Baltimore's Mansion*,[35] suggests that, at least in some quarters, emotions still run high. *Baltimore's Mansion* focuses on Johnston's father, Gord Johnston, a staunch supporter of the Responsible Government option who never came to terms with Newfoundland's entry into Confederation.

Some few years after the referendum, Joey Smallwood, now the Premier of Newfoundland, waged a campaign to entice expatriate Newfoundlanders to come home. Johnston's family came from far and wide to gather at Gord's house.

> This was the largest gathering of my relatives that I had ever seen. I was eight and knew from past experience that when more than four or five of them gathered in one place, it was inevitable that they would get going about Confederation.
>
> Almost anything could get my father going about it at almost any time. He would start off complaining about having the flu or about how awful the weather was and somehow wind up on the subject, though it was 18 years since our side had been defeated in the referendum, since Newfoundlanders had renounced independence by a heartbreakingly small margin.[36]

34. S.v. 'Newfoundland', *The McLelland and Stewart Canadian Encyclopedia Plus* (CD version, 1999).

35. Toronto: Alfred A. Knopf, 1999.

36. Johnston, *Baltimore's Mansion*, p. 53.

On this occasion, as on many others, Gord railed against the pragmatism that in his view had motivated many to vote, however reluctantly, for Confederation: 'How many Newfoundlanders, if they thought they had nothing to gain financially from joining Canada, would have voted to join? What would they be voting for? Who knew anything about Canada in 1949? It was patriotism versus pragmatism. And God help us, ladies and gentlemen, pragmatism won.'[37]

Joey Smallwood himself undertook to persuade the dissenters in several books and in frequent media appearances throughout his mandate as Premier. One such tome is entitled *No Apology from Me*.[38] Despite the title, this book is a defiant apologia that intended, as the title page notes, to reveal 'the truth about Confederation'. Smallwood recites at length the many benefits that Newfoundlanders experienced after joining Confederation:

> Was Newfoundland right or wrong, wise or foolish, to vote our country into Confederation? Might we not be better off today if we had spurned and rejected the many thousands of millions (that is, billions) of Canadian dollars that Ottawa has delivered to us these past thirty years, and is still delivering to us, but now at the rate of far above a thousand million dollars a year? Without Confederation would we, could we, have now, today, the 5000 miles of new roads built since 1949?... The 3000 miles of paving? The more than 1000 new schools?... The University?[39]

Johnston's memoir describes not only the contrast between the acquiescence and resistance to colonization, but also the conflict that this contrast can engender within the colonized group itself. A similar dynamic is evident, if only implicitly, in the Gospel account of the Baptist and his followers.

The 'Joey Smallwood' of the Baptist movement, that is, the individual who led the forces for joining with the 'colonizing' body, was John the Baptist himself. According to the Gospel, his efforts in this direction are based on a firm conviction both of Jesus's role as Messiah and his own role as witness. The source of John's certainty is an event he witnessed prior to Jesus's arrival on the narrative scene.

> The next day [John] saw Jesus coming toward him and declared, 'Here is the Lamb of God who takes away the sin of the world! This is he of whom I said, "After me comes a man who ranks ahead of me because he was before me". I myself did not know him; but I came baptizing with water for this reason, that he might be revealed to Israel'. And John testified, 'I saw the

37. Johnston, *Baltimore's Mansion*, p. 59.
38. Joey Smallwood, *No Apology from Me* (St John's: Newfoundland Books, 1967).
39. Smallwood, *No Apology*, p. 10.

Spirit descending from heaven like a dove, and it remained on him. I
myself did not know him, but the one who sent me to baptize with water
said to me, "He on whom you see the Spirit descend and remain is the one
who baptizes with the Holy Spirit". And I myself have seen and have
testified that this is the Son of God' (1.29-34).

John not only allows but actively encourages the 'colonization' of his
followers:

The next day John again was standing with two of his disciples, and as he
watched Jesus walk by, he exclaimed, 'Look, here is the Lamb of God!' The
two disciples heard him say this, and they followed Jesus... One of the two
who heard John speak and followed him was Andrew, Simon Peter's
brother (1.35-40).

That not all of John's disciples were eager to join forces with Jesus is
hinted at in the narrator's incidental reference to Jesus's baptizing
during the period before John's imprisonment (3.22-24). This reference
indicates that the movements remained separate for some time after
Jesus began his ministry, and leaves open the question of whether the
two groups worked together or as rivals.[40] The presence of some tension
between them is suggested most clearly by the 'discussion' that arose
between John's disciples and a Jew. John's disciples 'came to John and
said to him, "Rabbi, the one who was with you across the Jordan, to
whom you testified, here he is baptizing, and all are going to him"'
(3.25-26).[41]

40.   Scholars vary in their interpretation of the relationship between the Jesus and
Baptist movements. Some, such as Walter Wink (*John the Baptist in the Gospel Tradition*
[Cambridge: Cambridge University Press, 1968], p. 94), argue that Jesus and John the
Baptist were rival practitioners of the same rite, namely baptism. Others, such as
Jerome Murphy O'Connor ('John the Baptist and Jesus: History and Hypotheses',
NTS 36 [1990], pp. 363-66) suggest that Jesus's baptizing ministry, as described in the
Fourth Gospel, was initially an extension of the Baptist's and intended to further the
Baptist's aims rather than vice versa. He suggests that Jesus and the Baptist divided
up the territory in order to conduct a coordinated campaign among the Jews and the
Samaritans. Morton Enslin ('John and Jesus', *ZNW* 66 [1975], pp. 1-18) questions
whether Jesus and John even knew one another, and suggests that their entire
relationship may have been an invention of the early church. The variety of views
indicates that the interpretation of the Johannine material and the question of its
historicity are by no means clear. In my view, it seems likely that there was some
contact between John and Jesus. That there was some rivalry between them seems
more likely than the reverse.
41.   The text of Jn 3.25 is unclear with regard to the party or parties that were in
dispute with the disciples of John. Some manuscripts read μετὰ 'ουδαίου, meaning 'a
certain Jew'; others read μετὰ 'ουδαίων, meaning, 'certain Jews'. For detailed discussion, see John W. Pryor, 'John the Baptist and Jesus: Tradition and Text in John

This complaint implies that, from the point of view of these particular disciples, Jesus is usurping the activities of the group, taking away their clientele, 'treading on their turf'. A second hint in this direction may be found in 4.1, according to which 'Jesus learned that the Pharisees had heard, "Jesus is making and baptizing more disciples than John."' While we cannot know for certain the source of this report, it is not too farfetched to imagine that it might come directly or indirectly from those disciples of John the Baptist who are themselves distressed at Jesus' activities.

John is not open to the complaints of his disciples.

> John answered, 'No one can receive anything except what has been given from heaven. You yourselves are my witnesses that I said, "I am not the Messiah, but I have been sent ahead of him". He who has the bride is the bridegroom. The friend of the bridegroom, who stands and hears him, rejoices greatly at the bridegroom's voice. For this reason my joy has been fulfilled. He must increase, but I must decrease' (3.27-30).

The Fourth Gospel assigns an important but subordinate role to John the Baptist, as witness and friend to the 'bridegroom'. But beneath the surface of the Gospel's account of the Baptist's group we may detect at least some dissent among the ranks regarding the colonizing force of the Johannine Jesus, despite the model of acceptance provided by their leader.

Conclusion

In the interplay between modern Canadian and ancient Johannine texts, two points are clear. One is that, at least in these cases, colonized groups can also, from certain points of view, be viewed as colonizers. The second is that the groups at the margins, however those margins are defined, are not united in their response to colonization. In both cases we see evidence, explicit or implicit, of a twofold response of the margins vis à vis the centre: acceptance of or acquiescence to the colonized power and the experience of colonization on the one hand, and resistance to them on the other hand. This twofold response also creates the possibility for conflict or controversy within the colonized group. This is evident in all of the Canadian examples, and adumbrated in the Johannine ones, most clearly in the divisions between the Jewish crowds and the Jewish

3.25', *JSNT* 66 (1997), pp. 15-26. The variant readings do not affect the import of this passage with respect to the concern of the Baptist's disciples over Jesus's baptizing activities.

authorities on the one hand, and between various of the Baptist's disciples on the other hand.

Through an intertextual reading, the initial obstacles that seemed to stymie a postcolonial reading of the Fourth Gospel do not entirely disappear, but they do not seem quite so formidable as at first. The shifting definitions of colonizer and colonized can be accommodated simply by acknowledging the shift and then choosing one or more perspectives upon which to focus. The inability of the Gospel to provide direct access to the voices at the margins is both a consequence of its strongly rhetorical purpose—to persuade others to adopt its views about the person and significance of Jesus as Christ and Son of God—and an inevitable corollary to the narrative form per se, in which the words and deeds of all characters are controlled and conveyed by the narrative voice.

The exercise of reading this text in dialogue with those that belong to my own geographical and national location has convinced me of the value of postcolonial readings of texts such as the Fourth Gospel. First, applying a postcolonial perspective to the Canadian scene provided me a way of thinking differently about my own Canadian identity and for learning more about the history and peoples that live here. Second, a postcolonial reading of the Fourth Gospel allowed me to look at this very familiar text with new eyes. Looking at the Gospel from the point of view of the marginalized, however they are defined, is a form of resistant reading. Not only does one focus on the presence, or absence of resistance to colonization, but as a postcolonial scholar one is also engaged in a twofold act of resistance to the historical-critical center of Johannine studies as a discipline, and to the long-familiar paths and methods that we have shaped our own work on this text.

Ambiguous Admittance: Consent and Descent in John's Community of 'Upward' Mobility

TAT-SIONG BENNY LIEW*

Introduction

This essay does not assume that John's Gospel is a product, and thus a reflection of a so-called 'community of the beloved disciple'. Instead, it sees John as a site of struggle for community.[1] In other words, it will not provide a view of what John's community 'was actually like' through the 'window' of the Fourth Gospel, but will focus rather on how John's Gospel constructs community. It takes as its point of departure what Anthony P. Cohen calls 'the symbolic construction of community',[2] or

* I would like to thank Colleen Conway and the New Testament Faculty Group of the Association of Chicago Theological Schools (ACTS) for commenting on and responding to this paper. Unfortunately, time constraint does not allow me to revise the paper in light of their many constructive criticisms and insightful ideas.

1. For arguably the most influential attempt to reconstruct the community behind John's Gospel, see Raymond E. Brown, *The Community of the Beloved Disciple: The Life, Loves and Hates of an Individual Church in New Testament Times* (New York: Paulist Press, 1979). Despite recent emphasis that language *constitutes* reality, the deep-rooted understanding that language reflects reality dies hard. For example, Sharon H. Ringe, in her recent study of John, proceeds to spend an entire chapter describing (or more accurately, in-scribing) the 'language', 'location' and the 'social composition' of the Johannine community (*Wisdom's Friends: Community and Christology in the Fourth Gospel* [Louisville, KY: Westminster/John Knox Press, 1999], pp. 10-28) almost immediately after a brief comment that 'performative language...builds...community' (Ringe, *Wisdom's*, p. 2). Likewise, Adeline Fehribach ends her fine analysis by briefly questioning whether reconstructions of an egalitarian Johannine community honestly take into consideration John's androcentric and patriarchal characterization of women (*The Women in the Life of the Bridegroom: A Feminist Historical-Literary Analysis of the Female Characters in the Fourth Gospel* [Collegeville, MN: Liturgical Press, 1998], pp. 178-79). What is at issue for her then is the result, not the nature of such reconstructionist projects. Lest I be misunderstood, I will clarify that my resistance to historical reconstructions does not mean that I advocate an ahistorical understanding, or practice an a-contextual interpretation of John.

2. See Anthony P. Cohen, *The Symbolic Construction of Community* (New York:

what Benedict Anderson calls 'imagined communities'.[3] Both A. Cohen
and Anderson emphasize the formation of community through a myriad
of symbols, including language or literary texts. Or, to adapt the alli-
teration of Homi K. Bhabha, they claim a close relation between neigh-
bor(liness) and narration.[4] In contrast to Craig R. Koester's attempt to
demonstrate how specific symbols *within* John's Gospel bring together
'apparently contradictory ideas' (given the root meaning of 'symbol' as
'putting together'),[5] this essay will explore how John's Gospel functions
as a symbol to put people together in a community.[6] More particularly, it

---

Tavistock and Ellis Horwood, 1985). It is important to point out that for A. Cohen,
this shift of emphasis (from our reconstruction of John's community to John's construction of community) should not be understood simplistically as a shift from an etic
view of the outsider to an emic view of an insider, because any singular emic view may
itself be an etic view of an interpreter (see A. Cohen, *Construction*, p. 72).

   3.   See Benedict Anderson, *Imagined Communities: Reflections on the Origin and
Spread of Nationalism* (New York: Verso, rev. edn, 1991). Admittedly, Anderson's work
has a narrower focus than A. Cohen's. Anderson is interested in the emergence of
nation-states since the end of the eighteenth century, but I believe his thesis that
imagination brings about a sense of (be)longing is still applicable to other forms of
communities from an earlier time. This is particularly so given (1) Anderson's own
account of the many parallels between the imaginings of earlier religious and later
nationalist communities (Anderson, *Imagined Communities*, pp. 10-19); and (2) the
parallel between Anderson's emphasis on nation as a 'non-face-to-face' community
(Anderson, *Imagined Communities*, p. 6) and John's concern to construct a community
that overcomes geographical and temporal distances (11.52; 17.20-26). Anderson's
'imagined communities' thesis is, of course, not without problems. In fact, the thesis
seems to have a colonizing (under)current that attributes the 'models' of imagining
nations solely to Europe and the Americas (67-82). For an attempt to de-colonize
Anderson, see Partha Chatterjee, 'Whose Imagined Community?' in Gopal Balakrishnan (ed.), *Mapping the Nation* (New York: Verso, 1996), pp. 214-25.

   4.   See Homi K. Bhabha, 'Introduction: Narrating the Nation', in Homi K.
Bhabha (ed.), *Nation and Narration* (New York: Routledge, 1990), pp. 1-7.

   5.   Craig R. Koester, *Symbolism in the Fourth Gospel: Meaning, Mystery, Community*
(Minneapolis: Fortress Press, 1995), p. 27.

   6.   In his last chapter, Koester does address the relationship between John's
symbolic construction and community construction (*Symbolism*, pp. 220-56). His
insights into this topic, however, are muddled by his attempt to reconstruct the
Johannine community behind the Gospel (thus the chapter ends up demonstrating a
'mix-and-match' attitude towards the historical-critical, the literary-rhetorical, and the
social-scientific approach to John). This illustrates, yet once more, the hegemonic
power of the 'text-as-window' mentality, because Koester actually prefaces his reconstruction with warnings against such endeavors (*Symbolism*, pp. 221-23). Since most
studies on community within New Testament scholarship continue to focus on definition, structure and social fact (see, for example, Richard S. Ascough's survey on such
studies of Pauline churches, *What are They Saying about the Formation of Pauline*

will give attention to John's construction of consent, descent and ascent. As many readers will recognize, the phrase 'consent and descent' has been used by Werner Sollors to identify a powerful cultural code in the US.[7] I borrow his phrase, along with another powerful cultural code in the US (that of 'upward mobility') in the essay's subtitle to situate my reading of John within the context and contest of US (multi)cultural dynamics.[8]

Writing Boundary on Papyri

Building community is clearly the purpose of John's Gospel. As Koester points out, the appearance of Jesus's mother at Cana (2.1-12) and at Golgotha (19.16-27) presents an *inclusio* for Jesus's ministry.[9] If the prompting of this 'woman' leads to Jesus's inaugural 'sign' (2.3-5, 11), Jesus's facilitation of a new adoptive relationship between this same 'woman' and the beloved disciple fulfills his work on earth, because John immediately comments, 'After *this* [what amounts to the formation of a new relational community], when Jesus knew that *all* was now finished...' (19.28; my emphasis).

John certainly sees the crucifixion as the 'glorification', the goal and the climax of Jesus's ministry (3.14-15; 12.27-28; 17.1), but John is also adamant that his readers relate Jesus's death to the establishment of 'one flock, one shepherd' (10.14-16) and the 'gather[ing] into one the dispersed children of God' (11.49-52). Jesus's farewell prayer further confirms that community is the completion of Jesus's ministry and the intention behind Jesus's crucifixion. Jesus prays for two things before his

---

Churches? [New York/Mahwah, NJ: Paulist Press, 1998]), it is worth pointing out that for A. Cohen, moving to focus on the symbolic construction of community is a helpful shift to bring to the foreground the long-neglected questions of culture and meaning.

7. Werner Sollors, *Beyond Ethnicity: Consent and Descent in American Culture* (New York: Oxford University Press, 1986).

8. The Bible has, of course, been a galvanizing force within US national and nationalist politics for a long time; see Sollors, *Ethnicity*, pp. 40-65. For an insightful account that has relevance for the dynamics of 'internal colonization' within the US in both the past and the present, see Priscilla Wald, 'Terms of Assimilation: Legislating Subjectivity in the Emerging Nation', in Amy Kaplan and Donald E. Pease (eds.), *Cultures of United States Imperialism* (Durham, NC: Duke University Press, 1993), pp. 59-84. 'Internal' and 'external' colonization are, of course, related and provide fuel for each other; see, for example, Anderson, *Imagined Communities*, pp. 83-111; and John Carlos Rowe, 'Melville's *Typee*: US Imperialism at Home and Abroad', in Donald E. Pease (ed.), *National Identities and Post-Americanist Narratives* (Durham, NC: Duke University Press, 1994), pp. 255-78.

9. Koester, *Symbolism*, pp. 214-15.

arrest and passion: first, he asks God to glorify him (17.1, 5); and second, he asks God to protect the unity, or the community of his present and future followers (17.9-11, 20-23).[10]

According to Raymond Williams, the lexical root of the word 'community' is 'relations or feelings'.[11] A. Cohen suggests that community, as a relational idea, is most concerned with boundary; that is, where community begins and ends.[12] This is true whether a community comes into being because of external oppression, internal cohesion, or both.[13] This emphasis on relations and boundary leads A. Cohen to highlight one common strategy of community construction: that of contrastive definition, which may include naming or even name-calling.[14] As A. Cohen puts it, 'the finer the differences between people, the stronger is the commitment people have to them'.[15]

10. Community is also what Jan A. Du Rand seems to mean when he concludes that John's entire plot has to do with 'God's commitment through *relationships* for salvation renewal' ('Reading the Fourth Gospel Like a Literary Symphony', in Fernando F. Segovia [ed.], *'What is John?'* II. *Literary and Social Readings of the Fourth Gospel* [Atlanta: Scholars, 1998], p. 17, my emphasis). John's connection between crucifixion, glorification and community is also rather intricate. Crucifixion is glorification for both God and Jesus in John, because it manifests Jesus's unity with God, and this manifestation of unity will result in a community that also manifests the unity between God and Jesus. This double manifestation will, in turn, be a witness that leads to belief, and thus even greater glorification (13.31-35; 17.11, 20-23).

11. Raymond Williams, *Keywords: A Vocabulary of Culture and Society* (New York: Oxford University Press, rev. edn, 1985), p. 75.

12. A. Cohen, *Construction*, pp. 12-13.

13. Sollors, *Ethnicity*, pp. 175-76. Two projects that deal with similar issues (racial or ethnic communities in the US) end up taking these opposing emphases regarding the reason behind the formation of such communities. For Michael Omi and Howard Winant, racial formation is a result of domination (*Racial Formation in the United States: From the 1960s to the 1990s* [New York: Routledge, 2nd edn, 1994]). For Paul Spickard and W. Jeffrey Burroughs, ethnic community is the result of internal group processes ('We Are a People', in Paul Spickard and W. Jeffrey Burroughs [eds.], *We Are a People: Narrative and Multiplicity in Constructing Ethnic Identity* [Philadelphia: Temple University Press, 1999], pp. 1-19). As we will see in John's mixing of consent and descent, religion and race/ethnicity have a rather curious relationship. While Anderson talks about the practice to 'ethnicize' religion with the example that Malays were equated as Islamic during the days of colonial Malaya (*Imagined Communities*, p. 170), Wayne A. Meeks has also suggested that early Christians were often ridiculed as 'the third race' (*The Origins of Christian Morality: The First Two Centuries* [New Haven: Yale University Press, 1993], p. 9). For those who want to further explore this complicated relationship, Sollors (*Ethnicity*, pp. 21, 54-56) provides a good place to start.

14. A. Cohen, *Construction*, pp. 58, 109-10, 115. See also Sollors, *Ethnicity*, pp. 25, 28.

15. A. Cohen, *Construction*, p. 110.

Contrastive definition is a major strategy in John. One can find it at work within an episode as well as between successive episodes. For example, in another episode that involves a woman (12.1-8), Jesus's friend and foe are clearly defined by Mary's willingness to spend a costly pound of perfume on Jesus's feet, and Judas's accusation of her extravagance.[16] In fact, John 'ousts' Judas with two parenthetical statements: one about Judas's habitual greed (12.6), and the other about his eventual decision to betray Jesus (12.4). Similarly, lines are drawn between a Jewish man who comes to Jesus at night in ch. 3, and a Samaritan woman who is approached by Jesus at noon in ch. 4. While Nicodemus leaves Jesus in silent ambivalence (Nicodemus gives no response to Jesus's long answer to his question, 3.9-21), the unnamed woman leaves Jesus in spirited communication (4.28-30, 39).

Naming and name-calling are also part of John's repertoire to construct community. In contrast to 'disciples' who believe (2.11; 16.27, 29-30), remember or continue in Jesus's word (2.17-22; 8.31; 12.16), and bear fruit (15.8), the 'crowd' seeks but misunderstands Jesus's signs (6.2, 22-26; 7.12; 12.17-18, 34-37). In distinction from 'disciples' whom Jesus cleanses (13.3-10; 15.3), teaches (13.31–16.33), prays for and calls his own (17.6-26), 'Jews' consider Jesus a sinner and demon-possessed (8.48, 52; 9.18-24) and are in turn condemned by Jesus (5.37-47; 8.21-26, 44-47; 10.24-26). Unlike 'Galileans' who welcome Jesus (4.45), 'Jews' complain about Jesus (6.41-42, 52; 7.14-15, 35-36; 8.22, 27), persecute him and his followers (5.16; 9.18-22; 19.38) and seek to kill him (5.18; 7.1; 8.57-59; 10.31-33; 19.7).[17] John basically uses these names to characterize 'insiders' and 'outsiders' vis-à-vis Jesus's community.[18] Later on in the narrative, when Nicodemus speaks up briefly on Jesus's behalf, John indirectly and partially changes his earlier designation of him as 'a Pharisee' and 'a leader of the Jews' to that of a 'Galilean' (3.1; 7.45-52).

16. Many have pointed out the relationship between this episode and Jn 13, where we find Jesus washing the disciples's feet as well as Judas departing to betray Jesus. See, for example, J. Massyngbaerde Ford, *Redeemer, Friend and Mother: Salvation in Antiquity and in the Gospel of John* (Minneapolis: Fortress Press, 1997), pp. 136, 140.

17. Although John also names 'the chief priests' and 'Pharisees', and sometimes distinguishes them as the leaders of the 'Jews' (3.1; 11.45-47), John basically groups them together by giving them common perceptions and actions against Jesus. For example, both groups call Jesus a 'sinner' (9.13-16, 18-24), try to arrest/kill him (10.31-39; 11.45-50, 53, 57), harass his followers (9.22; 12.10, 42), and finally demand that Pilate crucify him (19.6, 14-16). The most telling sign of their interchangeability may be the way John identifies those who send people to interrogate John the Baptizer first as 'the Jews' (1.19), and later as 'the Pharisees' (1.24).

18. Koester, *Symbolism*, p. 263.

On the contrary, the Roman governor Pilate ironically identifies himself as a 'Jew' when he interrogates Jesus for the 'Jews' (18.33-35). After all, Jesus hides and stays away from the 'crowd' and from 'Jews' (11.54; 12.34-37), but he stays with 'disciples' (1.35-39; 3.22), and addresses them as 'friends' (11.11; 15.14-15) and 'brothers' (20.17-18; 21.23).

John uses yet another 'name' to perform his contrastive construction of Jesus's community. Despite the difference that John sometimes draws between the 'crowd' and the 'Jews', both are subsumed under what he calls the 'world'.[19] This term signifies what is earthly and what is from below, in contrast to Jesus who comes from above. As Jesus is not part of the 'world', his community is also not part of the 'world' (8.23; 14.18-21; 15.19; 17.6-9, 14). What belongs to the 'world', whether it is the provision of food or the power to rule, is also not comparable to what comes from above (6.25-33; 19.8-11).

As the passages above indicate, John does not construct community just through a categorization of (in)difference. He also does it by placing his 'community-under-construction' under siege. Jesus's farewell prayer for divine protection over his community is occasioned by a hostile and hateful 'world' that rejoices at the community's suffering (16.20). With the tactic of name-calling, John categorizes the 'world' as ignorant (1.10; 14.17), and attributes its intolerance to (1) desire for attention (5.44; 12.42-43);[20] and (2) association with the deceitful and murderous devil (3.20; 7.7; 8.44). As a result, the 'world' will pursue those who belong to Jesus with the same intensity that it persecutes Jesus (15.20; 16.1-2; 21.18-19). John's naming and name-calling function to highlight the peril that faces Jesus, and those who believe in him and thus belong to Jesus. Re-cognizing a nemesis, however, can result in a 'fortress mentality' that fosters community.[21] It is the same dynamic as singing the song

19. John says that the 'crowd' is, for example, afraid of the 'Jews' (7.12-13), but uses the verb, 'astonished' (θαυμάζω), in the same episode to describe the response to Jesus on the part of both groups (7.15, 20-21). Correspondingly, while the 'chief priests and Pharisees' accuse the 'crowd' of being ignorant of the law (7.49), their own knowledge of the law is immediately shown to be inadequate (7.50-51; Koester, *Symbolism*, pp. 60-61). Depending on how one interprets the genitive, one may well argue that John is identifying the 'crowd' with the 'Jews' with his curious turn of phrase, 'the great crowd of the Jews' (12.9). As I mentioned earlier, John makes it clear that Jesus distances himself from both groups (11.54; 12.34-37).

20. Koester (*Symbolism*, p. 165) suggests that some of John the Baptizer's disciples also demonstrate their membership within this 'worldly' group by virtue of their jealous resentment to Jesus's popularity (3.25-26, 31; 4.1).

21. 'Fortress mentality' is the term that Philip E. Hammond and James D. Hunter use to describe the outlook of evangelical college students in the US ('On Maintaining Plausibility: The Worldview of Evangelical College Students', *SSR* 22 [1984], pp. 221-

'You and Me Against the World'; every time you sing it, the 'you-and-me' part becomes closer, stronger and more real. Without telling us, John actually shows us the desired effect of this emphasis on nemesis in a couple of episodes. The more viciously the 'Jews' attack the congenitally blind beggar healed by Jesus, the more tenaciously he commits himself to his healer (9.1-38). Likewise, in response to repeated attempts to stone Jesus on the part of the 'Jews' (8.59; 10.31; 11.7-10), Thomas concludes with the following announcement to his fellow 'disciples': 'Let us also go [with Jesus to Judea], that we may die with him' (11.16).

Contrastive construction of community also often involves humor or jokes. Sollors talks about how 'communities of laughter arise at the expense of some outsiders', because 'a sense of we-ness' develops in laughing with others and/or at others.[22] Irony is, of course, an effective literary strategy for this end.[23] Since there is already a major monograph as well as a major review essay on John's use of irony,[24] I will just give some brief examples. A boundary comes up between readers and the 'world' when the former reads and laughs about the latter's inconsistencies: they belong to the devil while they accuse Jesus of demon-possession (7.20; 8.48, 52; 10.20); they circumcise on the Sabbath while they criticize Jesus for healing on the same day (7.19-23); they reject Jesus's Galilean origin while they remain ignorant of Jesus's origin from above (7.25-29, 52); they murder God's child while they remember the gracious Passover of God with rigid insistence on details to avoid ritual defilement (18.28; 19.31); they charge Jesus with treason against the Roman empire while they ask for the release of a known bandit (18.38-40; 19.12); and they concede loyalty to the Roman emperor while they

---

38; quoted in Rudy V. Busto, 'The Gospel According to the Model Minority? Hazarding an Interpretation of Asian American Evangelical College Students', in David K. Yoo [ed.], *New Spiritual Homes: Religion and Asian Americans* [Honolulu: University of Hawaii Press, 1999], p. 180). Koester (*Symbolism*, p. 224) also has a good discussion of this mentality in John filtered through the work of John Elliott (*A Home for the Homeless: A Social-Scientific Criticism of 1 Peter, its Situation and Strategy* [Minneapolis: Fortress Press, 1994]).

22. Sollors, *Ethnicity*, p. 132.

23. See R. Alan Culpepper, *Anatomy of the Fourth Gospel: A Study in Literary Design* (Philadelphia: Fortress Press, 1983), pp. 165-80; Mary Ann Tolbert, *Sowing the Gospel: Mark's World in Literary-Historical Perspective* (Minneapolis: Fortress Press, 1989), pp. 98-103; and Linda Hutcheon, *Irony's Edge: The Theory and Politics of Irony* (New York: Routledge, 1994).

24. Paul D. Duke, *Irony in the Fourth Gospel* (Atlanta: John Knox, 1985); and R. Alan Culpepper, 'Reading Johannine Irony', in R. Alan Culpepper and C. Clifton Black (eds.), *Exploring the Gospel of John: In Honor of D. Moody Smith* (Louisville, KY: Westminster/John Knox Press, 1996), pp. 193-207.

crucify Jesus for blasphemy (10.33; 19.7, 15). On the other hand, walls of laughter come up *around* readers and Jesus when they read the comment of the unsuspecting steward after Jesus's first 'sign', that the 'bridegroom' was not like 'every man' (πᾶς ἄνθρωπος, 2.9-10; see also 3.27-30); when they read about the opening of the 'door' to God through Jesus and the closing of the synagogue door by the 'Jews' (9.22; 10.7-10; 12.42; 16.2); or when they read that 'the light of the world' exercises authority over those who come with weapons and artificial lights to arrest him in a garden (8.12; 9.5; 18.1-12).

John's use of irony is closely connected with his other strategy of boundary construction. His Gospel is like a shroud of mystery that rises and falls on its characters as well as its readers, thus provoking a potential division between the initiated (those who understand) and the uninitiated (those who do not). Or, to use Norman R. Petersen's language, John uses a 'special language' or 'anti-language' to create 'an anti-society'.[25] A. Cohen reminds us that 'the boundaries of communities perform the same function as do the boundaries of all categories of knowledge'.[26] Alternatively, Anderson refers to the linguistic diversity that results from the dethroning of Latin, and results in the imagination of plural communities.[27] What we learn from both A. Cohen and Anderson is that knowledge, language and community are intricately bound. That is to say, what makes people become conscious of their belonging to and participating in a community is the sharing of the same educational and linguistic boundaries. Because of that, the capacity to hold back information or deny linguistic facility is 'an essential social and communal weapon'.[28] Language, then, has the capacity to create or crush community by conferring or withholding knowledge and information. My use of the word 'or' in the previous sentence, however, does not imply two neat and clear separations. In other words, conferring and

25. Norman R. Petersen, *The Gospel of John and the Sociology of Light: Language and Characterization in the Fourth Gospel* (Valley Forge, PA: Trinity Press International, 1992), pp. 5-6.

26. A. Cohen, *Construction*, p. 14.

27. Anderson, *Imagined Communities*, pp. 42-43.

28. A. Cohen, *Construction*, p. 87; see also pp. 84, 89. Anderson (*Imagined Communities*, p. 148, especially n. 2) argues for the political implication of linguistic boundary by pointing to the 'massacre' or 'retreat' of native language, and the manufacture of 'venomous argots' in colonial situations (like 'gooks'). For Anderson, gaining access to a foreign language is a form of social penetration. Colonizers often produce and employ argots like 'gooks' to vent their frustration over their inability to penetrate the language world of the natives, as opposed to the ability and need of the colonized to penetrate the language world of the colonizers.

withholding knowledge and information can both be used to create or crush community. In my opinion, John constructs community precisely by maneuvering his language simultaneously to confer *and* withhold understanding from his characters and his readers.[29]

Sometimes John does so by manipulating double meanings, like 'to be born again and/or to be born from above' (γεννηθῇ ἄνωθεν, 3.3), or 'spring water and/or living water' (ὕδωρ ζῶν, 4.10). Other times, he does so by mixing metaphorical and literal usages of a word within a single episode, like 'temple' in 2.19-21, 'food' in 4.31-34, 'bread' in 6.32-35, or 'sleep' in 11.11-14.[30] Either way, divisions are drawn as some characters within the Gospel become perplexed or misunderstand, while others are able to follow. At the same time, readers are involved in a similar double movement of understanding and misunderstanding as they follow the mixture of comprehension and incomprehension experienced by the characters. Not only will this encounter (much like irony) ally readers with characters who get the picture *over* against characters who do not,[31]

29. For me, the *impasse* within current discussions about John's language (includeing his use of irony) has much to do with a rigid assumption that John uses *either* 'stable irony' (resulting in a scenario where readers of the Gospel understand clearly what characters within the Gospel do not), *or* 'unstable irony' (resulting in a scenario where readers of the Gospel, along with characters within the Gospel, fail to understand and thus feel victimized). See, for example, Culpepper, 'Johannine Irony'; and Koester, *Symbolism*, pp. xi, 232). Instead, John can be using *both*, and misunderstanding, understanding, and lack of understanding in reading John can be an open, continual and shifting process. Using Herbert A. Simon's notion of 'satisficing' (*Models of Man, Social and Relational* [New York: John Wiley & Sons, 1957]), Eric Rothstein points out that intriguing texts always involve their readers in a dance between understanding *and* not understanding ('Diversity and Change in Literary History', in Jay Clayton and Eric Rothstein [eds.], *Influence and Intertextuality in Literary History* [Madison: University of Wisconsin Press, 1991], pp. 124-27). In Johannine terms, it is this mixture that keeps 'drawing' its readers back to the 'well'. If John uses only 'stable irony', and readers always understand, as Culpepper claims, Culpepper would have relatively little motivation to read John over and over again in the 'last fifteen years' ('Johannine Irony', p. 205).

To prepare for the development of this essay, let me also point out that there is a difference between the claim that John uses 'unstable irony' to victimize readers (Culpepper, 'Johannine Irony', pp. 193-94), and my view that John is himself betrayed by the contradictions or ambiguities of his own construction.

30. For Petersen, John's creation of a 'special language' depends on a heavy dose of 'contrast, negation, and inversion' regarding 'everyday experience' in general, and the Mosaic traditions in particular (*Gospel*, pp. 5-6).

31. I emphasize the word 'over' because, as John's Jesus makes 'blindness' an occasion for revelation (9.3), the inability to understand on the part of some characters reveals that (in accordance with Johannine understanding) they are from below and of

its instability will also lure or seduce readers into community with the implied author. The three-step process that Ted Cohen identifies for the functioning of metaphors in a verbal situation is equally applicable to the reading of John's Gospel: '(1) the speaker [John] issues a kind of concealed invitation; (2) the hearer [reader] expends a special effort to accept the invitation; (3) this transaction constitutes the acknowledgment of a community'.[32] This 'transaction' that results in community is premised on the extension and acceptance of an invitation rather than a clear and complete understanding of a metaphor. That is to say, the outcome of a challenge is often secondary to the primary bonding experience of participating in the challenge.

A Community of Confessing Consenters

It should be clear by now that in contrast to those who (1) seek perishable food and drinking water and (2) thus make up a deceitful and hateful 'world', John is constructing a community (or in Petersen's terms, an 'anti-society') around Jesus, who is the 'bread from heaven', the source of 'living water', the witness to truth and the manifestation of love (3.16; 4.13-14; 6.35; 18.37). Jesus's self-identification as 'the door' (10.7) certainly indicates an inside and an outside. Moreover, his following elaboration of the metaphor explains not only that Jesus handles all membership exclusively, but also that his community has no previous enrollment (10.8-10). According to John, there is only one way to see, know, believe and follow God, and that one way is Jesus. All other ways are hazardous and bogus (10.27-30; 12.44-50; 14.6-7). If the 'door' metaphor indicates that membership in Jesus's community is exclusive, the 'true vine' metaphor illustrates that this membership also requires absolute dependence (15.1, 4-6).[33] These metaphors establish a 'centripetal effect, bringing believers into relationship with each other by reinforcing their common relationship to Jesus'.[34] With the cleansing of the temple (2.13-17) and the conversation with the woman at the well

---

the 'world', unlike those who understand and will join Jesus in the realm above (8.21-27; 14.1-3).

32. Ted Cohen, 'Metaphor and the Cultivation of Intimacy', *Critical Inquiry* 5 (1978), pp. 3-12; quoted in Koester, *Symbolism*, pp. 231-32.

33. The 'fruitlessness' of discipleship independent of Jesus is later exemplified by Peter's fishing expedition (21.1-6). The 'disciples' are not able to catch anything by themselves; with Jesus's company and command, they have a full catch.

34. Koester, *Symbolism*, p. 230; see also pp. 5, 84-85.

(4.1-30, 39-42), Jesus replaces both the Jewish and Samaritan centers of worship, and becomes the new center of a new community.[35]

What this christocentric construction of community means is that members must confess Jesus. What confessing Jesus means, in turn, is that membership is based on consent instead of descent. As an alternative community to the 'world', Jesus's community is not built upon heredity or ancestry, but on choice and judgment. John makes this point in the first chapter of his Gospel, where he contrasts a nat(ur)al relation to a super-nat(ur)al relation (1.13), and promises community to 'all' (ὅσοι) who believe (1.12). Before John's Jesus performs his first 'sign' to begin his ministry, Jesus distances himself from a blood relationship with this statement to his mother, 'Woman, what do you have to do with me' (τί ἐμοὶ καὶ σοί, γύναι, 2.4). As we have already mentioned, the 'echo' of this episode in Cana is the scene at the cross, where Jesus addresses his mother again as 'woman', and 'from that hour', brings her and the beloved disciple together in an adoptive familial relation (19.25-27). This 'replacement relation' is particularly unusual because John is clear that Jesus is not the only son in the family; for he concludes the episode at Cana by identifying Jesus's brothers separately from his mother and his 'disciples' (2.12). Later on in the Gospel, John will spell out the reason for this separation by having Jesus's brothers issue a sarcastic remark about Jesus's need to go public for the sake of the 'disciples' (7.1-4). After that remark, we find another parenthetical statement by John: 'For not even his brothers believed in him' (7.5). As far as the Gospel is concerned, Jesus and his brothers seem to part ways from that point on (7.6-10), and we find the resurrected Jesus identifying the 'disciples' as his new 'brothers' near the end of the Gospel (20.17-18). In John, then, community with Jesus is not based on biological descent of the family.

Another illustration of this differentiation between faith and family can be found in the confession on the part of the blind beggar and the aversion on the part of his parents (9.18-23). While the beggar openly confesses Jesus's healing power to the 'Jews', his parents deny any knowledge of or association with Jesus. Since John gives great emphasis to the congenital nature of the beggar's blindness (9.1, 18-20, 32), one may argue that what this 'sign' reveals (9.3) is Jesus's ability to overcome the limits of descent, whether it is biological, familial, or ethnic/national. Jesus, as 'the light of the world' (8.12; 9.5), is not limited to Israel. In

35. Anderson's work (*Imagined Communities*, pp. 15-16, 19-20, 53-58, 121-32) suggests that imaginings of (national) communities often involve a center, whether it is realized vertically (as in belief in God or loyalty to a king), or experienced geographically (through religious, administrative, or educational pilgrimages).

contrast to the manna of Jewish ancestry, Jesus as 'the bread of life' is everlasting, life-giving, and given to 'who[m]ever': 'anyone', 'all', and 'everyone' who comes in faith (6.29-51). Jesus, as 'the good shepherd' (10.11, 14), is concerned to bring in 'other sheep' from 'other folds' (10.16). The rest of Jesus's statement to his mother ('My hour has not yet come,' 2.4) is repeated several times in John (7.8c, 30; 8.20c). When Jesus finally announces that his hour has come, he is responding to the coming of the Greeks (12.20-23; see also 7.32-36).[36] This 'gather[ing] into one the dispersed children of God' (11.52) is further signified by the multilingual sign above the cross (19.19-20).

This emphasis on consent over descent is evident in the way John attributes the rejection experienced by Jesus to various ancestral concerns of the 'Jews.' They are, for example, baffled by Jesus's untraceable intellectual lineage, or his Galilean origin (6.41-42; 7.14-18, 27, 40-52). They are unable to hear Jesus's message because they are adamant about being descendants of Abraham (8.31-59), and 'disciples of Moses' (9.28). They are ready to sacrifice Jesus because they grant priority to the preservation of the 'Jewish' nation (11.45-50). In many ways, their problem is Nicodemus's problem. Nicodemus, the 'Pharisee ... [and] leader of the Jews' (3.1), is stuck by the 'how-can' question, which he asks Jesus twice (3.4, 9). He is stuck because he is not able to shed what is impossible in the old paradigm of biological descent, in order to receive what is now possible in the new paradigm of spiritual consent.[37]

Jesus, however, is able to do for the Samaritan woman what he cannot help Nicodemus overcome. For Sollors, marriage is characteristic of consent relations,[38] and it is by now a familiar understanding within Johannine scholarship that the meeting between Jesus and the woman at the well amounts to a betrothal type-scene.[39] John sets the stage for this

36. Note also that the coming of the Greeks is, in turn, preceded by the ironic remark by the 'Pharisees' that 'the world has gone after him' (12.19). This 'world' thus carries the implication of tribes and traditions that go beyond those of the 'Jews'.

37. I am indebted to Ingrid Rosa Kitzberger ('How can This Be?' [John 3.9]: A Feminist-Theological Re-reading of the Gospel of John', in Fernando F. Segovia [ed.], 'What is John?' II, pp. 19-41) for using paradigmatic vacillation as a lens to view the interaction between Jesus and Nicodemus. Yet, Kitzberger never identifies the paradigms at play *within* this Gospel narrative; instead, she is using this narrative as a launching pad to put into dialogue two methodological paradigms in Johannine studies (feminist and theological interpretations).

38. Sollors, *Ethnicity*, p. 6.

39. See, for example, Robert Alter, *The Art of Biblical Narrative* (New York: Basic Books, 1981), pp. 51-62; Fehribach, *Women*, pp. 47-58. Sollors's idea of marriage is, of course, based on the romantic notion of courtly love. Since courtly love is a European development in the medieval period, it should not be confused with ancient practices

betrothal by (1) having Jesus take over the bridegroom's duty to provide wine at the wedding at Cana with his first 'sign' (2.1-12); (2) having John the Baptist refer to Jesus as the 'bridegroom' (3.25-30); and (3) specifying that the well that forms the backdrop in the meeting between Jesus and the Samaritan woman is none other than the ancestral well of Jacob (4.5-6a). When Jesus approaches the woman for water, she raises several descent-related concerns: (1) the long-standing barrier between Jews and Samaritans because of the latter's mixed lineage (4.9); (2) Jesus's status vis-à-vis 'our ancestor Jacob' (4.12); and (3) the different locations of worship according to ancestral traditions (4.19-20). Despite these concerns, her encounter with Jesus ends in her proclamation and the confession by many Samaritans that Jesus is the 'savior of the world' (4.28-30, 39-42).[40] In other words, by centering on Jesus, John is constructing a community that goes beyond the limits of descent. Its construction is based on a different paradigm. It is based on faith, confession or consent.

John's consent, however, should not be understood just as an opposition to descent; it should also be seen as the opposite of dissent. That is to say, John is also constructing a community that emphasizes assent or agreement around the central figure of Jesus.[41] Unlike those

---

of betrothal and marriage. Without equating these different understandings of love and marriage, one should still realize that ancient marriage was often also an arrangement by consent, although this consent was generally not made between the bride and the groom, but their respective fathers/guardians (see Riet van Bremen, *The Limits of Participation: Women and Civic Life in the Greek East in the Hellenistic and Roman Periods* [Amsterdam: Gieben, 1996], p. 265 n. 100).

40. Exactly how Jesus brings about this change in the Samaritan woman is, of course, a matter of interpretation. He seems to have done so by (1) clarifying the superior nature of the 'living water' that he has to offer (4.10, 13-14); (2) detailing her personal marital history (4.16-18); and (3) 'spiritualizing' true worship that transcends traditional prescription and geographical location (4.21-24). Although the woman's personal marital history is placed in the middle of the progression, according to her own confession (4.29), that is the most effective of Jesus's strategies. If one is willing to take this piece of marital history as a reference to Samaria's national history (2 Kgs 17.24), one may understand 4.16-18 as an important exchange over matters of lineage. See Fehribach, *Women*, pp. 63-69.

41. In that sense, John is constructing what Anderson calls 'a community of verticality' (*Imagined Communities*, pp. 20, 24). According to Anderson, this principle of community construction (linking members vertically to a central figure, be it king, God or Jesus) overcomes temporal separation, and lies behind the sexual politics of dynastic marriages which bring diverse populations together. We can see both of these factors at work in John: Jesus's farewell prayer includes a petition for unity between his present and future followers (17.20-21), and we have already looked at the 'betrothal' between Jesus and the Samaritan woman (4.1-30, 39-42).

who find Jesus's words offensive and leave (6.60-66), the twelve acknowledge his words as 'words of eternal life' (6.67-69). Unlike the 'Jews' who
refuse to hear what they are told (9.27), the congenital blind beggar
follows Jesus's instruction to wash in Siloam, and gains sight for the first
time in his life (9.6-7, 11). 'Disciples' must abide in Jesus's love by
obeying his commands (14.15, 21, 23-24; 15.9-10). Or, as Jesus's mother
explains to the servants at Cana, 'Do whatever he [Jesus] tells you' (2.5;
see also 13.12-17). Just like the official who hears Jesus's command to
return home and thus witnesses his son's healing (4.46-54), a sheep that
belongs to Jesus's flock is identifiable by its hearing of the shepherd's
voice (10.3, 16, 27; see also 3.29-30; 5.24-25; 8.43, 47; 18.37).

To construct this community of consent, John proceeds to show and
tell the exemplary unity between Jesus and God (17.11). Rather than
seeking glory from people like 'Jews' do (5.44; 12.43), Jesus and God
form a 'mutual glorification society' (5.41; 8.50, 54). Jesus glorifies God
by living a life of compliance, which involves, first of all, being God's
'ventriloquized voice'.[42] Jesus does not speak for God, but God speaks
through him, and Jesus has no voice of his own (7.16-18; 8.28-29; 12.49-
50; 14.24). Secondly, Jesus does nothing on his own. He copies whatever
God does, and does whatever God says (5.16-17, 19-21, 30). The clearest
proof, and thus the climax of this life of compliance is his crucifixion, or
his willingness to sacrifice himself in accordance with God's command
(10.17-18; 14.30-31; 18.11).[43] As Jesus completes this life in consent to
God's decree, God will be glorified and God will glorify Jesus in return
(12.27-28; 17.1, 4-5). Thus, Jesus's community is to be a carbon copy of
this consenting or assenting relation: to obey Jesus as Jesus obeys God
(14.23-24; 15.15; 16.13). What Jesus hears from God and gives to his
community is a command to love one another (13.34-35). What Jesus
does in obedience and in service to God for his community is also part of
that command to love; that is, to be willing to serve and give up life for
one another (13.34-35; 15.12-14). In other words, the unity between

42. I borrow this term from the title of Elizabeth D. Harvey's recent study on
gender politics and gendered poetics during the Renaissance (*Ventriloquized Voices:
Feminist Theory and English Renaissance Texts* [New York: Routledge, 1991]).

43. As Koester suggests, John's passion account is full of correlations between
Jesus's 'experiences' and Hebrew scriptures, thus showing that Jesus's suffering and
death are indeed in fulfillments of God's will (*Symbolism*, pp. 194-96). In a typical
move of Johannine irony, this unique unity that Jesus claims to have with God is what
the 'Jews' consider profane and what they kill him for (5.18; 10.33; 19.7). While they
think they are stopping Jesus from blasphemy by depriving him of life, they actually
facilitate Jesus's living out this life of compliance and self-sacrifice that he claims is
demanded by God.

Jesus and God becomes a model for the community's relating with Jesus, as well as its relating with each other within the community.

Notice that John often re-presents this emphasis on consent through unity with the language of love. Jesus's obedience to God is a result of God's love for him, causes God to love him, and demonstrates his own love for God (3.35; 10.17; 14.31). Likewise, Jesus loves those who belong to him. Those who belong to him will demonstrate their love for him by obedience, and they will be loved because of their obedience (11.5; 13.1; 14.15, 21, 23-24). What we have then, in John, is a community in the form of an irregular triangle. This is a triangle where God, Jesus and 'disciples' are united by (1) an obedience that goes in one direction and stops at the top (from 'disciples' to Jesus, and from Jesus to God);[44] and (2) a love that runs in a circular motion and in both directions (3.16; 15.9; 17.23, 26). In John, obedience, unity, and love are so intertwined that they are essentially inseparable.

What I am suggesting is that John constructs a community that requires confession and demands consent with a rhetoric of unity and love. I think this merging or blurring of consent, unity, and love is also at work behind the mystifying role that the beloved disciple plays within the Gospel. As we have already seen, the beloved disciple, being entrusted by Jesus to take care of Jesus's mother (the scene of the cross), is the representative figure John uses to announce the emergence of this new community of consent (19.26-30). John also claims to base his writing on the witness of this beloved disciple (21.24), but he is never named. In fact, he is mentioned late and seldom within the Gospel.[45] While John credits him as the first believer in Jesus's resurrection (20.8), John also states that (1) he, like Peter, 'did not understand the scripture, that he [Jesus] must rise from the dead' (20.9; see also 2.19-22); and (2) Mary Magdalene was the first one to proclaim Jesus's resurrection. Moreover, John, with one exception (19.26-27), always mentions the beloved disciple along with Peter. In these narratives where they appear

---

44. I readily admit that there are some passages in John that imply Jesus and the 'disciples' have an influence on God, like 9.30-31; 11.22, 41-42; 14.12-14, 16; 15.7, 16; 16.23-24. While these verses promise that God will hear or listen to either Jesus or the 'disciples', the verb that describes what Jesus and the 'disciples' do is not 'command' (ἐντέλλω), but 'ask' (αἰτέω or ἐρωτάω). Needless to say, these two verbs imply very different power relations.

45. He is only specifically mentioned in 13.23-26; 19.26-27; 20.1-10; 21.7, 20-24. His presence at the scene of the cross (and his habitual association with Peter) may suggest that he is also the unnamed disciple who accompanies Peter in Peter's attempt to follow Jesus after Jesus's arrest (18.15-18).

together, John always names Peter first, and devotes generally more coverage to Peter.

What can be the benefit to this rhetorical effacement of the beloved disciple in light of John's community construction?[46] First, I think this effacement strengthens John's attempt to construct a community around Jesus. Keeping the spotlight on Jesus, in turn, strengthens John's community construction by making it 'Jesusian' rather than one that is exclusively tied to the particular lineage of the beloved disciple. Associating Peter with the beloved disciple allows John not only to incorporate Peter's authority when needed, it also bolsters John's emphasis on consent by re-presenting a sort of consensus that Peter and the beloved disciple share as followers of Jesus. It is a move that gives John the flexibility of multiplicity, and, at the same time, the authority of unity. It gives credibility as well as content to John's symbolic construction of a consenting community.[47]

An Up-Coming, Never-Ending, and Ever-Growing Community

John's emphasis on consent as both confession and consensus should remind us not to read the preceding section in separation of boundary construction. Arguing against descent and dissent does not just construct intra-communal dynamics, it gives 'vitality to boundary'.[48] Those who do not make a conscious choice to concur with John's Jesus are left out in

46. I owe much of the following development to Denise Kimber Buell, whose work on Clement of Alexandria's writings provokes many of my thoughts regarding John's strategic employment of the beloved disciple as a representative figure in his Gospel (*Making Christians: Clement of Alexandria and the Rhetoric of Legitimacy* [Princeton, NJ: Princeton University Press, 1999]; see particularly pp. 7, 84-86). I am also grateful to my colleague at Chicago Theological Seminary, Laurel Schneider, who not only introduced me to Buell's book, but in true collegial spirit, also allowed me to use her own personal copy of Buell's book.

47. The potential problem John faces in pushing the figure of the beloved disciple more to the foreground may be illustrated in Anderson's discussion about the 'backfire' that dynasts after the mid-nineteenth century risked in identifying themselves with the 'particular-national' tendencies within their empires (*Imagined Communities*, pp. 84-85). John's double reference to his having left out from his Gospel 'other' materials about Jesus (20.30; 21.25) may be another power move on his part. As we have discussed earlier, there is power in withholding knowledge and information. Doing so (or at least claiming to have extra materials not accessible in writing) may not only reinforce John's own place in the community he seeks to construct, it can also further enhance its uniformity by keeping its members 'deprived' and dependent.

48. A. Cohen, *Construction*, pp. 35-36.

the dark, deprived of light and direction (12.35-36c). They will remain in the 'world' below, and die in their sins (8.23-24). In contrast, members of the community are destined to move up. John stresses that Jesus is from above, and repeatedly refers to his crucifixion as an 'up-lifting' experience, or as a prelude to his ascending return to God (3.13-15; 6.62; 8.28; 12.32-34; 13.1, 3; 14.12, 28; 16.4-5, 10, 28; 17.11a-c, 13a; 20.17).[49] Thus, John's Jesus promises that while 'outsiders' cannot follow where he goes (7.32-36; 8.21-24), his followers will follow him in this 'upward mobility' (12.26; 13.36; 14.1-4; 17.24). As Jesus tells Nathanael in their first encounter, Jesus is both the hub and vehicle of heavenly communication (1.51).

This 'upward mobility' is what John means by 'eternal life' (3.16, 36; 5.24; 6.47; 10.28a-b; 12.25, 49-50; 17.3). It includes not just being raised up from physical death (6.39-40, 44, 54; 11.25-26), but also a rise in the quality of life (8.51-53; 10.10; 17.2-3). While Jesus's own resurrection (20.1-20, 24-29), as well as his raising of Lazarus (11.1-44) show the first nuance of 'eternal life,'[50] Jesus's other 'signs' portray the second nuance of 'eternal life' in John. With Jesus, his followers experience plainness changing into sumptuousness (2.1-12), sickness into health (4.46-5.9b), paucity into plenty (6.1-14), terror into peace (6.16-21), and darkness into light (9.1-7).

In John's construction, this upward swing will entail a soaring in the community's membership as well. We have already seen that for John, Jesus's crucifixion, or his being 'lifted up', will result in community. John's Jesus is so confident in the 'draw' of the cross, and the 'fruit-bearing potential' of his 'disciples' that he ends his farewell prayer interceding for his next generation(s) of followers (12.24, 32; 17.18-23). The success of this growth to come is depicted in the miraculous catch of fish orchestrated by the risen Jesus (21.1-8, 11).[51] Just as Jesus taught

49. Despite their shared anxiety over influence (whether John is influenced by Jewish, Hellenistic or Gnostic texts), both Meeks ('The Man from Heaven in Johannine Sectarianism', *JBL* 91 [1972], pp. 44-72) and Charles H. Talbert ('The Myth of a Descending-Ascending Redeemer in Mediterranean Antiquity', *NTS* 22 [1976], pp. 418-40) have done much to alert Johannine scholars to this downward and upward emphasis in the Fourth Gospel.

50. Koester (*Symbolism*, p. 110) argues that Lazarus's resurrection functions to foreshadow Jesus's resurrection rather than the resurrection to be experienced by believers, because Lazarus obviously will die again. But if Lazarus's second death disqualifies it from being a model of the promised resurrection of believers, why is it acceptable for Jesus's resurrection? In other words, why is the implication of a second death not agreeable for believers, but agreeable for Jesus?

51. John's idea(l) of an expanding community can be seen in his emphasis on the

them earlier (15.4-5), the 'disciples' come up empty when they go fishing on their own. But when they follow Jesus's direction, they have a large catch. In fact, John makes a point to describe repeatedly the abundance of this catch (21.6, 8, 11).

This up and coming community of John's construction is characterized by honor, glory and expansion. With the freedom and power to conquer (8.31-32; 12.31; 16.33; 17.2), it will march in strides (11.9-10). As John declares not once, but twice in one verse, 'The one who comes from above is above all... The one who comes from heaven is above all' (3.31). In sum, Jesus's community is qualitatively and quantitatively appealing, both in terms of the present and the future.[52] With this construction, John provides an enticing invitation to those outside, but also reinforces the boundary for those inside.

Legitimation, Convolutions and Contra-dictions

According to A. Cohen, symbolic construction of community often refers to the past for legitimation.[53] This strategy has been identified by Anderson as fashioning a community 'up time' rather than 'down time',[54] or by Eric Hobsbawm and Terence Ranger as 'the invention of tradition'.[55] In other words, selective memory or creative composition is used to fabricate a history or precedent to make the present construction look valid and natural. A. Cohen underscores the emotional investment of this strategy, and thus compares it to Victor W. Turner's 'condensation symbols'.[56] It is such a significant part of imagining community that

---

need for the 'disciples' to testify or 'bear fruit' (see 1.19-51; 4.28-30, 39-42; 9.13-34; 15.1-8, 16, 27; 17.18, 20). Of course, the aforementioned emphasis on a 'world' that 'hates' and 'persecutes' will lead to trials, and trials are but another forum for testimonies. In other words, I do not think that one can rigidly divide between an emphasis on communal survival and an emphasis on communal expansion, since the two are intricately related in John.

52. In other words, John gives priority to what is on top, on high and in bulk. Admittedly, John does connect glorification with death (12.23-26), and emphasizes God rather than humans as the true giver of honor (5.41, 44; 8.50, 54; 12.42-43). The promise of an escalating membership shows most clearly, in my opinion, that these moves on John's part provide nothing more than different routes of travel to the same destination. That is to say, John employs rather than contests the existing 'cultural capital' of honor, power and number in constructing Jesus's community.

53. A. Cohen, *Construction*, p. 99.

54. Anderson, *Imagined Communities*, p. 205.

55. Eric Hobsbawm and Terence Ranger (eds.), *The Invention of Tradition* (New York: Cambridge University Press, 1992).

56. A. Cohen, *Construction*, p. 102. See also Victor W. Turner, *The Forest of Symbols:*

Anderson spends an entire chapter of his book on it,[57] and examples of it actually spill over into the other chapters. Whether it is through the 'primordialness of language', production of 'historical maps' or exhibits in a museum, Anderson shows how looking old can be looking good.[58]

Sollors describes one particular maneuver of this 'retrospective' and 'retroactive' strategy that is, in my opinion, important for John. We may call it the 'I am third' strategy, although Sollors himself refers to it as the psychoanalytic concept of a 'grandfather complex'.[59] Those who practice this strategy basically claim a third-generation status, thus positioning themselves to 'surpass the old ones [second generation or parents] in the name of even older ones [first generation or grandparents]'.[60]

We have already talked about the struggle between John's Jesus and the 'Jews' over lineage (6.41-42; 7.14-18, 27, 40-52; 8.31-59). What we must not lose sight of is how consistently John has Jesus invoke an older authority figure to circumvent his opponents. In fact, John has the Baptizer state the operating principle behind the 'grandfather complex' early in his Gospel: 'After me [the Baptizer] comes a man [Jesus] who ranks ahead of me because he was *before* me' (1.30; my emphasis [see also 1.15]). It is the priority of precedence. Thus John finds it important, for example, to clarify that circumcision is not from Moses but from the patriarchs (7.22). When the 'Jews' claim the authority of the paramount patriarch, Abraham, John has Jesus either assert his own prior existence (8.48-59), or debate whether they are actually faithful to Abraham (8.39-40). The trump card is, of course, that everything can be overridden in the name of God as '(Grand) Father [*sic*]' (5.15-24; 6.30-33, 43-51, 57-58; 9.28-33). By resorting to the strategic argument of origins, Jesus is able to deflect the criticism about his disregard for the law, with the mantra 'I am not swerving, Moses or Abraham. I am serving and fulfilling God. I am I AM'.[61] Jesus is the 'good wine' that is delayed (2.9-10). In other words, the 'grandfather complex'—in terms of Jesus's pre-existence with/as God (1.1-4, 17-18), and/or Jesus's obedience to God—allows John to argue that his community, though late in coming, is 'consistent

Aspects of Ndembu Ritual (Ithaca, NY: Cornell University Press, 1967).

57. Anderson, *Imagined Communities*, pp. 187-206.

58. Anderson, *Imagined Communities*, pp. 44, 144-45, 174, 181.

59. Sollors, *Ethnicity*, pp. 221-23, 230-33.

60. Sollors, *Ethnicity*, p. 230.

61. See Sollors, *Ethnicity*, p. 230. As I have been trying to argue throughout this paper, the double 'I-am' seeks to duplicate John's manipulation of language. It can function as an emphatic affirmation of what precedes (the fulfillment of divine purposes), and it can mean something more; namely, the claim to be divine (Jesus is not only fulfilling God, but is God).

with the law but not derived from the law'.[62] The 'Jews' may have been constructing a temple for forty-six years (2.20), but John is going to write the 'real' community into existence in twenty-one chapters.

The power of this construction lies in its flexibility to invoke and revoke tradition, because it constructs an 'antitype, the redemptive fulfillment of types, of original ancestors'.[63] It allows John to do so with Moses (5.45-47; 6.30-33, 49-51, 58; 10.8), or to consider Nathanael the 'true Israelite' who has no deceit over against the first Israelite (Jacob) who was deceitful (1.47). As the Word that has been there from the beginning and in whom everything has its beginning (1.1-4), Jesus proves himself to be greater than Jacob or any other founding figure. As such, he is able to accuse the 'Jews' of making false claims to paternity (6.70-71; 8.42-44), or is able to incorporate the traditions of Samaria as well as those of the world (4.12, 28-29, 39-42).[64]

This move for legitimation through the 'invention of tradition', however, brings to the surface a tension within John's symbolic construction of community. One should remember that Anderson's term for nations, 'imagined communities', has a double nuance. In addition to the idea that communities are constructed by the power of imagination, Anderson means for the term to connote also the thought that comradeship and unity are imaginations that cover up actual inequalities and differences.[65] Or, in the words of A. Cohen, 'the symbolic repertoire of a community...[seeks to construct] the reality of difference into the appearance of similarity', because boundary is the 'public mask' that a community puts on to conceal private differences.[66] Anderson's emphasis on imagination as a camouflage is also one of the reasons why Bhabha links nation or community to language.[67] Language is inseparable from the construction of nation or community; but nation or community is also like language, because both are full of ambivalence or ambiguities. Bhabha signifies the instability of both nation and language with another

---

62. Koester, *Symbolism*, p. 136.

63. Sollors, *Ethnicity*, p. 230.

64. John shows that A. Cohen's differentiation between 'creation of community' (signified by a rejection of existing norms) and 'continuity of community' (signified by a re-assertion of existing norms) is not sustainable in practice (*Construction*, p. 63). While the distinction may be helpful conceptually, these two emphases are more often than not combined in the actual practice of community construction.

65. Anderson, *Imagined Communities*, p. 7. See also Etienne Balibar, 'Racism and Nationalism', in Etienne Balibar and Immanuel Wallerstein, *Race, Nation, Class: Ambiguous Identities* (New York: Verso, 1991), pp. 37-67.

66. A. Cohen, *Construction*, pp. 21, 108-109.

67. Bhabha, 'Introduction', pp. 1-5.

playful signifier, 'DessemiNation'.[68] In other words, nation, like language, disseminates and disintegrates in the Derridean sense of *différance* and ambiguity. Why? Because the exterior (boundary) of a nation or community erodes, and its interior interrupts. Bhabha suggests, then, in one's study of nation or community, one should pay attention to the 'margins of the nation-space and...the boundaries *in-between* nations and peoples'.[69]

What would Bhabha's suggestion help uncover in John's community construction? In spite of his claim that his community is based on consent instead of descent, descent resurfaces throughout his narrative. After all, the entire Gospel, in re-telling Jesus's story, is itself a form of 'reversed ventriloquism' that creates and claims the authority of lineage or descent by 'speak[ing] for the dead'.[70] As we have just seen, John is concerned about the future expansion of the community. And this concern, in turn, betrays his concern about the next generation, the passing on of his construction as tradition, and thus his own concern with descent. The same can be said regarding John's selective use of Hebrew Scriptures (2.22; 5.39; 6.45; 7.38; 12.13-16, 38-41; 13.18; 15.25; 17.12; 19.23-25, 28; 19.36-37),[71] as well as John's pervasive use of kinship and familial language. While hanging on the cross, Jesus brings his mother and the beloved disciple into a fictive familial relation, asking them to address each other as 'son' and 'mother' (19.26-27). And after the resurrection, he refers to his 'disciples' as 'brothers' (20.17-18).

John's use of the kinship metaphor goes much deeper. Confessing Jesus is re-presented as an experience of (re)birth that results in a parent–child relationship with the divine (1.12-13; 3.3). Although John starts his Gospel by (1) contrasting birth by 'blood' and by 'will' (1.13); and (2) referring to this (re)birth as one of 'water and spirit' (3.5), John ends his Gospel by showing that this (re)birth does involve blood. When the soldier spears Jesus's body after the crucifixion, John tells us that 'blood and water came out at once' (19.34). In fact, one should remember that John's Jesus does not just come into the world through a descent from above like the Holy Spirit (1.32-33; 6.38), but he comes as a

68. Homi K. Bhabha, 'DissemiNation: Time, Narrative, and the Margins of the Modern Nation', in Homi K. Bhabha (ed.), *Nation and Narration* (New York: Routledge, 1990), pp. 291-322.

69. Bhabha, 'Introduction', p. 4.

70. Anderson, *Imagined Communities*, p. 198.

71. Since implicit allusions to Hebrew Scriptures can be matters of intense debate, I am limiting my examples here to John's explicit quotations. I do not deny, however, that John may contain many other allusions to Hebrew Scriptures that are not explicitly stated.

descendant, a child of God, so that more divine descendants may be (re)born (1.12, 3.3-7, 13-16).[72] As the Word was a progenitor from the beginning (1.3-4), Jesus will continue to birth a community.[73]

John's emphasis on consent over against descent is also weakened by traces where will and choice are revealed to be limited in power. All the talk about confessing Jesus notwithstanding, John himself confesses several times that confessing Jesus is impossible without divine initiative. God has to allow it to take place (3.26-27; 6.37, 64b-65), and then also has to make it happen with some kind of a divine magnet-like pull (6.44; 12.32). Quoting the prophet Isaiah, John asserts that without this divine permission and pull, people will not be able to understand and confess Jesus (12.37-41).

This motif of misunderstanding or incomprehension is, of course, all over John's Gospel.[74] And we know that it is not solely due to human refusal, but also results from divine repudiation. From the beginning, John's contrast between birth by blood and birth by will actually contains a specific reference to birth by human will. These traces of emphasis on divine prerogative over human initiative may show that John is not using it as simply another reference to physical birth (a reiteration of birth by blood), but also as a reference to the (futile) human desire and determination to confess Jesus. Given this emphasis on divine descent and a rather deterministic view that is associated with it, I cannot help but wonder if these forms of self-legitimation are not fundamentally in conflict with John's emphasis on consent.

72. Anderson also relates this invention of fictive kinship to the patriotic demand for self-sacrifice, since such a demand becomes more cogent when connected with 'purity and fatality' (*Imagined Communities*, p. 143). Anderson's suggestion itself becomes more pertinent in light of John's emphasis on sacrifice. John's Jesus defines a 'good shepherd' by his or her willingness to sacrifice their life (10.11-18), and John later links Jesus's thrice-repeated command to Peter to care for the flock with Peter's upcoming martyrdom (21.15-19). All this becomes even more alarming when one remembers John's affirmative response to Caiaphas's statement that sacrificing one person to save a nation is an expedient arrangement (11.50-52).

73. Buell helpfully reminds us that procreation language and kinship language are both symbols that function to 'naturalize' one's proposition. As such, both are deeply imbricated with power, particularly the power to claim legitimacy and demand conformity. In that sense, John's descent language is in line with his construction of a compliant community, if not in line with his contrast between consent and descent. Buell is careful to point out at the same time that argumentation using these symbols has 'vastly different consequences according to the relative cultural, social, or political power of its proponents' (*Making Christians*, p. 9; see also pp. 3-4, 12-13).

74. See Culpepper, *Anatomy of the Fourth Gospel*, pp. 152-65.

Descent also takes a detour and returns to haunt John's construction of a multi-ethnic community that supposedly finds unity by overcoming descent with consent. We have already seen how John has Samaritans and Greeks coming to confess or admit Jesus (4.28-30, 39-42; 7.32-36; 12.20-23). We have yet to note, however, John's own admission that Jews do occupy a place of priority in his community of united consensus. John's Jesus admits, for example, to the Samaritan woman that he is a 'Jew,' and that 'salvation is from the Jews' (4.9, 22). Furthermore, this Jewish priority is given away by the way John puts the Jewish expression, 'messiah', in the Samaritan woman's mouth (4.25, 29), although Samaritans of John's time did not use this term to refer to the prophetic figure whom they awaited.[75] What looks like a consent of equals may turn out to be a relation of dependence, especially in light of the (patriarchal) marriage metaphor. In John's episode of (communal) erotics, the Samaritans are re-presented as a woman who must subject herself to the primacy of the male lover. Jesus, as the 'Jew' and the 'bridegroom', is the one who takes the initiative to approach her and brings salvation to her.[76]

These fissures in John's construction of a consenting community are not only applicable to the understanding of consent in contrast to descent, but also applicable to understanding consent in opposition to dissent. In other words, there are cracks in the wall that John constructs to cut off two consensus camps. While John generally assumes the 'crowd', the 'Jews' and the 'world' to be monolithically anti-Jesus, he occasionally admits that they are 'divided' within (σχίσμα, 7.43; 9.16; 10.19). They debate about Jesus, with opinions ranging from Jesus being the messiah and a prophet, to Jesus being demon-possessed (7.31, 40-41; 10.20-21). They take opposing positions about Jesus being a 'good man' or a 'con man' (7.12). They disagree about whether the messiah's origin is known or unknown (7.27, 42). When a vestige of faith in Jesus is disclosed by the 'temple police' (7.45-46), an attempt is made to cover up

75. Koester, *Symbolism*, p. 43.

76. The qualifying statement of the Samaritans also establishes male and Jewish primacy, when they say that their belief is predicated on Jesus's own words rather than the woman's testimony (4.39-42; see Fehribach, *Women*, pp. 75-79). This confession of the Samaritans may have yet another implication. Given the classical Athenian equation of marriage with procreation (see Buell, *Making Christians*, p. 36 n. 14), their confession may signify a birthing on the part of the Samaritan woman, and thus the consummation of the betrothal between Jesus and the woman. For an insightful critique of marginalization of women within so-called 'progressive' communities, see Rey Chow, *Ethics after Idealism: Theory-Culture-Ethnicity-Reading* (Bloomington/Indianapolis: Indiana University Press, 1998), pp. 55-73.

this fissure in the camp with a reference to the 'united' front among the 'authorities' and the 'Pharisees' against Jesus (7.47-48). Yet John divulges later that there is also no 'unity' among those groups (9.16; 12.42). According to John, dissenters within the 'crowd' and the 'authorities' have to refrain from confessing Jesus because they are afraid of the 'Jews' and the 'Pharisees' respectively (7.13; 12.42-43). Nevertheless, we have already seen that consensus among the 'Jews' and the 'Pharisees' regarding Jesus is itself a hallucination (8.30-31; 9.16; 11.45; 12.9-11).

In like manner, there is dissension and contra-diction within Jesus's camp, despite John's rhetoric of unity and love. Judas Iscariot is, of course, the obvious example. Not only does he steal from the 'public purse', he complains about Mary's anointing of Jesus's feet as balmy waste, and finally betrays Jesus to the 'other' side (6.70-71; 12.1-6; 13.10-11, 17-18, 21-30). While Judas provides an obvious example, he is not the only example. We find within John other 'disciples' who become deserters (6.60, 64, 66), deniers (13.36-38; 18.17, 25-27) or even dissidents who desire Jesus's death (8.31-37).[77]

The relationship between Peter and the beloved disciple affords more ambiguities. It is true that John generally gives Peter first billing as well as more action and conversation. At the same time, John is clear that the beloved disciple precedes Peter in knowing the identity of the betrayer (13.21-26), in reaching and seeing the empty tomb (20.3-5), in believing in Jesus's resurrection (20.8) and in recognizing the risen Jesus beside the sea of Tiberius (21.7). I commented earlier on John's attempt to unite Peter and the beloved disciple in his community construction, but this attempt is seething with underlying tensions and competition. In fact, one may argue that John's attempt to incorporate Peter in his construction of a united community of love blows up at the end, when the risen Jesus tells Peter to care for Jesus's followers *without* concerning himself with the future of the beloved disciple (21.15-17, 20-22).

This discussion surrounding the beloved disciple and Peter leads us to yet another crevice in John's intra-communal and inter-communal construction. If the unnamed disciple who accompanies Peter to the high priest' house after Jesus's arrest is indeed the beloved disciple, then the beloved disciple would have also preceded Peter in entering the courtyard of the high priest (18.15-16).[78] Regardless of the identity of this

77. It is telling that within the short span of one chapter, John uses the same verb, 'complain' (γογγύζω; 6.41, 61) to describe the response that the 'Jews' and the 'disciples' make to Jesus (Koester, *Symbolism*, p. 59).

78. In addition to the unknown identity of the unnamed disciple, this episode also contains the confounding identity of the high priest (Annas or Caiaphas). For a

unnamed disciple, this episode unveils the mingling of Jesus's 'friends' and 'foes'. Peter is able to bypass the guard of the high priest only because Peter's fellow follower of Jesus is 'known to the high priest' (18.15c, 16b-c). In other words, not only are there schisms within each camp, and not only do people change camps, there are ongoing relations between Jesus's 'friends' and 'foes' even when their attitudes towards Jesus remain unchanged. John's 'Jews', for example, are there to 'console' Mary and Martha because of Lazarus's death (11.19, 31), and they weep together along with Jesus (11.33-37). As Bhabha writes, 'The "other" is never outside or beyond us; it emerges forcefully, within cultural discourse, when we *think* we speak most intimately and indigenously between ourselves'.[79] If the 'world' below cannot shut out a Jesus who descends from above, then neither can the 'disciples' be completely shielded from the 'Jews'.[80]

Contra-dictions are also present in the center figure around whom John is constructing community. While Jesus announces that 'true Israelites' are, unlike their trickster founder Jacob, people without 'deceit' (1.47), we find this founding figure of John's community deceiving and double-talking to his brothers about his plan regarding the festival of Booths (7.1-10; see also 7.18). In contrast to his own praise of his pioneer, John the Baptizer, as 'a burning and shining lamp' (5.35), Jesus pronounces that '*all* who came before me are thieves and bandits' (10.8, my emphasis; see also 1.6, 26-27, 29-30). Despite John's attempt to suppress both descent and dissent in his symbolic construction of community, both ascend to the surface to contradict his own narrative.[81]

fascinating reading of this bewildering question, see Jeffrey L. Staley, *Reading with a Passion: Rhetoric, Autobiography, and the American West in the Gospel of John* (New York: Continuum, 1995), pp. 85-109.

79. Bhabha, 'Introduction', p. 4.

80. The ambiguity, contradiction and confusion around John's construction of the 'Jews' is already recognized by Culpepper, who then proceeds to question the practice of translation ('The Gospel of John as a Document of Faith in a Pluralistic Culture', in Fernando F. Segovia [ed.], *'What is John?': Readers and Readings of the Fourth Gospel* [Atlanta: Scholars Press, 1996], p. 115). For discussions related to the translation of the word 'Jews' in John, see Adele Reinhartz, 'On Travel, Translation, and Ethnography: Johannine Scholarship at the Turn of the Century', in Fernando F. Segovia (ed.), *'What is John?'* II, pp. 254-55; and Daniel Boyarin, 'The *Ioudaioi* in John and the Prehistory of Judaism' (unpublished paper presented at the Annual SBL Meeting, Denver, CO, 19 November 2001).

81. At times, both Anderson and A. Cohen give the impression that a nation or community inevitably sows its own seed of further break-up as it constructs its boundary. Anderson does this more through examples, showing how the teaching of European 'national history' and administrative pilgrimages in colonies end up contributing

Ambiguous Admittance, Ambiguous Alterity, and Asian Americans

Chow points out that the word 'community' is closely related to the word 'admittance,' and that this latter, ambiguous word has at least three different meanings or connotations.[82] Admittance means, first of all, a permission to enter a physical space, like going into a country. It means, secondly, a form of social recognition or acknowledgment that implies a sense of belonging, like being validated as worthy to be part of a school or association. Finally, the word means confession, like surrendering to face the consequences of a crime, or repenting as a result of a conviction or conversion.

   I find Chow's explication of the word extremely helpful in approaching the deep and layered ambiguity in John's symbolic construction of community. For John, admittance into his community (Chow's second definition) hinges on one's admitting faith in Jesus (Chow's third definition). As John requires and demands admittance of Jesus (in the sense of conversion or conviction), will John himself admit the problems that are involved in his construction (in the sense of wrongdoing or crime)? What I find in John is a contradictory impulse to invoke and revoke the power of descent, as well as a contradictory impulse to oust 'outsiders' and increase 'insiders'. As a result, the power of consent that he emphasizes so much actually has hidden limits. Complex relations are reduced into one-dimensional, neatly separable 'friends' or 'foes'. Seepage through and differences within the community of his construction are smoothed over and covered up. Despite his best efforts, what we find in his Gospel is a community that is (1) torn between consent and descent; (2) simultaneously open and closed; and (3) often threatened by potential rupture of difference. Also disturbing is the fact that his symbolic construction of community implies not just boundary, but dehumanizing hierarchy. Those who do not come to Jesus in confessing consent become, in John's construction, part of the 'world' below (8.23), 'children of the devil' (6.70-71; 8.42-44), devoid of 'life' and 'light' (1.5; 3.18-21, 36; 6.53; 8.12, 24; 11.9-10; 12.35-36, 46). Using 'Jews' as representative figures of

to anti-colonial nationalism (*Imagined Communities*, pp. 110-11, 118, 113-40, 163-85). A. Cohen, on the other hand, states that community construction contains 'the domino theory of politics: once one group marks out its distinctiveness, others feel compelled to follow suit' (*Construction*, p. 110). If one is willing to follow Brown's traditional stance that 1 John reflects a later development of the Johannine community, then one may also claim to have a biblical example of this 'domino theory'.
   82. Chow, *Ethics*, pp. 56-57.

this fallen 'world', John amounts to what a Jewish scholar calls 'a gospel of Christian love and Jew hatred'.[83]

Chow's distinction between the first and second meaning of 'admittance' also helps me think about John in terms of US cultural politics. We live in a society where an entire apparatus of immigration red tape, structural limits and glass ceilings functions to 'erase', or make invisible different groups of people despite their physical presence within US national borders.[84] In fact, John's construction of community, particularly with its emphasis on consent and 'upward' mobility, sounds a lot like the dominant discourse of US society. Although Sollors ends up being more optimistic about the cultural politics of the US than are many scholars from racial and ethnic minorities (myself included), he has correctly identified that (1) 'the biblical diatribes against Pharisees and hypocrites were mimicked eagerly by the scribes [of the US]' in the rhetoric of consent over descent;[85] and (2) in the tension between consent and descent as 'the root of the ambiguity' surrounding US racial/ethnic interaction.[86] Since the early days of the nation, when consent was used to define itself against its European roots, the dominant culture has been trying to construct and legitimate national unity with John's naturalizing codes like rebirth and love. It is this rhetoric of consent over descent that makes someone like Milton Gordon suggest the so-called 'liberal expectancy', when all racial/ethnic affiliation will

83. Quoted in Culpepper, 'Gospel', p. 112.

84. David Leiwei Li concurs that a nation is made up of both 'the institutional and the imaginary, the political that regulates the juridical and territorial boundaries, and the cultural that defines origins and continuities, affiliations and belongings' (*Imagining the Nation: Asian American Literature and Cultural Consent* [Stanford: Stanford University Press, 1998], p. 7). This differentiation (and contradiction) notwithstanding, Li further points out that the 'cultural wars' over nation and community are tied to the understanding of the institutional and the political. For Li, the US rhetoric of 'volitional allegiance' is consistently opposed by an insistence on the nation's power to refuse consent to membership, thus giving the established community undue favors over the rights of the prospective citizen (*Nation*, p. 3). According to Li, this opposition itself results from the simultaneous embrace of Lockean 'individualistic liberalism' and the Machiavellian spirit of imperial governance within the understanding of 'Atlantic Republicanism'.

85. Sollors, *Ethnicity*, p. 92.

86. Sollors, *Ethnicity*, p. 5; see also pp. 4, 6-8. For specific references to John in the construction of consent in the US, see Sollors, *Ethnicity*, pp. 85-86, 94. Part of Sollors's (over)optimism is due to his (over)readiness to make race an aspect of ethnicity. For a good critique of this elision of race and ethnicity, see Omi and Winant, *Formation*, pp. 14-23, 53-91.

become insignificant in the US.[87] The emphasis on consent is, of course, intertwined with the accentuation of independence, self-reliance, and thus the myth of upward mobility.

This cultural rhetoric of consent and mobility is, like John, full of contradictions and cover-ups. As Sollors himself admits, US history is spotted with 'descent-based discrimination' like slavery and segregation, and the discourse about 'an immigrant nation' suppresses the violence done to Native Americans, African Americans and Chicano Americans.[88] From the perspective of Omi and Winant, the US has long been a 'racial dictatorship' that marginalizes and ostracizes non-whites.[89] What appear as 'opportunities' in this land are often constraining circumstances.[90] Likewise, for many in this country, what appear as issues of 'free choice' and 'individual consent' are often nothing but 'necessary' compromises. John's ambiguous admittance is especially intriguing to Asian Americans, whom David Kyuman Kim has described as the 'ambiguous alterity' within the US.[91] Kim's term clearly elucidates the 'almost-white-but-not-quite' status of Asian Americans in this country. We are part of the 'other' of white America, but we are excluded or included by white America, depending on the time and occasion. For example, long before the uproar about university admission by affirmative action, Asian Americans were ineligible to receive admission scholarships based on affirmative action in the University of California system. In that sense, we were considered whites. On the other hand, when the Los Angeles Police Department decided to protect the white districts after the verdict involving the police officers who arrested Rodney King, Koreatown was not included in the plan of protection. In that case, we were not considered whites. We are given the title of 'model minority' to reinforce the cultural rhetoric of upward mobility, but this image only turns us into 'middleman [sic] minorities' who do the bidding of our oppressors above, and deflect the menace of the oppressed below.[92] We are also an

87. Milton Gordon, *Human Nature, Class, and Ethnicity* (New York: Oxford University Press, 1978); quoted in Sollors, *Ethnicity*, p. 20.

88. Sollors, *Ethnicity*, pp. 8, 37.

89. Omi and Winant, *Formation*, pp. 65-66.

90. For an excellent discussion of the 'politics of mobility' from one Asian American perspective, see Sau-ling Cynthia Wong, *Reading Asian American Literature: From Necessity to Extravagance* (Princeton, NJ: Princeton University Press, 1993), pp. 118-65.

91. David Kyuman Kim, 'Enchanting Diasporas: Asian Americans, Religion, and Race' (unpublished paper presented at the Asian and Pacific Americans and Religion Research Initiative, University of California, Santa Barbara, 23 June 2000).

92. Jonathan H. Turner and Edna Bonacich, 'Toward a Composite Theory of Middleman Minorities', *Ethnicity* 7 (1980), pp. 144-58. According to Busto, this 'model

'ambiguous alterity' because many whites cannot (or will not) differentiate the different ethnic groups within Asian America; we are simply lumped together as an 'obscure other'. The strategies John uses in his symbolic construction of community are strategies that we know well as Asian Americans. For many of us, 'naturalization' is not just a strategy of self-legitimation, but a process filled with loops and loopholes. We have been victimized by stereotypical re-presentations and racial jokes. Our consent to the nation and national competence have been questioned on the basis of descent, despite the cultural discourse on consent. Many of us have also experienced the linguistic barrier to include and exclude that John manipulates.[93] Finally, the ambiguous meaning of descent has been used to disqualify other Asian Americans in terms of racial lineage, although they were born in the US.

Conclusion

Symbolic construction of community is as important for John as it is for contemporary Asian Americans. As Maxine Hong Kingston writes, 'Community is not built once-and-for-all; people have to imagine, practice, and re-create it'.[94] After reading and thinking about John in light of US cultural politics, I have to admit that I remain ambivalent towards John's ambiguous admittance. On the one hand, I find appealing John's radical vision in which consent or choice frees one from past constraints, and I appreciate the way John gives community a place of prominence, especially in light of the US culture of 'possessive individualism'.[95] On the other hand, I am apprehensive about John's hierarchical boundary, since within US history

> ...seizure of territory and goods, the introduction of slavery...not to mention the practice of outright extermination...all presupposed a worldview

minority' image also functions to pressure young Asian Americans into subscribing to the cultural emphasis on material success and conformative citizenship ('Gospel', p. 178). For an interesting illustration and insightful critique of this kind of cultural consent to upward mobility, see Gish Jen, *Typical American* (Boston: Houghton Mifflin, 1991).

93. Li, *Nation*, pp. 29, 38.

94. Maxine Hong Kingston, *Tripmaster Monkey: His Fake Book* (New York: Alfred A. Knopf, 1989), p. 306.

95. Li, *Nation*, pp. 103-104. Let me say that I, for one, am grateful for Jen's reminder that 'relationships count so heavily that to say something *has no relationship* in Chinese—*mei guanxi*—is to mean, often as not, *it doesn't matter*' (*American*, pp. 177-78).

which distinguished Europeans, as children of God, full-fledged human-beings, etc. from 'others'.[96]

I am also suspicious of John's emphasis on consent, which after all, is part of Antonio Gramsci's understanding of hegemony.[97] One must not forget many structural limits that we face as Asian Americans 'exist in a definite historical context, having *descended* from previous conflicts'.[98] John himself is eventually unable to sustain his dualistic opposition of consent and descent, because both are power-laden social constructs.[99] In addition, I resist the way John links his articulation of community to consensus, which is akin to what David Spurr has identified as a 'colonial rhetoric of affirmation' that (dis)misses difference.[100] Although John's appeal to 'grandparents' is undoubtedly effective (and, in fact, employed by many Asian Americans for resistance),[101] I wonder if this strategy, with its emphasis on 'origins', does not lock us to the past and prevent us from looking into the future. Like Buell, I also question how this strategy assumes, and thus reinforces, the patriarchal power differential between (grand)parents and (grand)children.[102]

---

96. Omi and Winant, *Formation*, p. 62.

97. For Gramsci, the difference between hegemony and ideology lies precisely in the difference between consent and contest, or between calm practices and clamorous protests (see *Selections from the Prison Notebooks* [ed. and trans. Quinton Hoare and Geoffrey Nowell Smith; New York: International, 1971]). That is to say, when articulation is needed to defend or argue for a position, that position is already exposed as contestable ideology. Hegemony (or the highest form of ideology), on the other hand, is what we do in silence and live out as 'it-goes-without-saying'. It is taken for granted, it is understood as a given, it is simply assumed; there is no question raised or any inquisition made. In sum, it is given in consent.

98. Omi and Winant, *Formation*, p. 58; my emphasis.

99. For an explication of ethnicity as a social construction, see A. Cohen, *Construction*, pp. 104-105.

100. David Spurr, *The Rhetoric of Empire: Colonial Discourse in Journalism, Travel Writing, and Imperial Administration* (Durham, NC: Duke University Press, 1994), pp. 122-24. Much of what Drucilla Cornell calls 'the postmodern challenge to the ideal of community' concerns issues of consensus, difference and 'otherness' ('The "Postmodern" Challenge to the Ideal of Community', *The Philosophy of the Limit* [New York: Routledge, 1992], pp. 39-61). In recent years, some reflections and suggestions have been made on how communities may exist and persist *with* conflict and disagreement. See, for example, Kathryn Tanner, who focuses on the community of Christendom (*Theories of Culture: A New Agenda for Theology* [Minneapolis: Fortress Press, 1997]); and Georgia Warnke, who focuses on the community of US society (*Justice and Interpretation* [Cambridge, MA: MIT, 1992]).

101. Li, *Nation*, pp. 39-41, 77-78, 139-40.

102. Buell, *Making Christians*, p. 99.

Finally, I remain ambivalent towards John's Gospel because as A. Cohen reminds us, symbols (including literary texts) that construct community are themselves ambiguous, and subjected to different interpretations.[103] To emphasize this ambiguity of symbols, A. Cohen suggests that the passing and receiving of symbolic construction of community is more akin to a form of regurgitation than a simple digestion.[104] In other words, people have the agency to negotiate and manipulate other people's symbolic constructions, and turn them into something else. Sollors has demonstrated that this is indeed the case with the Exodus narrative, which means rather different things in the hands of the Puritans and the African Americans.[105]

Likewise, Koester's study of symbols *within* John has come to a similar conclusion: symbols are ambiguous, and people 'may appeal to the same symbol to support conflicting points of view'.[106] For example, David Rensberger has read John as a helpful voice of protest and emancipation for the African American community, arguing that the contrastive definition used in John's community construction has a liberating political meaning for a community under siege.[107] On the other hand, even if Rensberger is right that John was written out of a context of oppression, one cannot deny its role in inciting and justifying oppression within history. In others words, adapting Ania Loomba's comments about Shakespeare's *Othello*, 'even if [John] was originally not [oppressive], its history has made it [so]... Historicizing [John] cannot be a scholarly project that denies us our own histories and politics'.[108] My relationship with this part of my Christian heritage can therefore be hardly categorized in terms of a simple consent or dissent. Instead, it is more accurately described by what Emmanuel Levinas says about his Heideggerian

103. A. Cohen, *Construction*, pp. 14-21.
104. A. Cohen, *Construction*, p. 46.
105. Sollors, *Ethnicity*, pp. 42-48.
106. Koester, *Symbolism*, p. 235; see also pp. 14, 17, 24, 221-22.
107. David Rensberger, *Johannine Faith and Liberating Community* (Philadelphia: Westminster, 1988). See also Wes Howard-Brook, *Becoming Children of God: John's Gospel and Radical Discipleship* (Maryknoll, NY: Orbis Books, 1995). If interested, one can find two more examples of liberational reading of John in Culpepper, 'Gospel', pp. 119-21.
108. Ania Loomba, 'Local-manufacture Made-in-India Othello Fellows: Issues of Race, Hybridity and Location in Post-colonial Shakespeares', in Ania Loomba and Martin Orkin (eds.), *Post-Colonial Shakespeares* (New York: Routledge, 1998) p. 150; see also Culpepper, 'Gospel', pp. 112-14.

lineage: I feel indebted, but this sense of indebtedness is simultaneously filled with regrets.[109]

Despite my own ambiguous admittance towards John's ambiguous admittance, there are certain things that I do not want to be ambiguous about. First of all, my ambivalence does not imply a mindless suspension of meaningful judgment or political intervention. It honestly admits that interpretation of politics and politics of interpretation are messy and complicated businesses, but it does not deny the many differences that exist between oppression and liberation. Second, my ambivalence implies an earnest plea that our interpretations of John be carried out in a contextually concrete and specific manner. One must be clear about one's point(s) of departure, goals and interests, as well as the socio-political and ethical implications of one's interpretation. Last but not least, my ambivalence implies a commitment to 'persistent critique'.[110] If the Gospel is an ambiguous symbol that is open to a range of inter-pretation and contains both blindness and insight (to use Paul de Man's terms),[111] then our own texts of interpreting the Gospel are also part of what Spivak calls 'a practical politics of the open end'.[112] We must admit that de-colonizing John and our interpretations of John, like de-colonizing the US, is a continuous process of revision and re-evaluation that requires humility, courage and vigilance.

109. Emmanuel Levinas, *Dieu, la mort et le temps* (Paris: Grasset, 1993); quoted by Jacques Derrida, *Adieu to Emmanuel Levinas* (trans. Pascale-Anne Brault and Michael Naas; Stanford: Stanford University Press, 1999), p. 12.

110. Gayatri Chakravorty Spivak, *The Post-Colonial Critic: Interviews, Strategies, Dialogues* (ed. Sarah Harasym; New York: Routledge, 1990), pp. 41, 63.

111. Paul de Man, *Blindness and Insight: Essays in the Rhetoric of Contemporary Criticism* (revised edn, Minneapolis: University of Minnesota Press, 1984).

112. Spivak, *Critic*, p. 105.

Bibliography

Achebe, Chinua, *Hopes and Impediments: Selected Essays* (New York: Doubleday, 1989).

Adams, Howard, *Prison of Grass: Canada from the Native Point of View* (Toronto: General Publishing, 1975).

Ahn, J., *Silverstallion: A Novel of Korea* (New York: Soho, 1990).

Allen, Paula Gunn, *Off the Reservation: Reflections on Boundary-Busting, Border-Crossing Loose Canons* (Boston: Beacon Press, 1998).

Alter, Robert, *The Art of Biblical Narrative* (New York: Basic Books, 1981).

Amour, E.T., *Deconstruction, Feminist Theology, and the Problem of Difference: Subverting the Race/Gender Divide* (Chicago: The University of Chicago Press, 1999).

Anderson, Benedict, *Imagined Communities: Reflections on the Origin and Spread of Nationalism* (New York: Verso, 1983).

Anzaldúa, G., *Borderlands/La Frontera* (San Francisco: Aunt Lute, 1987).

Applebaum, S., 'The Zealots: The Case for Revaluation', *JRS* 61 (1971), pp. 154-70.

Ascough, Richard S., *What are They Saying about the Formation of Pauline Churches?* (New York/Mahwah, NJ: Paulist Press, 1998).

Ashcroft, Bill, Gareth Griffiths and Helen Tiffin, *The Empire Writes Back: Theory and Practice in Post-Colonial Literatures* (London and New York: Routledge, 1989).

Ashcroft, Bill, Gareth Griffiths and Helen Tiffin (eds.), *The Post-Colonial Studies Reader* (London: Routledge, 1995).

Ashton, John, *Understanding the Fourth Gospel* (Oxford: Clarendon Press, 1991).

Assman, Aleida, 'Space, Place, Land—Changing Concepts of Territory in English and American Fiction', in Reif-Hüsler (ed.), *Borderlands*, pp. 57-68.

Bakhtin, Mikhail, *The Dialogic Imagination: Four Essays* (ed. Michael Holquist; trans. Caryl Emerson and Michael Holquist; Austin: University of Texas Press, 1981).

Bal, Mieke, J. Crewe and L. Spitzer (eds.), *Acts of Memory: Cultural Recall in the Present* (Hanover, NH: University Press of New England, 1999).

Balch, David L., and John E. Stambaugh, *The New Testament in its Social Environment* (Philadelphia: Westminster Press, 1986).

Balibar, Etienne, 'Racism and Nationalism', in Etienne Balibar and Immanuel Wallerstein (eds.), *Race, Nation, Class: Ambiguous Identities* (New York: Verso, 1986), pp. 37-67.

Barnstone, Willis, *The Other Bible: Ancient Esoteric Texts* (San Francisco: Harper & Row, 1984).

Barrett, C.K., *The Gospel According to St. John* (London: SPCK, 1978).

Baylis, C.P., 'The Woman Caught in Adultery: A Test of Jesus as the Greater Prophet', *BSac* 146 (1989), pp. 171-84.

Bennington, Geoffrey, 'The Politics and the Institution of the Nation', in Bhabha (ed.), *Nation and Narration*, pp. 121-37.

Berlant, Lauren G., *The Anatomy of a National Fantasy* (Chicago: University of Chicago Press, 1991).

Berman, B.J., 'Ethnicity, Patronage and the African State: The Politics of Uncivil Nationalism', *African Affairs* 97 (1998), pp. 305-41.

Berry, Wendell, *A Place on Earth* (San Francisco: North Point, rev. edn, 1983).

Beverley, J., 'The Margin at the Center: On *Testimonio* (Testimonial Narrative)', *MFS* 35 (1989), pp. 11-28.

Bhabha, Homi K., 'Dissemination: Time, Narrative, and the Margins of the Modern Nation', in Bhabha (ed.), *Nation and Narration*, pp. 291-322.

—'Introduction: Narrating the Nation', in Bhabha (ed.), *Nation and Narration*, pp. 1-7.

—*The Location of Culture* (New York: Routledge, 1994).

Bhabha, Homi K. (ed.), *Nation and Narration* (London: Routledge, 1990).

Binney, Judith, *Redemption Songs: A Life of Te Kooti Arikirangi Te Turuki* (Auckland: Auckland University Press, 1995).

Binney, Judith, G. Chaplin and C. Wallace (eds.), *Mihaia: The Prophet Rua Kanana and his Community at Maungapohatu* (Auckland: Auckland University Press, 1996).

Blaut, J.M., *The Colonizer's Model of the World: Geographical Diffusionism and Eurocentric History* (New York: Guildford, 1993).

Blunt, Alison, *Travel, Gender, and Imperialism: Mary Kingsley and West Africa* (New York: Guildford, 1994).

Blunt, Alison, and Gillian Rose (eds.), *Writing Women and Space: Colonial and Postcolonial Geographies* (New York: Guildford, 1994).

Boehmer, Elleke, *Colonial and Postcolonial Literature* (New York: Oxford University Press, 1995).

Borg, Marcus, *Jesus in Contemporary Scholarship* (Valley Forge, PA: Trinity Press International, 1992).

Boyarin, Daniel, 'The *Ioudaioi* in John and the Prehistory of Judaism' (unpublished paper presented at the Annual SBL Meeting, Denver, CO, 19 November 2001).

Brandon, S.G.F., 'The Defeat of Cestius Gallus, A.D. 66', *History Today* 20 (1972), pp. 38-47.

Brenner A., and C. Fontaine (eds.), *A Feminist Companion to Reading the Bible* (The Feminist Companion to the Bible, 11; Sheffield: Sheffield Academic Press, 1997).

Brock, R.N., and S. Thistlethwaite, *Casting Stones: Prostitution and Liberation in Asia and the United States* (Minneapolis: Fortress Press, 1992).

Brown, Peter, *The Cult of the Saints: Its Rise and Function in Latin Christianity* (Chicago: University of Chicago Press, 1981).

Brown, Raymond E., *The Community of the Beloved Disciple: The Life, Loves and Hates of an Individual Church in New Testament Times* (New York: Paulist Press, 1979).

—*The Gospel According to John: I–XII* (AB, 29; Garden City, NY: Doubleday,1966).

—*The Gospel and Epistles of John* (Collegeville, MN: Liturgical Press, 1988).

Brueggemann, Walter, *The Land: Place as Gift, Promise, and Challenge in Biblical Faith* (Philadelphia: Fortress Press, 1977).

Buell, Denise Kimber, *Making Christians: Clement of Alexandria and the Rhetoric of Legitimacy* (Princeton, NJ: Princeton University Press, 1999).

Bultmann, Rudolf, *The Gospel of John: A Commentary* (trans. G.R. Beasley-Murray; Oxford: Basil Blackwell, 1971).

Burge, Gary M., 'Territorial Religion, Johannine Christology, and the Vine of John 15', in Joel B. Green and Max Turner (eds.), *Jesus of Nazareth, Lord and Christ:*

Essays on the Historical Jesus and New Testament Christology (Grand Rapids: Eerdmans, 1994), pp. 384-96.

Burton-Christie, Douglas, 'Into the Body of Another: *Eros*, Embodiment and Intimacy with the Natural World', *ATR* 81 (1999), pp. 13-37.

—'Living Between Two Worlds: Home, Journey and the Quest for Sacred Place', *ATR* 79 (1997), pp. 413-32.

—'A Sense of Place', *The Way* 39 (1999), pp. 59-72.

—'Words Beneath the Water: Logos, Cosmos, and the Spirit of Place', in Dieter T. Hessel and Rosemary Radford Ruether (eds.), *Christianity and Ecology: Seeking the Well-Being of Earth and Humans* (Cambridge, MA: Harvard University Press, 2000), pp. 317-34.

Busto, Rudy V., 'The Gospel According to the Model Minority? Hazarding an Interpretation of Asian American Evangelical College Students', in David K. Yoo (ed.), *New Spiritual Homes: Religion and Asian Americans* (Honolulu: University of Hawaii Press, 1999), pp. 169-87.

Butler, J., and J.W. Scott (eds.), *Feminists Theorize the Political* (New York: Routledge, 1992).

Butler, S., 'An Alliance under Fire', *U.S. News and World Report* 119 (2 Oct. 1995), pp. 54-56.

Campbell, J.B., *The Emperor and the Roman Army 31 B.C.–A.D. 235* (Oxford: Clarendon Press, 1984).

Casey, Edward, *Getting Back into Place: Toward a Renewed Understanding of the Place-World* (Bloomington: Indiana University Press, 1993).

Casey, Maurice, *Is John's Gospel True?* (London: Routledge, 1996).

Cassidy, Richard J., *John's Gospel in New Perspective: Christology and the Realities of Roman Power* (Maryknoll, NY: Orbis, 1992).

Castronovo, R., 'Compromised Narratives along the Border: The Mason–Dixon Line, Resistance, and Hegemony', in D.E. Johnson and S. Michaelson (eds.), *Border Theory: The Limits of Cultural Politics* (Minneapolis: University of Minnesota Press, 1997).

Castro, P., 'La mujer en la pastoral de Jesús y de los fariseos', in I. Foulkes (ed.), *Teología desde la Mujer en Centroamérica* (San José: Seminario Bíblico Latinoamericano, 1989), pp. 105-19.

Cave, Terence, *Recognitions: A Study in Poetics* (Oxford: Clarendon Press, 1988).

Chadwick, St. John, *Newfoundland: Island into Province* (Cambridge: Cambridge University Press, 1967).

Chatterjee, Partha, 'Whose Imagined Community?', in Gopal Balakrishnan (ed.), *Mapping the Nation* (New York: Verso, 1996), pp. 214-25.

Chow, Rey, *Ethics after Idealism: Theory-Culture-Ethnicity-Reading* (Bloomington/Indianapolis: Indiana University Press, 1998).

Chrisman, Laura, and Patrick Williams (eds.), *Colonial Discourse and Postcolonial Theory: A Reader* (New York: Columbia University Press, 1994).

Cliff, Michelle, *No Telephone to Heaven* (New York: Penguin, 1996).

Cohen, Anthony P., *The Symbolic Construction of Community* (New York: Tavistock and Ellis Horwood, 1985).

Cohen, Ted, 'Metaphor and the Cultivation of Intimacy', *Critical Inquiry* 5 (1978), pp. 3-12.

Coleman, B.W., 'The Woman Taken in Adultery [John 7.53–8.11]', *Theology* 73 (1970) pp. 409-10.

Comaroff, John L., and Jean Comaroff, *Of Revelation and Revolution: The Dialectics of Modernity on a Southern African Frontier*, Vol. 2 (Chicago: University of Chicago Press, 1997).

Combs, James, 'Gardens of Earthly Delight', *The Cresset* 63 (2000), pp. 27-30.

Comfort, P., 'The Pericope of the Adulteress', *BT* 40 (1989), pp. 145-47.

Conrad, Joseph, *Heart of Darkness and the Secret Sharer* (New York: Bantam Classics, 1902).

Cornell, Drucilla, 'The "Postmodern" Challenge to the Ideal of Community', in Drucilla Cornell (ed.), *The Philosophy of the Limit* (New York: Routledge, 1992), pp. 39-61.

Counet, Patrick Chatelion, *John, A Postmodern Gospel: Introduction to Deconstructive Exegesis Applied to the Fourth Gospel* (Biblical Interpretation Series, 44; Leiden: E.J. Brill, 2000).

Cresswell, Tim, *In Place/Out of Place: Geography, Ideology, and Transgression* (Minneapolis: University of Minneapolis Press, 1996).

Culbertson, Diana, *The Poetics of Revelation: Recognition and the Narrative Tradition* (Studies in American Biblical Hermeneutics, 4; Macon, GA: Mercer University Press, 1989).

Culpepper, R. Alan, *Anatomy of the Fourth Gospel: A Study in Literary Design* (Philadelphia: Fortress Press, 1983).

—'The Gospel of John as a Document of Faith in a Pluralistic Culture', in Fernando F. Segovia (ed.), *'What is John': Readers and Readings of the Fourth Gospel* (Atlanta: Scholars Press, 1996), pp. 107-27.

—*Gospels and Letters of John* (Interpreting Biblical Texts; Nashville: Abingdon Press, 1998).

—'Reading Johannine Irony', in R. Alan Culpepper and C. Clifton Black (eds.), *Exploring the Gospel of John: In Honor of D. Moody Smith* (Louisville, KY: Westminster/John Knox Press, 1996), pp. 193-207.

Dabgarembga, T., *Nervous Conditions* (Seattle: Seal, 1988).

Davidson, Allan K., *Aotearoa New Zealand: Defining Moments in the Gospel–Culture Encounter* (Geneva: WCC, 1996).

—'The Interaction of Missionary and Colonial Christianity in Nineteenth Century New Zealand', in *Studies in World Christianity*, Vol. 2; Part 2 (Edinburgh: Edinburgh University Press, 1996), pp. 145-66.

—Unpublished personal correspondence to the author (26 April 2000).

Davidson, Allan K., and Peter J. Lineham, *Transplanted Christianity: Documents Illustrating Aspects of New Zealand Church History* (Palmerston North, NZ: Massey University Printery, 3rd edn, 1995).

Davies, C.B., and E.S. Fido (eds.), *Out of Kumbla: Caribbean Women and Literature* (Trenton, NJ: African World Press, 1990).

Davies, W.D., *The Territorial Dimension of Judaism* (Minneapolis: Fortress Press, 1992).

Dei Verbum, 'Dogmatic Constitution on Divine Revelation', in W.M. Abbot (ed.), *The Documents of Vatican II* (New York: America Press, 1967), pp. 111-28.

Delany, C., 'Seeds of Honor, Fields of Shame', in D.D. Gilmore (ed.), *Honor and Shame and the Unity of the Mediterranean* (Washington, DC: American Anthropological Association, 1987), pp. 35-48.

Delavignette, Robert, *Christianity and Colonialism* (New York: Hawthorn, 1964).

De Man, Paul, *Blindness and Insight: Essays in the Rhetoric of Contemporary Criticism* (Minneapolis: University of Minnesota Press, rev. edn, 1984).

Derrett, J.D.M., 'Law in the New Testament: The Story of the Woman Taken in Adultery', *NTS* 10 (1964), pp. 1-26.

Derrida, Jacques, *Adieu to Emmanuel Levinas* (trans. Pascale-Anne Brault and Michael Naas; Stanford: Stanford University Press, 1999).

Desjardins, Michel, *Peace, Violence and the New Testament* (The Biblical Seminar, 46; Sheffield: Sheffield Academic Press, 1997).

Dickason, Olive Patricia, *Canada's First Nations: A History of Founding Peoples from Earliest Times* (New York: Oxford University Press, 1992).

Donaldson, Laura E., *Decolonizing Feminisms: Race, Gender, and Empire-building* (Chapel Hill: University of North Carolina Press, 1992).

Dooley, Margaret Anne, *The True Story of the Novel* (New Brunswick, NJ: Rutgers University Press, 1996).

Dube, Musa W., 'Batswakwa: Which Traveler Are You (John 1:1-18)?', in Gerald West and Musa W. Dube (eds.), *The Bible in Africa* (Leiden: E.J. Brill, 2000), pp. 150-62.

—*Postcolonial Feminist Interpretations of the Bible* (St Louis: Chalice, 2000).

—'Savior of the World but not of this World: A Postcolonial Reading of Spatial Construction in John', in R.S. Sugirtharajah (ed.), *The Postcolonial Bible* (Sheffield: Sheffield Academic Press, 1998), pp. 118-35.

—'Towards a Post-colonial Feminist Interpretation of the Bible', *Semeia* 78 (1997), pp. 11-23.

DuBois, W.E.B., 'The Negro and Imperialism (1944)', in Philip S. Foner (ed.), *W.E.B. DuBois Speaks 1920–1963*, II (New York: Pathfinder, 1970).

—'The Souls of Whitefolk', in *Darkwater: Voices from within the Veil* (New York: Schocken Books, 1920).

Duke, Paul D., *Irony in the Fourth Gospel* (Atlanta: John Knox Press, 1985).

Dundes, A., *From Game to War: And Other Psychoanalysis Essays on Folklore* (Lexington, KY: The University Press of Kentucky, 1997).

Dunn, J.D.G., *Christology in the Making: An Inquiry into the Origins of the Doctrine of the Incarnation* (London: SCM, 2nd edn, 1989).

—*The Parting of the Ways between Christianity and Judaism and their Significance for the Character of Christianity* (London: SCM Press, 1991).

Du Rand, Jan A., 'Reading the Fourth Gospel Like a Literary Symphony', in Fernando Segovia (ed.), *What is John?* II, pp. 5-18.

Eagleton, Terry, *The Idea of Culture* (Malden, MA: Blackwell, 2000).

Ehrman, Bart D., 'Jesus and the Adulteress', *NTS* 24 (1988), pp. 24-44.

Eliade, Mircea, *Cosmos and History: The Myth of the Eternal Return* (trans. Willard R. Trask; New York: Harper Torchbook, 1959).

—'A New Humanism', in *The Quest: History and Meaning in Religion* (Chicago: The University of Chicago Press, 1969).

—*Patterns in Comparative Religion* (trans. Rosemary Sheed; New York: Sheed & Ward, 1958).

—*The Sacred and the Profane: The Nature of Religion* (trans. Willard R. Trask; New York: Harcourt Brace, 1959).

Elliott, John, *A Home for the Homeless: A Social-Scientific Criticism of 1 Peter, its Situation and Strategy* (Minneapolis: Fortress Press, 1994).

Elsmore, Bronwyn, *Like Them that Dream: The Maori and the Old Testament* (Tauranga: Tauranga Moana, 1985).

—*The Religion of Matenga Tamati* (Auckland: Reed, 1997).

Enslin, Morton, 'John and Jesus', *ZNW* 66 (1975), pp. 1-18.

Epp, M., 'The Memory of Violence: Soviet and East European Mennonite Refuges and Rape in the Second World War', *Journal of Women's History* 9 (1997) 58-87.

Fehribach, Adeline, *The Women in the Life of the Bridegroom: A Feminist Historical-Literary Analysis of the Female Characters in the Fourth Gospel* (Collegeville, MN: Liturgical Press, 1998).

Ford, J. Massyngbaerde, *Redeemer, Friend and Mother: Salvation in Antiquity and in the Gospel of John* (Minneapolis: Fortress Press, 1997).

Fortna, R.T., and B. Gaventa (eds.), *The Conversation Continues: Studies in Paul and John in Honor of J. Louis Martyn* (Nashville: Abingdon Press, 1990).

Foucault, Michel, *The Archaeology of Knowledge* (trans. A.M. Sheriden-Smith; London: Tavistock, 1972).

Freedman, Diane P., Olivia Frey and Frances Murphy Zauhar (eds.), *The Intimate Critique: Autobiographical Literary Criticism* (Durham, NC: Duke University Press, 1993).

Fuchs, Esther, 'Structure and Patriarchal Functions in Biblical Betrothal Type-Scenes: Some Preliminary Notes', *Journal of Feminist Studies in Religion* 3 (1987), pp. 7-13.

Gandhi, Leela, *Postcolonial Theory: A Critical Introduction* (New York: Columbia University Press, 1998).

Gellner, Ernest, *Nations and Nationalism* (Ithaca, NY: Cornell University Press, 1983).

George, F.C., 'The Promotion of Missiological Studies in Seminaries', *Mission Studies: Journal of the IAMS* 26 (1998), pp. 13-27.

Gerson, J., 'I Refuse', *The Bulletin of the Atomic Scientists* 52 (1996), p. 26.

Gilmore, D.D., 'Introduction: The Shame of Dishonor', in D.D. Gilmore (ed.), *Honor and Shame and the Unity of the Mediterranean* (Washington, DC: American Anthropological Association, 1987), pp. 2-21.

Goldie, Terry, and Robert Gray (eds.), 'Postcolonial and Queer Theory and Praxis', *Ariel* 30 (1999).

Goldsworthy, A.K., *The Roman Army at War: 100 BC–AD 200* (Oxford: Clarendon Press, 1996).

González, Justo L., *A History of Christian Thought: From the Beginnings to the Council of Chalcedon* (Nashville: Abingdon, rev. edn, 1987).

Gordon, Milton, *Human Nature, Class, and Ethnicity* (New York: Oxford University Press, 1978).

Gramsci, Antonio, *Selections from the Prison Notebooks* (ed. and trans. Quinton Hoare and Geoffrey Nowell Smith; New York: International, 1971).

Grant, George, *Lament for a Nation: The Defeat of Canadian Nationalism* (Toronto: McClelland & Stewart, 1965).

Greenblatt, S., 'Culture', in Lentricchia and McLaughlin (eds.), *Critical Terms for Literary Study*, pp. 225-32.

Grewal, I., *Home and Harem: Nation, Gender, Empire, and the Cultures of Travel* (Durham, NC: Duke University Press, 1996).

Grewal, I., and C. Kaplan (eds.), *Scattered Hegemony: Postmodernity and Transnational Feminist Practices* (Minneapolis: University of Minnesota Press, 1994).

Habermas, Jürgen, 'Struggles for Recognition in the Democratic Constitutional State', in Amy Gutmann (ed.), *Multiculturalism: Examining the Politics of Recognition* (Princeton, NJ: Princeton University Press, 1994).

Habinek, T., and A. Schiesaro (eds.), *The Roman Cultural Revolution* (New York: Cambridge University Press, 1997).

Hall, Stuart, 'Gramsci's Relevance for the Study of Race and Ethnicity', *Communication Inquiry* 10 (1986), pp. 5-27.

—'The Toad in the Garden: Thatcherism among the Theorists', in Cary Nelson and Lawrence Frossberg (eds.), *Marxism and the Interpretation of Culture* (Urbana: University of Illinois Press, 1988).

Hammond, Philip E., and James D. Hunter, 'On Maintaining Plausibility: The Worldview of Evangelical College Students', *SSR* 22 (1984), pp. 221-38.

Hanson, K.C., and D.E. Oakman, *Palestine in the Times of Jesus: Social Structures and Social Conflicts* (Minneapolis: Fortress Press, 1998).

Harlow, Barbara, *Resistance Literature* (New York: Methuen, 1987).

Harvey, A.E., *Jesus on Trial: A Study in the Fourth Gospel* (London: SPCK, 1976).

Harvey, Elizabeth D., *Ventriloquized Voices: Feminist Theory and English Renaissance Texts* (New York: Routledge, 1991).

Heil, J.P., 'A Rejoinder to "Reconsidering 'The Story of Jesus and the Adulteress Reconsidered'"', *ET* 25 (1994), pp. 361-66.

—'The Story of Jesus and the Adulteress (John 7.53–8.11) Reconsidered', *Bib* 72 (1991), pp. 182-91.

Hendricks, O.O., 'Guerrilla Exegesis: A Post-modern Proposal for Insurgent African-American Biblical Studies', *JITC* 22 (1994), pp. 92-109.

Hicks, G., *The Comfort Women: Japan's Brutal Regime of Enforced Prostitution in the Second World War* (New York: W.W. Norton, 1995).

Hobsbawm, Eric J., *Nations and Nationalism since 1780: Programme, Myth, Reality* (Cambridge: Cambridge University Press, 1990).

Hobsbawm, Eric, and Terence Ranger (eds.), *The Invention of Tradition* (New York: Cambridge University Press, 1992).

Hodges, Z.C., 'The Woman Taken in Adultery (John 7.53–8.11): Exposition', *BSac* 137 (1980), pp. 41-53.

—'The Woman Taken in Adultery (John 7.53–8.11): The Text', *BSac* 136 (1979), pp. 318-32.

Hong Kingston, Maxine, *Tripmaster Monkey: His Fake Book* (New York: Alfred A. Knopf, 1989).

Howard-Brook, Wes, *Becoming Children of God: John's Gospel and Radical Discipleship* (Maryknoll, NY: Orbis Books, 1995).

Howard-Brook, Wes and Anthony Gwyther, *Unveiling the Empire: Reading Revelation Then and Now* (Maryknoll, NY: Orbis Books, 1999).

Huffard, Evertt. W., 'Missions and the Servants of God (John 5)', in J. Priest (ed.), *Johannine Studies: Essays in Honor of Frank Peck* (Malibu: Pepperdine University Press, 1989), pp. 84-96.

Huie-Jolly, Mary R., 'Like Father, Like Son, Absolute Case, Mythic Authority: Constructing Ideology in John 5.17-23', *SBLSP* 36 (1997), pp. 567-95.

—'The Son Enthroned in Conflict: A Socio-rhetorical Interpretation of John 5.17-23' (unpublished PhD dissertation; Dunedin, New Zealand, University of Otago, 1994).

—'Threats Answered by Enthronement: John 5.17-27 with Reference to the Divine
    Warrior Myth in Psalm 2 and Daniel 7', in C.A. Evans and J.A. Sanders (eds.),
    Early Christian Interpretations of the Scriptures of Israel: Investigations and Proposals
    (JSNTSup, 148; SSEJC, 5; Sheffield: Sheffield Academic Press, 1997), pp. 191-
    217.

Hutcheon, Linda, *Irony's Edge: The Theory and Politics of Irony* (New York: Routledge,
    1994).

Hutton, J., *Aristotle Poetics* (New York: W.W. Norton, 1982).

Isaac, B., *The Limits of Empire: The Roman Army in the East* (Oxford: Clarendon Press,
    1990).

James, S.A., 'The Adulteress and the Death Penalty', *JETS* 22 (1979), pp. 45-53.

Jen, Gish, *Typical American* (Boston: Houghton Mifflin, 1991).

Jennings, D.L., *Raspberries and Blackberries: Their Breeding, Diseases and Growth* (New
    York: Academic Press, 1988).

Johnson, A.F., 'A Stylistic Trait of the Fourth Gospel in the Pericope Adulterae?',
    BETS 9 (1966), pp. 91-96.

Johnson, D.E., and S. Michaelsen, 'Border Secrets: An Introduction', in D.E. Johnson
    and S. Michaelsen (eds.), *Border Theory: The Limits of Cultural Politics* (Min-
    neapolis: University of Minnesota Press, 1997), pp. 1-39.

Johnson, L., 'Breaking Silence: Beijing Permits Screening of Najing Massacre Film',
    Far Eastern Economic Review (24 Aug. 1995), p. 40.

Johnston, Wayne, *Baltimore's Mansion* (Toronto: Alfred A. Knopf, 1999).

Käsemann, Ernst, *The Testament of Jesus: A Study of the Gospel of John in Light of Chapter
    17* (trans. Gerhard Krodel; Philadelphia: Fortress Press, 2nd edn, 1968).

Katrak, K.H., 'Decolonizing Culture: Toward a Theory for Postcolonial Women's
    Texts', *MFS* 35 (1989), pp. 157-79.

Keating, A.L., 'Myth Smashers, Myth Makers: (Re)Visionary Techniques in the Works
    of Paula Gunn Allen, Gloria Anzaldúa, and Audre Lorde', *Critical Essays: Gay and
    Lesbian Writers of Color* 26 (1993), pp. 73-95.

Keith, Michael, and Steve Pile (eds.), *Place and Politics of Identity* (New York: Routledge,
    1993).

Kellum, B., 'Concealing/Revealing: Gender and the Play of Meaning in the Moments
    of Augustan Rome', in Habinek and Schiesaro (eds.), *The Roman Cultural
    Revolution*, pp. 158-81.

Kerr, Heather, and Amanda Nettelbeck (eds.), *The Space Between: Australian Women
    Writing Fictocriticism* (Nedlands: University of Western Australia, 1998).

Khalidi, Rashid I., 'Contrasting Narratives of Palestinian Identity', in Patricia Yaeger
    (ed.), *The Geography of Identity* (Ann Arbor: University of Michigan Press, 1996),
    pp. 187-222.

Kim, David Kyuman, 'Enchanting Diasporas: Asian Americans, Religion, and Race'
    (unpublished paper presented at the Asian and Pacific Americans and Religion
    Research Initiative, University of California, Santa Barbara, 23 June 2000).

Kim, E.H., and C. Choi (eds.), *Dangerous Women: Gender and Korean Nationalism* (New
    York: Routledge, 1997).

Kim, J.K., '"Uncovering her Wickedness": An Intercontextual Reading of Revelation
    17 from a Postcolonial Feminist Perspective', *JSNT* 73 (1999), pp. 61-81.

Kim, R., *Clay Walls* (Sag Harbor, NY: Permanent Press, 1986).

Kipling, Rudyard, 'The White Man's Burden', in L. Synder (ed.), *The Imperialism Reader* (New York: D. Van Nostrand, 1962).

Kitzberger, Ingrid Rosa, 'How can This Be?' (John 3.9): A Feminist-Theological Re-reading of the Gospel of John', in Segovia (ed.), *'What is John'*, II, pp. 19-41.

Koester, C.R., 'The Savior of the World (John 4.42)', *JBL* 109 (1990), pp. 665-80.

—*Symbolism in the Fourth Gospel: Meaning, Mystery, Community* (Minneapolis: Fortress Press, 1995).

Koester, C.R., R.E. Brown and J.L. Martyn, 'Johannine Studies in Retrospect', *BTB* 21 (1991), pp. 51-55.

Kossen, H.B., 'Who Were the Greeks of John xii 20?', *Studies in John* (Leiden: E.J. Brill, 1970), pp. 97-110.

Kwok, Pui Lan, 'Jesus/The Native: Biblical Studies from a Postcolonial Perspective', in Fernando F. Segovia and Mary Ann Tolbert (eds.), *Teaching the Bible: The Discourses and Politics of Biblical Pedagogy* (Maryknoll, NY: Orbis Books, 1998), pp. 69-85.

Kysar, Robert, 'The Gospel of John', in *ABD*, III (1992), pp. 912-31.

—*John: The Maverick Gospel* (Louisville: John Knox, 1976).

Lauterbach, Jacob Z., *Melkita de Rabbi Ishmael. II* (trans. Jacob Z. Lauterbach; Philadelphia: The Jewish Publication Society of America, 1976).

Lavie, Smadar, and Ted Swedenburg (eds.), *Displacement, Diaspora, and Geographies of Identity* (Durham, NC: Duke University Press, 1996).

Leach, William, *Country of Exiles: The Destruction of Place in American Life* (New York: Random House, 1999).

Lentricchia F., and T. McLaughlin (eds.), *Critical Terms for Literary Study* (Chicago: University of Chicago Press, 1994).

Levinas, Emmanuel, *Dieu, la mort et le temps* (Paris: Grasset, 1993).

Leyerle, Blake, 'Landscape as Cartography in Early Christian Pilgrimage Narratives', *JAAR* 64 (1996), pp. 119-43.

Li, David Leiwei, *Imagining the Nation: Asian American Literature and Cultural Consent* (Stanford: Stanford University Press, 1998).

Lind, Christopher, *Something is Wrong Somewhere: Globalization, Community and the Moral Economy of the Farm Crisis* (Halifax, Nova Scotia: Fernwood, 1995).

Lindars, B., *The Gospel of John* (NCB; London: Oliphants, 1972).

Loomba, Ania, 'Local-manufacture Made-in-India Othello Fellows: Issues of Race, Hybridity and Location in Post-colonial Shakespeares', in Ania Loomba and Martin Orkin (eds.), *Post-colonial Shakespeares* (New York: Routledge, 1998), pp. 143-63.

Lozada, Jr, Francisco, *A Literary Reading of John 5: Text as Construction* (Studies in Biblical Literature, 20; New York: Peter Lang, 2000).

Luttwak, E.N., *The Grand Strategy of the Roman Empire: From the First Century A.D. to the Third* (Baltimore: The Johns Hopkins University Press, 1979).

Maccini, R.G., *Her Testimony is True: Women as Witnesses According to John* (JSNTSup, 125; Sheffield: Sheffield Academic Press, 1996).

MacMullen, R., *Soldier and Civilian in the Later Roman Empire* (Cambridge, MA: Harvard University Press, 1963).

Malina, Bruce J., *The Gospel of John in Sociolinguistic Perspective* (Protocol of the Forty-Eighth Colloquy; Berkeley, CA; Center for Hermeneutical Studies in Hellenistic and Modern Culture; Graduate Theological Union and the University of California, 1985).

Maluleke, Tinyiko S., 'What Africans are Doing to Jesus: Will He Ever Be the Same Again?', in C.W. Du Toit (ed.), *Images of Jesus* (Pretoria: University of South Africa, 1997), pp. 187-205.

Manor, F.S., 'Are They Really the New Romans?', in John. H. Redekop (ed.), *The Star-Spangled Beaver* (Toronto: Peter Martin Associates, 1971), pp. 106-13.

Marsot, A.L.A., *A Short History of Modern Egypt* (Cambridge: Cambridge University Press, 1985).

Martyn, J. Louis, *The Gospel of John in Christian History: Essays in Interpretation* (New York: Paulist Press, 1978).

—*History and Theology in the Fourth Gospel* (Nashville: Abingdon Press, 2nd edn, 1979).

Massey, Doreen, *Space, Place, and Gender* (Minneapolis: University of Minnesota Press, 1994).

Maunier, René, *The Sociology of Colonies: An Introduction to the Study of Colonies*, Vol. 1 (London: Routledge, 1949).

McClintock, A., '"No Longer in a Future Heaven": Gender, Race and Nationalism', in McClintock, Mufti and Shohat (eds.), *Dangerous Liaisons*, pp. 90-112.

McClintock, A., A. Mufti and E. Shohat (eds.), *Dangerous Liaisons: Gender, Nation, and Postcolonial Perspectives* (Minneapolis: University of Minnesota Press, 1997).

McDonald, J.I.H., 'The So-called Pericope De adultera', *NTS* 41 (1995), pp. 415-27.

McPherson, Robert S., *Sacred Land Sacred View: Navajo Perceptions of the Four Corners Region* (Charles Redd Monographs in Western History, 19; Salt Lake City: Charles Redd Center for Western Studies, Brigham Young University, 1991).

Meeks, Wayne, 'Equal to God', in Fortna and Gaventa (eds.), *The Conversation Continues*, pp. 309-21.

—'The Man From Heaven in Johannine Sectarianism', *JBL* 91 (1972), pp. 44-72.

—*The Origins of Christian Morality: The First Two Centuries* (New Haven: Yale University Press, 1993).

—*The Prophet King* (Leiden: E.J. Brill, 1967).

Meffe, Gary, and Ronald Carroll, *Principles of Conservation Biology* (Sunderland, MA: Sinauer Associates, 1994).

Mehic, D., 'We are Dying of your Protection', *The Bulletin of the Atomic Scientists* 51 (1995), pp. 41-44.

Mendel, D., *The Rise and Fall of Jewish Nationalism: Jewish and Christian Ethnicity in Ancient Palestine* (Grand Rapids: Eerdmans, 1992).

Metzger, B.M., *A Textual Commentary on the Greek New Testament* (New York: United Bible Societies, 1971).

Minear, Paul S., 'Writing on the Ground: The Puzzle in John 8.1-11', *HBT* 13 (1991), pp. 23-36.

Mitchell, Robert D., *Commercialism and Frontier: Perspectives on the Early Shenandoah Valley* (Charlottesville: University of Virginia Press, 1977).

Moi, T. (ed.), *The Kristeva Reader* (New York: Columbia University Press, 1986).

Moloney, Francis J., *Signs and Shadows: Reading John 5–12* (Minneapolis: Fortress Press, 1996).

Momaday, N. Scott, *House Made of Dawn* (New York: New American Library, 1996).

Moore, Stephen D., 'Postcolonialism', in A.K.M. Adam (ed.), *A Handbook of Postmodern Biblical Interpretation* (St Louis: Chalice, 2000), pp. 182-88.

—'True Confessions and Weird Obsessions: Autobiographical Interventions in Literary and Biblical Studies', *Semeia* 71 (1995), pp. 19-50.

Morales, A., 'Dynamic Identities in Heterotopia', in J.A. Gurpegui (ed.), *Alejandro Morales: Fiction Past, Present, Future Perfect* (Tempe: Bilingual Review, 1996).

Morris, L., *The Gospel According to John* (Grand Rapids: Eerdmans, 1995).

Mosse, G., *Nationalism and Sexuality: Respectability and Abnormal Sexuality in Modern Europe* (New York: H. Fertig, 1985).

Moulthrop, Stuart, 'Rhizome and Resistance: Hypertext and the Dream of a New Culture', in George P. Landow (ed.), *Hyper/Text/Theory* (Baltimore: The Johns Hopkins University Press, 1994).

Mowat, Farley, 'Letter to my Son', in Purdy (ed.), *The New Romans*, pp. 1-6.

Moynihan, Daniel Patrick, *Pandaemonium: Ethnicity in International Politics* (Oxford: Oxford University Press, 1993).

Mudimbe, V.Y., *The Idea of Africa* (Bloomington: Indiana University Press, 1994).

—*The Invention of Africa: Gnosis, Philosophy, and the Order of Knowledge* (Bloomington: Indiana University Press, 1988).

Newman, B., and E. Nida, *A Translator's Handbook on The Gospel of John* (New York: United Bible Societies, 1980).

Neyrey, Jerome H., *An Ideology of Revolt: John's Christology in Social-Science Perspective* (Philadelphia: Fortress Press, 1988).

—'Jacob Traditions and the Interpretation of John 4.10-26', *CBQ* 41 (1979), pp. 419-37.

Ngugi wa Thiong'o, *Decolonising the Mind: The Politics of Language in African Literature* (London: James Currey, 1986).

—*Moving the Centre: The Struggle for Cultural Freedoms* (London: James Currey, 1993).

Nobles, Gregory H., 'Breaking into the Backcountry: New Approaches to the Early American Frontier, 1750–1800', *William and Mary Quarterly* 46 (1989), pp. 641-70.

O'Connor, Jerome Murphy, 'John the Baptist and Jesus: History and Hypotheses', *NTS* 36 (1990), pp. 359-74.

O'Day, Gail R., 'The Gospel of John: Introduction, Commentary and Reflections', in *The New Interpreter's Bible*, IX (Nashville: Abingdon Press, 1994), pp. 496-865 (630).

—'John', in C.A. Newsom and S.H. Ringe, (eds.), *The Women's Bible Commentary* (Louisville, KY: Westminster/John Knox Press, 1992), pp. 293-304.

—'John 7.53–8.11: A Study In Misreading', *JBL* 111 (1992), pp. 631-40.

—*Revelation in the Fourth Gospel* (Philadelphia: Fortress Press, 1986).

—*The Word Disclosed: John's Story and Narrative Preaching* (St Louis: CBP, 1987).

Odin, Jaishree K., 'The Edge of Difference: Negotiations Between the Hypertextual and the Postcolonial', *MFS* 43 (1997), pp. 598-630.

Okure, T., *To Cast Fire upon the Earth: Bible and Mission Collaborating in Today's Multi-cultural Global Context* (Natal: Cluster, 2000).

Omi, Michael, and Howard Winant, *Racial Formation in the United States: From the 1960s to the 1990s* (New York: Routledge, 2nd edn, 1994).

Opitz, May, Katharina Oguntoye and Dagmar Schultz (eds.), *Showing our Colors: Afro-German Women Speak Out* (trans. Anne Adams; Amherst: University of Massachusetts Press, 1992).

Organization for Economic Co-operation and Development, *SOPEMI: Trends in International Migration. Annual Report* (Paris: OECD, 1994).

Overman, Andrew J., *Matthew's Gospel and Formative Judaism: The Social World of the Matthean Community* (Minneapolis: Fortress Press, 1990).

Pagels, Elaine H., *The Johannine Gospels in Gnostic Exegesis: Heracleon's Commentary on John* (SBLMS, Atlanta: Scholars Press, 1973).

Park, Robert E., and Ernest W. Burgess, *Introduction to the Science of Sociology* (Chicago: University of Chicago Press, 1921).

Park, S., C. Kim and U. Kim (eds.), *Our Kum-I* (Seoul: The Committee on the Murder of Kum-I Yun by American Military in Korea, 1993).

Passerini, L., *Fascism in Popular Memory* (Cambridge: Cambridge University Press, 1987).

—'Women's Personal Narratives: Myths, Experiences, and Emotions', in Personal Narrative Group (ed.), *Interpreting Women's Lives*, pp. 89-97.

Patte, D.M., *Ethics of Biblical Interpretation: A Reevaluation* (Louisville, KY: Westminster/ John Knox Press, 1995).

Personal Narrative Group (ed.), *Interpreting Women's Lives: Feminist Theory and Personal Narratives* (Bloomington: Indiana University Press, 1989).

Petersen, Norman R., *The Gospel of John and the Sociology of Light: Language and Characterization in the Fourth Gospel* (Valley Forge, PA: Trinity International Press, 1992).

Pfeil, Fred, *White Guys: Studies in Postmodern Domination and Difference* (New York: Verso, 1995).

Phillips, Gary A., 'The Ethics of Reading Deconstructively or Speaking Face-to-Face: The Samaritan Woman Meets Derrida at the Well', in Edgar V. McKnight and Elisabeth Struthers Malbon (eds.), *The New Literary Criticism and the New Testament* (Valley Forge, PA: Trinity Press International, 1994).

—'"What is Written? How are You Reading?" Gospel, Intertextuality and Doing Luke-wise: Reading Lk 10.25-42 Otherwise', *Semeia* 69/70 (1995), pp. 111-48.

Phillips, Gary A., and Danna Nolan Fewell, 'Ethics, Bible, Reading as if', *Semeia* 77 (1997), pp. 1-21.

Philo, 'The Confusion of Tongues', in *Philo. IV. Loeb Classical Library* (trans. F.H. Colson and G.H. Whitaker; Cambridge, MA: Harvard University Press, 1932).

Pospisil, Leopold Jaroslav, *Anthropology of Law: A Comparative Theory* (New York: Harper & Row, 1971).

Prior, Michael, *The Bible and Colonialism: A Moral Critique* (The Biblical Seminar, 48; Sheffield: Sheffield Academic Press, 1997).

Pryor, John W., 'John the Baptist and Jesus: Tradition and Text in John 3.25', *JSNT* 66 (1997), pp. 15-26.

Pui-Lan, Kwok, Notes from unpublished lectures, 18–19 August (University of Otago Dunedin, New Zealand, 1997).

Purdy, A.W. (ed.), *The New Romans: Candid Canadian Opinions of the U.S.* (Edmonton: M.G. Hurtig, 1968).

Quint, David, *Epic and Empire* (Princeton, NJ: Princeton University Press, 1993).

Raditsa, L.F., 'Augustus' Legislation Concerning Marriage, Procreation, Love Affairs and Adultery', *ANRW*, II. 13, pp. 278-339.

Raisanen, Heikki *et al.*, *Reading The Bible in The Global Village, Helsinki* (Atlanta: SBL, 2000).

Raper, Mark, 'Refugees: Travel under Duress', *The Way* 39 (1999), pp. 27-38.

Reif-Hülser, Monika (ed.), *Borderlands: Negotiating Boundaries in Post-Colonial Writing* (ASNEL, Papers 4; Atlanta: Rodopi, 1999).

Reinhartz, Adele, 'The Johannine Community and its Jewish Neighbors: A Repraisal', in Segovia (ed.), *What is John?*, II, pp. 111-38.

—'On Travel, Translation, and Ethnography: Johannine Scholarship at the Turn of the Century', in Segovia (ed.), *What is John?*, II, pp. 249-56.

—*The Word in the World: The Cosmological Tale in the Fourth Gospel* (Atlanta: Scholars Press, 1992).

Renan, Ernest, *Qu'est-ce qu'une nation* (Paris: Presses Pocket, 1992).

Rensberger, David, *Johannine Faith and Liberating Community* (Philadelphia: Westminster Press, 1988).

Ridderbos, H., *The Gospel of John: A Theological Commentary* (Grand Rapids: Eerdmans, 1997).

Ringe, Sharon H., *Wisdom's Friends: Community and Christology in the Fourth Gospel* (Louisville, KY: Westminster/John Knox Press, 1999).

Robinson, J.A.T., 'The Destination and Purpose of St. John's Gospel', *NTS* 6 (1959–60), pp. 117-31.

Roetzel, Calvin J., *The World that Shaped the New Testament* (Atlanta: John Knox Press, 1985).

Rogers, Lawrence M. (ed.), *The Early Journals of Henry Williams 1826–40* (Christchurch: Pegasus, 1961).

Rosaldo, R., *Culture and Truth: The Remaking of Social Analysis* (Boston: Beacon Press, 1993).

Rothstein, Eric, 'Diversity and Change in Literary History', in Jay Clayton and Eric Rothstein (eds.), *Influence and Intertextuality in Literary History* (Madison: University of Wisconsin Press, 1991), pp. 114-45.

Rowe, John Carlos, 'Melville's *Typee*: US Imperialism at Home and Abroad', in Donald E. Pease (ed.), *National Identities and Post-Americanist Narratives* (Durham, NC: Duke University Press, 1994), pp. 255-78.

Roxburgh, Irvine, *The Ringatu Movement: A Phenomenological Essay on Culture Shock in New Zealand/Aotearoa* (Christchurch, NZ: Cadsonbury, 1998).

Saadawi, N.E., *The Hidden Face of Eve: Women in the Arab World* (Boston: Beacon Press, 1980).

—*Woman at Point Zero* (trans. Sherif Hetata; London: Zed Books, 1983).

Said, Edward, *Culture and Imperialism* (London: Chatto & Windus, 1993).

Saldarini, A.J., 'Pharisees', *ABD* V (1992), p. 297.

Saliba, T., 'On the Bodies of Third World Women: Cultural Impurity, Prostitution, and Other Nervous Conditions', *College Literature* 22 (1995), pp. 131-46.

Salmond, Anne, *Two Worlds: First Meetings Between Maori and Europeans 1642–1772* (Auckland: Viking, 1991).

Salvoni, F., 'Textual Authority for John 7.53–8.11', *Restoration Quarterly* 4 (1960), pp. 11-15.

Sanders, E.P., *Judaism: Practice and Belief 63 BCE–66 CE* (Philadelphia: Trinity International, 1992).

Schilling, Frederick A., 'The Story of Jesus and the Adulteress', *ATR* 37 (1955), pp. 91-106.

Schnackenburg, Rudolf, *The Gospel According to St. John*, II (New York: Seabury, 1980).

—*The Gospel According to St. John*, I (New York: Crossroad, 1982).

Schnapper, Dominique, *La communauté des citoyens: Sur l'idée moderne de nation* (Paris: Gallimard, 1994).

Schneiders, Sandra, *The Revelatory Text: Interpreting the New Testament as Sacred Scripture* (San Francisco: HarperCollins, 1991).

Schüssler Fiorenza, Elisabeth, *Rhetoric and Ethic: The Politics of Biblical Studies* (Minneapolis: Fortress Press, 1999).

Schwartz, R.M., 'Adultery in the House of David: The Metanarrative of Biblical Scholarship and the Narratives of the Bible', *Semeia* 54 (1991), pp. 35-55.

Segovia, Fernando F., 'And They Began to Speak in Other Tongues: Competing Modes of Discourse in Contemporary Biblical Criticism', in F.F. Segovia and M.A. Tolbert (eds.), *Reading from This Place*. I. *Social Location and Biblical Interpretation in the United States* (Minneapolis: Fortress Press, 1995), pp. 1-32.

—'Biblical Criticism and Postcolonial Studies: Toward a Postcolonial Optic', in R.S. Sugirtharajah (ed.), *The Postcolonial Bible* (The Bible and Postcolonialism, 1; Sheffield: Sheffield Academic Press, 1998), pp. 49-65.

—'Cultural Studies and Contemporary Biblical Criticism: Ideological Criticism as Mode of Discourse', in F.F. Segovia and M.A. Tolbert (eds.), *Reading from This Place*. II. *Social Location and Biblical Interpretation in Global Perspective* (Minneapolis: Fortress Press, 1995), pp. 1-17.

—'The Journey(s) of the Word: A Reading of the Plot of the Fourth Gospel', *Semeia* 53 (1991), pp. 23-54.

—*The Farewell of the Word: The Johannine Call to Abide* (Minneapolis: Fortress Press, 1991).

—*Interpreting Beyond Borders* (Sheffield: Sheffield Academic Press, 2000).

—'Notes Toward Refining the Postcolonial Optic', *JSNT* 75 (1999), pp. 103-14.

—'Postcolonialism and Diasporic Criticism in Biblical Studies: Focus, Parameters, Relevance', *Studies in World Christianity* 5.2 (1999), pp. 177-95.

Segovia, Fernando F. (ed.), *What is John?': Literary and Social Readings of the Fourth Gospel*, II (Atlanta: Scholars Press, 1998).

Seton-Watson, Hugh, *Nations and States: An Enquiry into the Origins of Nations and the Politics of Nationalism* (Boulder, CO: Westview, 1977).

Shadbolt, Maurice, *Season of the Jew* (Auckland, NZ: Hodder and Stoughton, 1986).

Shammas, Anton, 'Autocartography: The Case of Palestine, Michigan', in Patricia Yaeger (ed.), *The Geography of Identity* (Ann Arbor: University of Michigan Press, 1996), pp. 466-75.

Sheldrake, Philip, 'Travelling Through Life? Subversive Journeys', *The Way* 39 (1999), pp. 5-15.

Shirres, Michael P., *Te Tangata: The Human Person* (Auckland, NZ: Snedden & Cervin, 1997).

Silko, Leslie Marmon, 'Fences against Freedom', *Hungry Mind Review* (Fall 1994) http://www.bookwire.com/hmr/Review/silko.html.

Silva, N., 'Mother, Daughters and "Whores" of the Nation: Nationalism and Female Stereotypes in Post-colonial Sri Lankan Drama in English', *JGS* 6 (1997), pp. 269-76.

Sim, S. (ed.), *The A–Z Guide to Modern Literary and Cultural Theorists* (London: Prentice–Hall, 1995).

Simon, Herbert A., *Models of Man, Social and Relational* (New York: John Wiley & Sons, 1957).

Sinclair, Keith, *Kinds of Peace: Maori People after the Wars, 1870–85* (Auckland, NZ: Auckland University Press, 1991).

Smallwood, Joey, *No Apology from Me* (St John's: Newfoundland Book, 1967).

Smith, Abraham, 'Cultural Studies', in John H. Hayes (ed.), *Dictionary of Biblical Interpretation A–J* (Nashville: Abingdon Press, 1999), pp. 236-39.

Smith, Jonathan Z., *To Take Place: Toward Theory in Ritual* (Chicago: University of Chicago Press, 1987).

Smith, Neil, and Cindi Katz, 'Grounding Metaphor: Towards a Spatialized Politics', in Keith and Pile (eds.), *Place and Politics of Identity*, pp. 67-83.

Snyder, Louis L. (ed.), *The Imperialism Reader: Documents and Readings on Modern Expansionism* (Princeton, NJ: Van Nostrand, 1962).

Sollors, Werner, *Beyond Ethnicity: Consent and Descent in American Culture* (New York Oxford University Press, 1986).

Spickard, Paul and W. Jeffrey Burroughs, 'We are a People', in Paul Spickard and W. Jeffrey Burroughs (eds.), *We Are a People: Narrative and Multiplicity in Constructing Ethnic Identity* (Philadelphia: Temple University Press, 1999), pp. 1-19.

Spivak, Gayatri Chakravorty, 'French Feminism Revisited', in Butler and Scott (eds.), *Feminists Theorize the Political*, pp. 54-85.

—*Outside in the Teaching Machine* (New York: Routledge, 1993).

—*The Post-Colonial Critic: Interviews, Strategies, Dialogues* (ed. Sarah Harasym; New York: Routledge, 1990).

Spurr, David, *The Rhetoric of Empire: Colonial Discourse in Journalism, Travel Writing, and Imperial Administration* (Durham, NC: Duke University Press).

Staley, Jeffrey L., 'Changing Woman: Postcolonial Reflections on Acts 16.6-40', *JSNT* 73 (1999), pp. 113-35.

—'Narrative Structure (Self Stricture) in Luke 4.14–9.62: The United States of Luke's Story World', *Semeia* 72 (1995), pp. 173-213.

—'The Politics of Place and the Place of Politics in the Gospel of John', in Fernando F. Segovia (ed.), *'What is John?'* II, pp. 265-77.

—*The Print's First Kiss: A Rhetorical Investigation of the Implied Reader in the Fourth Gospel* (Atlanta: Scholars Press, 1998).

—*Reading with a Passion: Rhetoric, Autobiography, and the American West in the Gospel of John* (New York: Continuum, 1995).

—'Stumbling in the Dark, Reaching for the Light: Reading Character John 5 and 9', *Semeia* 53 (1991), pp. 55-80.

Stegner, Wallace, 'The Sense of Place', in *Where the Bluebird Sings to the Lemonade Springs: Living and Writing in the West* (New York: Penguin, 1992), pp. 199-206.

Stern, D., 'The Captive Woman: Hellenization, Greco-Roman Erotic Narrative, and Rabbinic Literature', *PT* 19 (1998), pp. 91-127.

Stibbe, Mark W.G., 'The Elusive Christ: A New Reading of the Fourth Gospel', in Mark W.G. Stibbe (ed.), *The Gospel of John as Literature: An Anthology of Twentieth-Century Perspectives* (Leiden: E.J. Brill, 1993).

Storey, J., *Cultural Studies and the Study of Popular Culture: Theories and Methods* (Athens: University of Georgia Press, 1996).

Stream, C., 'Jesus vs. Sanhedrin', *CT* 42 (1998), pp. 48-50.

Streete, G.C., *The Strange Woman: Power and Sex in the Bible* (Louisville, KY: Westminster/John Knox Press, 1997).

Strobel, Margaret, *European Women: And the Second British Empire* (Bloomington: Indiana University Press, 1991).

Sturdevant, S.P., and B. Stolzfus (eds.), *Let the Good Times Roll: Prostitution and the U.S. Military in Asia* (New York: The New Press, 1992).

Sugirtharajah, R.S., *Asian Biblical Hermeneutics and Postcolonialism: Contesting the Interpretations* (Maryknoll, NY: Orbis Books, 1998).

—'A Brief Memorandum on Postcolonialism and Biblical Studies', *JSNT* 73 (1999), pp. 3-5.

—'A Postcolonial Exploration of Collusion and Construction in Biblical Interpretation', in R.S. Sugirtharajah (ed.), *The Postcolonial Bible* (The Bible and Postcolonialism, 1; Sheffield: Sheffield Academic Press, 1998), pp. 91-116.

Swanson, Tod D., 'To Prepare a Place: Johannine Christianity and the Collapse of Ethnic Territory', *JAAR* 62 (1994), pp. 241-63.

Szymanski, Albert, *The Logic of Imperialism* (New York: Praeger, 1981).

Talbert, Charles H., 'The Myth of a Descending-Ascending Redeemer in Mediterranean Antiquity', *NTS* 22 (1976), pp. 418-40.

—*Reading John: A Literary and Theological Commentary on the Fourth Gospel and the Johannine Epistles* (New York: Crossroad, 1994).

Tanner, Kathryn, *Theories of Culture: A New Agenda for Theology* (Minneapolis: Fortress Press, 1997).

Tanzer, Sarah J., 'Salvation is for the Jews: Secret Christian Jews in the Gospel of John', in Birger Pearson (ed.), *The Future of Early Christianity: Essays in Honor of Helmut Koester* (Minneapolis: Fortress Press, 1991), pp. 285-300.

Taylor, J.E., *The Immerser: John the Baptist within Second Temple Judaism* (Grand Rapids: Eerdmans, 1997).

Thomas, Norman E., *Classic Texts in Mission and World Christianity* (Maryknoll, NY: Orbis Books, 1995).

Thompson, Marianne, *The Humanity of Jesus in the Fourth Gospel* (Minneapolis: Fortress Press, 1988).

Tiffin, Chris, and Alan Lawson (eds.), *De-scribing Empire: Post-colonialism and Textuality* (London: Routledge, 1994).

Tolbert, Mary Ann, 'Afterwords: Christianity, Imperialism, and the Decentering of Privilege', in Fernando F. Segovia and Mary Ann Tolbert (eds.) *Reading from this Place: Social Location and Biblical Interpretation in Global Perspective*, II (Minneapolis: Fortress Press, 1995), pp. 347-61.

—'Afterwords: The Politics and Poetics of Location', in Fernando F. Segovia and Mary Ann Tolbert (eds.) *Reading from this Place: Social Location and Biblical Interpretation in the United States*, I (Minneapolis: Fortress Press, 1995), pp. 305-17.

—'Protestant Feminists and the Bible: On the Horns of a Dilemma', in Alice Bach (ed.), *The Pleasure of her Text: Feminist Readings of Biblical and Historical Texts* (Philadelphia: Trinity Press International, 1990).

—*Sowing the Gospel: Mark's World in Literary-Historical Perspective* (Minneapolis: Fortress Press, 1989).

Tombs, D., 'Crucifixion, State Terror and Sexual Abuse', *USQR* 53 (1999), pp. 89-109.

Totontle, Mositi, *The Victims* (Gaborone: Botsalo, 1993).

Trafzer, Clifford E., *The Kit Carson Campaign: The Last Great Navajo War* (Norman: University of Oklahoma Press, 1982).

Trinh, T.M., *When the Moon Waxes Red: Representation, Gender, and Cultural Politics* (New York: Routledge, 1991).

Trites, A.A., 'The Woman Taken in Adultery', *BSac* 131 (1974), pp. 137-46.

Turner, Jonathan H., and Edna Bonacich, 'Toward a Composite Theory of Middleman Minorities', *Ethnicity* 7 (1980), pp. 144-58.

Turner, Victor W., *The Forest of Symbols: Aspects of Ndembu Ritual* (Ithaca, NY: Cornell University Press, 1967).

Ukpong, Justin S., 'Towards a Holistic Approach to Inculturation Theology', *Mission Studies: Journal of the IAMS* 26 (1999), pp. 100-24.

Valaskakis, Gail Guthrie, 'Indian Country: Negotiating the Meaning of Land in Native America', in Cary Nelson and Dilip Parameshwar Gaonkar (eds.), *Disciplinarity and Dissent in Cultural Studies* (New York: Routledge, 1996), pp. 149-69.

Van Bremen, Riet, *The Limits of Participation: Women and Civic Life in the Greek East in the Hellenistic and Roman Periods* (Amsterdam: Gieben, 1996).

Van Dommelen, P., 'Colonial Constructs: Colonialism and Archaeology in the Mediterranean', *World Archaeology* 28 (1997), pp. 305-23.

Van Unnik, W.C., 'The Purpose of St. John's Gospel', in Kurt Aland *et al.* (eds.), *Studia Evangelica: Papers Presented to the International Congress on 'The Four Gospels in 1957' at Oxford, 1957* (Berlin: Akademie-Verlag, 1959), pp. 382-411.

Von Wahlde, Urban C., 'The Johannine "Jews": A Critical Study', *NTS* 28 (1982), pp. 33-60.

—'The Relationships Between Pharisees and Chief Priests: Some Observations on the Texts in Matthew, John and Josephus', *NTS* 42 (1996), pp. 506-22.

Wainwright, Elizabeth, 'Rachel Weeping for her Children: Intertextuality and the Biblical Testaments—a Feminist Approach', in Brenner and Fontaine (eds.), *A Feminist Companion to Reading the Bible*, pp. 452-69.

Wald, Priscilla, 'Terms of Assimilation: Legislating Subjectivity in the Emerging Nation', in Amy Kaplan and Donald E. Pease (eds.), *Cultures of United States Imperialism* (Durham, NC: Duke University Press, 1993), pp. 59-84.

Wallace, D.B., 'Reconsidering "The Story of Jesus and the Adulteress Reconsidered"', *NTS* 39 (1993), pp. 290-96.

Wallace-Hadrill, A. (ed.), *Patronage in Ancient Society* (New York: Routledge, 1989).

Warnke, Georgia, *Justice and Interpretation* (Cambridge, MA: MIT, 1992).

Watson, G.R., *The Roman Soldier* (Ithaca, NY: Cornell University Press, 1969).

Weaver, Jace, *That the People might Live: Native American Literatures and Native American Community* (New York: Oxford University Press, 1997).

Webster, J., 'Necessary Comparisons: A Postcolonial Approach to Religious Syncretism in the Roman Provinces', *World Archaeology* 28 (1997), pp. 324-38.

Webster, Peter, *Rua and the Maori Millennium* (Wellington, NZ: Price Milburn for Victoria University Press, 1979).

Weil, Simone, *The Need for Roots: Prelude to a Declaration of Duties toward Mankind* (trans. Arthur Wils; New York: Harper, 1952).

White, E.F., 'Africa on my Mind: Gender, Counter Discourse and African-American Nationalism', *Journal of Women's History* 2 (1990), pp. 73-97.

Wiggins, James B., *In Praise of Religious Diversity* (New York: Routledge, 1996).

Williams, Raymond, *Keywords: A Vocabulary of Culture and Society* (New York: Oxford University Press, rev. edn, 1985).

Wink, Walter, *John the Baptist in the Gospel Tradition* (Cambridge: Cambridge University Press, 1968).

Wong, Sau-ling Cynthia, *Reading Asian American Literature: From Necessity to Extravagance* (Princeton, NJ: Princeton University Press, 1993).

Yaeger, Patricia, 'Introduction: Narrating Space', in Patricia Yaeger (ed.), *The Geography of Identity* (Ann Arbor: University of Michigan Press, 1996), pp. 18-30.

Yoon, J., *Reins* (Seoul: Poolbit, 1988).

Young, Brad, '"Save the Adulteress!": Ancient Jewish Response in the Gospels?', *NTS* 41 (1995), pp. 59-70.

Zago, M., 'The New Millennium and the Emerging Religious Encounters', *Missiology* 28 (1997), pp. 5-18.

Zurbrugg, N., 'Burroughs, Barthes, and the Limits of Intertextuality', *Review of Contemporary Fiction* 4 (1984), pp. 88-97.

INDEX

INDEX OF REFERENCES

INDEX OF AUTHORS